# IN ORDER
# THAT
# JUSTICE
# MAY BE DONE

D0735801

# IN ORDER
# THAT
## JUSTICE
## MAY BE DONE

---

The Legal Struggle of the Turtle Mountain
Band of Pembina Chippewa, 1795–1905

by John M. Shaw

NDSU NORTH DAKOTA STATE
UNIVERSITY PRESS

Fargo, North Dakota

# NDSU NORTH DAKOTA STATE UNIVERSITY PRESS

Dept. 2360, P.O. Box 6050, Fargo, ND, 58108-6050
www.ndsupress.org

*In Order That Justice May Be Done: The Legal Struggle of the Turtle Mountain Band of Pembina Chippewa, 1795–1905*
By John M. Shaw

Copyright © 2023 by North Dakota State University Press
First Edition
First Printing

All rights reserved. No part of this book may be used or reproduced in any manner without written permission, except in the case of brief quotes in critical articles or reviews. For more information, contact North Dakota State University Press, NDSU Dept. 2360, P.O. Box 6050, Fargo, ND 58108-6050, ndsu.press@ndsu.edu.

LCCN: 2022951183
ISBN: 978-1-946163-56-1

Cover design by Jamie Trosen
Interior design by Deb Tanner
Cover photograph used with permission of the National Anthropological Archives, Negative No. 51,107, by Charles M. Bell, Washington, D.C.
Cover photograph colorization by Kade M. Ferris, Turtle Mountain Chippewa/Metis, Dibaajimowin.com

The publication of *In Order That Justice May Be Done: The Legal Struggle of the Turtle Mountain Band of Pembina Chippewa, 1795–1905* is made possible by the generous support of donors to the NDSU Press Fund and the NDSU Press Endowed Fund, and other contributors to NDSU Press.

Stephenson Beck, Interim Director
Suzzanne Kelley, Editor in Chief
RoseE Hadden, Administrative Assistant
Kyle Vanderburg, Assistant Acquisitions Editor
Hannah Slater, Editorial Intern

Printed in the USA

Publisher's Cataloging-in-Publication
(Provided by Cassidy Cataloguing Services, Inc.).

Names:    Shaw, John M., 1950- author.

Title:    In order that justice may be done : the legal struggle of the Turtle Mountain Band of Pembina Chippewa, 1795–1905 / by John M. Shaw.

Description:    First edition. | Fargo, North Dakota : North Dakota State University Press, [2023] | Includes bibliographical references and index.

Identifiers:    ISBN: 978-1-946163-56-1

Subjects:    LCSH: Turtle Mountain Band of Chippewa Indians of North Dakota--Government relations--History--19th century. | Turtle Mountain Band of Chippewa Indians of North Dakota--Land tenure. | Indian reservations--Law and legislation--North Dakota. | Federally recognized Indian tribes--North Dakota. | BISAC: LAW / Indigenous Peoples. | SOCIAL SCIENCE / Ethnic Studies / American / Native American Studies. | HISTORY / Indigenous Peoples of the Americas.

Classification:    LCC: E99.C6 S43 2023 | DDC: 977.00497333--dc23

# TABLE OF CONTENTS

# INTRODUCTION

*Only looking back is there a pattern. There is a story to it the way there is a story to all, never visible while it is happening.*[1]
—Louise Erdrich

Examining the history of the Turtle Mountain Band of Pembina Chippewa provides an intriguing case study of one Native nation's struggle for justice against nineteenth-century federal policy. Tribal relations with the United States ran counter to the federal government's professed adherence of dealing honorably with Native American peoples. Reacting to the U.S. government's unilateral 1884 Executive Order reducing their reservation from twenty to only two townships without any compensation, tribal member and solicitor of the Turtle Mountain band John B. Bottineau asked "whether these Indians have some constitutional rights in this great Republic, which a court of justice is bound to respect as well as the President of the United States."[2] His inquiry lies at the heart of their legal struggle.

Although assuring government protection in exchange for vast areas of Native peoples' territory, promises of federal guardianship spurred rather than deterred European American settlement. Conveniently acknowledging not following the "rule of law," the commissioner of Indian Affairs conceded in 1879 that the federal government's "guardianship" over the lands of its Native "wards" produced another policy failure:

> There is hardly a reservation within the limits of the United States which has not been subject to [European American]

encroachments. They resort to all kinds of devices and schemes to obtain a foothold on Indian soil, and offer ready and varied excuses for their continued unlawful occupancy.[3]

The commissioner's observation sums up the situation of the Turtle Mountain people from 1863 to 1905.

Heeding persistent calls from Native American Studies specialists for an "increase in the diversity of voices heard," this work provides a comprehensive narrative about the legal struggles of the Turtle Mountain Chippewa.[4] Too many scholars have failed to appreciate the history of the band. The reasons for this oversight stem from three main factors. First, the group's geographic remoteness in north-central North Dakota on the border with Manitoba, Canada. Second, its unique evolution as a "composite band" of full-blood Chippewa (along with Cree) in the minority and mixed-blood Métis in the majority. And third, being a peaceful people avoiding attention-grabbing wars with the United States.[6]

To help fill the void, this study examines various nineteenth-century federal policies and their impact on one tribe's struggle to retain their homeland, culture and sovereignty.[8] While being forced to cede millions of acres of land in return for an inadequate reservation, they never received a suitable tract of land for the promised reservation. Following decades of contention and indecision, a local superintendent noted in 1906 that "this failure was due largely to the rapid absorption of available lands by the rush of white settlers."[9] The band protested to the commissioner of Indian Affairs that:

> no attempt has been made to keep settlers from occupying our lands. The Turtle Mountain Indians regard these mountains as their own and express a strong desire to have a reservation definitely located for them in that region, before white settlers shall further encroach upon them.[10]

This testimony demonstrated that despite adverse circumstances, the peoples of Turtle Mountain resisted being pawns or victims. Their Native witness is crucial in illuminating the contradictions of nineteenth-century federal policy. The various representatives of the band discerned accurately the motivations and practices of those European Americans who shaped, articulated, and handled Indian affairs.

This investigation focuses on the historical context and political expression of Turtle Mountain Chippewa sovereignty with particular attention to their relationship with the federal government of the United States throughout the nineteenth century. Such an inquiry reveals how the band sought to determine their own existence within the confines of European American political hegemony, economic stratification, and racial exclusion. The analytical emphasis is on this tribe's abilities to act in their own best interest while resisting hostile external forces. In terms of power relations and economic adaptation, they creatively attempted to maximize their cultural and political survival amidst European American domination.

By utilizing Harold Lasswell's classic definition of politics—"who gets what, when, and how"—we can better understand the political context of how the Turtle Mountain Chippewa contested federal Indian policy implementation.[11] They affirmed their claims to the utmost of their considerable political abilities. Such a legacy, discerned from their prayers, addresses, memorials, letters, legal briefs, and delegations, exemplified Edward Said's important insight that "nations themselves are narrations."[12] A significant part of the Turtle Mountain band's fight to survive derived from the power to narrate their side of the story. They asserted "a common history, language, culture, traditions, political consciousness, laws, governmental structures, spirituality, ancestry and homeland." These assertions enabled them to maintain their right of self-determination in an effective manner.[13] They also contested the disingenuous counterclaims of various federal, state, territorial, and local officials and private profiteers who coveted their territory.

The inclusion of a specific Native peoples' perspective adheres to Richard White's call to look at "the historical construction of Indian nations."[14] As articulated by Lumbee legal scholar Robert A. Williams, Jr., the main reason for the consistent failures of federal policy derived from the fact that "the Indian voice was either not heard, not heeded, or falsely reported."[15] It is not enough to simply acknowledge the disastrous effects of this policy on Native communities. Scholars should delve into the history of tribal-federal dialogue to understand the basis of policies hyped by its advocates as "benevolent." While most articles focus on a more specific time period, this study analyzes a connected series of transformative eras throughout the nineteenth century. Since federal policies mirrored larger historical trends, one of the most insightful ways to analyze and interpret the dynamic interplay between tribal-federal relations is to focus on one Native community's experiences over an extended period of time.

The legal struggles of the Turtle Mountain community as seen from their point of view provides valuable insights into the dysfunctional nature of nineteenth-century federal policy. This tribal case study recounts and analyzes the political relationship between the Turtle Mountain band of Chippewa and the United States. By taking a history from the bottom-up approach, combined with a focus on tribal self-representation, the abilities of the Turtle Mountain Chippewa to make their own way in the world becomes self-evident. The goal of this investigation is to make the compelling story of one tribe's political relationship with the United States accessible to a wider audience.

The Turtle Mountain Chippewa comprise the only predominantly Métis community in North America to secure a reservation in the United States or a reserve in Canada. Such a singular achievement should have been explored comprehensively long before now. They proved capable of thinking and acting for themselves during a series of difficult situations. How many nineteenth-century tribes had a member as their attorney, litigating and lobbying actively on their behalf for forty years (1871–1911)?[17] They developed economic and political strategies to sustain their sovereignty and contest external threats. Through peaceful and diplomatic means, the band fought to maintain the core elements of their Indigenous peoplehood.[18]

Another fascinating discovery concerns the rare issuance of "halfbreed" scrip (i.e., a coupon that could be redeemed for land or cash) by the United States government. Some North American Indian history has focused on how this worked in Canada or has explored the few instances where some Métis received specific U.S. treaty allotments. Yet the existence of "half-breed" scrip provisions in treaties has been overlooked. In the wider historical context of applications of "mixed-bloods" for land or scrip under treaties with various bands of Chippewa in Wisconsin and Minnesota, the Pembina and Turtle Mountain experience with "half-breed" scrip constitutes one of the most important findings of this undertaking.[19]

The political history of the Turtle Mountain Chippewa's relations with the United States government calls into question many assumptions about federal law and policy. The "history of Indian-White relations" has frozen policy eras into static removal, reservation, assimilation, and allotment epochs. Studies of tribal relations with the federal government became shoehorned into top-down, discrete policy period paradigms.[20] Historian Patricia Limerick observed accurately that they "overplay[ed] the significance of federal policy" by creating an "illusion of a purposeful sequence of events," rather than reflecting the "swirl" of an "unsettling" and "persistent muddle."[21] An account of tribal-federal relations from a distinctive tribal perspective can amend this situation by paying "careful attention to the actual facts of a particular controversy."[22]

To increase our understanding of the varied experiences of the Turtle Mountain Chippewa, an "Indian-centered history" should do more than highlight Indigenous peoples as historical actors in their own right.[24] Yet Native agency can become diminished if constrained within existing top-down tribal-federal relations paradigms. "Policy is what the government says and does about perceived problems."[25] The government's perception of an alleged "Indian problem" was framed by various county, territorial, and state interest groups and officials in conjunction with the federal bureaucracy and Congress. To get inside its formulation, this study proposes the alternative archetype of a "grab-bag" for federal policy, as it relates to the "garbage-can" model of organizational theory.[26] Both the metaphor and the model applies all too accurately to the historical experiences of the Turtle Mountain Chippewa with the U.S. government throughout the nineteenth century.

The testimony of the Turtle Mountain Chippewa confirms that they confronted the handling of federal Indian affairs as capricious expediencies rather than coherent policies. Their attorney attorney, John B. Bottineau, complained that "they have been subjected to . . . half a dozen or more policies or regimes, under different administrations and agents, each having a policy or regime of his own."[27] He concluded that "the authorities of the government have really done nothing for these Indians," while "endeavoring to remove them from their home on Turtle Mountain."[28] As a result, the Turtle Mountain Chippewa rejected all of the government's proposals "lest the abandonment of the country claimed by them might be looked upon as a willing relinquishment of their title."[29] If the grab-bag pattern conforms to how the Turtle Mountain Chippewa perceived federal policy, perhaps it can better explain the experiences of other tribes as well. The Department of the Interior and the BIA used the most expedient means and then sought the best rationale for the action taken. As a result, the grab-bag model helps explain the persistent failures of federal policy.[30]

In the realm of tribal-federal relations, it is imperative to determine not just what happened, but the policy behind it. Not surprisingly, solutions from the policy grab-bag always missed their mark because little or no concern was given to the interests and aspirations of Native peoples. Federal policies constituted "collections of choices looking for problems."[31] With little if any Native input and no meaningful evaluative feedback loop, the federal affairs echelon recycled its way through the policy grab-bag until they declared the problem solved, regardless of the actual outcome or its detrimental impact on Native communities.[32] To have been effective, federal administrators should have at least consulted with Native peoples, yet they did not in any meaningful way.

The Turtle Mountain band's fortitude against marginality, injustice, and the reduction of their homeland fits Native scholar Philip J.

Deloria's stipulation that the best Native American scholarship must be a "thoroughly cross-cultural history" that looks at "Indians and non-Indians in a changing world."[35] Examining a wide array of sources shows Native Americans and Métis as actors in the assertion and defense of their inherent rights to land and sovereignty. Rather than rely upon the federal government's ethnocentric preconceptions, they defined themselves and their goals. John Bottineau confirmed that the Turtle Mountain Chippewa "are as well qualified today to judge for themselves as to what may be needed for their best interest as any other class of people."[36]

This analysis is also concerned with how and why nineteenth-century federal policy failed consistently to achieve any of its "benevolent" goals. Instead, it resulted in the dispossession, dislocation, and marginalization of Native peoples. This outcome raises important questions with both historical and contemporary significance. If everyone agrees on the failures of policy, then it becomes more important to look at how and why the policy was formulated and implemented. Although a well-intended plan might go wrong, can an incoherent array of quick fixes ever achieve success? Was treaty administration part of a systemic national policy framework, or just an aberration? In spite of all the benign rhetoric about securing Native American title and conferring the benefits of "civilization," the primary goal of nineteenth-century federal policy coincided with the national goal of furthering European American settlement and bringing more resources from the peripheral areas of the West into the industrializing national economy of the United States.[37]

It was not the imperatives of the European American market economy that disrupted the Turtle Mountain Chippewa. Around 1800, they emerged as a distinct Plains-Ojibwe people intermarried with French Canadian fur traders at Pembina, North Dakota, in the Red River Valley of the North. Evolving beyond their origins as a trading post band, by 1810 they extended farther west as wintering bands of hivernants in the Pembina and Turtle Mountains. They became hunters, trappers, provisioners, guides, interpreters, and transporters living and working within an entrepreneurial milieu that valued their labor and skills. In this pre-commercial farming and pre-industrial era, they adapted sufficiently to many economic changes and participated actively in a market economy until the demise of the buffalo in the 1880s.[38]

It was not their inability to understand market economics or to compete in an increasingly European American world that led to their dispossession and dislocation. The Turtle Mountain Chippewa adapted successfully to external market forces in a variety of ways until the intrusion of the railroads and the decimation of the buffalo ended Native control of the region's natural resources and means of production. Yet in the end, demographic disparity and aggressive European American settler encroachment—countenanced by federal policymakers—overran the Turtle Mountain Chippewa. A series of Executive Orders, commissions, and agreements whittled down the ten-million-acre Turtle Mountain Chippewa domain to a two-township allotted reservation. These actions left most of the band landless and scattered across the public domain of the northern Plains, while "worthy" European Americans would champion their self-made economic independence in America's heartland.[39]

Understanding the history of the Turtle Mountain Chippewa requires us to discard the assumption that the course of Native American-European American relations was unalterable or inevitable. We should not accept the rationalizations of the federal apparatus at face value. We need to look beyond the contradictions between policy rhetoric, formulation, and implementation. This tribal case study addresses historian Richard White's concern that "the history of Indian-white relations has not usually produced complex stories."[40] A more nuanced analysis is required to better assess the causes and effects of federal policy on one Native community "insisting on their rights" and adherence to "equity and justice."[41]

After a half-century (1851–1905) of legal wrangling with U.S. officials, incursions by European Americans, and harassment by local non-Native authorities, the Turtle Mountain Chippewa relented to an "obnoxious agreement" imposed by the federal government. But they continued to reiterate that "there is ample evidence showing the merits of the claim of the Turtle Mountain Indians, and the great wrongs and injustice in their treatment by this Government."[42] The generation of a substantial body of official government records affirmed their case and documented their struggle against cultural annihilation, economic devastation, and injustice. Modern tribal chairman Richard LaFromboise summarized this perspective eloquently:

> the story of the Turtle Mountain People is a record of endurance, of survival, of adaptation, and creativity in the face of overwhelming obstacles. It is a record of enormous contributions to this country—to its art and culture, its strength and spirit, its sense of history, and its sense of purpose.[43]

The Turtle Mountain Chippewa persevered to retain some semblance of their self-governing autonomy and land tenure. These two essential components of Indigenous peoplehood lay at the heart of their long legal struggle with the federal government. The Turtle Mountain Chippewa wanted to stay on their reserved tribal lands, and they demanded protection from unwanted intruders and fair compensation for the land taken from them. The band's representatives believed that by adhering to peaceful relations and the rule of law, their sovereign legal status and land title would be upheld by the United States. Yet their modest needs clashed with the expansionist demands of European American settlement. The principled and persistent effort of the Turtle Mountain Chippewa should be a shining example for all Native American tribes to follow in their quest to maintain tribal rights. Their compelling story cries out for an extensive analysis. It may be only a slight exaggeration to agree with attorney Bottineau when he concluded that "there is no tribe of our American Indians that has ever been so ill-treated as these Turtle Mountain Indians. It is but justice to acquaint the facts to the American people."[44]

# CHAPTER 1

# The Origins of the Pembina and
# Turtle Mountain Chippewa, Pre-1795–1824

*Before the boundaries were set.*[1]

Access to and control over land and its resources has always been the major issue of contention between American Indians and European Americans.[2] As stated by historian Wilcomb Washburn, "the greatest legal gap between the two cultures has been the respective attitudes toward that commodity."[3]

Whether land was obtained by purchase or conquest from Native Americans, it was never free. Understanding the culturally and legally contested concepts of land and its uses and ownership are crucial to analysis of federal policy and Native political resistance. As Stephen Cornell perceived, "dispossession was not merely an aspect of frontier history." For Native Americans, "it was the fundamental event on which much of the American future turned."[4] United States territorial expansion and economic development depended upon Native displacement.

This context leads to several questions. Who are the Turtle Mountain band of Pembina Chippewa? Where did they come from? What territory did they regard as their homeland? How and when did they coalesce as an identifiable community with a distinct tribal organization holding "Aboriginal title" to the lands they possessed? Moreover, why did their cultural identity, political organization, and territorial claims create such a conundrum for federal policymakers?

Native peoples have definite ideas about the origins and extent of their homeland. Many European Americans justified their expropriation of Native lands by claiming that bands or tribes did not practice recognizable European American forms of land ownership. This falsehood became a dangerous rationalization. From the *Johnson v. McIntosh* Supreme Court decision in 1823, to the 1892 "ten-cent treaty" forced upon the Turtle Mountain Chippewa, a long line of U.S. officials maligned the different cultural practices of Native peoples to concoct elaborate legal justifications for claiming superior rights to their lands. Federal policy invented various devices to impair Native land ownership and tribal sovereignty. The officials wanted the "empire of liberty" envisioned by Thomas Jefferson to expand at a rapid pace with minimal costs to the United States. When European Americans began to encroach on the Turtle Mountain Chippewa in the mid-nineteenth century, the band complained about the "damages and wrongs perpetrated upon our people under the guise of law."[6]

The Turtle Mountain and Pembina communities considered their lands and resources as a sacred endowment from the "Master of Life [who] placed us here and gave [this land] to us for an inheritance."[7] The death of warriors, the burial of ancestors, and the use of certain portions of land for specific purposes—such as ceremonial rites—confirmed its sacredness. The "ancient bloody feud" with the Dakota led the Chippewa to consider their lands as "blood earned country." "The Ojibway exclaims with truth when asked by the grasping 'Long Knife' to sell his country that it is strewed with the bones of his fathers and enriched with their blood."[8] Such entitlement showed they had a clear notion of "adverse possession" by birthright or battle. Within this territory, the Turtle Mountain band loosely controlled the use of diverse ecological niches by various kinship groups, who acted as stewards rather than exclusive owners. As part of their seasonal subsistence pattern, a variety of extended family groups used vast non-residential territories for hunting. They saw their land and resources as part of a larger interdependent relationship, to be used in culturally sanctioned ways that fulfilled their sacred obligations of stewardship. But a key question remained: what extent of territory did the Turtle Mountain band of the Pembina Chippewa have owner rights in, based upon continuous occupation for many generations?

In the Northwest Ordinance of 1787, the United States pledged to discharge its "utmost good faith" in relation with Native Americans: "Their land and property shall never be taken from them without their consent."[9] In contrast to the Ordinance's promised "laws founded in justice and humanity," a tribal spokesman responded that, "we submit that there is ample evidence showing the merits of the claim of the Turtle Mountain Indians, and the great wrongs and injustice in their treatment by this Government."[10] While the issues of sovereignty and land have always been paramount to tribes and the federal government, Native communities like the Turtle Mountain Chippewa did not aspire to any European American form of a sovereign state. The crucial benchmarks for nation-state or tribal sovereignty comprised exclusive control over a defined territory by an identifiable and autonomous group of people exercising some controlling authority.[11] Yet the Turtle Mountain Chippewa also sought some degree of freedom from the impositions of European American law and governance. The legal dispute at the heart of this study emanated from the battles for political control between the United States and the Turtle Mountain band over what would become northeastern and north-central North Dakota.

From approximately 1680 to 1780 the migrations and territories of the Anishinaabeg, Ojibwe, or Chippewa arced across the woodlands of the Great Lakes region from eastern Canada to western Minnesota. After 1780 some of these people extended further across the prairies of the Great Plains through north-central North Dakota (see Image 1).[12] The term Plains-Ojibwe became the designation for the Chippewa bands who moved west from the Great Lakes and adapted their modes of subsistence and cultural practices to the environmental conditions on the northern Great Plains (see Image 2).[13] Bands formed around localized, autonomous, extended-family kinship groups. They usually

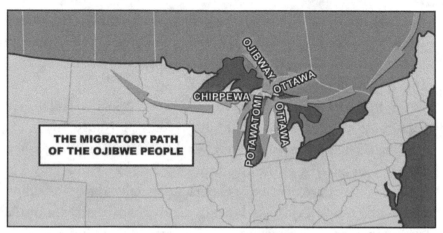

Image 1. Migratory Path of the Ojibwe People. The arrow points to Turtle Mountain, ND. *Adapted from the Benton-Benai, Land of the Ojibwe, Minnesota Historical Society, 1973; State Historical Society of North Dakota: North Dakota Studies.*

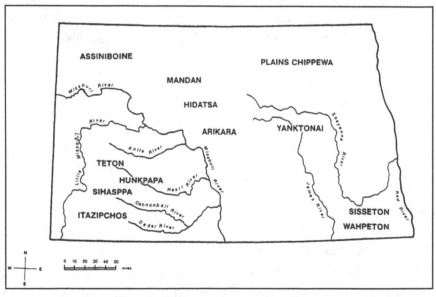

Image 2. Indian tribes before 1850 in what will become North Dakota. Plains Chippewa is another name for the Turtle Mountain Band of Pembina Chippewa. *State Maps on File (North Dakota), New York: Facts on File, 1984, Figure 5.14.*

became identified by the geographic place name associated with their primary residence (e.g., Pembina or Turtle Mountain) or with the name of a distinguished leader (e.g., Little Shell).

These eighteenth-century Ojibwe movements coincided with the British crown's pretensions of sovereignty over the thinly populated aboriginal regions of northern North America. Britain's territorial claim derived from its assertion that Henry Hudson "discovered" Hudson's Bay. In 1670, King Charles II of England claimed dominion over the vast drainage of Hudson's Bay. This vaguely defined expanse extended as far south as the headwaters of the Red River of the North (see Image 3).[14] It included the Pembina River that flowed from the

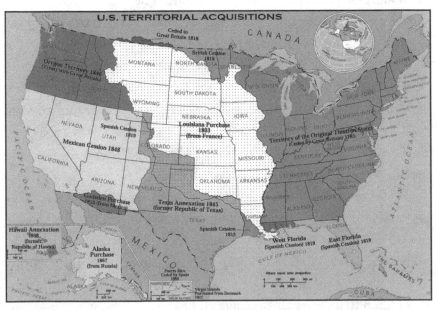

**Image 3. The British Cession of 1818 created the boundary between British North America and the United States** as a line starting in the east from Lake of the Woods to the 49th parallel, and then west along the parallel to the Stony (Rocky) Mountains. The original homeland of the Turtle Mountain Band of Pembina Chippewa was situated within the western portion of the cession, the area west of the Minnesota-North Dakota border formed by the Red River of the North. *Image available in public domain.*

eastern portion of Turtle Mountain and the northward flowing Souris River flanking the western part of the Turtle Mountains. The king granted an exclusive charter for the monopoly of trade and governance to the private stock Hudson's Bay Company (hereafter referred to as the HBC). Its domain became known as Rupert's Land, in honor of the monarch's cousin Prince Rupert, the first governor.[15]

An English colony like Rupert's Land represented a hypothetical claim of royal sovereignty over a territory and all of its Native inhabitants. Theoretically, property rights in land were held by the British crown, in the interests of the commercial imperatives of British colonialism in North America. In reality, the existence of even sparse Native populations subverted any European colonizer's pretensions about coercing Native autonomy or land rights. The westward expansion of the French inland fur trading empire from lower Canada and the English Hudson's Bay from upper Canada contributed significantly to the movement of Chippewa bands. More than any other European nation, the Ojibwe "learned to love the French." Aside from the bonds created by extensive intermarriage, this strong affinity stemmed from the Chippewa discernment that the French understood and respected their "totemic clans," "governmental polity," and "religious rites and ceremonies," unlike the British or Americans.[16]

The French connection stemmed from their activities as trappers and hunters with French traders and voyageurs. It resulted also in the early acquisition of guns and ammunition through the fur trade, which gave them a technological advantage over tribal rivals farther west. This association left a legacy of "unbounded" French influence. In addition to the French language and Roman Catholic religion, numerous and large families of half-blood children provided the most obvious outcome.[17] As a consequence, they became trading middlemen with other Indian groups. In the subsequent phase, they established themselves as permanent residents, adapting their cultural ways and subsistence modes to new environmental conditions west of the Great Lakes and toward the Great Plains.

During the initial phase of western migration, "the Prairie region was, at first, a strange and unfamiliar environment to these Woodland people."[18] Their shift beyond the "water roads" and river valleys out onto the prairie resulted in cultural changes. They transformed themselves from being an Eastern Woodlands people (e.g., living in bark-covered wigwams, gathering wild rice, growing corn, traveling by canoes, and tapping maple trees for sugar) to adopting many characteristics of Great Plains cultures (e.g., living in tipis, riding horses, hunting buffalo, and engaging in the Sun Dance ceremony), while retaining lake fishing, deer, elk, and moose hunting, fur trapping, and some of their older burial customs and religious society (Midaewaewin) practices. They represented an "unparalleled example of mixed culture," aware of and relishing "the best of two worlds" (see Images 4 and 5).[19]

**Image 4. This trade cloth shirt once belonged to Standing Elk, Turtle Mountain, Plains-Ojibwe.** Today it is in the Plains Indian Museum, Browning, Montana. The beaded arm strips have integral disks, and the beadwork on red cloth around the neck and cuffs has Woodland border patterns. The shirt probably dates from the 1880s. *Caption text and image reproduced here with permission of Greene Media Ltd., copyright owner of the* Encyclopaedia of Native Tribes of North America.

**Image 5. Turtle Mountain Ojibwe and Cree at the Canada–Dakota border (1889).** Left to right, back row: Little Boy, Black Thunder; middle row: Burning Ground, Yellow Robe, Little Wound, Eee-noo; front: A. C. J. Farrell (Misko Makwa/Rev. Bear), Prairie Chicken (son of Black Thunder). Note that Burning Ground wears a trade cloth shirt similar to the one depicted in Image 4. *State Historical Society of North Dakota, 66509.*

From his location near the mouth of the Yellowstone River, the artist and chronicler George Catlin noted that approximately six thousand Cree, Assiniboine, and "Ojibbeways" "occupied a vast extent of country" to the northeast as far as Lake Winnipeg (i.e., the Red River Settlements). These tribes "lived as neighbors on terms of friendship." Turtle Mountain in North Dakota comprised one center of this "vast extent of country." It had long been a main intertribal trading, resource and refuge center of accommodation and conflict for the Dakota, Plains Cree, and the Assiniboine. This area of natural beauty—made lush by above-average rainfall, covered with a variety of trees, and containing hundreds of small lakes—may have reminded the Plains-Ojibwe of their ancestral Eastern Woodlands around the Great Lakes. The landscape certainly met their interrelated subsistence and spiritual needs on the northern Plains.[20] In terms of subsistence, it not only provided food, water, timber, shelter, small game, and furs, but the hills served as an excellent jumping off point for buffalo hunting out on the prairie and refuge for wintering herds.

Their close ties with the fur trade facilitated this cultural shift. They established diplomatic and trade relations with the British after they defeated and displaced New France in the French and English (Indian) or Seven Years War in 1763. Although official Ojibwe relations with the French king and his representatives ended, a Chippewa chief reminded a British official that, "although you have conquered the French, you have not conquered us. We are not your slaves." The Cree, Assiniboine and Ojibwe began trading principally with the British. The intrepid Alexander Henry the Elder became the first British trader with whom the Ojibwe resided.[21] This new relationship enabled them to acquire horses from their Cree and Assiniboine allies in exchange for the steady supply of guns, knives, and axes they procured through the fur trade with the British. The Ojibwe battled more successfully against rival Plains tribes (most notably the Dakota) and began forging a new homeland for themselves and their descendants by the 1790s in what would become northeastern and north-central North Dakota.

The acquisition of horses constituted the most significant factor in the cultural shift of the Plains-Ojibwe from an Eastern Woodlands to a Plains orientation.[22] Evidence for this alteration appears in the material culture, historical record and the oral traditions of contemporary Turtle Mountain Chippewa families. "Thus, a formidable body of the tribe had gradually congregated on this remote northwest frontier." Joined by some Ottawas, they "flourished" under an alliance with the Assiniboine and Cree relations at Red River, Pembina, and Turtle Mountain against the Dakota.[23] Elder, spiritual leader, and former tribal chairman Francis Cree confirmed that, "way back there the Chippewa, Crees, and Stone Sioux lived together in the Turtle Mountains . . . I'm in three parts: I'm Cree, Chippewa, and Assiniboine Sioux." [24] These testimonies accurately express identity as it relates to family, community, and culture.

Parallel to, and sometimes converging with, these tribal migrations, alliances, conflicts, and cultural adaptations, European colonizers came into increasing conflict with each other throughout the eighteenth-century up until 1783, when the United States attained its independence from Great Britain. Significant challenges arose in that year. Thirteen Atlantic coast colonies won their independence from Britain after eight years of war in the American Revolution. While the terms of the Paris Peace Treaty of 1783 did not impact directly on Canada or the Hudson Bay Company's Rupert's Land, the United States won all British territory south of the Great Lakes, north of Florida, and east of the Mississippi River. This new nation-state represented a still weak, yet potentially aggressive and expansionist, country whose national self-interest seemed destined to dispossess Native peoples.

Even before winning its independence from Britain in 1783, or ratifying the Constitution in 1789, the former colonies that became the United States continued the policies of Britain. From the outset, acquiring and reselling Native lands became a potential source of federal funds. The original and short-lived governing principles of the Articles of Confederation (1781–1788) established the important legal process for "the mode of disposing of Lands in the Western Territory" (i.e., territory west of the original thirteen states, and east of the Mississippi River). The guidelines of the Land Ordinance of 1785 instituted the methods for administering the ceded Indian lands that would become the nation's "public domain." The "use" right of "Indian title" had to be extinguished legally and purchased through a treaty. Then they had to be surveyed prior to any legal sale or settlement of public land or private property.

Aside from its aforementioned "utmost good faith" clause, the Northwest Ordinance of 1787 concerned itself primarily with the conveyance of property, along with the inviolable nature of property rights and private contracts. It also outlined the procedures for incorporating new territories into the United States as an interim step to becoming new states on an "equal footing" with the existing states. These expansionist goals precluded equitable and just tribal-federal relations. The aggressive taking of Native lands became normalized and legalized.[25]

The first part of this process involved making treaties with Native peoples as sovereign nations. In theory, treaty-making created a government-to-government legal relationship between the United States and various Native nations. But the actual text in these treaties, taken from the Articles of Confederation, asserted U.S. control and undermined Native autonomy. Article IX of the 1785 *Treaty of Hopewell* with the Cherokee nation exemplified this conundrum:

> For the benefit and comfort of the Indians, and for the prevention of injuries or oppressions on the part of the citizens or Indians, the United States in Congress assembled shall have the *sole and exclusive right* of regulating the trade with the Indians, and *managing all their affairs* in such manner as they think proper.[26] [emphasis added]

This stipulation did not just apply to one tribe in a single treaty. The following year it became enshrined in the Ordinance for Regulation of Indian Affairs enacted by Congress.[27] This "sole and exclusive right" of the U.S. Congress to manage "all" the affairs of a tribe without their consent became known as the doctrine of plenary authority. Such assertions undermined the whole idea of tribal sovereignty. In reality, tribal sovereignty deteriorated into various levels of diminished sovereignty with the degree of reduction determined by the resistance of Native people against the impositions of the U.S. government.

Neither plenary power nor diminished sovereignty had any clear constitutional basis. Despite the major diplomatic, trade, and military roles Native Americans played in the European imperial struggles in North America that produced the United States, the federal Constitution referred to Indians only once explicitly. Article I, Section 8 (the Commerce Clause), stated that "The Congress shall have Power . . . to regulate Commerce with foreign Nations, and among the several States, and with the Indian Tribes." Unlike the Articles of Confederation, this section did not give Congress the plenary power to manage tribal affairs. In fact, no part of the Constitution granted Congress that power, although the Supreme Court sometimes ruled otherwise, most notably in *Johnson v. McIntosh* in 1823.

The Commerce Clause only authorized Congress to regulate interstate commerce and the federal government's or its own citizens' commercial relations with tribes. While the Constitution excluded Native Americans from the federal republic, the Naturalization Act of 1790 limited citizenship to a "free white person." Native Americans did not become citizens (with many exceptions) until 1924. Tribes were neither foreign nations nor states. This rendered the original legal status of American Indian polities as "extra-constitutional." Such exclusion presented a problem when the United States decided to follow Britain's practice of negotiating treaties with Indian tribes. A treaty represented a compact between two or more sovereign nations. Article VI, Paragraph 2 (the Treaty or Supremacy Clause) declared that "all Treaties . . . shall be the supreme law of the Land." This meant that treaties were on a par with international law. They trumped federal, state, or local statutes that attempted to abrogate a treaty. This is why Native communities like the Turtle Mountain Chippewa have asserted consistently that their legal status and inherent rights have been recognized as the highest law of the land through their treaty relationship with United States.

One of the most important criteria for the recognition of a sovereign nation-state or tribe entailed exclusive control over a defined territory by a recognized authority. As a result of winning independence, the United States declared that such a victory over Britain gave it a superior sovereignty over all Native peoples, and title to all their lands, without their consent. Secretary of War Henry Knox, whose department became responsible for federal Indian policy, noted that the "Indians . . . entertained a different opinion." United States claims to the great expanse of territory from the Appalachian Mountains to the Mississippi River met significant Native American resistance over the next fifty years. Nevertheless, George Washington assumed that the "gradual extension of our settlements" would prevail over "a liberal system of justice . . . for the various Indian tribes within the limits of the United States," and ensure European American demographic dominance.[28]

These founding principles would not touch the Turtle Mountain region for another thirty years. A more immediate hazard faced by the HBC after 1783 involved the banding together of various independent fur trade rivals under the protection of the North West Company (NWC). Based in Montreal and owned and operated by Scots and French-Canadian entrepreneurs, it challenged the HBC's fur trade monopoly in innovative ways. Although it required many portages, the NWC's main trade route linked Montreal to the Great Plains and beyond via the St. Lawrence River and the Great Lakes. This route was shorter, and therefore potentially more profitable, than the HBC's reliance on its Hudson's Bay outlet. The less hierarchical structure, and more reliance on the initiative of its *gens libre* (freemen) traders, as opposed to the HBC's *engages* (servants), represented a significant NWC organizational innovation. The NWC utilized the old French inland empire approach by thrusting their traders deeper into Native country.

The NWC located their posts at or near Native villages or at the junctures of major waterways. This move compelled the HBC to do the same. For almost four decades these two organizations engaged in an intense rivalry over the fur trade of the Old Northwest. Although the HBC tried to disparage NWC opposition as disloyalty to its British charter, the "bitter antagonism" of the NWC "extended no further than a staunch and persistent opposition to the chartered monopoly" of the HBC.[29]

The Plains-Ojibwe came into contact with these British rivals, as the lucrative and competitive fur trade expanded westward in the late eighteenth and early nineteenth centuries. This convergence occurred within the territory then known as "Red River Chippewa Indian country."[30] The fur-rich region, with its numerous navigable waterways draining into the Red River of the North, created expanded possibilities for trade. By 1795 these conditions had attracted Chippewa, Métis, European Canadians, and European Americans to this area. Centered at the small trading hub of Pembina linking northern Minnesota and North Dakota, major trade routes extended north sixty miles to the convergence of the Assiniboine and Red Rivers at Winnipeg, southeast to St. Paul, and westward along the Pembina River through the Pembina Mountains to the Turtle Mountains one hundred miles away. The sources of the Pembina River originated on the northern and northeastern slopes of Turtle Mountain to the west, while the north–south range of hills known as the Pembina Mountains formed the western boundary of the Red River Valley of the North, and the eastern edge of the drift prairie which stretched west to the Missouri Plateau (see Image 6). These two adjacent ecological zones fit the subsistence and cultural needs of the Pembina and Turtle Mountain Chippewa. They devised a unique blend of Eastern Woodlands and Great Plains lifeways, "standing one foot on the deep eastern forests, and the other on the broad western prairies."[31]

The Chippewa band at the heart of this study coalesced around the small trading post village of Pembina in the 1790s. From 1795 to 1800 the NWC began establishing a series of semi-permanent trading posts to exploit the prairie fur trade in a region untapped by the HBC.

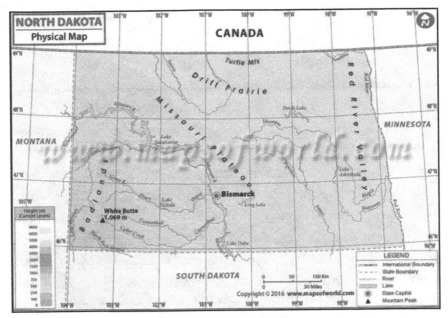

**Image 6. North Dakota Physical Map, locating the Turtle Mountains, Red River Valley, Drift Prairie, Devils Lake, and the Red, Pembina, Sheyenne, and Souris Rivers.** *https://www.mapsofworld. com/usa/states/amp/north-dakota/physical-map-of-north-dakota.html.*

They ranged westward from Pembina to the Turtle Mountains. The viability of these outposts depended on Chippewa and Cree hunters and trappers. North West Company traders and trappers like Peter Grant, Charles Jean Baptiste Chaboillez, Alexander Henry, David Thompson, and John Tanner based themselves in this region. They competed successfully against the rival HBC and XY fur trading companies and traveled all over northern North Dakota, including the Turtle Mountains, to expand their business.[32]

The Pembina-based fur trade provided the impetus for the formation and development of more cohesive and settled Plains-Ojibwe bands. This association of the Chippewa with the fur trading posts at Pembina deviated from the regular pattern of convergence. Usually, an NWC fur trader established a station at or near a Native village. In this case the fur trading posts preceded Chippewa settlement. Between 1801 and 1808, a permanent Plains-Ojibwe band coalesced around NWC fur trader Alexander Henry's post, Fort Pembina. This band formed the nucleus of the Pembina and Turtle Mountain Chippewa.[33]

Pembina served as a Red River haven amidst familiar surroundings and old allies. It also provided a staging ground for Chippewa cultural transformation as they began securing an extensive and sufficiently diverse, resource-rich domain across northeastern North Dakota. Gradually they positioned themselves in a series of semi-permanent villages accessible to nearby "buffalo grounds" at Pembina, Grand Forks. Stump Lake, Devils Lake, Dog Den, Des Lacs River, Souris River, Turtle Turtle Mountain, and St. Joseph (Walhalla) in the Pembina Mountains (see Image 7).[34] Operating within a system of seasonal migrations focused on semi-annual buffalo hunts, these strategic locations appear calculated to maximize survival and contradict any notion of a community of people without fixed habitation.

Chaboillez and his successor, Henry, both dealt primarily with the local Pembina Chippewa, who acknowledged Old Wild Rice (Manomin'e) as their most prominent leader. According to tribal historian Charlie White-Weasel, "the Old Wild Rice descendants intermarried with the mixed-blood and [NWC] white trade group, contributing to the eventual mixed blood majority in the Pembina [and Turtle Mountain] band memberships." J.B. Bottineau's grandfather, Charles Joseph Bottineau, worked from 1803–1808 as a voyageur for Alexander Henry the Younger at Pembina. The elder Bottineau married Margaret Songab (or Songup), a full blood Chippewa of the Ahdik Reindeer clan of the Pembina and Turtle Mountain bands.[35] Tanner, who had great affection for the Ottawa mother who adopted him and her maternal relations, married an Ojibwe woman. So did Henry, while Thompson married a Scots-Irish/Cree Métis woman. All such intimate relations conformed with the combined Native and European marriage rite known as the "custom of the country," or a la facon du pays. While the frontier as "battleground" has dominated American popular

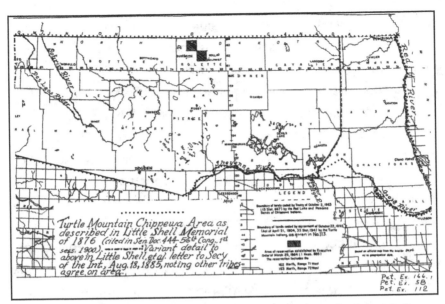

Within the map image:

Turtle Mountain Chippewa Area as
described in Little Shell Memorial
of 1876 (cited in Sen.Doc.444 56ᵗʰ Cong., 1ˢᵗ
sess. 1900). ••••• Variant detail to
above in Little Shell, et al. letter to Secy
of the Int., Aug.18,1885, noting other tribes
agree on area.

LEGEND

Pet. Ex. 166,1
Pet. Ex. 58
Pet. Ex. 112

## Image 7. Turtle Mountain Chippewa Area, as described in *Little Shell Memorial* of 1876:

"Your memorialists, the Turtle Mountain band of Chippewa Indians, respectfully represent that they and their forefathers for many generations have inhabited and possessed, as fully and completely as any nation of Indians on this continent have ever possessed any region of country, all that tract of land lying within the following boundaries, to wit: On the north by the boundary between the United States and the British possessions; on the east by the Red River of the North; on the south their boundary follows Goose River up to Middle Fork; thence up to the bead of Middle Fork; thence west-northwest to the junction of Beaver Lodge and Sheyenne River; thence up Sheyenne River to its headwaters; thence northwest to the headwaters of Little Knife River, a tributary of the Missouri River; and thence due north to the boundary between the United States and the British possessions. That their possession of this country has never been successfully disputed by any of the neighboring nations or tribes of Indians, but has at all times been recognized as the country of the Turtle Mountain band of the Great Chippewa Nation, of which the three Chippewas, Little Shell, Grandfather, Father and Son, have been principal chiefs for the past fifty years, and that they have never, by general council by their chiefs or by any authorized delegates, entered into any treaty with the United States by which they ceded any portion of their possessions." *Indian Claims Commission, Docket 113/Petitioner's Exhibits 3, 58, 112, 166, p. 104*
*"Collection of Interpretive Maps*
*. . . Prepared by Nancy O. Lurie.*

consciousness, we should not lose of sight of it as a "marrying ground" of "cultural merging."[36] Sexual relations often formed part of the nexus for establishing trade and acquiring power for Native American tribes.

Intermarriage bolstered the population of Native groups and fostered alliances with new and potentially powerful external allies. Native women acted customarily as the main trade intermediaries for their male kin and family. The success of a fur trader's operation often relied on marrying an influential Native leader's daughter and relying on her social and economic skills.[37] For example, another principal chief of the Pembina band circa 1800, known as Cottonwood, older brother of Little Shell I, became Alexander Henry's father-in-law. This "country marriage" gave Henry potential access to the elaborate Pembina Chippewa reciprocal kinship network essential to his fur trading business, while Cottonwood's immediate and extended relations secured a steady supply of goods and gifts from his son-in-law. After Cottonwood's death, Little Shell I took his place in accordance with the Chippewa custom of hereditary chieftainship transmitted patrilineally.[38]

What little that we know of Little Shell I (or Little Clam, Aisainse), is that he became the most prominent leader of the nascent Pembina Chippewa. He personified their physical migration to, and cultural shift in, the Red River region by residing at Devils Lake (Minnewaukan, or Spirit Lake) and trading at Pembina. In accordance with the Ojibwe totemic patrilineal clan system, Little Shell I belonged to the clan of his father.[39] This mode of kinship reckoning, considered to be a gift from the Creator, provided the basis for Ojibwe social order and political organization.

The prominent Crane Clan "claim[ed] . . . the chieftainship over the other clans of the Ojibway." Being a member of this highly regarded tribal lineage imbued him to become concurrently a chief, an acknowledged orator of the tribe, and a spiritual leader. The applicability of the name Little Shell probably originated in a dream of his father. It was also associated with an emblem of the Midewiwin spirituality. Ascendancy to Ojibwe leadership roles did not derive exclusively from heredity. Little Shell I ascended to his chieftainship through a combination of prized Chippewa cultural characteristics. Others recognized that, as a notable warrior and hunter, he had a significant amount of good medicine, or spiritual power. Such attributes meant that he had enough power to protect his people and enough expansive foresight to lead the way. In Ojibwe culture, authority vested in individuals still had to be conferred by a consensus of the band's members. Traders and tribesmen acknowledged his personal attributes of generosity, bravery, and diplomacy. As a result, Little Shell I became known as the most prominent "British Ojibwa chief of Red River."[40]

His example indicates that the political organization of pre-reservation Native communities like the Turtle Mountain Chippewa cannot be conveyed by European American concepts of administrative government, statehood, or nationhood. Because these culturally constructed notions did not conform to Native governing practices, federal policy makers often dismissed the claims of tribal government as inconsequential, trivial, or superficial. Native American political organization handled the public affairs of their society. It provided for the coordination of behavior to achieve the goals of survival, order, and stability, and it assumed a variety of forms. "Like other people the Indian needs at least a germ of political identity, some government organization of his own. Exclude him from this, and he has little else to live for."[41] Despite the inherent disparity in the tribal-federal government-to-government relationship, a case study focused on the legal battles of a tribal community with the United States must consider Native law and political organization. In the case of the Turtle Mountain Chippewa, assumptions that only the United States had genuine law and government remain unsupported by the historical evidence.

The Plains-Ojibwe comprised several egalitarian, decentralized, autonomous, and localized bands. Each constituted a political and territorial unit. Several factors inherent in such a structure worked against formalized political federation. The modest size of band, lack of hierarchy, and relative equity precluded the need for representation or stringent social control mechanisms. The Chippewa also placed a high cultural value on group and individual autonomy. Kinship provided the major counterforce to any divisive tendencies.

As illustrated above, kinship linked to a totemic clan system provided the principal means of social and political organization.[42] The Turtle Mountain band consisted of small extended-family kinship groups. Low population density (a few hundred) suited a subsistence economy of hunting and foraging based upon seasonal migrations. These shifts in subsistence and locus reduced potential strains on any one resource or area, provided maximum flexibility, individual responsibility, and mobility to gain or maintain an adaptive advantage. This form of political organization suited the metamorphosis of the Pembina and Turtle Mountain Chippewa into a Plains-Ojibwe culture.

They subsisted primarily as seasonal hunters who lived off the great herds of buffalo across northern North Dakota and Montana and southern Manitoba and Saskatchewan. The band united itself around various common-interest societies that served to integrate the entire group for subsistence, military, ceremonial, social, or political purposes.[43] The political organization of the Plains-Ojibwe derived from this structure of social relationships. It enabled leadership to be diffuse. In addition to the principal chief, the band had sub-chiefs, or ogimaag, who acted as leaders of their own family-based sub-groups. Different types of chiefs—clan, civil, diplomatic, war, and ceremonial—exercised distinct types of authority under various delineated circumstances.[44] Band governance and law rested upon kinship relations, social customs, and cultural values. While this uncontrived assemblage lacked the coercive authority of a European-derived nation-state government with well-defined functions and powers, the head chief and his council still served the basic purpose of government.

Anthropologist Maurice G. Smith concluded from his study that "the council was the most important political institution among the Plains tribes."[45] The council comprised prominent elders and warriors. In the case of the Turtle Mountain band, the head chief (Little Shell I) also served as the leading member of the council. They coordinated the use of resources, defined relationships among members of society, established authority to impose sanctions, and regulated behavior by deterring the violation of social norms. It should be noted that the political system of the Turtle Mountain Chippewa, like their cultural norms, was derived from Native American and Métis structures. Documentary evidence referring to Little Shell III noted that the chief referred to the tribal council as a Loge Soldat (a soldiers' lodge). This body, "according to their laws, customs, and traditions, is the council or legislative body of said Turtle Mountain Indians, and the only representative and authority with whom business may be transacted."[46] Historian Verne Dusenberry claimed that this arrangement was "strictly democratic," since "both the chief and the members of the soldier society were elected by the people themselves."[47]

Two key interrelated factors worked toward formalized political organization. Warfare, which was endemic—especially with the Dakota—and seasonal migratory subsistence patterns created the need for effective governance. The semi-annual communal buffalo hunts had to be highly organized to maximize the accumulation of this most vital resource and minimize its dangers. It functioned like a hierarchical military enterprise. The head chief and sub-chiefs of the council elected a hunt chief. This leader had unprecedented authority for the duration of the hunt.[48] The council also organized an Ogichidaa or "strong-hearted men" police society from the most prominent warriors and scouts. They lived in a separate tipi, had their own songs, dances, apparel, and identifying emblems. Their duties exempted them from labor and blood vengeance obligations because they had the authority to kill anyone who disobeyed their orders three times.[49]

These soldier societies organized the trip, the people, and the hunt. Moving as a group over vast expanses of prairie, they maintained a sharp lookout for buffalo and enemies. Their duties also included finding campsites, making camp, organizing a defense perimeter, breaking camp, and maintaining overall order and discipline. Any un-

sanctioned straying away from the group or individual hunting endeavors had the potential to jeopardize the entire band. In a culture that
valued personal autonomy highly, it is notable that the Ogichidaa had
the power to compel obedience and punish offenders. A first offense
resulted in shaming, ostracism, or the destruction of personal property
(e.g., a saddle and bridle or a bow). A second transgression brought
about corporal punishment (e.g., flogging) or banishment. If a third
infraction occurred, it meant execution.

While trying to make a case for the absence of Native American
law, a commissioner of Indian Affairs asserted that "the first condition
of civilization is protection of life and property through the administration of law."[50] If we take his word for it, then the measures noted above
fulfilled the basic functions of law and governance. They preserved the
hunt in particular and the social order in general by deterring conduct
inimical to well-being and survival.[51] The Pembina and Turtle Mountain bands, along with their interrelated and corresponding Métis kin,
organized themselves politically around the basic tenets of Indigenous
law and governance. Specific rules prescribed proper behavior in their
communities. Definable approaches to dispute resolution existed. They
resulted in "observable regularities in everyday behavior" as noted by
many contemporary informants.[52]

As alluded to above, the dangers posed by the Dakota constituted
the most persistent factor that necessitated a "regular system of government polity" by the Chippewa.[53] The coalescence of the Pembina
and Turtle Mountain Chippewa and their Métis kin occurred during
a time of heightened conflict with the Yankton Dakota over lands
west of the Mississippi and in the Red River valley. From 1801 to 1804
pitched battles took place at Cross Lake, Long Prairie, and Pembina. At
the latter place, at large party of Dakota attacked the Red River Ojibwe. During the bloody melee, a Dakota warrior killed and scalped Little Shell's favorite son and stripped him of his honorary British medal.
Despite being outnumbered, "the Ojibways were so exasperated at the
loss of their young chief that they fought with unusual fierceness and

hardihood." Outraged over the fate of his son, Little Shell I charged into the ranks of the Dakota, killed the attacker, then cut off his head. He held it aloft for everyone to behold, and "yelled his war-whoop." The awestruck Dakota made no move against him. His conspicuous bravery inspired the members of his band. Under Little Shell's leadership, they preserved their encampment and drove off the Dakota attackers. As a result of this victory and others, the Chippewa drove the Dakota out of Minnesota and west of the Red River Valley. In alliance with the Cree and Assiniboine tribes, they now had greater freedom to trap beaver and chase the buffalo in this abundant region. Thus, several formidable Ojibwe bands, including the Pembina and Turtle Mountain Chippewa in the westward vanguard, "gradually congregated on this remote northwest frontier."[54]

This Native borderland remained superficially part of British North America even after the American Revolution. References to British Natives, with British chiefs wearing British medals, amidst British traders always dismayed U.S. officials. They perceived the prospects for western expansion impeded by the southern extent of Rupert's Land projecting down the Red River Valley of the North (see Image 3) and potential British or Spanish territorial aspirations beyond its Mississippi River boundary. About the same time as Little Shell's Pembina Chippewa band originated, external events converged to alter circumstances in the region forever. Yellow fever and the success of a slave rebellion in Haiti thwarted Napoleon's dreams for a revived North American French empire centered in the Caribbean and supplied from New Orleans as the strategic gateway of the Mississippi River. He decided to sell quickly the vast French domain west of the Mississippi to the United States to help finance France's greater territorial ambitions in Europe.

Although President Thomas Jefferson thought he had a good chance to secure the vital port of New Orleans from France for a good price, the news from the U.S. negotiators that France wanted to sell all of Louisiana stunned him. For fifteen million dollars, the size of the

United States almost doubled in 1803. The dreams of the ardent expansionist who envisioned the U.S. as an "empire of liberty" overcame
his constitutional qualms about whether the president of the United
States could authorize such an arrangement. The Louisiana Purchase
secured trans-Appalachian commerce on the Mississippi River within
the United States, ended any future French aspirations in North America, made the British and Spanish possessions even more peripheral,
and opened the trans-Mississippi West for Jefferson's agrarian republic.

Three prominent North American natural landmarks bounded
Louisiana Territory: the Mississippi River to the east, the Gulf of Mexico to the south, and the Rocky Mountains to the west. Given the
paucity of first-hand geographic knowledge and the vagaries of map-
making, the Louisiana Purchase never precisely defined the northern
border of this immense area, other than imprecise references to an area
drained by the Missouri River. Not surprisingly, in all such transactions, the European or European-settler nation-states claimed dominion without consulting the Native peoples who lived in and controlled
various parts of the region.

The Indigenous territory of the Turtle Mountain band of the
Pembina Chippewa remained independent from Louisiana, although
the French may have claimed a tenuous *de jure* sovereignty beyond
their rightful bounds. The royally sanctioned Hudson's Bay Company,
with its legally significant, if very vague, British charter for Rupert's
Land, still prevailed over the region in terms of European sovereignty.
Because the homeland of the Pembina and Turtle Mountain bands of
Chippewa Indians encompassed approximately the northeastern quad-
rant of what became North Dakota, it resided east and north of the
Missouri River drainage, beyond the northern extent of the Louisiana
Purchase. It stayed within the southwestern edge of Rupert's Land,
including the portion of North Dakota drained by the Red River Val-
ley of the North in the east, the Sheyenne River in the south, and the
Souris River in the west (see Image 3).[55]

President Jefferson launched a series of exploratory expeditions
into and beyond this new domain of the United States. From 1804 to

1806, Lewis and Clark sought the Northwest Passage continental waterway to the Pacific Ocean. They traveled along the Missouri River south and west of the Turtle Mountain band's territory and the British Possessions. Zebulon Pike's failed 1805–1806 search for the source of the Mississippi in northern Minnesota became noteworthy for only one reason: "The visit of this officer [was] an event of considerable importance to the Ojibways of the Upper Mississippi, as they date their first intercourse with the 'Long Knives,' or citizens of the United States." The main messages of these heavily armed U.S. expeditions passed among all the Native communities and their associated French-Canadian traders in the region. The United States proclaimed its sovereignty, tried to interpose diplomatic relations to deter enmity and alliances between various tribes, and attempted to woo trade and any residual loyalty away from the British.[56] Such external impositions increased the internal tensions within the Native communities of the region.

Around 1808, Native American communities of the Old Northwest relayed messages of spiritual revival coming from, or parallel with, the revelations of Tecumseh's brother Tenskwatawa, known as the Shawnee Prophet.[57] Between the close of the American Revolution and the end of the War of 1812, a fundamental shift began to occur in the balance of power between various Native peoples and European Americans pushing into the trans-Appalachian West. Many Native Americans (e.g., Seneca, Shawnee, Cherokee, Creek) exhibited various forms of spirited resistance against these intrusions and federal policy. As the United States expanded westward, Native American territorial, political, and cultural integrity declined.

Spiritual revitalization movements became a significant and widespread Native response to cultural stress. Threatened increasingly by the outside influences from European American encroachment, Native prophets envisioned a return to an idealized former way of life. In 1808, an Ojibwe messenger brought news revealing the wishes of the Great Spirit or Creator (Kitchi Manitou or Kizhi Manido). The chiefs of the Red River region assembled at the trading house in Pembina. Little Shell I took it upon himself to interrogate the messenger and assisted in conveying the pronouncement to the assemblage. The maxims forbade intertribal warfare, lying, stealing, drunkenness, and partaking of non-Native foods or drink. These axioms harmonized with the codes of ethical conduct prescribed by the "great rules of life" of Ojibwe Midewiwin (from mino [good] daewaewin [hearted]) spirituality.[58] Since they seemed easier to observe than the decrees of the Shawnee prophet, "their influence was manifest for two or three years in the more orderly conduct, and somewhat amended condition of the Indians."[59] These prophetic movements offered hope and attempted to restore some sense of power and self-sufficiency to demoralized Native Americans.

Not all Indigenous peoples in the region heard or heeded such pronouncements. Endeavors to gain strength and cultivate resistance via multi-tribal alliances could not be sustained. European American infringement intensified intertribal aggression due to increased competition for fewer resources. After the gathering broke up, Little Shell I invited many of the attendees (including John Tanner, who, declined and went hunting instead) to return with him to his home on Graham's Island at Devils (Spirit) Lake.[60] "Ten men together with great numbers of women, accepted his invitation and went with him." Unfortunately, the next day at their encampment, a band of Dakota cut off the whole party and killed them all, except one young man who escaped to report the attack. The bodies of the men, women, and children were strewn around the campground, with "the stout body of Little Shell stuck full of arrows." Tanner, who did not give out compliments lightly, noted that Little Shell I was "the last of the considerable men of his age." The noted warrior and sub-chief Black Duck succeeded Little Shell I as head chief of the Turtle Mountain band until Little Shell II came of age. Black Duck's village was at Stump Lake, just southeast of Devils Lake. This noted warrior's territory extended southwest to the entry of Goose River into the Red River. He had "distinguished himself for bravery" in an 1805 battle with the Yankton Dakota led by Wa-nah-ta over this vital confluence of waterways.[61]

The Plains-Ojibwe battles with the Dakota bands would continue for another half century. A more transformative process occurred during this time that had a much longer lasting effect. This profound development tipped the region's balance of power in favor of the Chippewa and their Métis relations. The major legacy of the close relationship between the Red River fur traders and the Red River Native Americans proved to be a unique cultural amalgamation that transformed the Turtle Mountain band forever. Due to the intermarriage of mostly Chippewa (and some Cree and Ottawa women) with mainly French Canadian and some Scots and English NWC traders (e.g., Charles Joseph Bottineau) and trappers, a new and unique Métis cultural (and ultimately national) identity emerged by 1805 in the Red River borderland.[62] The "true descendants" of the Turtle Mountain band consisted primarily of "individuals of mixed Chippewa blood" and "the Pembinas and other mixed bloods and their descendants" who resided primarily west of Pembina, along the Pembina River, and at Turtle Mountain. The Ojibwe referred to the mixed-blood children of European men and Chippewa and Cree women as "half-burnt-wood" males or females. "They call the half-breeds so, because they are half-dark, half-white, like a half-burnt piece of wood." The French dubbed them *bois brule*, or scorched wood.[63] Many of the surnames of Chaboillez's and Henry's voyageurs (e.g., Grant, Delorme, Belgarde, Dejarlais, Dubois, Larocque, etc.) have been on the various Turtle Mountain Chippewa tribal rolls since their inception and remain prominent families associated with the tribe.

Contemporary tribal member and family historian Ruth Irene Belgarde verified that "it is such a thrill to trace an ancestor from France, to Quebec, to Winnipeg, to Pembina, and to the Turtle Mountains." This sense of deriving a unique identity from a peerless history matched that of the Chippewa worldview. "The Ojibways [were] traditionally well possessed of the most important events which have happened to them as a tribe." [64]

The Turtle Mountain Chippewa became the only predominantly Métis band to secure a reservation in the United States or a reserve in Canada. This singular and bittersweet attainment against a variety of cultural, legal, and bureaucratic obstacles was a significant accomplishment that has often been misunderstood. In terms of language, geography, and affinity as a Plains-Ojibwe culture, Belgarde pointed out, "Our people are so unique." [65] Degrees of blood quantum inherent in terms like "full-blood" or "mixed-blood" did not indicate who was, or was not, a Native or a non-Native or a tribal member. From the Native American perspective, "an Indian is someone who has Indian relatives." [66] Belgarde recounted Turtle Mountain childhood memories of many grandmas, grandpas, uncles, aunts, and cousins. "Only in later years," she said, "did I realize that they were not all my near blood relatives. However, that didn't make them any less loved by us." [67]

In addition to extensive intermarriage, the practice of adopting other Natives and non-Natives contributed to the admixture of non-blood relations. By 1800 the Pembina Chippewa contained an Ottawa segment. "A resourceful matriarch" known as Netnokwa led this contingent. She and her Chippewa husband adopted a white boy named John Tanner (nicknamed The Falcon). He had been captured in Kentucky by an Ojibwe raiding party in 1790 to replace a deceased son. In 1792, his captor sold him to Netnokwa. [68] A few years later Tanner and his new family moved to the Red River region near Lake Winnipeg to join his stepfather's Chippewa relations. This instance demonstrated that the Native community decided who it considered one of its own regardless of their biological origins. The aptness of this criteria derived from the emphasis on self-identity as it related to family, kinship, and community. These factors had more relevance to the actual process of identity formation than federal government blood quantum formulations for tribal enrollment, or other bureaucratically imposed notions about Native Americans.

Blood quantum did not matter to the predominantly intermingled Turtle Mountain band. Self-identification, kinship, and being part of a Native community trumped blood quantum. The oral tradition of many Métis and Chippewa families living in the Turtle Mountain region recounted the common experiences of buffalo hunts and Dakota attacks, creating a common and proud heritage that transcended ethnic boundaries. Belgarde exclaimed that she is "a descendant of those early buffalo hunters and . . . proud of each and every one of them."[69] Within a single family, some identified as Chippewa, others identified as Métis, and others attempted to "pass" into Canadian or U.S. society as French Canadian or European American. Yet distinct cultural differences in terms of language, spirituality, and social customs existed between those tribal members who identified themselves as primarily Chippewa or Métis.[70]

The best evidence for the very lengthy and relatively amicable blending of the two cultures at Turtle Mountain comes not only from family oral traditions, but from linguistic studies of their unique Michif language. Much of the scholarship about Native Americans agrees that language is *the* major component of cultural identity because language structure, style, and content reveal the cultural core of a community. According to linguistics scholar John C. Crawford, "[T]here are indications that linguistically as well as socially the Métis constituency and the Michif language have been dominant and increasing influences on the reservation for a considerable period."[71] Michif is a unique language. Its development can only be explained as the result of prolonged polyethnic Cree-Ojibwe and French contact. Such cultural blending is evidence of a sustained multi-lingual community, because "people who speak the same language also hold most of their culture in common." For instance, Turtle Mountain resident Andrew DeCoteau Sr., spoke Chippewa, French, Cree, Sioux, and English fluently.[72] Through this proficiency, they "constructed a common, mutually

comprehensible world" of accommodation and common meaning."
Transculturation through intermarriage, community-building, and
the blending of Cree–Ojibwe and French elements evolved into a new
people known as the Turtle Mountain Chippewa. Their unique Michif
(French–Cree) language is still spoken by a few elders, although—as on
every reservation or reserve—English predominates today.[73]

Unfortunately, the U.S. federal bureaucracy could not comprehend or categorize such nuanced cultural realities. They devised their
own gradations. The term Chippewa became the sanctioned label giv-
en to various Native tribes and their Métis members by both the U.S.
and Canadian governments. While the United States and Canada applied the legal term Chippewa to many federally recognized tribes,
bands, or sub-groups, the opposite happened with the Métis. In the
United States, Métis did not meet the criteria of an Indigenous "identifiable group" according to the census bureau, the Bureau of Indian
Affairs, or the courts. They therefore had no legal rights to land based
upon "Aboriginal title." They had to be content with occasional concessions of land grant scrip.[74] The misunderstanding over the legal status of the Métis in both the United States and Canada complicated the
specific outcomes regarding the land, sovereignty, and membership
claims of the Turtle Mountain Chippewa.

To forestall the influence of a separate and demographically
dominant Métis population in the Red River region and to bolster its
commercial monopoly against growing competition with the NWC,
a leading stockholder of the Hudson's Bay Company, the Earl of Selkirk, planted an agricultural colony named Assiniboia in the Red River
Valley in 1812. Although the HBC always asserted its self-appoint-
ed superior sovereignty over the region's Native peoples, British legal
precedent established by the royal Proclamation of 1763 obliged Lord
Selkirk to at least indulge in the formality of a treaty. For a modest annual gift (*not* a quit rent) of one hundred pounds of tobacco each to the
resident Chippewa (Saulteaux) and Cree bands, the Treaty of Selkirk

(1817) extinguished their "Indian title," securing a large and lucrative section of the North American heartland for almost nothing. Selkirk's view of the treaty terms differed from the Native understanding. The leading hereditary chief of the Saulteaux, Peguis, complained to the British years later that neither he nor his people had been asked for permission or compensated financially by the "Silver Chief." Peguis only signed the treaty "for the sake of peace," expecting "to be paid well for my tribes' lands." Selkirk also neglected to obtain the consent of the "half- breeds," who formed nearly half of the settlement. Noting their growing sense of distinction and entitlement, NWC factor William McGillivray wrote that the Métis "look upon themselves as members of an independent tribe of natives, entitled to property in the soil."[75] The colony's intrusion into the Red River settlements only increased tensions with the resident inhabitants.

In theory, the colony would cut the heavy cost of importing food for HBC fur trading posts and brigades by producing local foodstuffs, providing a refuge for retired traders or ex-*engages* and their families, and countering the political aspirations of the Métis. The colony failed initially from 1812 to 1821 on all counts. Not surprisingly, the Métis freemen resented the Highland Scots and De Meuron Swiss settlers and the advent of an agricultural colony that would impair their hunting and trapping lifeways and subsistence, while swallowing up the land, including their tenuous property claims. Armed clashes occurred, most notably the so-called Seven Oaks massacre in 1816, where Cuthbert Grant (some of whose descendants became enrolled members of the Turtle Mountain band) and a party of NWC Métis encountered a similar sized HBC party led by Governor Semple. They exchanged rash words and threats, which escalated suddenly into gunfire and hand-to-hand combat. The governor and three quarters of his retinue "were shot down and tomahawked."[76] Uneasiness subsided only when the British government sent a military guard to protect the Selkirk colony from the Métis and—after the Earl's death in 1819—intervened to bring about a merger of the two companies in 1821 under HBC governance.

The rather precise HBC grant of Assiniboia to Lord Selkirk took advantage of the poorly defined northern boundary of the Louisiana Purchase. It also encouraged British fur traders to expand their long-standing alliances with the Plains-Ojibwe bands in the region. Based on perceived insults to the nation's honor and economic distress from Britain's maritime policies, U.S. political leaders viewed present British intrusions and injustices since 1783 as threats to America's national development. The strong desire for territorial growth and westward expansion, combined with mounting anti-British resentment stemming from maritime disputes, led to the War of 1812.

The United States wanted to thwart the British in Canada, the Spanish in Florida, and their Native allies in the Northwest Territories and the Mississippi Valley. Although militarily inconclusive in terms of territory won or lost, the War of 1812 had far-reaching consequences. It diminished British influence throughout the Great Lakes region, by compelling the abandonment of their forts, replacing them with U.S. military and trading posts. These establishments provided a preliminary stepping stone for increased U.S. westward expansion in the Old Northwest.

The war had disastrous consequences for the Native Americans, especially for the pan-tribal confederacies of the Great Lakes region allied with the British. First, the preservation of their fur trade dominance could not be sustained under the expansionist designs of the United States. Fear of the continuing influence of British traders on Native Americans within the United States, plus a desire to keep the profits of the peltry business in American hands, resulted in an 1816 Act of Congress excluding non-citizens from the trade. This overturned the "free passage" right agreement in the Jay Treaty of 1794. Article 3 permitted Indigenous peoples from either side to move freely back and forth across the international boundary. Second, large-scale family-unit communities, based upon harvesting crops, grazing livestock, and cutting down forests, required lots of land and left little or no room for Natives or fur trapping. During the peace Treaty of

Ghent negotiations, the British tried to retain most of the Northwest by reverting to the Greenville Treaty line of 1795 as a permanent boundary and forbidding the purchase of Indigenous peoples' lands by either country. However, resurgent U.S. nationalism, fueled by the war, refused to consider any proposals that could limit territorial expansion.[77] Weakened and scattered tribes could no longer militarily resist the ever-increasing encroachment of European American settlements into their tribal lands. Federal policy continued its practices of coercion and paternalism, which proved equally fatal to the welfare of Native Americans. The tribes that remained intact became diminishing islands amidst a tide of European American towns stretching to the Mississippi River.

The post-War of 1812 era represented a significant epoch in American history. Most aspects of Native and non-Native life in the United States underwent major demographic, domicile, economic, and political changes. Although the conflict ended the "middle ground" in the Great Lakes region, according to Richard White, it provided the impetus for a new middle ground centered in the Red River watershed of the north and farther west. This situation drew more Chippewa, Métis, European Canadians, and European Americans to the Pembina area. Nonetheless, the frequency of major spring floods diminished Pembina's development. Its strategic location meant that it would never be abandoned entirely, but most of the early trading posts, some Chippewa extended families, and the growing Métis population moved thirty miles west along the river to higher ground at St. Joseph in the Pembina Mountains (see Image 6).[78] Connected by the lower fur trade posts of Winnipeg (at the confluence of the Assiniboine and Red Rivers), and the upper fur trade posts at Pembina (at the convergence of the Pembina and Red Rivers), these river junctions melded the fate of Assiniboia and the fur trade of the Hudson's Bay territories of Canada with the Pembina and Turtle Mountain Chippewa on the northern plains of the United States.

By 1815, Little Shell II (Weesh-e-damo) had matured enough to assume his mantle as a hereditary chief of the Pembina band. Two major considerations besides the floods influenced him, and a significant number of the band's members, to migrate farther west. First, because of his father's fate and the prior death of a brother during another Dakota raid at Pembina, they decided to move away from Black Duck's village and the Devils Lake/Goose River area to a safer refuge in the Pembina and Turtle Mountains. Despite this precaution, mortal danger followed them. In December 1815, only three of thirty-six Chippewa warriors survived a Dakota assault. This implacable inter-tribal rivalry and warfare between the Chippewa and the Dakota fueled the further fragmentation and westward migration of small family or sub-groups of Chippewa.[79] Second, by 1815, the declining beaver and muskrat fur trade in the Red River basin and the lure of more westerly buffalo herds induced Little Shell II's sturdy band to begin wintering, trapping, and hunting as far as one hundred miles to the west in the bountiful Turtle Mountains of north-central North Dakota. By 1818, they upgraded from "wintering in the bush" to a dwelling settlement to be near the buffalo. In this bountiful place, "[T]hey'd eat buffalo all winter," despite the sub-zero temperatures and heavy snowfalls. With their Red River carts, the "half-breed traders generally followed with goods and ammunition, buying their furs, buffalo hides, dried meats, and pemmican." This hybrid culture of Native and European ancestry "were talkin' mixed Cree, Chippewa, and French . . . and that's what they were, and that's [Michif]."[80] A unique polyethnic community emerged.

Their beneficent adopted homeland of elevated terrain straddled the later international border between North Dakota and Manitoba. Geographically, located at the heart of North America, Plains-Ojibwe oral tradition explained its origins and significance in their account of a great flood. After the deluge, the rounded shell of the Great Turtle (called Mekinok) remained as the only solid entity above water. It provided the foundation for the new world. "Mekinok became Turtle Island, the center of the world and the birthplace" of the Ojibwe people. As the land formed, Mekinok became covered with earth, known as Mikinaak Wajiw in Ojibwe (the mound of earth that is a turtle), or

Turtle Mountain.[81] Later government cartographers, like the French émigré Joseph Nicollet, who produced the first detailed and accurate map with place-names of the region between the Mississippi and Missouri Rivers, noted the aptness of Native Americans to accurately name places after "the form an object resembles." It seems that the Chippewa deciphered the unmistakable turtle-shape of this upland, with its head in the west and tail in the east, and always referred to the specific area in the singular as Turtle Mountain.[82]

Approaching these well wooded and watered rolling hills from the south and southwest after crossing the Souris (Mouse) River, Alexander Henry noted the "astonishing quantity of water," and that the "buffalo continued to appear in every direction around us." From the vantage point of the wide semi-arid sea of grasslands below, Henry referred to Turtle Mountain as a "low blue cloud."[83] Closer inspections revealed irregular hills rounded by receding glaciers, rising four hundred to eight hundred feet above the prairie below. They stretched over an area of twenty miles north and south, and forty miles east to west. Early observers, like the geographer David Thompson, found this unique terrain—which he labeled on his 1798 map as "Turtle Hill"—interspersed with hundreds of lakes (the larger ones with fishing), ponds, springs, marshes, and swamps. The terra firma was densely covered with hazelnut, pin cherry, and chokecherry bushes, amidst woodlands of small aspen, poplar, elm, ash, pine, and birch. The highlands and wetlands abounded with abundant wildlife like rabbits, grouse, prairie chickens, ducks, gophers, deer, moose, and bears. The Chippewa who traded with Alexander Henry at Pembina and hunted with John Tanner gathered the birch bark for their canoes, the ash wood for their bows, and Juneberry and chokecherry wood for their arrow shafts from the Turtle Mountains.[84] These foothills provided abundant sources of food and shelter and yielded a variety of pelts from beavers, muskrats, and raccoons.[85] Amidst "the traders' and trappers' paradise between the Red River country, the Turtle Mountains, and the Souris River, the Turtle Mountain country was *the* choice fur spot." These circumstances settled Turtle Mountain as the headquarters for the Plains-Ojibwe in the Old Northwest. [86]

Thus, between 1800 and 1818, the Turtle Mountain band had not only transformed themselves into a Plains-Ojibwe culture, but they also formed the nucleus for the "composite band" made up of full-blood Pembina Chippewa and mixed-blood Métis who emerged from the hybrid fur trading society in the Red River region. Their totemic clan and kinship systems enabled them to retain close relations with their kin in the Pembina band and to incorporate Métis-Chippewa descendants and members of other tribes (Ottawa, Cree) into the band through assigned clan designations.[87] The genesis of the Turtle Mountain Chippewa illustrated that Native cultures and identity are dynamic and characterized by intentional action and change.

The changing circumstances that brought the Turtle Mountain band into being demonstrated a fluid relationship between cultural attributes and identity. To survive growing and more intrusive European Canadian influence, the Turtle Mountain band's Chippewa culture and identity had to be redefined and renegotiated with their Métis relations.[67] They adapted to new circumstances and melded their cultural identity to survive. By 1818, they exhibited all the political attributes of an identifiable group of autonomous Native American and Métis people, with "possessory occupation" of, and controlling authority over, a defined territory.[89]

At the same time, the United States pressed its claims to the same territory. As a follow-up to the Treaty of Ghent, the United States and Britain agreed upon the land cession of the Convention of 1818 (see Image 3). This international agreement (*not* the Louisiana Purchase of 1803, as asserted by some) established U.S. jurisdiction over the upper part of the Red River Valley of the North (which formed the eastern border of North Dakota, the western border of Minnesota, and flowed north into Manitoba, Canada). The land cession also created a new northern boundary line along the forty-ninth parallel: "the said Parallel . . . shall form the Northern Boundary of the . . . United States . . . from the Lake of the Woods [Minnesota] to the Stony [Rocky] Mountains."[90] It is crucial to understand that from neither the Louisiana Purchase nor the British Cession of 1818 did the United States acquire sovereignty over, or territory from, the Native American inhabitants. In terms of the latter transaction with Britain, the United States only secured a "claim" of "jurisdiction" over "Territory, Places, and Possessions." It did not acquire ownership of territory or preclude "Indian title." It attained the exclusive right (i.e., it superseded any prior claims by France, Spain, or Britain) to acquire legal title by negotiating land cessions from the Native peoples of the region, including the Turtle Mountain Chippewa.[91]

As part of its separate and subdue policy in the Northwest Territory since the 1795 Treaty of Greenville, the United States began to assert ever greater jurisdiction over Chippewa tribes and bands. Prior to 1824, when the Office of Indian Affairs became a branch of the War Department within the federal government, the Secretary of War had primary responsibility for formulating and administering federal policy. Secretary of War John C. Calhoun articulated the core of that policy in 1818 when he stated:

> It is impossible . . . that [Indians] should exist as independent communities, in the midst of a civilized society. They are not in fact an independent people nor ought they to be so considered. They ought to be brought within the pales of law and civilization. Our views of their interest, and not their own, ought to govern them.[92]

These unilateral and ahistorical affirmations announced the future tenor of U.S. federal policy. They also foreshadowed that any subsequent treaty councils initiated by the federal government with representatives of "the great nation of the Chippewas," would attempt to place new restrictions upon their trade, territory, and autonomy.[93]

Two years before the policy of delimiting Native homelands began in earnest with the Treaty of Prairie du Chien in 1825, the U.S. Supreme Court rendered a landmark decision that had momentous consequences for the future legal status of all Native American lands. Because so many conflicting claims over land cessions and subsequent sales arose prior to 1823, the U.S. government had to settle this matter once and for all. Western expansion could not occur without valid land ownership, and these holdings could not be secured until the relinquishment of prior "Indian title." In English common law, a legal case needed a cause of action. In the Supreme Court case of *Johnson v. McIntosh,* the action was trespass.[94] The issue at stake concerned the validity of each European American party's land title, and the nature of Indigenous peoples' title. The principle of law before the Supreme Court and Chief Justice John Marshall considered whether the courts of the U.S. could recognize the title conveyed from a tribe to a private individual as valid. Marshall ruled that the title obtained under the original private land purchase in 1773 was invalid. Only the United States could acquire legal title to Native lands, not private citizens.

To bolster his decision, Marshall reprised several hundred years of colonial North American history and proclaimed the "doctrine of discovery" as the legal justification for his decision.[95] By impugning the character and religion of the Native Americans, he asserted that "conquest gives a title which the courts of the conqueror cannot deny."[96] This *fait accompli* became the foundation for the U.S. federal law doctrine of "Indian title," based on the diminished "use right" of occupancy. While their rights were not "entirely disregarded," they were "necessarily impaired."[97] This left Native Americans as tenants with "diminished" use, possession, and disposition rights to their land.[98] Impeded "Indian title" left them at the mercy of a U.S. government landlord who could assert its self-proclaimed superior sovereignty to evict them whenever the circumstances of European American agricultural settlement or commercial enterprise dictated.

To put this principle into practice for the recently acquired British Cession of 1818 sector, the United States needed to determine the northern extent of its territory at the forty-ninth parallel boundary with the British Possessions. In 1823, topographical engineer Major Stephen H. Long became the first official U.S. government-sponsored explorer to traverse through the homeland of the Pembina Chippewa when he traveled down the Red River from the Minnesota River, through Pembina, and up to Lake Winnipeg in Canada. His exploratory mission illustrated how closely the federal government involved itself in the earliest prelude to European American settlement of the region, including the feasibility of navigable river transportation in the Red River basin.

The main object remained locating the international boundary with the British Possessions at the forty-ninth parallel and "fix[ing] an oak post on it, bearing on the north side the letters G.B., and on the south side U.S."[99] They found that the entire village of Pembina (with the exception of one log cabin) remained inside the United States. Apparently this discovery pleased the local populace of approximately "350 souls," two-thirds of whom Long designated as "half-breeds" (or "Bois brules," for "burnt wood, from their dark complexion," i.e., Métis), because most of the buffalo would be on the American side of the line. The only dissatisfied parties turned out to be the HBC, who abandoned their trading post, some of the British Selkirk colonists who left with them, and the Catholic diocese, who abandoned the mission they had established in 1818. They all moved northward to the lower Red River settlements.[100]

Long, like many—but not all—U.S. officials, disparaged the Pembina Métis for not "possessing the qualifications for good settlers" because of their lack of farming and their preference for hunting and the fur trade, preferring the frugal and industrious Scots as good settlers. He denigrated the mixing of "inferior" Native American with "superior" European American bloodlines, maligning the Métis. Wedded to an idealized American racial homogeneity while ignoring the reality of post-contact *métissage*, Long ascribed heterogeneity as the causal factor for their "very low rank in the scale of civilization . . . but little superior to the Indians themselves."[101]

This attitude reflected the advent of scientific racism. It exhibited itself through an increase of racial stereotyping associated with the violent and self-righteous expansionism of Manifest Destiny that came to fruition during the 1840s. This dogma linked the destiny of the Anglo-Saxon "race" with U.S. continental expansion, and the extension of liberty and freedom to northern European Protestant men. Racial mixing could corrupt American and British Anglo-Protestants, and therefore, deter their destiny. Yet, the devaluation of mixed-blood populations (Native Americans, Métis, mulattos, Creoles, Mexicans) along gendered, religious (anti-Catholic), and class lines was also deployed to render them unfit for self-governance. All of these factors justified taking their lands and treating them as social or political inferiors, incapable of deciding what was best for themselves.[102]

Long's scorn of the Métis generalized and assigned negative values to imagined differences, "to the accuser's benefit and at his victim's expense, in order to justify the former's own privileges or aggression."[103] Such racism became insidious when it upheld the power and aggression of U.S. national policies such as Indian Removal in the 1830s and the Mexican War in the 1840s. In Rupert's Land, the Protestant clergy's middle-class British values aggravated racial tensions along gender lines by denigrating Native and mixed-blood women, their progeny, and interracial marriage. British mixed-blood, or "country-born" families, much more than the French Métis, increasingly shunned their Native origins, female relations, and Métis kin while assimilating themselves to Anglo cultural norms. This differentiation resulted in a much "more consciously stratified" fur-trade society.[104]

Long, like his Anglo-American predecessors in colonial New England, misunderstood and criticized how the Chippewa and Métis made a living. His ethnocentric concepts of "civilization" only compounded his ignorance about "productivity." To view buffalo hunting as random leisure activity rather than as a well-organized, quasi-military disciplined operation requiring dangerous, risky, and hard work to find, kill, butcher, process, and cart away the fruits of their labor, demonstrated how little "exploring" he really did.[105] Small-scale eastern U.S. farming was neither a practicable nor profitable endeavor on the northern plains in the pre-industrial era. The Métis engaged in small-scale agriculture, as part of a balanced economy of hunting, gathering, fishing, and trading. They raised horses, cattle, oxen, sheep, and swine, while growing hay, corn, squash, pumpkins, beans, and potatoes.[106] No viable markets or cost-effective transportation existed except for furs and limited merchandise. "While they could not sell the produce of their farms, they found it easy to sell the articles obtained in their hunts."[107] Scarcity of credit, capital, equipment, and labor, plus harsh winters, short growing seasons, floods, and insect plagues precluded farming beyond small garden plots. The ultimate irony of Long's misconceptions was that the Scots Selkirk colonists failed miserably to establish an agricultural colony, not because of any predilection for industry or lack thereof, but for all the reasons mentioned above. If it had not been for the timely interventions of the "lowly" yet hospitable Métis, they would have starved or been forced to abandon their colony sooner than they did.

What an outsider like Long failed to comprehend, insiders like Alexander Ross or Father Belcourt understood. The priest accompanied a Métis buffalo hunt across the southern borderlands of Turtle Mountain Chippewa territory in 1845. The bottom line of their venture should have intrigued rational self-interested men like Long and other U.S. officials. It certainly impressed the man of the cloth. In less than two months, fifty-five hunters among 309 people procured and processed 1,776 buffalo. At "the most moderate market prices," their net profit "remained 1,500 pounds sterling." Such an astounding profit margin amounted to "more money than all the agricultural class obtained for their produce in the same year."[108] This episode illustrated that the goal of the Chippewa and Métis political economy endeavored to obtain maximum abundance through the most efficient means. For the most part they succeeded until the depletion of the buffalo by European Americans in the 1870s. Yet, the ethnocentrism of Long and other federal policymakers precluded recognition that different modes of Native American or Métis economics sought similar ends. As noted by one of the keenest and biased resident observers in the Red River settlements, Alexander Ross, "they cherish freedom as they cherish life."[109] Their economic activities maximized their social goals of collective and individual liberty.

Such freedom can only be organized around and sustained by political organization and territorial sovereignty. By focusing on their emergence and geographical expansion, this chapter established that between 1795 and 1825 the Pembina and Turtle Mountain Chippewa coalesced as an identifiable and organized group of Native Americans meeting all the legal criteria for valid title to a defined territory. As an extended kinship group associated with a particular region, they contested for and occupied a hunting territory attributed to the impact of the changing economic realities of the fur trade. Indigenous title derived from the recognition of their right of possession by other regional tribes prior to European American colonization. The Pembina and Turtle Mountain Chippewa territorial sovereignty occurred prior to U.S. acquisition from the British Cession of 1818 treaty with Britain. This change in European-derived sovereignty set the stage for a contentious tribal-federal relationship throughout the remainder of the nineteenth century and beyond. A major source of this contention derived from the persistent U.S. assertion that "Indians must be brought gradually under our authority and laws" without acknowledging divergent Native interests and autonomy.[110]

# CHAPTER 2

# From "Middle Ground" to "Border Fixing," 1825–1862

*It is not that we want the country badly, but to make provision for you.*[1]
—Alexander Ramsey, Pembina Treaty Council, 1851

Since the founding of the United States, Native American autonomy conflicted with non-Native national interests. Federal policy assumed that Native peoples had little awareness of their own needs. Based on this erroneous assumption, government officials asserted that nothing limited their dictates to the Native peoples. This circular logic reveals the expedient nature of most tribal-federal treaties from 1825 to 1851. The federal government wanted to consolidate as many Chippewa bands on as few reservations as possible, leaving less land reserved for Native peoples, and more land for European American settlement.[2] Although compelled to negotiate under these circumstances, Ojibwe historian William Warren perceived accurately that "no good" could result from "bad and thoughtless policy."[3]

This keen observation held true for the Chippewa-Dakota demarcation line drawn by the Treaty of Prairie du Chien in 1825. And it had long term significance for the territorial claims of the Pembina and Turtle Mountain bands. Anticipating the need for a regional treaty conference with most of the Natives in the northwest, determining the extent of Native homelands and hunting territories became a task of Major Long's expedition. Long detected that "the Bois des Sioux is supposed to be the northernmost limit of the undisputed property of the [Dakota] on the Red River. Beyond this point they never hunt without being prepared for war" with the Chippewa (see Image 8).[4] While Long's observations proved accurate, his ethnocentrism created false impressions about the Native people in the region. His bias converged with similar anti-Native preconceptions shared by some of his superiors, like President James Monroe, Secretary of War John C. Calhoun, and Chief Justice John Marshall. With Long's demarcation of the international boundary with British Canada and Marshall's self-serving legal rendering of "Indian title," the power of their perceptions warped federal policy by privileging European American interests over those of Native Americans.

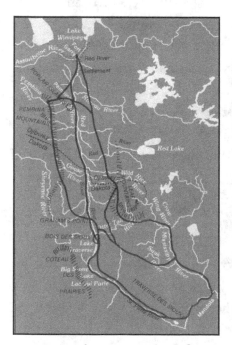
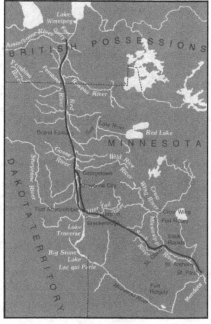

**Image 8. The map at the left accurately labels and denotes the Ojibwe-Dakota dotted boundary line of the 1825 Treaty of Prairie du Chien, extends it west of the Red River, and also identifies Pembina, the Pembina River, and the Pembina Mountains.**
Minnesota History *46, no. 3 (Fall 1978), p. 119, Minnesota Historical Society Press.*

To begin realizing this goal, the United States encouraged multi-tribal assemblies to establish mutual boundaries via multilateral treaties with most of the tribes in the Northwest Territory (i.e., north and west of the Ohio River, south and west of the Great Lakes, and east of the Mississippi River). In August of 1825, one of the most significant of these gatherings convened portions of the Chippewa (the Lake Superior bands), Dakota (Sioux), Sacs and Fox, Menominee, Iowa, Winnebago, Ottawa, and Potawatomi nations at Prairie du Chien (then within Michigan Territory, now in the state of Wisconsin). These tribes met with two U.S. commissioners: Superintendent of Indian Affairs William Clark and Michigan Territorial Governor Lewis Cass.

Article Five of the Treaty of Prairie du Chien became the most relevant portion for the Turtle Mountain band. It divided the Chippewa to the north and the Dakota (Sioux) to the south by a compromise line running in a northwesterly direction through Wisconsin and Minnesota as far west as the Red River (see Image 8).[5] These traditional enemies had fought each other as they migrated slowly westward throughout the eighteenth century. The Article One provision for "firm and perpetual peace" did not deter their animosity, which lasted until the advent of reservations and other agreements in the 1850s.[6] The Turtle Mountain and Pembina Chippewa bands neither attended these talks nor signed the treaty, because their lands extended west of the Red River beyond the line the United States designated at that time. Unfortunately, they bore the brunt of subsequent intertribal hostility, west of the Red River and east of the Missouri River during the first half of the nineteenth century. In the winter of 1824–1825, the Dakota attacked the Turtle Mountain band's substantial settlement at Buffalo Lodge. They razed the palisade, destroyed the surrounding cornfields, and drove the Chippewa out until 1850.[7]

Rather than seek compliance via intertribal negotiation, U.S. officials forced a compromise on both groups. Despite endorsing the treaty, neither tribe recognized it as binding in any way. The United

States wanted to begin the process of limiting hostilities to pave the way for future settlement and commercial development. Not achieving more peaceful Dakota-Chippewa relations at this early stage did not preclude the eventual attainment of these goals. Legally defining the territories of the two most powerful Native nations in the vicinity marked a significant achievement for U.S. policymakers at Prairie du Chien. Unbeknownst to the tribal delegates, it set the stage for future incremental land cession treaties.

Most of the inter-tribal warfare derived from colliding hunting parties despite Article Thirteen's "reciprocal right of hunting on the lands of one another, permission being first asked and obtained."[8] It would be inaccurate and ethnocentric to reduce this conflict to primitive uncontrolled blood feuds, as many European Americans then and since have supposed. Although the scale, organization and violence associated with European American and Native American warfare differed significantly, the Pembina and Turtle Mountain Chippewa fought against the Dakota for many of the same geopolitical aspirations as any European or European-derived state. "From the Indian point of view, warfare was part of their economic cycle. The occupancy of the Red River region by the Ojibwe rested upon their success in withstanding the inroads of the Dakota."[9] As confirmed by Alexander Ramsey, governor and superintendent of Indian Affairs in Minnesota Territory, "they acquired [a] vast tract of country, wresting it from warlike and generally more numerous foes." The "advantageous results of the contest have been altogether with" the Chippewa, "who have acquired by conquest and steadily maintained a beautiful and widespread territory."[10] United States officials respected this type of territorial sovereignty derived from coercive power. For the Pembina and Turtle Mountain bands, it meant that all neighboring tribes, and eventually the U.S. government, recognized their occupancy and adverse possession.

After the signing of the treaty of Prairie du Chien, some of the Chippewa and Dakota in attendance decided to extend the demarcation line between their territories beyond the Red River. This Chippewa-Dakota Sweet Corn Treaty agreed upon a dividing line west of the Red River and north of the Sheyenne River to where the Knife River meets the Missouri River (see Image 2).[11] A secondary chief of the Sisseton and Yankton Dakota bands, Sweet Corn (or Ojoupay, who was not a signatory of the Prairie du Chien treaty) gave his name to this pact. The principal chief of the Sisseton and Yankton Dakota bands, Wa-nah-ta (He-Who-Rushes-On), signed the Treaty of Prairie du Chien and seems to have been the initiator for this agreement. His father, Shappa (The Beaver), had been murdered with the foreknowledge of Flat Mouth, while on a peace overture in 1806. "During his [Wa-nah-ta's] lifetime he amply revenged the death of his father, by inflicting repeated blows on the Ojibways of Red River."[12] Twenty years before, he also fought against Turtle Mountain band chief Black Duck (Little Shell II's predecessor and father-in-law) for control over the region where the Goose River flowed into the Red River. Flat Mouth, a civil chief from Leech Lake, through the "force of his character" also represented the Northern or Red Lake Chippewa, including the Pembina band.[13] He still displayed his British medal and flag as a sign of being a former British ally. In contrast, he often demonstrated his displeasure with European American demands by making a show of throwing away his presidential badge of honor while haranguing U.S. officials. Within this international context, Chippewa leaders determined that setting boundaries amongst themselves, or with Britain and the United States, did not diminish their territorial sovereignty on the northern Plains.[14]

Although referred to vaguely in the Prairie du Chien treaty journal, U.S. representatives remained unaware of this separate arrangement until given a copy retained by Wa-nah-ta's son (of the same name) during U.S. treaty negotiations with the Sisseton-Wahpeton bands of Dakota in 1867 for their lands south of the Turtle Mountain Chippewa domain. These traditional tribal enemies had learned through bitter experience the potential value of written documents to uphold Anglo-American legal claims. Too often their oral renderings of treaties had been shunned by U.S. authorities, so they grafted European American legalistic practices onto their own Indigenous solutions to problems of human diversity and conflict in North American borderlands. As noted by historian Francis Jennings, such "treaty protocol was of Indian manufacture."[15] More importantly in this case, its submission by the Dakota to the treaty commissioners demonstrated tribal sovereignty by representing their own political interests.

Too much significance should not be read into this treaty between two Native nations. Nor should it be romanticized. As with the U.S.-imposed Prairie du Chien treaty, this independent arrangement somewhat mitigated, but did not stop, clashes of violence between various hunting parties until the 1850s. Yet the Sweet Corn treaty proved significant in two major ways. First, such self-directed action challenged many of the negative assumptions imposed on Native peoples by federal policymakers. This inter-tribal accord refuted the inaccurate claim of Commissioner William Clark, who probably had more firsthand knowledge of Native affairs than any U.S. representative. He claimed that tribes had no defined boundaries and did not know what belonged to each other.[16] It also disproved the U.S. allegation that Native Americans only retained "pretensions" of sovereignty. The actions of the Dakota and the Chippewa answered the fundamental policy question about whether the undiminished attributes of tribal sovereignty remained an "inherent right," or a right "bestowed" by the United States. Clearly both parties to the Sweet Corn treaty exercised their inherent right of self-government without any need for U.S. government authorization.

Representatives from both groups exercised their notions of self-preservation, not as wards under the guardianship of the United States. They had to settle this matter on their own because they had to live with the dangers of unresolved conflict. Federal policymakers remained self-absorbed and uninterested, as exemplified by President Monroe's last state of the union address to Congress in 1825. Up until then the United States had believed that the Native Americans east of the Mississippi River would continue to cede their lands willingly. But by the 1820s, they could no longer afford to give away anymore land and retain a semblance of tribal cohesion. Monroe's Secretary of War, John C. Calhoun, devised a new means to the same end of Native land cessions. They proposed the removal of eastern tribes to an unorganized territory carved out of the Louisiana Purchase west of the Mississippi River, creating a permanent Native American frontier for the tribes relocated to that region.[17]

Timed to coincide with the need to end inter-tribal wars and establish boundaries as instituted by the Prairie du Chien treaty, removal provided the basis for federal negotiators to arrange piecemeal land cessions that would be reallocated to relocated tribes. With this new designation of lands west of the Red River as "Indian territory," the self-proclaimed "general controlling power of the United States" asserted in the Prairie du Chien treaty provided no protection to the Chippewa or Dakota. Government officials viewed this region as an expedient dumping ground for relocated eastern tribes.[18] Yet despite these negative connotations, the Pembina and Turtle Mountain Chippewa benefited indirectly. The U.S. government recognized that the Chippewa had exclusive "Indian title" to all the Indigenous lands north of "Indian territory."[19]

In order to strengthen the chances of Chippewa compliance with the Prairie du Chien treaty, Lewis Cass teamed up with the head of the Bureau of Indian Affairs, Thomas McKenney, for a follow-up treaty at Fond du Lac at the western tip of Lake Superior in August of 1826.[20] The Chippewa delegates at Prairie du Chien never claimed to represent the interests of any absent bands. The United States recognized "the remote and dispersed situation of the Chippewas," and "the loose nature of the Indian government," while also believing that such an entity as the "whole Chippewa tribe" endured. Although such a unified body had never existed, pretending that it did, provided an expedient means to achieve the main U.S. treaty goal. As stated in Article 8, "the

Chippewa tribe of Indians fully acknowledge[d] the authority and jurisdiction of the United States, and disclaim[ed] all connection with any foreign power."[21] Potentially, such a concession applied to the Pembina and Turtle Mountain bands without their consent or knowledge, or any recognition of the territory they possessed.

To signify this presumed shift in allegiance, the commissioners distributed U.S. medals to various Native leaders. Unfortunately, "sufficient care was not taken in this rather delicate operation" of ranking chiefs from disparate bands. The distribution caused bewilderment among the Chippewa delegates. Instead of determining how each band organized themselves, Cass and McKenney relied on the recommendations of local European Americans.[22] These self-interested traders wanted whatever headman they had the most influence with elevated to chieftain status and recognized by the U.S. government. This "bad practice . . . of breaking and creating chiefs at pleasure" created a situation where federal authorities would "treat" with opportunist leaders, who lacked legitimate authority among the Chippewa, for more land cessions. Chippewa bands became further "split up by the *policy* of traders and U.S. agents" into more numerous factions "headed by new[ly] made upstart chiefs." Trader–U.S. agent collusion further undermined the already unequal Native American bargaining position when negotiating treaties. Such a "bad and thoughtless policy" set a dismal precedent for when the Pembina and Turtle Mountain Chippewa negotiated directly with the United States in 1851, 1863, and 1892.[23]

The Treaty of Fond du Lac included some standard provisions that the Pembina and Turtle Mountain Chippewa would face in subsequent direct negotiations with U.S. treaty commissioners. Article Three granted the mineral rights of the "Chippewa tribe" to the United States, without supposedly impairing their title or jurisdiction. Article Five alleged the "poverty of the Chippewas" and "sterile nature" of their domain, despite the inaccuracy of both claims. To help alleviate their supposed "destitution," the United States proposed a $2,000 annual annuity in money or goods. While the Native Americans may have thought such a payment, especially for relinquishing their mineral rights, would continue forever, its duration depended solely on the unreliable "pleasure of the Congress." This stipulation reflected the real "proof of regard on the part of the United States" for the Chippewa.[24]

The Fond du Lac treaty also contained a rare provision addressing the genuine "consideration of the affection" the "Chippewa tribe" bore to their "half-breed" relations and "of the interest which they feel in their welfare."[25] Cultural distinctions always existed between the two groups despite their extensive intermarriage and cultural borrowing.[26] Yet their common subsistence and mutual protection strategies provided an organizational basis for political solidarity. "The Ojibways . . . felt a deep love for the offspring of their women who had intermarried with the whites, and cherished them as their own children," resulting in strong extended-kinship networks. Hence the treaty provision insisted on by the Native delegates demonstrated "the great affection with which the Ojibways regarded their half-breeds."[27] Article Four granted six hundred and forty acres of land located in the Sault St. Marie region to each person on a list designated as "being half-breeds and Chippewas by descent."[28]

As always, the U.S. government considered such allotments to be a cornerstone of its "Indian civilization" policy. "The possession of permanent property and fixed residences stimulated exertion and improvement."[29] In this particular case, policymakers hoped that the full-blood Chippewa would be more willing to eventually embrace such a mode of existence if their mixed-blood relations showed them the path to European American ways of life. To help smooth the way, the United States even agreed to divert from its 1785 Land Ordinance rectangular survey grid pattern. Where circumstances permitted, the Métis grants would be "surveyed in the ancient French manner" of long narrow *rotures*, or lots, fronted on water, with the land stretching out miles behind.[30]

Unfortunately, as with all treaty allotments, the United States would not confer the ultimate attribute of "civilized" land ownership, known as fee simple title, to any Native Americans, mixed-blood or otherwise. These land grants would be held in "trust" by the federal government. As with most treaty arrangements of this type, the United States conferred eligibility for such allotments on the Native wives and mixed-blood children of European American traders. Distinguished beneficiaries included one section to each of the children ("being of Chippewa descent") of the guide and interpreter John Tanner, and one section to the prestigious mixed-blood Ojibwe historian William Warren.[31] Unfortunately, these less-than-favorable precedents would be carried over into future treaty negotiations involving the Pembina and Turtle Mountain bands. It would take another quarter of a century for them to engage directly in treaty negotiations with the U.S. government.

In the interim, four major developments impinged on the Pembina and Turtle Mountain Chippewa by the 1850s. Together they weakened the Plains-Ojibwe band's ability to resist European American encroachment reinforced by federal policy. First, the scourge of epidemic disease had a devastating impact on them. From 1837–1840, the "spotted sickness" of smallpox arrived with an American Missouri River steamboat at the Mandan villages in what would become south central North Dakota. It spread quickly from this regional trading center throughout the tribes of the Upper Missouri.[32] In 1849, the Roman Catholic missionary priest of Pembina territory, Father G.A. Belcourt, informed Major Samuel Woods, of a U.S. exploratory expedition, about the havoc wrought by the smallpox epidemic on the Plains-Ojibwe bands.

It had wiped out camps of Chippewa, leaving as few as one in ten alive. In a letter included in Woods' report to Congress, Father Belcourt reported that, "here on the banks of the Pembina there is not a spot near the river where the ploughshare does not throw out of the furrow quantities of human bones, remains of the destructive [smallpox] scourge."[33] For estimates of the surviving population almost a decade afterward, the priest tallied the population of the Red Lake, Reed Lake, Pembina, and Turtle Mountain bands at 2,400 Chippewa. In addition, he reported more than 5,000 Métis inhabitants in the Pembina region.[34]

Second, overhunting, drought, and disease began to take their toll on the bison herds. A decline in the availability of buffalo threatened Native American subsistence on the plains. The Commissioner of Indian Affairs report for 1851 stated that "the buffalo upon which they rely for food, clothing, and shelter are rapidly diminishing."[35] Although this decline was not yet the case farther north in the Turtle Mountain "buffalo grounds," it foreshadowed the dire future for the buffalo and the Great Plains peoples dependent on them. Third, the trickle of overland European American migrants in the 1840s heading for Oregon or Utah, turned into a flood with the discovery of gold in California in 1848. The increased scale and scope of westward migration via overland pioneer trails, wagon freight routes, and steamboat navigation of rivers, led to the Indian Office becoming more involved in facilitating the national priorities of westward expansion. These new circumstances shifted the Bureau of Indian Affairs from the War Department to the Interior Department in 1849. This bureaucratic shuffle constituted an inherent conflict of interest. The executive branch administration of Indian affairs clashed with the management of public lands by the General Land Office. The heightened pressures of territorial growth, unleashed by the end of the Mexican-American War, complicated the U.S. government's plans for a portion of the Trans-Mississippi West to remain as a permanent "Indian Territory" for removed eastern tribes.

Although far removed from the U.S. government's focus on what to do with Texas and the Mexican Cession in the Southwest or the disputes with Great Britain over the boundaries of Oregon territory, the region immediately west of the Great Lakes also came under greater federal scrutiny. This fourth development derived from the situation during the 1840s when most Plains Indians ignored, assisted, or levied fees on the small groups of European American migrants heading west. The torrent of "forty-niners," along with those who more profitably provided high-priced goods and services to the miners, escalated tensions. To forestall any small misunderstandings from intensifying into open warfare, the Bureau of Indian Affairs decided to more aggressively pursue tighter boundaries for Plains tribes.

They began by negotiating treaties for land cessions and rights-of-way through tribal territories in exchange for annual annuities of goods and services. The need to secure safe passage through Native American country motivated the United States to initiate negotiations with plains tribes. In 1851, with the Treaty of Fort Laramie, the United States began concentrating various Native groups onto unceded "reserved" portions of their Indigenous territory away from European American transit routes and farming and mining areas. The federal government attempted to negotiate similar treaties with every northern plains tribe, including the Plains-Ojibwe bands. Alexander Ramsey endorsed the "favorite scheme of the government to collect the scattered bands of Chippewa," and "concentrate them" on lands "entirely unsuited and undesirable for white occupation."[36] This scheme enabled the United States to initiate a process of tribal attrition by land cession treaty. It placed restrictions upon trade, territory, and autonomy. For federal officials, these restrictions represented the vanguard for subsequent European American settlement.

Although located north of the main flow of westward migration, the "vast and magnificent valley of the Red River" existed as an old corridor shared by Native American, Métis, European Canadian, and European American traders.[37] The valley formed what would later become the border between Minnesota and North Dakota. Although preceded by the U.S. Army's Fort Snelling in 1819, the Selkirk colony and Red River flood refugees founded nearby St. Paul, Minnesota, in 1826, at the confluence of the Mississippi and St. Peters Rivers. Their relocation coincided with a fundamental shift in the Red River fur trade after 1830. The American Fur Company (AFC) began expanding its territory and directly challenging the HBC. In 1834, Henry H. Sibley founded an AFC post opposite Fort Snelling. A decade later, he took on Norman Kittson, a Canadian trader, as a partner. Kittson founded a post at Pembina in 1844. From this base, he began consolidating the still profitable upper Minnesota and Red River fur trade away from the British HBC. Moreover, Kittson and the AFC found their Pembina locale well situated to take advantage of the emerging markets in pemmican and buffalo robes supplied mainly by the Pembina and Turtle Mountain Chippewa.

The Red River trade supported a diversity of cultures while pumping enormous amounts of wealth into St. Paul. The city grew as the vital commercial center linking the resources of the north (furs and buffalo hides) with manufactured items and commodities from the east (liquor, powder and shot, sugar and tea, apples, flour, pork and bacon, canned goods). Fed by twenty-seven tributaries, and traversed by many overland cart trails, the Red River flowed northward into Canada (see Image 9). It snaked through the Selkirk and Métis settlements centered at Fort Garry (Winnipeg) and emptied into Lake Winnipeg. The fur-trading-post town of Pembina served as the lynchpin of this trade, because it stood at the juncture of what would become Minnesota (1858), North Dakota (1889), and Manitoba, Canada (1870). Although the village and western district of Pembina would eventually be located in North Dakota, in 1851 it was still part of the newly established Minnesota Territory.

The region west of the Red River and north of Devils Lake remained the unceded domain of the Pembina and Turtle Mountain bands. The westward extent of Pembina County to the White Earth River coincided with the western periphery of Turtle Mountain Chippewa territory. During his official Red River expedition in 1849, Major Samuel Woods encountered twenty-five Red River carts from Selkirk loaded "with peltries and pemmican" and a larger train of sixty-five carts under the management of Norman Kittson en route to St. Paul from Pembina.[38] The major also received vital information about the Native inhabitants and the extent of the Pembina district from Father Belcourt. The resident priest reported, "the immense plains which feed innumerable herds of bison to the westward and from which the Chippewa and half breeds of this region obtain their subsistence, contains within their limits a country about 400 miles from north to south and more than 500 miles from east to west." Noting Pembina "as the gate to the prairies," Belcourt helped spread the word to federal authorities

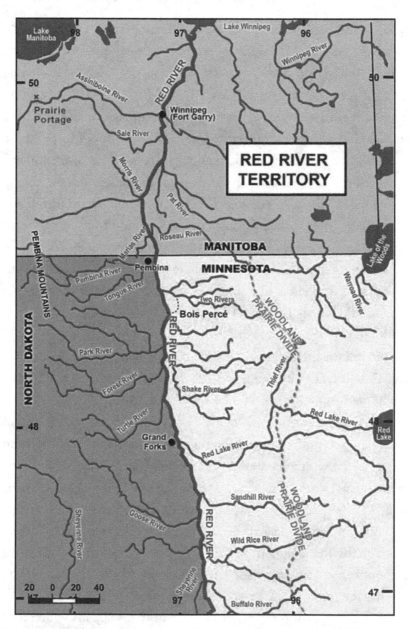

Image 9. Red River Territory. This map shows the Red River area during the Pembina fur trade era, around 1800. *Map by Cassie Theurer, adapted from Ethnohistory, 1959, p. 300; State Historical Society of North Dakota—North Dakota Studies, Red River Valley in Hickerson's "Genesis of a Trading Post Band"; https://www.ndstudies.gov/curriculum/high-school/turtle-mountain.*

about the "immense quantity of fertile lands easy of cultivation [and] ready to be settled."[39]

Such enticing news led to territorial reorganization. An Organic Act of Congress incorporated Minnesota Territory on March 3, 1849, as a result of Wisconsin becoming a state in 1848. President Zachary Taylor named Alexander Ramsey, a political opportunist from Pennsylvania, to be the territory's first governor and superintendent of Indian Affairs as a patronage reward for his diligent election campaign work. Only a few thousand European Americans inhabited the area.[40] Their settlement remained confined to the southeastern corner because the rest of Minnesota remained unceded Native American territory. Yet according to the General Land Office (GLO), it would not remain an "outpost of civilization" for long.[41] Its proximity to the "geographical and commercial center of our ocean-bound republic" caused the commissioner of Indian Affairs to declare it an "absolute necessity to obtain without delay a cession from the Indians on the west side of that river."[42] Thus, the creation of Minnesota Territory necessitated U.S. treaty initiatives with the Dakota, Chippewa, and Métis of the region.

At this point, territorial politicians and the entrepreneurs of St. Paul saw their immediate "manifest destiny" as trade and settlement to the north, rather than to the west. Such providential nationalism also pervaded Anglo-Canada. They increasingly perceived the Red River region as part their nation's future. Westward Canadian growth could thwart any U.S. northern ambitions.[43] This region's unceded territories remained more connected with established British fur trade interests than the new commercial ventures in the United States. Among various Indigenous groups, the Red Lake Chippewa held sway over the eastern bank and contiguous lands, while the Pembina Chippewa inhabited the opposite shore and its western adjoining territory, along with the Métis centered at St. Joseph in the Pembina Mountains. Unlike every other Chippewa band in Minnesota, these two bands had not entered into any diplomatic or treaty relations with the United States.[44]

As a prelude to any formal treaty negotiations, the United States once again launched a series of exploratory expeditions and sought information from prominent European Americans and Canadians in the region. The U.S. Army, not U.S. fur traders or farmers, led the way. Part of Captain John Pope's exploration from Fort Snelling (St. Paul) to Pembina searched for another suitable fort site to aid in deterring British traders, "extinguishing the Indian title to the lands in that quarter," and securing the international boundary.[45] The poorly defined northern extent of the Louisiana Purchase permitted British fur traders to continue their alliances with the Native peoples in the region. Forts acted as a counterbalance and foundation for future European American settlement.

Another proposal to secure and utilize the region envisioned the creation of a Native American state spanning the drift prairie grasslands from west of the Red River to east of the Missouri River.[46] This territory coincided almost exactly with the domain of the Pembina and Turtle Mountain Chippewa. Although it never came to be, the notion indicated how federal policy planned consistently to utilize the region for its own purposes, without consulting the Native inhabitants. For the time being, showing the flag backed by the military created an impressive opening tactic preceding upcoming treaty initiatives.

To control northwestern Minnesota, the United States had to win the loyalties of the Chippewa bands away from the British fur trade interests and "draw its savage neighbors within the pale of civilization."[47] Promising annuities in exchange for lands, they hoped to secure their loyalty and subsume their autonomy under the tutelage of the United States. In exchange for their land, they would be compensated by the government's "civilization" program. Compliance among the Natives would lessen their resistance to the primary objective of "opening the country to agricultural settlement." The incoming European American population would act as a buffer against the incursion of HBC fur traders or Métis and Indigenous hunters from Canada, who constantly overstepped the forty-ninth parallel border. They received the blame for the declining number of buffalo, clashes with the Dakota, and the diversion of approximately $400,000 per year into the coffers of the HBC from furs "largely obtained from the territory of the United States," including Turtle Mountain.[48]

The Pembina and Turtle Mountain Chippewa expressed similar concerns. One of their chiefs, Green Setting Feather, also complained about the band's "buffalo grounds" being overrun by Métis hunters. He noted their increasing numbers and profligate slaughter of the buffalo, while acknowledging that Chippewa men such as himself gave birth to, and raised up, the "half-breeds." As a result of this "blood relation," the chief observed how the "child has become master of my own dish," although "we wish it to be as our Father told us." He expressed the band's attachment to and love for their sacred homeland. "I only wish to be master and do as I please with what is my own . . . I love all of the Turtle Mountain."[49]

Green Setting Feather asserted that the Métis should live and hunt where they belonged, from St. Joseph to Pembina, and down to Devils Lake and further south. This demarcation referred to the territory of the Pembina band, east of the Turtle Mountain band's zone. He then asserted that "we reserved all north [and west] of this line for our own use." This invasion of the Turtle Mountain area without the consent of the Chippewa constituted a trespass that violated "our law," and required compensation in the form of a fine or a horse.[50] A contemporary of Green Setting Feather, the Mississagua Ojibwe Kah-ge-ga-gah-bowh (George Copway) confirmed this stipulation. "The hunting grounds of the Indians were secured by right, a law and custom among themselves. No one was allowed to hunt on another's land, without invitation or permission."[51] Both of these accounts confirm that Indian communities had their own unwritten yet effective codes of law.[52]

Father Belcourt, who had escorted his Métis flock on their buffalo hunts since 1845, confirmed the chief's claims. The priest noted that "in the Turtle Mountains, half-breeds had already established 'winter over' or hivernant villages."[53] Since these transgressions continued without the accustomed reciprocity, Green Setting Feather ended his address on a less than conciliatory note. As a chief, he pledged the continued friendship of the Chippewa of Turtle Mountain collectively for the "half-breeds" of Pembina. Yet on a personal level, he felt betrayed and unforgiving. "As for me, I do not ever intend to give my hand to the swine."[54] The chief's address conveyed a sense of Turtle Mountain tribal identity, based upon a sense of proprietorship, stewardship, and legal entitlement ("our law") over their land and its attendant resources, that he hoped would be sufficient to sustain the current and future generations of his community.

The letters and reports from Major Woods, Captain Pope, Isaac Stevens, and Governor Ramsey concurred on the richness of the Red River soil and its suitable fertility for any type of agriculture.[55] Along with Pere Belcourt's letters, which noted the presence of a Turtle Mountain Chippewa village of thirty huts, they also noted the relative affluence, industry, and preponderance of the Pembina Chippewa Métis population sustained by a mixed subsistence of buffalo hunting, fur trapping, husbandry, small gardens, gathering, and fishing. Other than the huge well-organized semi-annual buffalo hunts with their Native kinsmen and hundreds of accompanying Red River carts, their means of support differed marginally from other western frontier European American settlements.[56]

All of the glowing reports about the agricultural and commercial potential of the Red River Valley of the North, plus lobbying from territorial politicians like Henry H. Sibley and Henry M. Rice, prominent traders like Norman W. Kittson, and the territorial legislature, convinced Congress to appropriate $20,000 for treaty negotiations.[57] Alexander Ramsey, received a commission from the Secretary of the Interior "to treat with the Chippewa Indians of the Pembina and Red Lake Minnesota territory . . . for the relinquishment of a portion of their lands."[58] The subsequent treaty negotiations pitted tribal sovereignty against the expedient policies of a rapidly expanding United States.

Ramsey embarked from St. Paul for Pembina on August 18, 1851, along the North Dakota cart trail that ran along the higher ridgeline west of the Red River. Besides actually getting to the site of the treaty council, Ramsey wanted to gain sufficient knowledge to make a case for procuring federal funds to improve the Red River trails and establish a U.S. Army fort near Pembina. This small but still vibrant fur trading town had an estimated non-Native population of slightly over one thousand residents. It remained a comfortable and convenient locale for the Chippewa bands, the area's Métis inhabitants, and local businessmen. The prominent Pembina trader and entrepreneur Norman Kittson, assisted by his French-Canadian trading partner, "Jolly Joe" Rolette, and customs collector Charles Cavalier, provided Ramsey with accommodations and assistance in setting up the council.

In addition to the general desire to secure the rich agricultural and timber lands, federal officials and local representatives like Ramsey and Kittson coveted the opening of the Red River of the North to lawful non-Native passage and settlement. They wanted to secure the economic future of Minnesota (St. Paul) and impede the continuing British and HBC poaching of U.S. resources. Anglophobes like Ramsey and most other U.S. officials involved with Native matters, feared that the British might beat them at their own game. In his letter to the commissioner of Indian Affairs in 1849, Ramsey blustered against the British government for "evading its morality and stretching its pretensions of benevolence" in its dealings with Native Americans.[59]

The treaty council commenced on September 15, 1851. There were five Chippewa chiefs, accompanied by nine headmen, plus the president and council of the principal men of the "Half-Breeds" totaling ten members.[60] Governor Ramsey opened with declarations of benevolence and altruism. The only aim of the "Great Father"—the president of the United States—was "to attend particularly to the interests of his red children," who were poor and needed his help. The U.S. did not really "want the country badly." By purchasing "comparatively useless" lands and turning them over to his "white children" and "half-breeds" for cultivation, the money received by the Natives would enable them to become as "comfortable" as the whites, and as "civilized" as the Cherokee.[61] The dishonesty of such a statement by a U.S. representative, only a decade after the Trail of Tears, illustrated that Ramsey had little intention of acting with the "utmost good faith."

This deception foreshadowed the contentious nature of the treaty negotiations. The United States wanted the Red Lake Chippewa territory east of the Red River. What would become the northwest part of the state of Minnesota in 1858 ranged for thirty miles eastward and extended south from the Canadian border to Buffalo River. From the Pembina Chippewa to the west, the United States coveted an equally wide swath for thirty miles west of the Red River that stretched southward to the Goose River in what would become northeastern North Dakota in 1889 (see back cover image, "Chippewa Land Cessions in North Dakota"). The southern demarcation line coincided with the Chippewa-Dakota boundary drawn up in the 1825 Treaty of Prairie du Chien and the subsequent Sweet Corn agreement. This total area encompassed approximately five million acres of relatively level and treeless grasslands atop rich soil with great potential for farming—plus a vital waterway—linking the burgeoning commercial center of St. Paul with the Red River settlements. Many Minnesotans, including Governor Ramsey, not only desired increased trade with Canada, but also coveted it for annexation by the United States.[62]

The U.S. offer of $160,000 ($8,000 paid immediately, the remaining $152,000 deferred over twenty years) came to less than four cents per acre. Even if the Chippewa had no knowledge about the wrenching experience of Cherokee forced removal, they scorned Ramsey's bid. The paltry proposition made the Native delegates question the president's and Ramsey's benevolent intentions. One chief retorted that neither the "Great Father" (the president) nor the "Little Father" (Ramsey) acted in ways that coincided with Chippewa cultural norms of fatherhood, because they failed to "take notice of [their] children."[63] Red Lake Chief Mosomo declared they would not sell their lands for Ramsey's asking price, nor be restricted in the use of it. He even made a counteroffer of $40,000 immediately, plus $20,000 per year for twenty years (almost nine cents per acre, or more than double Ramsey's offer). Ramsey publicly acknowledged that such a large amount was not "improper." He conceded privately that his initial offer had been deliberately low. This confirmed the Chippewa suspicion that the financial trusteeship of their alleged "Father" was not being offered in the best interests of his "wards."

The same might be said for the estimated 1,100 Métis inhabitants of Minnesota Territory. Many contemporary observers noted that "the Chippewa and half-breeds are all related, either by marriage or other kindred ties."[64] The formally recognized presence of a "half-breed" president (or "chief"), Jean Baptiste Wilkie, and a council of principal men "freely elected by the half-breeds of Pembina" at the treaty negotiations signified that they had "laid a solid foundation for the fabric of social improvement," while constituting a major "political community" in the region.[65] If and when the Chippewa bands ceded their lands, the Métis wanted the U.S. government to attend to their land claims with fee simple title.

The United States had a different agenda concerning the "half-breed" population. They could not afford to disregard their claims out of hand, especially during negotiations when their considerable influence with their Native kinsmen might persuade the Chippewa bands to comply with Ramsey's demands. Although wary of their French-Canadian patrimony, Roman Catholicism, and close Native American associations, Anglo-American policymakers sought two potential benefits from securing Métis allegiance. First, they could act as a tactical shield defending U.S. interests in the region from any potential British incursions from Canada. Second, they might provide the core for an invasion strike force if it ever became necessary to "supplant the cross of St. George between the 49th parallel and Hudson's Bay." A couple of years before, Isaac Stevens also envisioned the Métis as the potential core of a frontier buffer zone that could provide "a controlling check upon the Indians."[66] Allotting fee lands from ceded territory could secure the loyalty of the Red River Métis population to the United States and away from the HBC and British Canada permanently.

After five days of intense negotiations, they reached a compromise agreement on September 20, 1851. Ramsey claimed that the Chippewa "might have been induced, under the pressure of their necessities," to agree to a final figure closer to his initial proposal rather than their counteroffer. The U.S. representatives and local traders, like Kittson and Rolette, plus territorial delegate Henry Sibley, wanted the land in the Red River Valley. So did the governor and local missionaries. The Chippewa feared the "mercenary ends" of the Americans "who . . . have made Mammon their God and have looked on the Indian but as a tool or means of obtaining riches." In this instance, the Reverend J. P. Bardwell cautioned the Chippewa "against overshooting the mark, and asking so high a price that they should get nothing." Observer J.W. Bond noted that the commissioners misrepresented the treaty payment to the Chippewa as a "present," alleging that the Native Americans would "be but little intruded upon" during their lifetime.[67] Although claiming otherwise, all the urgency came from the non-Native side of the bargaining.

While Ramsey continued to complain about the price for the ceded lands, it still constituted a staggering bargain at less than five cents per acre. The final amount added up to $230,000. The chiefs received $30,000 to provide for their mixed-blood relatives and "arrange their affairs." This provision was a standard treaty euphemism for disbursing promised outlays to first pay off alleged Native American debts to the traders in attendance, like Kittson and Rolette. Driving Native peoples into debt to force land concessions had been a covert part of federal policy since 1803. President Jefferson wrote in a private letter to William Henry Harrison that to induce Native peoples to "a cession of lands," the U.S. government should encourage "the good and influential [Native] individuals among them run into debt."[68] The 1851 treaties with the Dakota and the Chippewa exemplified this surreptitious policy.

While not mentioned directly in the 1851 treaty journals, Chief Little Shell II (whose real Ojibwe name was Weesh-e-damo, not

Zhow-ozh-ko-go-nay-bee, nor "Yellow Feather," as indicated on the final treaty document) fulfilled his dual responsibilities representing the Pembina and Turtle Mountain Chippewa during the council. The final version of the Pembina Treaty identified him as a signatory, referred to as "Little Chief of Pembina." Firsthand evidence indicating his direct participation came from a speech he made at the Old Crossing treaty negotiations in 1863. He stated that he had a "right to talk about the Pembina country, as his father [Little Shell I] owned all that country." Yet, he had come to the treaty council "with his mind made up to cede the country from the timber on the Red River (i.e., *not* the prairie) on both sides to the heads of the streams, as had been done *before* when he [i.e., Ramsey] made a treaty with them at Pembina in 1851."[69] This direct testimony demonstrated formal U.S. recognition of, and continuity within, the political leadership of the Turtle Mountain band. Such attributes contributed significantly to fulfilling the legal requisites of being an autonomous land-owning entity with "recognized title" to their lands.

To avoid confusion over the disparate labels applied to the same or closely related group of people, the Turtle Mountain band evolved from the Pembina Chippewa who lived west of the Red River, along the Pembina River, in the vicinity of the Turtle Mountains, and hunted further southward to Devils Lake and the Sweet Corn line. Ramsey knew about them, if not their specific name, and referred to them as the "Ojibwas to the far northwest" adjacent to the Assiniboine and the Cree.[70] Their territory remained west of the land Ramsey wanted to obtain. As hereditary chief, Little Shell II shared in the interests of the Pembina band, along with the Métis "chief" Jean Baptiste Wilkie, who also represented the interests of kin relations among both Chippewa bands. Little Shell II remained "distrustful" and unwilling to sell any of their prairie lands west of the Red River, even after Ramsey conferred U.S. recognition upon him via a medal "as chief of the Pembina section of the Ojibwa tribe."[71] This sign of formal U.S. political recognition bolstered the band's subsequent legal standing in future negotiations.

The final terms of the treaty proved to be a setback for the "half-breeds." They failed to secure any treaty provision recognizing them as being the rightful Indigenous claimants to land in Pembina by the U.S. government. Their similar inability to secure legal title to lands they had occupied and possessed in Rupert's Land (District of Assiniboia) under the Hudson's Bay Company fomented their discontent and fueled their separatist aspirations. The Chippewa bands secured a total of $10,000 per year for twenty years, minus as much as $2,000 per year for agricultural and educational purposes, which remained the hallmarks of the federal government's "civilization" policy. Yet as usual, the Native Americans, not Congress, had to pay for their own "civilization" after the traders skimmed a portion off the top. Because of this scam, the Pembina and Red Lakes spokesmen made it clear to Ramsey that they were not interested in even the modest offers of the federal government's "civilization" policy.

This part of Article III, Section 2 remained in the treaty despite the fact that Ramsey knew it displeased the Native Americans. He conceded privately in his report that "no part of the annuity is to be paid in goods" because "experience has taught us that cash annuities are, in the end, more beneficial to the Indian." Ramsey gloated that he could have held out for an even better bargain with the "poor, ignorant savages," but the dignity and honor of the United States guided his actions.[72] Of course this "dignity and honor" did not conform to the U.S. government's guardianship role of "giving them [the Native Americans] effectual protection against the wrongs from our own people."[73] The "liberal system of justice" standards of treaty making that the United States imposed on its treaty commissioners declared that "because bands and tribes of Indians lacked experience and knowledge of affairs of business and government," it was the financial obligation of the United States to protect its Native "wards in their property and rights, and to deal with them fairly and honestly."[74] But this policy rhetoric fell far short of reality, as indicated by the final terms of the treaty.

Yet this circumstance had nothing to do with why the treaty faced opposition from all sides. By the time the governor returned to

St. Paul, a letter of protest from Red Lake arrived. Two Chippewa chiefs claimed that they had been represented by non-authorized leaders.[75] Ramsey attempted to dismiss this charge in a letter to Luke Lea, the commissioner of Indian Affairs in Washington, D.C. In light of praising his own high-mindedness for not taking advantage of "poor, ignorant savages," he defended himself to his boss by stating that any tribal complaints occurred because of their poor comprehension of what had been agreed upon. Instead of taking responsibility as the territorial representative of the guardian "Great Father," who promised to "promote the prosperity and happiness" of his Native wards, Ramsey could only lash out at the dissatisfied chiefs as liars.[76]

In addition to some Native resistance, the U.S. Senate had its doubts about the treaty. Most European Americans who had visited the Red River watershed (e.g., Captain Pope, Agent Fletcher, J.W Bond, Isaac Stevens, Henry M. Rice) considered its agricultural and commercial transit potential to be as noteworthy as indicated by Major Woods, who stated, "agricultural pursuits [at Pembina] are rewarded by a bountiful harvest, and there is hardly a product that the farmer values that cannot be raised there in abundance." But it remained geographically remote from the main corridors of U.S. settlement and markets. Its northern climate and the deep and dense root system of the prairie grasses made it unprofitable for immediate farming. Woods confirmed that "there is no farming on our side of the line."[77] Given the other contending 1851 treaties to consider for ratification, the Pembina and Red Lake pact lingered low on the national priority list.

Thus the first attempt at a treaty between the United States and the Pembina Chippewa, ceding part of the Red River Valley, failed. To the vested powers and competing regional interests in the U.S. Senate, the "great bargain" did not seem worthwhile. Responding to the annexation of Texas (1846), the acquisition of Oregon (1846), the appropriation of northern Mexico (1848), and the California gold rush (1849), the Compromise of 1850 aggravated, rather than alleviated, the sectional crisis between the North and South over the potential exten-

sion of slavery into the new western territories. Due to these circumstances, all three of the 1851 Minnesota treaties faced stiff opposition
in the Senate. Southern Senators opposed anything that would bolster
the settlement of another northern territory and further undermine the
balance between free and slave states. Political and financial support for
the more geopolitically important Fort Laramie treaty, which secured
the vital overland rights-of-way across the territories of more central
northern Plains tribes to the new mining and farming districts in the
far West, required higher priority, attention, and appropriations from
policymakers and Congress.

With European Americans edging into southeastern Minnesota,
the Senate ratified the more pressing Traverse des Sioux and Mendota treaties.[78] Four bands of the eastern Dakota nation ceded most of
southern Minnesota west of the Mississippi River to the United States.
This nineteen-million-acre cession extinguished "Indian title" except
for the "reserved" lands one hundred miles long and twenty miles wide
along the Minnesota River. These agreements constituted quite a coup
for Commissioner Lea and Governor Ramsey. They placated the cad-
re of Minnesota traders, land speculators, and lumber special interests
for the rest of the decade.[79] The remote Red River Valley, with its
contentious mix of Chippewa and Métis peoples suspected of greater
loyalty to British than U.S. interests, could wait. The Senate rejected
the treaty on June 23, 1852. On June 26, Minnesota territorial delegate
Sibley wrote to Ramsey with the bad news. The treaty "went by the
boards" as a "conciliatory sacrifice" to the more pressing needs of the
St. Paul "friends" of the Traverse des Sioux ($3.7 million) and Mendota
($2.5 million) treaties.[80] But at least the United States recognized Little
Shell II as a chief of the Pembina band, and the Pembina and Turtle Mountain Chippewa retained their unceded lands and "recognized
Indian title."

Any subsequent attempts to entreat with the Pembina or Red
Lake Chippewa for passage through, or relinquishment of, their lands,
were overshadowed by the North-South sectional crisis. The "Sau-

teux of Pembina" and the "Métis de Pembina" still wanted a treaty, "the sooner the better." The Native Americans wanted to protect their subsistence resources and themselves, while the mixed-bloods wanted to secure legal land title.[81] After receiving no response to their 1852 petition to the president, they turned again to their beloved priest, Father Belcourt, who had been evangelizing among the Chippewa of the Turtle Mountain region during 1853.

In 1854, he traveled to Washington, D.C., and presented their "griefs and demands" to the commissioner of Indian Affairs. They indicated their willingness to cede some of their territory along the Red River, it "being now very poor in furs," in exchange for a contiguous reserve for Native Americans and fee patents so their Métis kin "could be firmly settled among them at Pembina."[82] This enduring Chippewa/Métis unity and desire to live in proximity to each other derived in large part from shared kinship and cultural ties. A strength-in-numbers strategy may also have played a unifying role. They wanted a treaty to secure U.S. government protection against the encroachments of the Hudson's Bay Company and Canadian Métis on their buffalo hunting grounds and raids by the Sisseton Dakota on their settlements.[83] While the president did not feel compelled to extinguish the region's "Aboriginal title" with a treaty yet, Congress appropriated funds for more federally sponsored territorial explorations, such as Isaac Stevens's 1853 survey for a transcontinental railroad route from Lake Superior to Puget Sound on the Pacific coast. Federal policy priorities could not have been more transparent.

But the lack of a "firm and perpetual peace" west of the Red River became flagrant enough that the Chippewa/Métis and Dakota felt the need to constrain their mutual hostilities. This realization derived from the numerically superior Dakota's shocking defeat after attacking a party of Red River Métis near Dog Den Butte just east of the Missouri River. This prominent landmark marked the southwestern corner of the Turtle Mountain Chippewa territory. As a consequence of the July 1851 "Battle of Grand Coteau," historian W. L. Morton surmised that "the Métis thereafter were masters of the Plains." Morton also noted that there "were as many Saulteaux [i.e., Chippewa] warriors who participated in the engagement."[84] Their mutual protection strategy prevailed against numerically superior tribal rivals.

Recognizing their failures to abide by the 1825 demarcation line and avoid hostilities, the sons of Sweet Corn and Wa-nah-ta decided to honor the Indigenous practice of refreshing treaty relations to restore harmony. They had their fathers' oral history of these transactions committed to paper. Changes in conditions or circumstances did not provide grounds for terminating an agreement. They mandated its renewal. Their actions contradicted the European American presumption that "savage Indians" could not manage their own affairs or govern themselves without the imposition of "civilized" Anglo-American law. The second Sweet Corn treaty exemplified the continuity of tribal sovereignty. Native communities had settled their differences belligerently and peaceably long before any external intervention.

The Dakota and Chippewa/Métis subsequently honored the renewed Sweet Corn boundary. The U.S. recognized this fact when they adopted it as the northern extent in the 1867 Sisseton-Wahpeton cession treaty, and a subsequent 1872 investigation into which bands possessed legitimate "Indian title" in this contested region. These developments had a direct bearing on determining the southern extent of the Turtle Mountain band's territorial claim. The treaty eliminated the possibility of any contending Dakota claim north of the line and confirmed the Turtle Mountain assertion of exclusive use and occupation. It verified that the lands they claimed had been recognized by neighboring tribes and had never been ceded to the United States.[85]

Amidst this inter-tribal treaty-making, the federal bureaucracy attempted to initiate another conference with the Red Lake and Pembina Chippewa. The advent of regular steamboat traffic made "safe transit" along the Red River more imperative than ever. United States officials believed correctly that passage could not be guaranteed and constituted legal trespass while the unceded lands adjoining both sides of the river belonged to the Native Americans. Federal policymakers still viewed the eight hundred Pembina and Red Lake Chippewa as impediments to European American expansion and development along this corridor of "progress."[86] No longer could a treaty commissioner like Ramsey maintain the pretense that Native American territory and its most vital resources would not be subsumed by U.S. determination to secure them for European American commerce and settlement. The failure of the U.S. Senate to ratify the Pembina Treaty of 1851 left the Red Lake band in possession of their homeland east of the Red River and north of the Prairie du Chien line, while the Pembina and Turtle Mountain bands retained their territory west of the Red River north of the Sweet Corn line.[87] Minnesota's territorial government, aided and abetted by the federal government, had procured almost all other Dakota and Chippewa lands within the state from 1849 to 1858. But these three Chippewa bands continued to stymie the U.S. government's and Minnesota's policy of expansion.

Governor Ramsey's justifications at the treaty council illustrated the fundamental conceit and contradiction of federal policy. The hunger for Native lands undermined any hope of bestowing European American "civilization." The desire to gain Native land for European American settlement and expansion always took precedence over promoting Native welfare. Thomas Jefferson considered these twin goals of policy to be mutually beneficial, or as he termed it, a "coincidence of interest."[88] Unfortunately it was neither a coincidence nor mutually beneficial. This rhetoric of assimilation and civilization served primarily as a means to the end of appropriating Native American land. The real goal of federal policy continued to be the continental expansion of U.S. political power and commercial interests at the expense of Native peoples.

The Red River Valley of the North proved resistant to these U.S. prerogatives in the short term. It remained a locale of intercultural rapprochement with fluid geographic and cultural borders.[89] This contested frontier region, shaped by imperial (French, British, U.S.), intercultural (Native American, Métis, European Canadian, European American), and national (Canada and the U.S.) rivalries, created what anthropologist Jack D. Forbes called an "inter-group contact situation" where no one culture, people, or nation prevailed.[90] The situation in the Red River borderland serves as reminder that contrary to Frederick Jackson Turner's famous frontier thesis of 1892, the European aspect of the North American frontier experience was neither exclusively Anglo-American in nature, and neither did it move in a linear progression from the Atlantic coast to the Pacific. The Red River watershed and adjacent prairies encompassed a unique region categorized by fluid relations between Native peoples and European newcomers.[91] By examining this notable North American borderland, we can more fully understand the process where the independent Pembina and Turtle Mountain Chippewa bands and the Red River and Pembina Métis attempted to negotiate favorable terms for trade, land, resources, sovereignty, and compromise with competing European Americans and European Canadians.

Historian Richard White has defined this type of North American region as an area of cooperative and contentious accommodation. Instead of being the nexus of unrelenting opposition between European American "civilization" and Native American "savagery," White posited that in spite of some inherent conflict, this kind of borderland acted as a "middle ground." The ethnic mixing of different peoples and cultures (including formal and informal intermarriage) created "common meaning" through borrowing and adapting various cultural traits and practices based on shared circumstances.[92] The common experiences of buffalo hunts and Dakota attacks related by the oral traditions of many Métis and Chippewa families living in the Turtle Mountain region created a common heritage that transcended ethnic boundaries and united them as a unique group.[93]

An incident in 1850 further solidified this sense of community. Father Belcourt survived a severe winter storm traveling to Turtle Mountain. To give thanks for his survival, he said a Mass and erected an oak cross on the highest butte in the Turtle Mountains. Since this happened on the feast day of St. Paul, it became commemorated as St. Paul Butte (northwest of Dunseith, ND).[94] Because the priest had shared the rigors of many buffalo hunts with them, he was beloved by the Chippewa and Métis from Pembina, to St. Joseph, to Turtle Mountain. His outward acknowledgement of the sacredness of their land base further endeared him to this heterogeneous and predominantly Roman Catholic community and affirmed their affiliations.

This collective "middle ground" of the Red River and Pembina regions continued up until 1858. By the 1850s, U.S. and Canadian authorities began initiating the process of border fixing and constraining people's trade partners, hunting practices, and land rights along ethnic and national lines. This contingent and inclusive borderland (e.g., the District of Assiniboia) became the site of increasingly contentious and exclusive nation-state rivalries (the United States and Canada), and inter-tribal warfare (Chippewa, Dakota, and Métis). In Assiniboia, an HBC backlash against the Métis resulted in Father Belcourt being transferred to eastern Canada in 1858. The HBC pressured the Catholic hierarchy at St. Boniface, Manitoba, to rein in their priest because of his advocacy for, and immense popularity with, the Native Americans at Turtle Mountain and the Métis at St. Joseph.[95] In the United States, the formal creation of Minnesota as a state in 1858 settled its boundaries permanently. It pivoted on a south-north axis framed by the Mississippi and Red Rivers with a diverse farming, lumbering, and mining economy centered in St. Paul.

The entrepreneurs of St. Paul knew that the Red River provided the vital link for a burgeoning regional trade. In 1859, 1,500 tons of merchandise annually—including $150,000 in fur sales alone—moved between Rupert's Land and the United States.[97] This natural north-south orientation superseded the artificiality of the international boundary created by the necessity of a diplomatic compromise forty years before. Ardent proponents of U.S. expansion in the region, like Alexander Ramsey, Henry H. Sibley, Henry M. Rice, Norman W. Kittson, and Father Belcourt, envisioned eliminating the monopolistic grasp of the HBC by annexing adjacent portions of the remains of the Assiniboia/Selkirk colony and the growing Red River settlements near Lake Winnipeg. Each of these prominent men, other than the priest, envisioned their future prosperity and political careers linked to the development of new regional markets based on farming, lumbering, and mining.

Since the Seven Oaks clash of 1816 and the grasshopper plague of 1818, the Red River settlements in the British Possessions (Canada) had been dependent economically on free trade with the United States. This dependency stymied the HBC's trade containment policies. During the 1840s, the growing U.S. economic dominance of the border trade—fueled by the commercial growth of Pembina, St. Joseph, St. Paul, and Mendota—bolstered the fur trapping, buffalo hunting, and carting economy of the Pembina and Turtle Mountain Chippewa/Métis. In terms of profit, by 1854 Sibley, Kittson, and Rolette of the American Fur Company lost the trade war with the HBC. Despite this setback, the AFC achieved the greater goal of establishing de facto U.S. sovereignty over the Red River up to the international boundary.

Ultimately, this sovereignty extended more potential for profit to a wider variety of American economic interests in the region. The HBC realized its own marginal economic survival in the area depended on lowering transportation costs. As part of a remarkable turnaround in 1860, they contracted with former rival Kittson to be their new importing agent. St. Paul, Minnesota, rather than Hudson's Bay, became the new center of HBC imports and exports for the Red River Valley. Transnational commerce negated the necessity for any formal or immediate U.S. political control north of the international boundary. Minnesota's territorial years had not only fostered increased commerce with Rupert's Land, it also fueled land and townsite speculations sustained by a booming population. Within the eight-year span between 1849 and 1857, it has been estimated that the European American populace of Minnesota Territory increased 333 percent. Travel, trade, rapid development, and population increase intensified after Minnesota became a state in 1858.[98]

The frequent flooding of the Red River hampered Pembina's development as a vital commercial waystation and precluded the practicality of a large permanent settlement. After the great Red River flood of 1852, Father Belcourt moved his Catholic mission, and Norman Kittson relocated his business headquarters from Pembina to higher ground at St. Joseph, thirty-five miles west along the Pembina River. A thriving Chippewa/Métis community of 1,200 developed at this settlement near the base of Pembina Mountain. The expanding buffalo trade—involving robes, hides, pemmican, and tallow—created a lucrative provisioning and carting commerce.

Antoine Gingras and Joseph Rolette became the leading merchants. Jean Baptiste Wilkie governed the Métis, while Green Setting Feather and Little Shell II led the Pembina and Turtle Mountain Chippewa. The European Canadians and Kittson's Red River and Pembina free-trade coalition valued this region for obvious reasons. St. Joseph linked the long-established Chippewa trade route from Turtle Mountain and the Souris (Mouse) River to Pembina and the booming illegal border traffic between the Red River settlements and St. Paul.[99] For the Native Americans and the Métis, St. Joseph's location served as an ideal jumping off point for the semi-annual buffalo hunts and provided a more than adequate supply of wood, water, forage and shelter during the non-hunting seasons.[100]

These Indigenous developments demonstrated that the area of what would become northeastern North Dakota still remained beyond the U.S. goal of bringing the peripheral areas of the Trans-Mississippi West into the national economy. The devolution of the borderland immediately west of the Red River, including Pembina, to the status of a federal "unorganized territory" from 1858 to 1861, confirmed its "colonial hinterland" status.[101] It should be noted that the lands of the Pembina and Turtle Mountain Chippewa bands coincided with the northeastern portion of this territorial wedge. So, for the moment, the Native nations in this area remained beyond the jurisdiction of the U.S. federal territorial system.

The significance of this development is important to reiterate, especially in the context of later legal wrangling over the Native possession of this land. The United States probably had no weaker claim to, or less interest in, any unceded Indigenous territory in the lower forty-eight states than in this region. This area had not been part of the United States from 1783 to 1817. Even after becoming part of the United States in 1818, from the federal government's perspective, it remained on the outer fringe of a series of varying territories. For example, the postal address of Henry Sibley's AFC post at Mendota started as being in Michigan Territory in 1834, then changed to Wisconsin Territory in 1836, followed by another change to Iowa Territory in 1838 until the creation of Minnesota Territory in 1849.[102] These shifting territorial boundaries and designations illustrated the lack of U.S. adherence to its own professed "utmost good faith toward the Indians," while imposing inconsistently higher standards on tribal groups like the Pembina and Turtle Mountain Chippewa. From 1858 to 1861, other than being below the northern boundary line of the United States, no federal or state institutions or laws existed in this locale. Only the Native and Métis inhabitants occupied or possessed this region until the creation of Dakota Territory in 1861. The Chippewa thrived in their hard-won lands hardly aware of all the foreign names and boundary lines brought to bear on their domain.

This lack of recognition led a growing number of European American settlers farther south to memorialize Congress for a new territory. Nevertheless, their quest fell victim to the sectional stalemate over the issue of slavery in the western territories. The Republicans in Congress insisted that no new territory could be brought into being without a prohibition on slavery. Their position could not prevail until the Southern Democrats seceded just before President Lincoln's inauguration in 1861. But this situation did not curtail renewed local interest in extinguishing any remaining "Indian title" impeding the commercial trade and transportation development of the Red River Valley. "No communications to the north [could] be had except across their territory."[103]

The U.S. Senate's rejection of the 1851 Pembina Treaty magnified the mistrust and discord during those council negotiations. The fact that approximately thirteen thousand square miles in the northwest corner of Minnesota remained unceded Native American country left territorial and state politicians like Ramsey, Sibley, and Kittson more anxious than ever about the manifest destiny of their region. In 1854 and 1855, significant treaty-based Chippewa land cessions immediately to the south and east increasingly isolated the Red Lake and Pembina bands. The Native peoples living on both sides of the Red River grew alarmed at the burgeoning boat traffic, especially the arrival of steamboats. They also had to fend off the related increased logging of their timber. All of these European American activities constituted illegal trespass. Yet, the Native Americans had almost no means or avenue of redress to stop any wrongful interference or damages. They protested politely, yet vehemently, because they feared that any acquiescence would be misinterpreted as giving up of their rights, or a form of abandonment, jeopardizing their "Indian title."[104]

As threatening as these encroachments appeared to be, the advent of an even greater danger imperiled their future. Due to its long freezing winters, steamboats only had access to St. Paul via the Mississippi River for little over half the year. This limitation could be overcome easily by another implementation of steam power: the railroads. Territorial politicians like Henry M. Rice lobbied Congress for railroad land grants. As a result, Minnesota received its first grant in 1856. Along with a five-million-dollar loan from the territorial legislature, they financed four major rail lines disseminating from St. Paul. The commissioner of Indian Affairs noted the building of villages by the settlers of Minnesota "in the remote valley of the Red River of the North," based on Isaac Stevens's survey touting Pembina as the future eastern rail terminus for the northern transcontinental railroad to Puget Sound.[105]

Word of trouble brewing in the region finally reached Washington, D.C., in 1859. To force European American acknowledgement of their pre-existing land rights, the Red River Chippewa began exacting payments under threat of force from some of those sailing up and down the river.[106] The commissioner of Indian Affairs advocated another treaty conference with the Red Lake and Pembina Chippewa to insure safe transit along the Red River. Allegedly, safe commerce could not be guaranteed while the lands adjoining both sides of the river belonged to the Chippewa. The extensive trade over the Red River Valley cart trails refuted this false assumption. Once again, federal policymakers found it convenient to only perceive Native Americans as impediments to European American westward expansion.

Local agents considered their removal and "concentration upon one reservation" to be "exceedingly desirable."[107] Tribal lands in tribal hands restrained the pursuit of profit. The cultural expectations of European Americans conceived of progress in terms of an orderly settlement dominated by cultivated farmland. Indigenous possession of land and its accompanying waterways impeded the "rapid development of the country."[108] Because they had a different set of economic priorities, U.S. policy framers overlooked Chippewa/Métis participation in the British-Canadian market exchange economy of buffalo hides for trade goods. Alexander Ramsey maintained that "no finer country exists anywhere in the Union."[109] With the decline of the fur trade, Native American fertile lands and vital waterways needed to be integrated into the expanding U.S. national economy. In February 1860, the new legislature of Minnesota petitioned the president to extinguish the "possessory title" of the Red Lake and Pembina Chippewa that embraced large portions of the valley of the Red River of the North by treaty. The Red Lake band had already relinquished any prior claims to the territory west of the Red River. The federal government, Minnesota Territory, and the Red Lakers recognized this area as being in the sole possession of the Pembina band. By July 1860, the lobbying efforts of the commissioner of Indian Affairs and Henry M. Rice of Minnesota paid off. Congress appropriated funds for a treaty conference.[110]

In September 1860, federal commissioners convened a council with tribal representatives of the "Red River Chippewas," but the negotiations fell short of the desired "extinguishment of their title." The federal commissioners used the excuse that the absence of some important chiefs precluded the possibility of concluding an agreement. [111] In fact, the bargaining failed because the Natives asked for more than the United States would pay. These bands had long been involved in the give-and-take of the fur trade. They knew the value of commodities that European Americans wanted and how to drive a hard bargain. Due to their closer proximity to European American settlement, the treaty commissioners offered twice as much to the Red Lakers as the Pembina band. Nevertheless, the federal government's revived interest resulted in both Chippewa bands, especially the Minnesota-side Red Lakers, being more cognizant of their land's market value and less willing to part with it for the paltry sums offered by the United States.

The inability to reach an accord did not curtail "the prospective increase of [European American] population."[112] The Chippewa could not envision the relentless demographic tide abetted by land speculators and new technologies that would soon spill over into their lands and tip the balance of power against them. As a prelude and an impetus to this development, the federal government did not need a treaty to incorporate the last "unorganized" territorial remnant within what would become the lower forty-eight states of the United States. But the GLO could not survey land or issue patents. So, a determined land-speculation outfit decided to fill the void and create a sense of urgency. With the governor of Minnesota as its president, the Minnesota Legislature chartered the Dakota Land Company in 1857. Their assertive townsite speculation led to the organization of counties and an elected legislature without any authorization from the federal government. This dubious creation of a quasi-Dakota Territory prior to its formal creation by Congress in 1861 had far-reaching consequences. In spite of all its subsequent developments, for the rest of the nineteenth century North Dakota remained a colonial hinterland of the railroad, banking, lumber, and grain elevator interests of St. Paul and Minneapolis, Minnesota.[113] As a result, Congress merged it with the northeastern portion of Nebraska Territory and created the new Dakota Territory in 1861 with an Anglo population of 2,128.[114]

The Civil War propelled this territorial integration. President Abraham Lincoln and the northern Republican-dominated Congress sought to incorporate as much of the vast, loosely organized western territories into the Union as possible. In addition to the establishment of new territories, Congress passed the Homestead Act and the first Pacific Railroad Act in 1862. To secure greater national allegiance and accelerate westward expansion, the United States began to give away public domain lands so citizens and corporations could transform them into private property, while the non-citizen status of Native Americans prevented them from acquiring homesteads.[115] This landmark legislation placed existing unceded lands at greater risk of loss to European American settlers and speculators. Both of these huge land grants meant that the federal government had to pursue Native land cessions more aggressively. Facilitating European American settlement required securing legal "Indian title." This consolidation of federal territory to secure areas of vital natural resources and overland transportation routes did not bode well for Native homelands. Various U.S. expeditions and commissions had observed how the "extremely fertile and valuable" territories of the Red Lake and Pembina Chippewa made the Red River region and the Turtle Mountain lands farther west "well adapted for agricultural purposes" and homesteading.[116]

Because the Supreme Court designated their legal status as "domestic dependent nations" and non-citizens, the United States did not feel obligated to obtain consent from any Native Americans in the new territory, including the Pembina and Turtle Mountain Chippewa. Yet in an ironic legal twist that would have significant future implications, the authority of Congress to create the new territory under the precedent established by the Northwest Ordinance of 1787 directly acknowledged the de facto sovereignty of the concerned tribes. In the enabling act creating the Territory of Dakota, Congress continued the same general policy of reserving to itself any extinguishing of Indigenous land ownership within federal domains. In this case, the creation of a new territory did not inherently diminish Native rights. Congress specified that "nothing in this act shall be construed to impair the rights of person or property now pertaining to the Indians in said Territory, so long as such rights shall remain unextinguished by treaty between the United States and such Indians." [117] This specification meant that the Pembina and Turtle Mountain Chippewa had as valid a claim to the northeastern and north-central territory of North Dakota as any Native people could have under the legal doctrine of Indigenous title.

The Dakota Territory's disclaimer clause confirmed that treaties did not grant rights to Native Americans. Only through consent could Native Americans give up or convey any of their inherent rights to land or self-governance as a consequence of the treaty process. This crucial aspect of federal law became known as the reserved rights doctrine: Rights not explicitly given up in a treaty were retained, or reserved, by the tribe. The self-governing authority of the Turtle Mountain band came from the consent of its own community members. They pre-dated U.S. sovereignty over their autonomous area and the creation of Dakota Territory. Any territory ceded by a Native tribe required the consent of the tribe for it to be included within the territorial limits or jurisdiction of a state or territory. This doctrine meant that "all unced-ed Indian territory shall be excepted out of the boundaries and consti-tute no part of the Territory of Dakota."[118] Since these provisos applied to Dakota Territory (1861) and the state of North Dakota (1889), they should have provided legal protection to the territory and rights of the Turtle Mountain Band of Chippewa within those jurisdictions. In actuality, such disclaimer clauses sought only to protect federal juris-diction over Native affairs instead of tribal sovereignty.

But other unresolved issues that had aggravated tribal-federal re-lations since 1851 eclipsed the creation of Dakota Territory. In addi-tion to failing to reach a settlement with the Pembina Chippewa in 1860, a greater regional upheaval intervened to forestall another trea-ty council. The eruption of Dakota band frustrations, known as the

Dakota War of 1862 (although most of the Dakota opposed the war) resulted in an explosion of violence that shocked white Minnesotans. This upheaval precluded temporarily any peaceful Native American and European American interactions in the region. Most local European Americans and federal policymakers blamed the intractable nature of the Dakota for the violent outbreak. A few dispassionate observers like Bishop Henry Whipple believed "that this massacre was the legitimate fruit of our Indian system" stemming from the fraudulent 1851 treaties.[119] With peace (but not justice) restored by 1863, continued informal communications between the Red River Chippewa bands and U.S. Indian Affairs representatives indicated that both sides still desired a treaty, although most of the impetus came from the United States. Along with setting up a new treaty council came renewed formal recognition by local BIA officials of Little Shell II as the chief of the Turtle Mountain band.[120] This recognition set the stage for the first formal treaty council between the United States and the Pembina and Turtle Mountain Chippewa since 1851. While the Native Americans would seek protection and recognition of their inherent legal status as sovereign nations, the United States would focus almost exclusively on land cessions. As a consequence, the imposition of federal law and policy onto tribal societies weakened their institutions and customs. The treaty process establishing U.S. political relations with the Chippewa in the first half of the nineteenth century initiated the federal erosion of tribal authority. These intrusions derived from selfish economic interests rationalized by moral imperatives. Significantly, the rule of law would not result in justice for the Pembina and Turtle Mountain Chippewa.

# CHAPTER 3
## The Old Crossing Treaty, 1863–1864

*The Master of Life placed us here and gave it to us for an inheritance.*[1]
—Little Rock, Red Lake Chippewa "Talking Chief,"
Old Crossing Treaty Council, 1863

Treaties created the original legal relationship between the U.S. government and Native American nations.[2] They provide glimpses into the intercultural relations between Native peoples and the U.S. federal government during specific historical eras. Article VI, Paragraph 2 (known as the Treaty or Supremacy Clause) of the U.S. Constitution dealt implicitly with Native peoples. It declared that "all Treaties . . . shall be the supreme law of the Land." Treaties acknowledged a legal alliance between two sovereign but not necessarily equal governments. This is why Native peoples, like the Pembina and Turtle Mountain Chippewa, have asserted to this day that their inherent sovereign status and accompanying legal rights have been recognized by the United States through their treaty relationship.

Treaty negotiations provided the main forum for a government-to-government relationship of Native peoples with the United States. Yet the well-documented focus on the negative ramifications of broken treaties misses a fundamental flaw in this process.[3] The negotiations doomed most treaties to failure because the United States usually acted in "bad faith."[4] In 1863, a few months before the Old Crossing council, the Minnesota Indian agent reported to the Commissioner of Indian Affairs (CIA) that "the government should at once abandon the treaty system . . . and compel the Indians to submit to the authority" of the United States.[5] By the mid-nineteenth century, the United States did not need American Indians as trading partners or military allies. It wanted their lands to unlock the potential economic wealth of western North America. Besides the fact that the United States responded to the contractual obligations it had dictated with consistent failure, the treaty documents often conceal, rather than reveal, what actually occurred at a treaty council.

The treaties themselves fail to connect us to what Vine Deloria, Jr., described as the "emotional context of history which enables us to understand the flesh of historical processes."[6] Native testimony comes from their diplomatic council speeches recorded in the treaty journals, since they had little or no voice in the treaties themselves. A focus on what Native spokesmen said during a treaty council makes the proceedings come alive and helps us to learn about the distinctive features of Indigenous historical narrative, or what Peter Nabokov calls, "American Indian forms of historical consciousness."[7] A close examination of the treaty-making process between U.S. commissioners and Native Americans sheds light on almost every facet of tribal-federal relations.

As part of the extensive effort during the Civil War (1861–1865) to incorporate all of the remaining western Native tribes into a more formal relationship under U.S. control, commissioner of Indian Affairs William P. Dole selected Minnesota Senator Alexander Ramsey as the federal government representative empowered to treat with the Red Lake (northwestern Minnesota) and Pembina (northeastern Dakota Territory) Chippewa in 1863. Based on the instructions Dole received from the Secretary of the Interior, the commissioner set forth the goals of the treaty council. The "main object" was to secure uninterrupted navigation of the Red River. This objective could be achieved only by extinguishing "Indian title" to a substantial portion of territory on both sides of the waterway. In addition to the cession, Dole issued instructions to Ramsey indicating that "removal of the bands to positions remote from our white settlements" embodied the "primary objective" of the treaty.[8] Ramsey undertook the mission reluctantly. After his experience with the unratified Pembina Treaty of 1851, he asked Dole why "the government should place itself on an equal footing in treating with hordes of savages."[9] A few months before the Old Crossing council, an Indian agent from Minnesota reported to the commissioner of Indian Affairs that "the government should at once abandon the treaty system . . . and compel the Indians to submit to the authority" of the United States.[10] These sentiments became so prevalent, that it is surprising the United States decided to re-negotiate a treaty with the Red Lake and Pembina Chippewa. But the imperative of obtaining the prized Red River Valley compelled the United States to continue with the expediency of treaty-making.

In the fall of 1863, Ramsey set out from St. Paul, Minnesota, with a grand entourage and military escort. The apprehension generated by the horrors of the Dakota War of 1862 still reverberated throughout the region. These anxieties provided an unfortunate anti-Native context for the negotiations, despite the fact that the Pembina, Turtle Mountain, and Red Lake Chippewa bands had no connection with any violence. Although they provided food to, and accepted gifts from, some of the Dakota fleeing to Canada, the Ojibwe never menaced any European American settlers or the U.S. government during the regional crisis.[11] Ramsey's uneasiness accounted for the larger than usual military presence at the treaty council. As he had for the treaty entourage that negotiated the unratified treaty at Pembina in 1851, Pierre Bottineau acted as the commission's guide and as an adviser to the Pembina and Turtle Mountain Chippewa. He also assisted as an interpreter at the treaty council since he spoke French, English, Dakota, Ojibwe, Cree, Mandan, and Winnebago. The U.S. representatives valued his usefulness as a "mixed-blood" because he "thoroughly understood the temperament and inclinations" of both the Chippewa and the Métis participants.[12]

En route to their destination, Ramsey described the lands east of the Red River as "extremely fertile, and if reclaimed from the overflow, would be equal to the bottoms of the Nile in its productiveness of cereals."[13] After two and a half weeks, the party reached the Old Crossing, located conveniently at the intersection of a ford on the Red Lake River and a Red River cart trail.[14] The agent from Crow Wing, Ashley C. Morrill, arrived on the same day, having brought the Red Lake band. The Pembina band of Red Bear and the Turtle Mountain band of Little Shell II (Little Chief) came the next day, comprised of 352 Native Americans and 663 "half-breeds."[15] The mixed-bloods' large presence threatened to destabilize the proceedings before they started. They insisted on acting as the guardians and legal representatives of the Pembina Chippewa, especially in all matters related to the "dispositions of their landed interests," as had been the case when they renewed the Sweet Corn peace agreement with the Dakota in 1858.[16] The commissioners had no choice but to accept their presence. Although Ramsey asserted that he would only negotiate directly with the Pembina Chippewa delegation consisting of Chief Red Bear, Chief Little Shell II, and their warriors, the existence of two Pembina Métis signatories to the final treaty indicated otherwise.[17]

In his opening speech, Ramsey framed the business at hand as being for the "welfare" of the Native Americans primarily. The Great Father had a "great heart" for all of his red, white, and black people, unless they committed any crimes. Ramsey tried to tie the self-interests of the U.S. and the Chippewa together by singling out the Dakota as a common enemy. He referred to the "perfidy" of their recent uprising in Minnesota by portraying the Dakota as being ungrateful for all the U.S. had done for them.[18] Ramsey conveniently ignored the broken promises that many European American observers believed caused the revolt.[19]

In contrast to his mischaracterization of the Dakota as "a base and treacherous people," Ramsey said that he was glad to meet with these Chippewa bands. They had never "violated the solemn faith of treaties," and "no white man's blood had ever been shed by a Chippewa." One regional agent concurred by considering them to be "an easily governed and tractable people."[20] These acknowledgements by

U.S. officials refuted the Secretary of the Interior's assertions about the "moral inferiority" of the Chippewa. But Ramsey focused on the reports of local Native officials about the European American population influx into the "fertile lands" of Red River region. "Settlements have been made upon that river up to the very limits of the ceded land," he warned, "and the whole of the valley . . . would be sought for settlement as soon as the Indian title should be secured by the government."[21] These waves of newcomers brought increasing demands for unimpeded travel and trade provided by steamboats and the railroads. Ramsey asserted proudly that, "this is what we call Progress." Not surprisingly, the commissioner—like so many U.S. politicians and missionaries—defined "progress" solely in terms of European American economic and technological development. He did not show any appreciation for the fact that the Chippewa's well developed socio-economic system had served them well up to this point.

Then Ramsey forewarned that uninterrupted trade with the British settlements in what would become Canada was of "the highest importance." The annual value of fur sales alone reached $250,000 in 1863.[22] He revealed that the Great Father's desire for commerce along the Red River constituted the real reason for these negotiations, rather than the welfare of the Native population. His claim did not shock the Native delegates. The same desires had been expressed by Ramsey and Kittson back in 1851 and by local agents and superintendents ever since.

To soften his urgency, Ramsey tried to calm the Natives' biggest fear. He stated dishonestly that the Great Father had no special desire to get possession of their lands. All he wanted was the privilege of unmolested travel through their country via wagons or steamboats. Then he applied pressure by making baseless allegations about the theft of the goods of peaceful merchants that dismayed the Great Father. Ramsey reported one or two occasions where Red River steamboats had been impeded or levied by the Chippewa. The most significant incident had involved his old political crony Kittson, who by 1860 had become the main overland and river transporter of goods between St. Paul, Minnesota, and the British Red River settlements. Kittson recounted the episode in a letter to the Superintendent of Indian Affairs at St. Paul. As the purchasing agent for the Hudson's Bay Company, and the leading private merchants in the Red River settlements, he made a claim against the Red Lake and Pembina Chippewa for "property taken at Grand Forks" on Sept 13, 1862, amounting to nearly $8,500.[23]

Kittson identified the immediate cause of the robbery as the disappointment of the Chippewa bands at the non-arrival of a treaty commission to negotiate with them, and their expectations of the usual presents and rations that accompanied such meetings. Apparently, these goods had been stored farther south at Fort Abercrombie in anticipation of a treaty council. The Dakota insurgency in August 1862 had depopulated the southwestern Minnesota frontier and hurt Kittson's business by curtailing trade throughout the region. He considered the perpetrators who "took a leading part" in the Grand Forks episode to be "scoundrels" and "wretches" who should be "made an example of." This included Little Shell II, identified as "Chief of the Turtle Mountain Band." Kittson claimed that Little Shell II was not "badly disposed." Although he thought the Turtle Mountain leader had the moral sense to know right from wrong, he regarded Little Shell as "entirely unfit to govern his land."[24] Such an attitude did not bode well for negotiations with the Pembina and Turtle Mountain leader.

As a private businessman and prominent politician, Kittson had benefited from the defrauding and dispossession of the Chippewa and Dakota that was part of the corrupt political patronage system in Minnesota Territory. His letter ended by weighing in on the long-term cause for the alleged depredation. Kittson reiterated the common charge that all Native problems stemmed from undue leniency on the part of the federal government. The U.S. government's "forbearance" and concessions constituted the sole cause for incidents of Chippewa pillage and Dakota violence.[25] Kittson refused to recognize that the Native Americans had any legitimate grievances.

One might think that he based his harsh opinions on bitter experience rather than malice. He concluded the letter with an obvious untruth that revealed his spitefulness. All reports from local agents, superintendents, and even Ramsey made clear distinctions between the "tractable" nature of the Chippewa versus the more combative temperament of the Dakota. Kittson overlooked these obvious differences. He attempted to conflate an incident involving $8,500 of property, with no injuries or deaths, against a horrific month of violence that turned Minnesota into a two-hundred-mile "track of blood" resulting in the death of nearly six hundred settlers.[26] Kittson accused the Chippewa of being as hostile to the United States as the Dakotas. Moreover, he claimed that if their role in the Grand Forks incident went unpunished, then "we may look forward and expect from them such scenes as have been enacted the past season by the Sioux."[27] Clearly, Kittson painted the Chippewa with as broad and tarnished a brush as necessary to get the full and speedy compensation to which he felt entitled. His accusations provided greater leverage to induce Chippewa concessions in a treaty that would bolster his business by securing various rights-of-way through the Red River Valley.

Ramsey concluded his thoughts on this matter by stating that the passage of boats or carts through their country did not harm the resident Natives in any way, or deprive them of anything.[28] He promised that they could still hunt and fish as usual. The United States would pay the bands "liberally" for these passage rights, even though such an arrangement took nothing from them which they "possessed." This offer to pay for "nothing" must have puzzled the Native delegates. The cutting of timber and intrusion of steamboats diminished the availability of fish and game, devaluing their territory. Of greater importance legally, their occupation and use of this area gave them "Indian title" to the region's lands and waterways. Despite the weak protection this legal doctrine provided for Native land claims, it still precluded European American passage or settlement until extinguished lawfully by the federal government. Although never stated forthrightly, the commission had to extinguish the "Indian title" through the legal instrument of a treaty.

A growing sentiment in Congress and Dole's bureau increasingly permitted negotiators like Ramsey to "eliminate any possibility that the treaty might be interpreted as a recognition of Indian title to the land."[29] Instead, Ramsey offered the Chippewa bands what he characterized as a "liberal" payment of $20,000 for the right-of-way. He followed immediately with an offhand alternative offer presented as, "or, if you want to sell your lands and retain a reservation for yourselves, say so."[30] Ramsey's offer of a generous payment for "nothing which you possess" amounted to legal deceit, defined as "the fraudulent representation of a material fact made with the knowledge of its falsity."[31] He had not come just to negotiate a right-of-way. River transit and routes for railroad and telegraph lines comprised high priorities, for which he and other prominent persons (i.e., Henry M. Rice, Henry H. Sibley, and Norman Kittson) had personal financial interests.[32] According to Commissioner Dole's instructions, this proposal represented only one of the treaty commission's goals. No matter which option the Chippewa chose, the end results would be the same: the opening of their territory to European American transit and settlement, almost total dispossession of Native lands except for a small reservation, and no preservation of their hunting and fishing rights.

The following day, the U.S. delegation yielded the speaker's forum to the Native Americans. Little Rock, of the Red Lake band, fulfilled the role of main spokesperson for both bands during the proceedings. As an example of the situational nature of Chippewa political leadership, they customarily chose an orator or "talking chief," who was not necessarily a chief, to speak for them in diplomatic settings. Since a significant part of the Pembina band traced their origins to the Red Lake band, they deferred to their elder brothers to speak for them in formal councils. Pointing to the assembled headmen, Little Rock stated, "I do not consider myself a chief, but I am going to interpret their words. I am a representative of them, as you are of the Great Father."[33] From his opening remark, the chiefs must have figured out that the U.S. called into question the Chippewa band's possessory rights to the lands on both sides of the Red River south of the British possessions.

Little Rock based their Indigenous claim on the highest authority possible. He asserted that, "I am going to show you how we came to occupy this land. The Master of Life placed us here and gave it to us for an inheritance."[34] This simple yet eloquent statement conveyed the sacred and inalienable nature of Native sovereignty. Ojibwe concepts of creation, identity and heritage derived from the Creator. They also perceived of land and its attendant resources as part of a larger holistic spiritual relationship. Land and resources did not belong just to the living members of their community, but for generations to come.[35] A large part of the chief's responsibility involved looking ahead to provide their people with a sustainable future.

To convey their sense of place, order, and continuity within a tradition that transcended time, Little Rock summarized migration stories recounted from Ojibwe oral tradition. He placed their grandfathers' origins "far to the East," while the tracks of their travels "strike away off to the West" (referring to the Turtle Mountain band and other Plains-Ojibwe). In case these migrations should be mistaken by the U.S. commissioners as the random movements of "roving bands," Little Rock made it clear that the territory currently under discussion "belongs to us." His affirmation of their sovereignty confirmed that Ramsey's devious presentation had not fooled them. In fact, his presumptuous offer offended them. "We should be very sorry for you to set a value upon the land for us and make us an offer . . . before you heard our offer."[36]

They took further offense at Ramsey's assertion that the Red River had little or no importance for them. To make it clear to the U.S. delegation, Little Rock elaborated upon the Chippewa's sovereign claim. "The Master of Life gave us the river and the water thereof to drink, the animals for food and clothing, and the woods and roads [referring to any river as a "road," which was the purpose it served for them, as depicted on Chippewa birch bark scrolls showing footprints on waterways] we depend on for subsistence, and [yet] you think we derive no benefits from them. The Master of Life gave it to us for an inheritance."[37] According to the Ojibwe worldview, land and resources should be used only in culturally-sanctioned ways that fulfilled their subsistence and spiritual needs based on sacred obligations of stewardship. As Indigenous peoples, they had prior occupation, no intention of moving and wanted to insure their children's future. In case Little Rock's eloquence had not expressed their dismay with the U.S. proposal, the Pembina chief Red Bear interjected. He reminded Ramsey that "you are here on a visit to lands that do not belong to you." Red Bear also denied any involvement with the incidents alleged by Ramsey, declaring, "I have been guilty of no crime." [38]

Ramsey tried to soothe the Natives' hurt feelings by confirming that European Americans also acknowledged the Master of Life. He speculated that perhaps Native Americans in adjacent regions, who had forgotten the lessons of the Great Spirit, fomented the recent troubles on the Red River. While these somewhat agreeable words could have shifted the negotiations in a more conciliatory direction, it seemed that Ramsey could rarely get beyond his overbearing nature. After launching into a diatribe on the inferior ways Native Americans used their lands and resources, he ended with a false assertion that they had been destitute before contact with Europeans. The commissioner boasted that the European American system of cultivation and settlement could support ten thousand times as many people in the region. All the good things the Chippewa had (e.g., guns, powder, shot, lead, blankets, cloth, etc.) came from European Americans or Canadians. Nevertheless, the Natives should not despair because "it is probable that the Great Spirit had in view the mutual advantage of both races in bringing them together."[39] In this statement, Ramsey invoked a version of the popular U.S. national expansion vision of manifest destiny. From this ethnocentric perspective, more white people meant more food and blankets for Native people and greater overall improvement in their condition, rather than dispossession and removal. The paternalistic and altruistic Great Father only wanted to "promote their welfare" by buying a right-of-way, and then taking them "under his care."[40]

Displaying his annoyance, Ramsey announced that if they considered this offer unacceptable, he would be open to another proposition. The commissioner reminded the Native delegates that the Great Father had several times offered to purchase their lands. The United States made such overtures not for settlement, but because they desired free passage to avoid quarrels between them, which might get out of control and lead to violent conflict. By selling their lands, the Chippewa would assure their own peace and security. In return, they would receive a yearly supply of money and goods. Ignoring Little Rock's rejection of his claim about the worthlessness of these lands, Ramsey reiterated that such an agreement did not deprive them of anything valuable. If they sold their territory, they could still occupy and hunt over it as before, "probably for a long time." He then made another dishonest statement, stating that this lucrative region would not be desired for European American settlement "before the youngest man among them was a gray-haired old man" (i.e., for approximately thirty-five years or circa 1900).[41]

Such untruthful exaggeration contradicted the report of the region's Superintendent of Indian Affairs, W. J. Cullen. Only four years before, he informed the commissioner of Indian Affairs that "settlement would be sought [by European Americans] as soon as the Indian title should be secured by the government."[42] Ramsey presented the Native Americans' choice as clear-cut. The obvious advantages for them required little or no reflection on their part to reach an agreement. On top of this, he made the unique nature of this offer quite clear. The Great Father did not usually ask his children, white or red, for the privilege of passing through their lands. He did so in this case only to "prevent difficulties" and "out of concern for their interest and welfare."[43] Ramsey conceded that the assembled chiefs had not committed any crimes. He reiterated that the "whites and Chippewas of this country have heretofore lived in peace."[44] This accurate assessment seemed to contradict his concerns about any "difficulties." Yet the commissioner still expected some sort of "explanation" or "apology," without clarifying what could be explained or atoned for if none of them had engaged in criminal activity.

Little Rock replied that "all our bands" desired "perpetual peace and friendship with the whites."[45] Nevertheless, he refuted Ramsey's notion of their dependence on trade goods, or destitution before contact with European Americans. Once again, he referred to the Red River not just as a passageway, but as a region of adjacent prairies and resources "where I get my living." Eloquently explaining the reciprocal relationship between spirituality and subsistence, Little Rock explained that "the Master of Life has placed upon these prairies animals from which I live. Their meat is my food, and their skins are my clothing."[46]

The increasing amount of steamboat traffic on the Red River since 1859 threatened the sustainability of these resources. Little Rock raised the crucial concern. Wrongful European American interference with the possession of unceded Chippewa lands (and waterways) constituted illegal trespass. He stated that, "it seems now that the white man is passing backward and forward and wrestling these prairies from our hands and taking this food from my mouth."[47] Crews cut wood to fuel the steamboats without paying. Based on these experiences, he challenged the self-proclaimed equity of U.S. justice. "When your young men steal anything, you make them pay. That is the way we look upon those white men who drive away the animals and the fish the Great Spirit has given us for our support."[48]

Ramsey refused to acknowledge the possibility of any negative consequences for the Native population from European American encroachment. It seemed he had not even heard Little Rock's perspective. He characterized the "whole tenor" of the Chippewa orator's speeches as little more than ingenious justifications for depredations without acknowledging that any had been committed.[49] Little Rock addressed the treaty commissioner's less than adequate offer. He wondered if Ramsey thought them ignorant and characterized the proposed U.S. payment for an unimpeded right of passage on the Red River as completely inadequate to either its worth to the Americans, or its loss to the Native peoples. Again, the former governor's obsession with the alleged pillaging caused him to miss Little Rock's rejection of his meager offer and its unfounded rationale. He thought Little Rock had begun to address the issue of compensation for depredations. Sensing that the U.S. representatives had still not gotten his message, the Native spokesman became more blunt and less diplomatic. "We want you to understand that the proposition you made us yesterday [i.e., $20,000 for the right-of-way] we do not accept. We do not think of it at all."[50]

The Ojibwe upbraided the U.S. delegation for not adhering to the custom of gift-giving required by Native diplomacy. Little Rock reminded them that, "when we come into council, we smoke all the time, and we have consumed all the tobacco you have given us."[51] Ramsey once again proved himself incapable of complying with what seemed like a reasonable request. He elevated a matter of protocol into a contentious issue. Clearly, he did not understand that the Native delegation interpreted the scarcity of presents as a lack of commitment to a satisfactory settlement. For the Ojibwe, generosity smoothed the way towards reconciliation. Believing that their request amounted to nothing more than a stalling tactic, Ramsey began complaining about the lateness of the autumn season, the onset of cold weather, and the long journey back to St. Paul. He did not believe that the Natives had used up all of their tobacco. They must be mistaken. Little Rock, tapping the empty bowl of his pipe, replied that "there is a mistake, but the place where it is, is in the bottom of my pipe."[52]

Ramsey noted that so far only the Red Lake Natives had taken an active and amenable part in the proceedings. As usual he attributed this situation to the wrong reasons. In addition to not understanding Little Rock's orator role for both bands during the negotiations, the commissioner came to the rather racist conclusion that the more amenable nature of the Red Lake Chippewa stemmed from their geographical isolation and unadulterated Native blood. Due to these circumstances, Ramsey believed they remained "among the purest representatives . . . of the Indian race," in contrast to the predominantly mixed-blood

Pembina band.[53] His attitude reflected the increase of biological racial stereotyping connected with the public discourse of manifest destiny.[54] Ramsey obviously had no knowledge of the long-standing kinship relations between the Red Lake and Pembina bands. Although the latter group had split off from the Red Lakers some time ago, they still deferred somewhat to their elder relations in political councils of great importance. While the right of Red River passage required the assent of the both bands, the closer proximity of the Minnesota Red Lake band to oncoming European American settlement resulted in the commissioners directing much more of their attention and flattery towards them, rather than the Pembina band in Dakota Territory.

Little Rock reminded the commissioners that he spoke for all the chiefs of both bands. He began his next oration on a note that Ramsey did not comprehend. Speaking metaphorically, he said that he liked "cleanliness." Responding privately in the journal (not publicly to the Native delegates), Ramsey could not resist denigrating the less than tidy appearance of the "talking chief's" shirt and misinterpreting the statement as a "boast."[55] Little Rock meant that these talks should have started with a clean slate. "Past offenses" should be overlooked or forgotten. He was not just referring to Ramsey's allegations of Native depredations. The major concern of the Chippewa bands focused on the illegal European American trespass into their territory, and the subsequent damages to their resources. To get beyond these mutual accusations, the Red Lake orator invoked an aspect of Indigenous Eastern Woodland diplomatic protocol known as the condolence ritual.[56] By asking that "the tracks of footprints everywhere, and the ravages [they have] made" be wiped away, Little Rock tried to open the door to more meaningful and less contentious negotiations. He conveyed the Native sense that any bad blood on either side must be "cleaned" before they could enter into a sacred treaty relationship.[57]

Little Rock felt compelled to try and get the U.S. representatives to understand that the Chippewa bands had not come to this council to discuss land merely in terms of property, territory, or resources. They had no right to do this because of their sacred connection to this particular land. "The Master of Life when he put you here never told you that you should own the soil, nor when the Master of Life put me here did he tell me that you should own the soil."[58] The Red Lake and Pembina Chippewa could not separate their particular place on earth from their lives and identity. They conceived of this unique relationship in sacred and symbolic terms that gave them meaning as a people.[59]

In a manner similar to other Native peoples, the Chippewa had an ominous insight about the coming of the European Americans. Little Rock recounted "the words that were given to [my great-grandfather] by the Master of Life: 'At some time there shall come among you a stranger speaking a language you do not understand. He will try to buy land from you, but do not sell it. Keep it for an inheritance to your children.'"[60] Since much of the cultural identity of Native American communities evolved from such prophecies, the Chippewa bands reflected upon the increasing tenuousness of their situation and drew strength from their oral tradition. As founder of postcolonial studies Edward Said remarked, such "stories are at the heart of [what] people use to assert their own identity and the existence of their own history."[61] In an appeal for greater empathy from the American delegation, Little Rock addressed Ramsey personally and said, "My friend, if you want to understand me more thoroughly, take away from me . . . what afflicts me in my feelings."[62] Once again, Ramsey misinterpreted the Native orator's plea for cross-cultural compassion, as an admission of guilt over the alleged pillaging deserving of some punishment. It seemed that Ramsey's obsession with depredations precluded him from comprehending what Little Rock told him about the Indigenous concept of sacred land and sense of place.

Sensing the commissioner's primary concern, Little Rock addressed the plundering issue directly but in accordance with the Chippewa ideal of autonomous responsibility. He reminded Ramsey that young warriors often behaved foolishly and acted in ways beyond the control of their elders. Even the usually hostile Kittson had confirmed this state of affairs. In his critical rendition of the incident at Grand Forks, Kittson praised Little Rock and the Red Lake chief Moose Dung (Mo-so-mo) in particular, for endeavoring to prevent trouble. Even though their efforts proved to be in vain, Kittson believed they deserved "some notice from the Government for their good intentions."[63]

Little Rock's response raised the issue of the lack of fair and equal justice in cases of Native-white crime. United States officials resorted to the same rationale about their inability to control the incursions and violence of its citizens on the borderlands of Native country. Yet, in his subtle way, Little Rock acknowledged "we know that you are powerful."[64] He implied that if the United States, with its legal, law enforcement, and military institutions could not control its unruly citizens, how could two weaker Ojibwe bands be expected to restrain their disruptive members?

Little Rock addressed the other issues raised by Ramsey. In regard to concluding the council sooner rather than later, the Red Lake orator reminded the commissioner that "we also are not without work to do." He reiterated Red Bear's reminder that "I have not gone to your house, but you have come to mine." Little Rock also refuted Ramsey's statement about the "destitution" of his people. "Formerly I did not consider myself poverty stricken at all, because there was plenty of game in the country. Now the game is going." He attributed this circumstance to an "evil spirit." [65]

Some of the commissioners seemed to realize that the Native negotiators had "a special esteem for their homeland that [went] beyond its cash value or level of productivity."[66] Yet Ramsey insisted that the the Native Americans "were in want of many things," such as powder, shot, guns, knives, axes, blankets, tobacco, and clothes. Nevertheless, God "sent a new race over here to supply their necessities," and as a consequence they have become "entirely dependent upon this race." Ramsey resorted to this denigration of Native peoples before proceeding to the real issue which concerned him. He did not bring up the need for a right-of-way but mentioned casually that "if they were now to turn over this land" to the United States, both races would benefit.[67]

Then he contradicted his previous statement by claiming that "we do not care so much about the land." The citizens of the United States only wanted to travel over it. Yet, if the Ojibwe wanted to sell their land, "they may reserve as much as they choose *within reasonable limits* for hunting and agriculture, and that a farm will be given to each of their half-breed friends."[68] For the first time during these negotiations, Ramsey broached the possibility of the Red Lake and Pembina bands each receiving a reservation on their respective sides of the Red River. Such a proposal ignored Little Rock's affirmation that the Chippewa derived an adequate living from, and felt a sacred connection to, their territory. The former governor insisted that their lands were "worthless to them." By relinquishing them, they would get provisions "every year" from the U.S. government, while continuing to hunt "for many years at least."[69] If the Native Americans agreed to these terms, they had nothing to lose and much to gain. Ramsey reminded them that they would need the money because they had debts to pay, plus reparations for their looting.

Little Rock responded that crime, lying, and theft annoyed him as much as it alarmed Ramsey. His frustrations with Ramsey's specious claims became more apparent. While the commissioner kept insisting that the Chippewa lived poorly before the arrival of the European Americans, Little Rock tried to convince him that the opposite was true. He told Ramsey that any final settlement must "take into consideration the animals that you kill and the wood that you burn."[70] The Red Lake orator also challenged Ramsey by stating, "I do not believe, as you say, that our land is worthless. I think the amount I asked of you is nothing but a fair equivalent for the land we cede to you. If you want to better my condition, you should give me enough to make me comfortable."[71] He reminded the commissioner that as long as he could remember, the Red River region had given him adequate sustenance. However, the coming of the steamboats had "driven away the game and made me poor." The Native spokesman then refuted Ramsey's false claim that their lands were worthless. "You say that the land is not of much value to us. It *is* of great value to us." "That river furnished me a living." It provided food, water, shelter and clothing. "It is there we used to get everything we had."[72]

Sensing that his tricks had made little headway with the Native Americans so far, the commissioner resorted to a divide and conquer strategy. He blamed the lack of progress in the bargaining on the "difficulty of doing business in a large council." Ramsey wanted to exclude Little Rock, the warriors, and the Métis from the negotiations. He believed it would be better for only the chiefs to meet with him and then come to an agreement.[73] The Chippewa saw right through this maneuver. The process was not the problem. The negotiations stalemated over the inability of the commissioners to understand that from the Native perspective, the United States refused to accept responsibility or offer compensation for its citizens' trespass into their territory and waterways. Little Rock told Ramsey that, "if you had wanted a right-of-way over roads and rivers, you would have consulted us first, *before you took it*."[74] To drive home his point about the inadequate sum of money offered by the United States, the Red Lake orator asked Ramsey how long it would be before the citizens of the United States ceased using the roads and rivers? His implication was clear. If Americans wanted to gain access to, and use something forever, then Native Americans should be compensated with enough financial consideration (to offset all they would lose permanently) to sustain their future generations.

Yet Ramsey either genuinely misunderstood or pretended not to understand. Even though Little Rock had made his points clearly and directly, Ramsey referred to his speeches as "enigmatical and non-committal." He insisted that the United States did not want to buy the Chippewa's land, but only wanted a right-of-way. He became increasingly irritable about their "refusal to sell," and could not understand why they would not sell their land for "money and blankets." Ramsey declared that if the bands did not "make a treaty," they "would be held answerable for the wrongs they had done, and the depredations they had committed."[75] In the aftermath of regional European American anger over the United States-Dakota War of 1862, such admonitions had ominous overtones.

Little Rock rejected any punishments for past depredations, because no guilt had been established. Even more significantly, he contended correctly that the "white man's laws" had no jurisdiction over the Red Lake or Pembina Chippewa, while they continued living in unceded country.[76] While this lack of federal jurisdiction over Native American country remained the law of the land until 1885, Ramsey's insinuation had the desired effect. They had heard many other European Americans in the vicinity, like Kittson, say that the recalcitrant Chippewa deserved the same fate as the rebellious Dakota. Little Rock pleaded that if the commissioners would promise "not to erect in this land *a bad tree* [i.e., gallows] for any of our people, or make a dark hole in the ground to lock us in [i.e., a dungeon], we shall come to an understanding."[77]

Ramsey agreed and began crafting the various treaty provisions. Although he asserted the final "arrangements" to be "fair and just" and in line with recent similar transactions with other bands, he already started back-pedaling. He claimed that other Ojibwe had "more desirable lands." Therefore, he could not give the Red Lake and Pembina bands more. If they ceded their lands, they would retain their "privilege" (rather than a "right") of hunting "for many years."[78] Sensing the strengthening of his position and the wavering of the Native Americans, Ramsey launched into a bizarre analogy more "enigmatical" than anything said by Little Rock. He equated the Native peoples ceding their land to a man selling a horse. When someone sells a horse, they lose the use of that animal forever. They either do without it or buy another horse. Analogous to the proposed land cession, the United States would pay the value of the horse, and then give them the horse back "to use as much as they choose."[79] Once again Ramsey misrepresented the true purpose of the treaty.

The bargaining got sharper over the issues of boundaries and money. Alluding to the proposed purchase price, Little Rock reminded the commissioner about the relative nature of wealth or poverty by rejecting Ramsey's assertions about their low standard of living. He upped the ante by stating that "we demand per head, $100 in money and $55.66 in goods, per annum . . . for 50 years." Ramsey exploded and launched into a diatribe without factual or legal foundation. He accused them of trying "to sell me a country which does not belong to them."[80] Referring to the contested southern boundary of the Sheyenne River west of the Red River, Ramsey asserted that the Dakota hunted along this watercourse more than the Chippewa. This was not true. While both tribes had contended for the lucrative buffalo grounds along this vital waterway, long before 1849 the Chippewa had established themselves as the dominant tribe north of the Sheyenne.[81] The Ojibwe and Dakota settled this matter between themselves and the Métis in the renewed Sweet Corn treaty of 1858. They recognized mutually that the Chippewa held the lands to the north of the river, and the Dakota controlled the territory to the south. This fact, which Ramsey ignored, became recognized formally by the U.S. government in the Sisseton and Wahpeton treaty of 1867. It acknowledged that Chippewa territory began just north of Devils Lake.[82] Since this western realm of the proposed treaty cession belonged to the Pembina band, Ramsey demanded to hear about it from their chiefs directly.

The Pembina chief Red Bear responded reluctantly and expressed his dismay with the commissioner and the entire proceeding. He told Ramsey, "I do not want to say anything to you." Red Bear found fault with the commissioner for the failure of the council to reach an agreement. In rebuttal to Ramsey's earlier insistence that he only wanted to deal with the chiefs, Red Bear stated, "my friend, what is the reason that when we want to talk with you, there are a great many here who trouble us with their breath? We have been in council before, but we were never so hard pushed by the whites." Red Bear's interjection showed that while the negotiations seemed centered on the sparring between Alexander Ramsey and Little Rock, other U.S. officials asserted more pressure and sharp bargaining behind the scenes and off the

official record. Red Bear stated repeatedly that "things do not go right."
He did not want to talk about any land cession, especially beneath a
flagpole flying the U.S. stars and stripes. He objected to its implication
of a superior authority over the higher powers of the Master of Life.
Red Bear also refuted the U.S. claim that the initiative for land cessions came from the Chippewa bands. They wanted to stop European
American trespass, rather than sell their lands. They perceived the ea-
gerness of Minnesota and the United States for their unceded territory
and sensed that this urgency could be used to their own advantage.
Red Bear observed, "whenever there is anything to be sold, the last
place to be ceded is always the strongest. We have the last place, and
we claim that we have a pretty strong thing."[83]

Ramsey once again interjected falsely that he had not come to this
treaty council to buy their lands. He wanted rights-of-way through
their unceded territory and compensation for depredations. The commissioner did not seem to realize that asking the bands for a right of
transit over the lands and waters where they lived recognized their "Indian title." Exasperated by the Ojibwe's ability to deflect his stratagems,
Ramsey asked bluntly what they intended to do about these particulars.
He wanted a quick and final answer, one way or the other. To reinforce
his demands and increase the pressure on the Chippewa, he reverted to
the baseless allegation that they had conspired with the Dakota during
the recent war. "Tell Mr. Red Bear that he and his friends are better
friends to the Sioux than to the whites." He accused the Pembina Natives and "half-breeds" of harboring Sioux runaways, supplying them
with ammunition, receiving stolen goods from various unspecified
robberies, and levying a tax upon several Red River steamboats.[84]

Red Bear replied indignantly that he did not harbor any Dakota.
"I can see nothing back of me [i.e., nothing in his past] of which I am
ashamed, and with all my band it is the same. My band has not been
guilty of any depredations."[85] Kittson and Ramsey knew their accusations about any Chippewa collusion with the Dakota in 1862 had no
credibility.[86] Ramsey tried to moderate this charge by stating that he

did not accuse the chief personally. However, he insisted on the collective guilt of the Pembina Chippewa because some Dakota had fled to the Red River Valley, Devils Lake, and the Pembina or Turtle mountains. While U.S. agents, missionaries, soldiers, and traders remained faultless when not fulfilling their trust responsibility and delivering food, supplies, and treaty annuities on time, they blamed Red Bear for not keeping Dakota refugees out of his band's territory. "If he cannot keep them out, why does he come here to make a fuss about a country which they don't own, but which is occupied by our enemies."[87] Ramsey's absurd denunciation had ominous implications.

If the Pembina band could not control its borders, they could not claim sovereignty over their domain. Therefore, they could not cede it legally or be entitled to any compensation from the U.S. through a treaty. As a negotiating ploy, Ramsey attempted to smear the "tractable" reputation of the Chippewa with unsubstantiated conspiracy theories in order to negate their sovereignty and land rights. Still, Ramsey overlooked the contradiction of his rationalizations. First, if the Pembina Chippewa had no sovereignty or control over the lands west of the Red River, why had the commissioner of Indian Affairs sent a treaty commission to negotiate a right-of-way or a land cession? Second, did the U.S. forfeit its sovereignty over twenty-three southwestern Minnesota counties when they were "virtually depopulated" by the Dakota revolt?[88]

Ramsey raged against recognized facts. He proclaimed that the Dakota had a greater claim to the lands in question than the Red Lake or Pembina Chippewa. Yet the latter bands had the nerve to ask for ten times as much as the land was worth.[89] The commissioner's tirade set off Red Bear. He did not know that these matters would be discussed at this council, and complained that nobody had gotten down to "business" yet. Both he and Little Shell had deferred from saying anything until the Red Lakers had finished. Then they would "make a bargain."[90] Again Ramsey misperceived Native diplomatic protocol and misinterpreted what Red Bear said. He replied that the Pembina band had not indicated that they wanted to negotiate separately from the Red Lake band. If they did, he did not care, as long as they did something at once.[91]

Little Rock interjected that urgency could not substitute for straight-forward negotiation. He felt compelled to challenge Ramsey's prior statements disparaging the Pembina Chippewa land claims west of the Red River in favor of the Dakota. Regarding "the tract of country you spoke of . . . and how we came to own this land," Little Rock indicated that "a tribe speaking a different language occupied it." This reference identified the Pembina and Turtle Mountain Chippewa as distinct Plains-Ojibwe bands who spoke a different Cree-influenced dialect of Ojibwe than their eastern woodland relations, like the Red Lake Chippewa. Little Rock conceded that a long time before, these lands had belonged to the Dakota. Nevertheless, "we drove them [westward], and when we had driven them off we claimed the land as our own." Their claim derived not only from the Master of Life. The Chippewa orator rebuffed Ramsey's denigration of their sovereignty and territorial possession. While the commissioner never substantiated his charges, Little Rock offered proof of his claim by saying, "we can show you our camps all along the Sheyenne River. We hunt down there always. It is still so—we still own that land, and we never want to shake hands with the tribe [the Sioux] you have mentioned."[92]

Ramsey deflected the Chippewa territorial claim by shifting his focus away from the land question and back to the free river-passage issue by claiming that, "we do not care about the lands. We want a right-of-way."[93] He insisted that "the roads and river must be unobstructed." Depicting the Chippewa bands as obstacles of progress, the commissioner warned them that "the world is going ahead, and those that can't go with it must stand aside."[94] Then the commissioner turned back to the land issue by denigrating the basis of the Chippewa claims and denying the fairness of their asking price. "They pretend to be very fond of their lands," and will not part with them "except at an extravagant price. I told them at the beginning that I did not want their lands." Ramsey persisted in misrepresenting the facts. Contrary to his own observations en route to the treaty council and the unanimous assessments of many other expeditions commenting on the tremendous agricultural potential of the Red River Valley, he stated that, "they are not the kind of lands that the white man want at all."[95]

Ramsey insisted that the United States only wanted a right-of-way to forestall trouble, settle past offenses, and avoid future difficulties. He accused the Chippewa of double-dealing. "They told me they wouldn't sell the right-of-way, and then offered their lands at a price they know would not be given." On top of his mischaracterizations, he went to greater lengths to belittle the bargaining position of the Natives. He accused them of not receiving "the offer of the Great father . . . in the spirit in which it was made." Because of this "the Great father would regard the price at which they offer their lands as ridiculous."[96]

After eight days of discussions, the U.S. delegation sought closure. Ramsey decried that "all this counciling comes to nothing. It is all talk-talk-talk and no business." He accused the Chippewa of "trifling" with him.[97] To overcome this predicament Ramsey offered to let the Native Americans in on a little secret. "The bad conduct of the Sioux had created a prejudice in the minds of a great many whites against *all* Indians. Congress and the "Great Father" had *all* begun to place a lower estimate upon 'Indian title' than heretofore."[98] Ramsey's threat attempted to intimidate the Chippewa delegates.

Congress and the president had suspended the 1851 Dakota treaties and reservations as a result of the 1862 war. But this unilateral termination, implemented amidst the crisis of the Civil War, did not signal any major shift in federal Native policy. In the past, many powerful U.S. officials, such as Chief Justice John Marshall, Secretary of War John C. Calhoun, and President Andrew Jackson, desired to "impair" the legal basis of "Indian title" to varying degrees. They usually made this claim on the erroneous grounds that Native Americans did not "use" their lands productively. Yet, in the immediate aftermath of the Dakota revolt, no new policy emanated from the federal government to "disregard" any other Native claims to occupy and possess their lands legally until purchased by the United States. Once again, Ramsey made false representation of the facts to enhance his bargaining position. Such intentional deception constituted legal fraud.[99]

The commissioner drew attention to the new political and financial realities of the Civil War. Earlier in the negotiations, Ramsey had reassured the "poor" Native delegates that the wealthy "Great Father" would "promote their welfare" and take them "under his care." Now he claimed that the "Great Father" had his "hands full" with an enormous military undertaking, costing unprecedented amounts of money. As a result, Congress looked more closely at the finances of treaties than they had before. Now was the time to make a treaty. It would probably be the Native Americans' only opportunity for several years.[100]

To begin the real business of treaty-making, Ramsey asked for a description of the boundaries from the Ojibwe representatives. Apparently, the right-of-way no longer constituted the primary issue. He wanted to know whether they considered the Goose River or the Sheyenne River as the southern Chippewa boundary with the Dakota. Little Rock reiterated that the latter waterway comprised the dividing line. He proclaimed that "the bones of the Chippewa are scattered all along the Sheyenne River, and that is the reason we consider it belongs to us."[101] Despite their seasonal mobility, the Chippewa had a clear sense of their territory, often marked by sacred and burial sites.

Getting nowhere with Little Rock, Ramsey turned his attention to the Pembina Chippewa. He reiterated that the recent Sioux uprising had "very much weakened popular respect for Indian titles."[102] This disingenuous statement ignored the fact that while there had been a relative amount of European American and Dakota harmony amidst the ethnic tensions on the Minnesota frontier since 1851, there had never been much—if any—"popular respect" for Native title. That lack of respect came as much from the federal government's acquiescence to land speculators and lumberman as from the interests of local traders and settlers. Despite Ramsey's assertion, the Dakota upheaval did not change the long-standing European American disregard for Native land rights. Since Supreme Court Chief Justice Marshall declared in 1831 that Native Americans "occup[ied] a territory to which we assert a title independent of their will," European American settlers remained indifferent to the fact that their encroachments violated the law.[103] They took up residence on unceded and reservation lands with little fear of removal or any legal consequences.

Red Bear asserted that in the aftermath of the Dakota uprising, the U.S. Army had driven them into Chippewa territory. Despite this unwanted intrusion of their traditional enemy, "we were trying to make peace when you interrupted it. You have counseled us to make peace, and we were trying to do so."[104] Ramsey backed away from his prior accusations and shifted the blame to certain "half-breeds" at St. Joseph who had traded ammunition to some of the fleeing Dakota. Since Ramsey mentioned his Pembina homeland, Red Bear took the opportunity to reassert his claim to it. "We had always lived at the mouth of the Pembina River," and his father had lived there before him. He and his band wished to retain a "spot" there.[105]

Little Shell jumped in and stated that he too had a "right to talk about the Pembina country, as his father *owned* all that country." He had come to the treaty council "with his mind made up to cede the country from the timber on the Red River [i.e., *not* the prairie] on both sides, to the heads of the streams," as had occurred before when he (i.e., Ramsey) made a treaty with them at Pembina in 1851.[106] Red Bear had a slightly different configuration in mind. He described a strip of land running along the north side of the Pembina River that he wanted reserved. It extended from the Red River to St. Joseph and encompassed the most valuable portion of that country. The Plains-Ojibwe leaders asserted that the territory west of any treaty cession boundary would continue to be held in common by both the Pembina and Turtle Mountain bands.

In return for ceding their land adjacent to the Red River, the Pembina and Turtle Mountain bands wanted clothing, fifty dollars per person, fifty horses (mares and stallions) with harnesses and bridles, and fifty cattle (oxen and cows). Ramsey responded in his usual disingenuous fashion. He would accede to their demands, but the "Great Father and his council" would wonder why he gave these Chippewa bands more than others had gotten in their treaties. This discrepancy could not be justified, especially since "we shall not want [these Chippewa lands] for fifty years, if *at all*."[107]  Once again, Ramsey misrepresented the goals of his commission, because he had admitted his concern previously about the imminent arrival of various railroads in the region. As an incorporator and director of four railroad lines holding grants through the area, he also had a personal financial interest in the outcome of the proceedings.[108]

After insisting that he did not really want their lands, Ramsey conceded that an agreement to sell them was a wise decision. Yet his patience with their "extravagant asking price" and "enormous demands" could not last forever.[109] He inferred that such demands meant that the Chippewa did not want a treaty. Refusal to reach an accord implied that the Native Americans did not want to live in comfort or atone for their alleged offenses. Ramsey's stingy counteroffer offended the Chippewa delegates. Despite his assessment of Moose Dung as the leader of the majority who wanted a treaty, the chief complained, "Is this all you can give to your children?" Ramsey considered the more combative principal Red Lake chief, May-dwa-gua-no-nind (He That Is Spoken To), as the main force behind the "surly minority" who opposed any treaty.[110] Not surprisingly, his response disconcerted Ramsey. The chief cried out, "My heart is bleeding when I hear you talk. I am sorry . . . that the Great Father thinks so lightly of our land." He rejected "the little you offer me. I want enough that my children should all benefit."[111]

The reason that the Ojibwe offer seemed too high derived from Ramsey's refusal to look beyond the immediate issues at hand and consider the permanent ramifications of his proposal. Little Rock reminded Ramsey that you "forget that the land will be yours as long as the world lasts. If you want to make a bargain on the proposition you have made us, I tell you frankly that I do not accept."[112] Ramsey upped his offer.

He increased the annual payment (divided equally between the Red Lake and Pembina bands) to $16,200, plus $2,000 worth of ammunition at the first installment. "For their interest," Ramsey urged the Chippewa to accept his offer "and make an end of it."[113]

Principal Chief May-dwa-gua-no-nind continued to object. In accordance with his role as a Chippewa chief, he felt that any agreement had to benefit the long-term interests of the entire tribe. Ramsey griped that "the chiefs who are trying to defeat a treaty do not understand their own interests."[114] The pleading by the Red Lake leaders for more considerations only strained Ramsey's patience further.

May-dwa-gua-no-nind considered Ramsey's current offer "impossible. There would not be enough that my children should benefit by it." Little Rock concurred, by saying, "his words and my words are one."[115] Ramsey accused them of bad faith towards the "Great Father," reiterated their alleged depredations, and demanded compensation. The principal chief replied respectfully, "my Father, I have nothing that I can pay away." Ramsey accused them of "trifling" with him and treating "their Great Father" with "disrespect," after all the "trouble" and "expense" he and the president had expended on their behalf.[116]

After nine days of contentious negotiations, Ramsey conceded that "all hope of effecting a treaty . . . seemed to be at an end."[117] In spite of his belief that May-dwa-gua-no-nind remained the only "obstacle" to a final agreement, Ramsey once again raised his offer. The annual payment to be divided between both bands rose to $20,000 per year, with $150 to each chief, $500 for each chief's house, $2,000 worth of provisions, and $100,000 to indemnify the damages resulting from their purported robberies.[118] The Red Lakers asked for and received an additional $5,000 for a road running from their reserve to Leech Lake. The Pembina "half-breeds" made a strong effort to procure treaty monies for their benefit, but Ramsey rejected this proposal.

Although both sides had been so far apart and some issues remained unresolved, they arrived at a final agreement rather suddenly. All the Chippewa chiefs, except May-dwa-gua-no-nind, who had left in disgust, made their marks as signatories to the Old Crossing Treaty on October 2, 1863.[119] No evidence uncovered so far can explain definitively what transpired behind the scenes during the last evening of the council. Determining the causes for such an abrupt turnaround can only be inferred. The treaty itself contained some telling provisions. The Pembina chief Red Bear and the Red Lake leader Moose Dung each obtained a reserve of 640 acres. Ramsey initiated this offer. The Native leaders did not request them. These grants to influential headmen can be viewed as inducements, or less favorably as bribes. Either way, they probably helped facilitate their acquiescence.

The Red Lake and Pembina Chippewa worked as hard as they could to get a fair price for their lands. They pushed Ramsey to increase the compensation for the land cession in Article Three to $20,000 per year for twenty years. Unfortunately, the Senate changed this and other provisions in an amended supplemental treaty the following year.[120] Allocating more for goods and less for per capita payments meant that local white businesses would benefit more than the Native Americans. Article Two of the revised treaty also reduced the payment period to fifteen years, or at the discretion of the president. This provided the United States with an escape clause in case of any disturbances like the Dakota rebellion. Despite all of his protestations during the council to the contrary, Ramsey confided to the commission's secretary that "no territorial acquisitions of equal intrinsic value have been made from the Indians at so low a rate per acre." [121]

As low as it was, Ramsey's final offer contained one significant concession that had not been on the table before. The $100,000 indemnity specified under Article Four constituted a major breakthrough. Despite Ramsey's repeated references to their alleged depredations, accompanied by his insistence that they would pay or else, this eleventh hour indemnity provision clinched the treaty. While the Chippewa still felt they did not get enough money for their land, especially compared to the far greater amount offered by the United States in the unratified 1851 Pembina Treaty, at least they got something. Their sparse annuity would not be siphoned off to pay debts to traders or damages for depredations.

Unfortunately, the 1864 treaty changed this provision. May-dwa-gua-no-nind led the Red Lake delegation, including Little Rock and Moose Dung, to Washington, D.C. Along with Red Bear from the Pembina Chippewa, they signed the amended treaty. Article Six reduced the depredation indemnity by $25,000 and distributed it to the chiefs, with May-dwa-gwa-no-nind getting a specific payment of $5,000. This represented more than a substantial inducement for their compliance. While other signatory chiefs received payments of $150 or $500 annually, and two leading chiefs obtained 640-acre land grants (worth only $51.20, or eight cents per acre), the only chief who refused to sign the 1863 treaty secured $5,000. Only after they signed did the chiefs find out they would not receive their payments. According to historian Ella Hawkinson, the money went to a special agent assigned to procure goods for them.[122] As a result, the Chippewa ceded a large portion of valuable territory for very little money, goods, or services in return.

While the amended 1864 treaty somewhat reduced and reallocated the monetary compensation stipulations of the original 1863 treaty, Articles Three, Four, and Five provided more goods, services (e.g., blacksmith, doctor, miller, farmer), and new technologies (i.e., a sawmill). Nevertheless, while some of these provisions appeared to be based upon generosity, others represented the expedient underside of alleged federal benevolence. Nobody asked the Native Americans what "may be deemed for their best interests." Unfortunately, the upshot of inducements "to adopt the habits and pursuits of civilized life" diverted Native monies into the hands of non-Native agents agents, businesses, tradesmen, farmers, and artisans.[123]

Little Shell II did not go with Red Bear to Washington, D.C., as part of the Pembina delegation. The fact that he signed the 1863 treaty but not the 1864 supplementary articles has led to some confusion in the scholarly literature on the Pembina, Turtle Mountain, and

Little Shell Chippewa. A few sources claim that he did not sign either treaty. Perhaps some of the consternation stems from the fact that the Old Crossing treaty did not create any reservation for the Pembina or Turtle Mountain Chippewa. This occurred because homesteading had become a major part of federal land administration in 1863. By promoting European American settlement, homestead policy sought political consolidation of the West through economic integration of the region with the rest of the nation. The process of homesteading coincided with the rapid addition of new territories and states after the Civil War.

The advent of homesteading also gave federal policymakers another solution in search of a problem to deploy from their grab-bag of options. Despite Commissioner Ramsey's attempts to dismiss the 663 Pembina Chippewa mixed-bloods, and preclude their inclusion in the treaty council or land cession compensation, they did play a role in the final outcome. This constituted a rare instance of a U.S. treaty that contained some land provision for kindred Métis.[124]

As the majority of the region's population, and allied closely with the Chippewa, the United States could not afford to disregard or alienate the mixed-bloods. To do so might disrupt the greater goal of securing the lands and resources of both groups. The treaty commissioners saw the Métis as useful, yet secondary, temporary allies who could be crucial to securing and solidifying the desired concessions from the Native Americans. The formal issuance of allotments or scrip as part of the final treaty agreement represented a small additional price to pay, since it helped pave the way to the ultimate goal of a huge land cession for a low price.

Article Eight of the 1863 treaty provided the best evidence for their influence. It contained a rather unique provision. Ramsey stuck to his insistence that the "half-breed" Chippewa not receive any treaty monies, even after the Pembina chiefs prepared a written request following the treaty signing for their mixed-bloods to receive $25,000.[125] Even the initial lack of any land scrip from the cession, did not exclude them from any legal regard. In "consideration" of the "cession" the treaty recognized implicitly that the mixed-bloods had some Indigenous interest in the ceded land. This constituted an exceptional occurrence in the annals of tribal-federal relations.

The United States agreed to provide for the homestead-like allotment of 160-acre quarter sections to each adult "half-breed or mixed-blood" male of the tribe. They could select their tract within the boundaries of the ceded territory, but only *if* European American settlers had not "occupied" it. Unfortunately, this stipulation subsumed Métis rights beneath the claims of "actual settlers." Securing legal land title could not be achieved unless they "adopted the habits and customs of civilized life," became U.S. citizens, and provided "due proof of five years' actual residence and cultivation," as stipulated by the Homestead Act. While these terms sounded fair and reasonable, they attempted to impose unrealistic European American agrarian standards on non-citizens who made their living from hunting buffalo, the fur trade, and carting goods. To be successful in these endeavors required mobility, not residential farming. The promised "homestead" in reality amounted to an unprotected "squatter's right" undermined eventually by European American citizen's claims.

Even these tentative provisions could have left too much land in the hands of mixed-bloods identified or affiliated with the Ojibwe. Article Seven of the revised 1864 treaty was agreed upon in Washington, D.C., without any Métis participation in those negotiations, other than the presence of Charles Bottineau as a witness. The supplemental treaty reverted to the older federal government practice of issuing land scrip in lieu of actual land. Scrip represented a form of currency and, therefore, a marketable commodity in the form of cash or land. Its negligible security did not convey a fee patent or land title. Land speculators usually acquired these certificates at a steep discount for ready cash soon expended by the mixed-bloods. The brokers resold them at a considerable markup or pressured the government into redeeming them at face value. Based on prior experiences with Native land allotments and Métis scrip, Indian Office and Land Office officials knew that lack of cash or credit, English language proficiency, local political connections, and legal know-how would soon see most Native and Métis holdings in the hands of European American speculators, banks, tax collectors, or farmers.[126]

No evidence can be found to indicate that allotment on the public domain ever intended to help the Turtle Mountain Chippewa become permanent residents on their land with clear legal title. Although the United States obtained a significant land cession for the fertile Red River Valley of the North at a very cheap price, one of its main goals remained unfulfilled. The "primary objective" of the treaty, as outlined in Commissioner of Indian Affairs Dole's directive to Ramsey, indicated that the main purpose of the council did not require a land cession. Instead, the treaty aimed at the "removal of the bands to positions remote from our white settlements."[127] This explains why the U.S. never granted the Pembina Chippewa a reservation. It also hindered the establishment and extent of the Turtle Mountain reservation decades later.

While the Red Lakers got a reservation in their homeland, the Pembina did not. Neither band insisted on retaining their reserved rights to hunt, fish, and gather in their ceded lands, like the Mille Lacs Chippewa did in their 1837 treaty. These concessions can be explained in part by how the Pembina and Turtle Mountain bands envisioned their immediate post-treaty future, as illustrated by the reminiscences of the Davis and Nolin families:

> When the Red River land was deeded to the U.S Government in 1863, William and Sarah (Nolin) Davis came with their families to settle in the Turtle Mountains, which they had regarded as their hunting territory. Like most Turtle Mountain Chippewa, they refused to settle on the White Earth Reservation in Minnesota which had been assigned to them.[128]

They considered the cession of their Red River lands (see image, back cover) as a trade-off that secured the much greater extent of territory west of the treaty line as a permanent home. They did not press for a reservation because they retained all their territory north and west of Devils Lake. This included land north of the Sheyenne River as far west as the intersection of the Knife and Missouri Rivers, then up the western loop of the Souris (Mouse) River to the international border, and back to their beloved Turtle Mountain (see Image 6). This vast unceded territory encompassed their vital buffalo hunting grounds. Although "the cession to the United States by the Pembina embraced a territory of about 278 townships equal to 10,000 square miles of the finest agricultural soil of the Northwest," the European American development of the Red River Valley as an avenue of commerce and agricultural settlement would not impinge on them for a while.[129] In the foreseeable future there remained plenty of land and resources for the Pembina and Turtle Mountain Chippewa, or so they thought. At least the Old Crossing treaties provided some legal foundation for their sovereignty and subsequent territorial claims.

# CHAPTER 4

# Encroachments into the Pembina and Turtle Mountain Homeland, 1865–1876

*They cling with tenacity to their old homes.*[1]
—Board of Visitors, 1871

Within a few decades after the Civil War, most aspects of Native American and European life underwent major changes. During this era, entrepreneurial capitalism generated fundamental changes in the organization of a growing industrial economy. Corporate economic reorganization brought about commercial farming, and industrial development focused aggressively on capital accumulation. Corporations became legal "persons" entitled to "due process" rights under the new Fourteenth Amendment, while Native Americans became "wards of the nation" with virtually no rights.[2]

Transcontinental railroads became the catalyst of this new political economy with their emphasis on efficiency, development, and European American settlement. Economic and demographic expansion increased contact between the emissaries of federal policy (agents, missionaries, soldiers, treaty negotiators, surveyors, commissioners) and Native peoples. Instead of leading to accommodation, European Americans' presumed superiority facilitated Native American displacement. As noted by sociologist Stephen Cornell, for Natives, "dispossession was not merely an aspect of frontier history; it was the fundamental event on which much of the American future turned."[3] Post-Civil

War U.S. economic development accelerated Indigenous peoples' dis-possession in the Trans-Mississippi West.

The Interior Department and the Indian Affairs office achieved their initial land cession goals with the Old Crossing treaties. In his annual report for 1864, the commissioner of Indian Affairs commented that "these treaties ceded to the government a large tract of fine agri-cultural lands"—on both sides of the Red River Valley—and a valuable route for the transportation of goods.[4] West of the treaty cession, the Turtle Mountain band of Pembina Chippewa retained an estimated ten million acres of unceded territory, consisting of equally valuable agricultural and timber lands.[5]

But the convergence of six powerful forces impacted the unceded territory of the Turtle Mountain Chippewa while the U.S. govern-ment dithered over whether it needed to enter into further negotia-tions to legalize non-Native access. First, the Homestead Act of 1862 unleashed the pent up non-Native demand for "free land" from the federal government. Qualifying citizens could acquire 160 acres of surveyed public domain land for only a nominal filing fee. By occupy-ing and improving the land, title could be acquired in five years. The prospect of nearly free farmland lured many settlers into and beyond the Red River Valley. Second, to protect these homesteaders and se-cure Dakota Territory from the Native inhabitants, the United States established a network of forts along vital transit routes and in areas of valuable resources. Third, the advent of the railroads onto the north-ern plains transformed the region. Fourth, in 1871 Congress declared an end to treaty-making with tribes as "domestic dependent nations." Fifth, a "wheat boom" in bonanza farming occurred in North Dako-ta. The sixth impetus emerged from the 1869–1870 Métis Red River resistance to Canada's annexation of Rupert's Land and the imposition of a new government without consulting the inhabitants of Manitoba. The cumulative effect of these forces constituted a "pattern of colonial-ism" that enabled European Americans to push west of the 1863 Old Crossing Treaty cession line illegally into the unceded territory of the Turtle Mountain Chippewa.[6]

The potential availability of copious amounts of fruitful land in various North American borderlands promised to be the ultimate means of alleviating most European American social, economic, and political problems. The siren song of abundant and cheap (not "free") land as the basis for American prosperity and liberty still resounded in the late-nineteenth-century American consciousness. In the form of private property, it remained the fundamental requirement for a home, status, and wealth. Freehold property owners held the franchise and the political power. An increasing European American population's hunger for more land became a central impetus of American development and the "free land" myth of the western frontier embodied in the Homestead Act of 1862.[7]

After the ratification of the Old Crossing Treaty in 1864, the influx of settlers into the Red River Valley induced the federal government to initiate the land survey process in 1866. The General Land Office surveyed Pembina County in 1867 and 1868. As a result, on June 15, 1868, Joseph Rolette, Jr., made the first homestead entry on public land at Pembina, in what would become North Dakota.[8] Like many such claims, Rolette had no intention of farming his 160-acre quarter-section. As a long-time trader associated with the American Fur Company, he acted as a "dummy entryman" for a partner's business interests. In 1870, he commuted his homestead claim after six months by paying the going rate of $1.25 per acre. This "first cash entry of public land in North Dakota" enabled Rolette to transfer the title to his partner, the entrepreneur and future railroad builder James J. Hill.[9] On this property, Hill built a bonded warehouse as part of the growing efforts by European Canadians and Americans to expand the lucrative trade between St. Paul and Winnipeg.

This example confirms the findings of land policy historian Paul W. Gates' extensive research into how land speculators and absentee owners took advantage of the Homestead Act.[10] In this case Hill was able to profit from the "structural impediments" of customs regulations and security deposit requirements that served to disrupt the primacy of the Métis carting business in the region.[11] For nearly half a century the Chippewa and Métis had been mainstays of the fur and buffalo-robe trade, and the provisioning and carting commerce connected with the Red River Valley and the northern Dakota Plains. With the end of the fur trade and a decline in buffalo-robe commerce, the Turtle Mountain Chippewa found themselves in a position of greater economic disadvantage. Outside economic interests exploited Dakota Territory as a peripheral region increasingly dependent on metropolitan investment, trade and political decision-making.[12] The fertility of the land in the Red River Valley and farther west attracted an increasing number of immigrants. By 1870 the European American population in northern Dakota Territory equaled 2,500, with 90 percent of families engaged in farming.[13] The ever-widening settlement pattern of preemption or homesteading on the ceded and unceded lands of the Pembina and Turtle Mountain Chippewa increased significantly.

Even before the signing of the Old Crossing Treaty in 1864 and the end of the Civil War in 1865, the United States began securing Dakota Territory. The establishment of nine U.S. Army posts inside Dakota Territory within twelve years demonstrated U.S. government resolve to contain the feared Dakota and Lakota bands, permit unimpeded railroad construction, and protect the increasing number of immigrants traveling west from Minnesota to Montana and beyond.[14] The proximity of five of these posts to the nonviolent Turtle Mountain Chippewa caused them to believe that the encirclement of their unceded territory constituted an attempt to, in the words of tribal historian Charlie White-Weasel, "put the squeeze" on them. They perceived the "plain objective" to be "the dispossession of their Aboriginal lands."[15] The overall effect of this substantial U.S. military presence provided greater security for waves of European American incursion and settlement on unceded Turtle Mountain land before any treaty.

The Chippewa bands objected to this illegal "taking" of their territory. They claimed that "every principle of equity and justice" required notification and compensation for the U.S. takeover of approximately 500,000 acres to create the Fort Totten Indian Reservation and Agency as a result of the 1867 Sisseton-Wahpeton treaty.[16] Adding insult to injury, the BIA agency at Fort Totten assumed jurisdiction over the affairs of the Turtle Mountain band until 1890.

At least the Pembina and Turtle Mountain Native Americans gained some indirect benefit from this 1867 treaty to which they were not a party. Article Two acknowledged the demarcation line that the Dakota bands and the Chippewa established between themselves in the Sweet Corn treaties of 1825 and 1858. The BIA had remained unaware of inter-tribal treaties in general and the most recent Sweet Corn treaty in particular until it was brought to their attention by two Dakota chiefs in 1867.[17] The treaty reconfirmed that the northernmost extent of Dakota Indian territory extended only as far as the Goose River, settling the southern boundary of the Turtle Mountain Chippewa's domain. Such a stipulation recognized implicitly that the Turtle Mountain band had "exclusive use and occupancy" of the lands they claimed and bolstered the legal status of their "Aboriginal title." The confirmation of this material fact by the United States helped substantiate the undisputed nature of the Chippewa land tenure north and west of Devils Lake in relation to any other tribe in the region.

With a southern extent agreed upon, the federal government remained concerned about the United States and the Turtle Mountain band's northern boundary. By 1867, the lack of a definitive international boundary along the forty-ninth parallel between the United States and the British Possessions caused increasing anxieties on both sides of the border. The United States still feared potential incursions from remnants of the Dakota bands who sought refuge north of the border (some even camped near Turtle Mountain) after their failed 1862 uprising in Minnesota. At the urging of the Minnesota Legislature in 1868, the War Department agreed to the establishment of Fort Pembina to help safeguard the border and the Customs House at Pembina. Among calls for the United States to annex western Canada by persons like Senator Alexander Ramsey of Minnesota, and fears that the

Métis Red River resistance might involve Native communities south of the border, the installation of Fort Pembina (1870–1895) secured the Northeast corner of the Chippewa domain and Dakota Territory beginning in 1870.[18] With U.S. manifest destiny ambitions towards Rupert's Land stymied by the colonization efforts of the new Dominion of Canada, federal officials also wanted to impede any "half-breed" migrations from Métis leader Louis Riel's failed provisional government in Manitoba. On December 9, 1867, Senator Ramsey introduced a resolution for Canada to cede all of its territory west of longitude $90^0$ to the United States for $8 million. This resolution represented the last U.S. attempt at annexation prior to the creation of the Dominion of Canada.[19] The timing and location of the fort also figured prominently in plans to protect the construction of the Northern Pacific and St. Paul & Pacific railroads westward and to facilitate the expected rapid European American settlement of the region. Not coincidentally, the first North Dakota Land Office also opened at Pembina in 1870.[20]

These events illustrate how North Dakota conformed to the general pattern of development followed by most western states. After the military posts quelled the Native inhabitants and pushed them away from the main corridors of transit and onto reservations, the railroads conveyed the European American population necessary for them to make a profit. The railroads created the web of mutual connections for a burgeoning industrial national economy. They provided the technological infrastructure for western development centered on farming, ranching, natural resource (mining and timber) extraction, and speculative investment. These raw materials supplied foreign export markets and the growing eastern urban manufacturing centers manned by record numbers of cheap immigrant labor. In turn, the manufactured products found new markets in the rapidly growing West. By linking the far and intermountain West with the East, the railroads overcame the expansiveness and non-navigable rivers of the Great Plains. They opened the region's territories and states, including North Dakota, to rapid European American settlement and commerce.

Rapid overland railroad expansion into new regions, like Dakota Territory, became the mainstay of a national government policy to develop territories into states. Local efforts worked in tandem towards the same end. In 1871 the Dakota Legislature created a Bureau of Immigration. It distributed Dakota newspapers, pamphlets, and reports throughout the country, especially in eastern cities.[21] They contained overstated accounts intended to attract European American settlers. Even with all this effort, federal and state endowments to the railroads far exceeded colonization schemes and homestead land grants. The U.S. government subsidized railroads with vast quantities of public domain land, estimated to total as much as 155 million acres. As noted by Richard Franklin Bensel, "the land grant railroads became the premier promoters of western settlement."[22]

Only by filling new territories and states with settlers could railroads be profitable. Yet to become profitable, the railroads had to get settlers on their land grants quickly. So they also devised promotional campaigns for colonization schemes. Their advertisements claimed to provide the "best homes" for ten million people along their transcontinental route. In North Dakota the Northern Pacific railroad land grant cut a swath that almost covered the entire southern half of the state. The company touted "six million acres" of "choice agricultural and grazing" lands "at the lowest prices ever offered by any railroad company." They even published foreign language booklets full of embellished claims to entice landless European immigrants. The prices for the best wheat and farming lands in the "world" ranged from $2.50 to $5.00 per acre, while grazing lands cost $.75 to $3.00 acre. Either type could be had with only a one-sixth to one-tenth cash down payment, and the remainder in five to ten annual installments, at 6 percent interest.[23] Land speculation companies purchased most of this acreage for as little as one dollar per acre. Then, they resold it in small parcels to individual settlers.

These interlocking economic, technological, and demographic developments created new pressures on Great Plains Native communities and their lands. In contrast to the pre-Civil War East, the post-Civil War plow followed the railroad tracks. Union war hero General William T. Sherman considered western railroad development to be the decisive vanguard "in the great battle of civilization with barbarism."[24] Like the military brass, top civilian federal policymakers also welcomed the spread of the railroads as the means for solving the "Indian problem." Commissioner of Indian Affairs Francis A. Walker declared that "if they stand up against the progress of civilization and industry . . . they must yield or perish." By predicting that the "Indians of Dakota" would be "reduced to a habitual condition of suffering from want of food," he foretold the bleak prospects faced by the Turtle Mountain Chippewa beginning in the late 1870s.[25]

The railroads pried open the territory of the Turtle Mountain band and its adjacent lands to profitable resource exploitation before the tribe agreed to sell or cede any of it. Since the federal government gave the railroads access to their lands before negotiating any land cession, the tribe wanted to be paid one-fourth of the profits that the government derived.[26] After years of sharp dealing during the fur trade and treaty conferences, the Turtle Mountain Chippewa were neither naive nor ignorant about commerce. Their demand demonstrated the band's understanding about European American regard for land as a marketable commodity. At the same time, the railroads brought in a large, non-Native settler population. Transportation expansion, capital formation, and demographic migration encroached steadily on the ten-million-acre Turtle Mountain Chippewa homeland. The band's representatives seemed well aware that these forces and interests had little regard for legal precedents like "Indian title" or the inviolability of unceded land. Based on experience, they had little faith in government promises to provide any protection for their land. Prior treaty councils had shown them that federal policy served as a mopping-up operation for European American technological, demographic, economic, and political goals intended to override equitable legal principles designed to protect Native American land tenure.[27]

The most direct impact on the Turtle Mountain Chippewa came from the Great Northern Railway system since the Northern Pacific Railroad ran just south of their domain. James J. Hill bought out the St. Paul & Pacific after its construction from the Twin Cities in Minnesota to Winnipeg stalled as a result of the Panic of 1873. If the line could not be finished, its land grant would be forfeited. Hill renamed it the Manitoba Railroad and retained the land grant. It competed successfully with the Northern Pacific along the Red River Valley from St. Paul to Winnipeg in 1878. His investors and partners (including ex-fur trader and shipper Norman Kittson) then looked to run a transcontinental main line, with a web of feeder lines, stretching from St. Paul to Seattle. Unlike the St. Paul & Pacific, Hill financed the rest of his railways with private U.S. and European capital, along with elaborate subsidy schemes for settlers, instead of government land grants. Yet variations in the means to fund construction did not alter the wrenching effect on Native inhabitants. The vastly increased demand for food in the urbanizing and industrializing parts of the eastern United States and Western Europe created a surge in the expansion of farming worldwide. These circumstances facilitated the agricultural invasion of the Great Plains. As noted by North Dakota historian Elwyn B. Robinson, "outside finance, trade, and manufacturing" launched the railroads that led to the great Dakota land boom of the late 1870s and 1880s.[28]

The St. Paul, Minneapolis, and Manitoba Railway Company organized formally in 1879. It reorganized as the Great Northern Railway the following year and crossed the Red River at Grand Forks. It reached Devils Lake in 1885, Minot in 1886, and Montana in 1887, thus completing its run through unceded Turtle Mountain Chippewa country. Its feeder lines spread their tentacles across northern Dakota Territory and ultimately, according to Robinson, "controlled the economic and political lives of North Dakotans." [29] The railroad eventually sprouted new towns like Rolla, Dunseith, St. John, and Bottineau. These towns came into and remained in existence because of the railroad, while the Turtle Mountain Chippewa's commonwealth receded steadily.

These interconnected economic booms produced other negative consequences for northern Dakota's Native communities and the security of their land tenure. They also led to over-development, mismanagement, and a speculative frenzy of over-investment. Railroad stock prices skyrocketed beyond their true value, emboldening Wall Street firms to float bonds and advance risky loans to railroad companies such as the Northern Pacific Railroad (NPRR). Since 1862, the NPRR received almost fifty million acres of public domain land grants. Even with all of this federal government generosity, major railways failed to sell enough bonds or land to cover their corrupt practices. The glut of misleading advertising promising enormous profits to purchasers of railroad lands did not match inflated construction costs and mounting debts. In 1872 the Crédit Mobilier scandal further undermined investor confidence in railroad stocks.[30]

When over-extended companies failed, an economic depression—known as the Panic of 1873—gripped the United States the next four years. The stock market collapsed, banks and brokerage houses failed, and large numbers of industrial workers faced wage cuts, layoffs, or unemployment. The depression interrupted the railroad boom briefly. The Northern Pacific Railroad crossed the Red River, and then extended to Bismarck, North Dakota. But it halted there for lack of funds because railroad stocks had plummeted. Although it accused "greedy capitalists" of ruthless and counterproductive speculation, the Bismarck Tribune used the economic crisis to call for more aggressive dispossession of Native Americans. As a result of the depression, "the American people need the country the Indians now occupy."[31]

This first corporate industrial "bust" in U.S. history redirected some devalued railroad capital into new channels that would leverage Native lands.[32] Like an impeded flow of water always finding another outlet, corporate industrial capital could be diverted from failed investments and pumped into new profitable ventures. Frantic railroad officials tried to revive investment by offering newly opened Red River wheat lands to wealthy investors in exchange for their devalued certificates. Ironically, the bursting of a national economic bubble set in motion the advent of commercial wheat agriculture in the Red River Valley and onto the Dakota plains.

Prior to 1870, wheat had not been grown in Dakota Territory. The Métis living in the prairie villages of the old Pembina District lived mostly by hunting and fishing. Some accounts have created the false impression that they depended entirely upon the buffalo and engaged in little or no farming.[33] On the contrary, they grew vegetables in small family garden plots and raised barley, hay, and oats to feed their horses. Since they did not have mills to grind wheat, they had to buy flour from the Selkirk settlement north of the border. Yet at least some Métis, with close ties to the Pembina and Turtle Mountain Chippewa, began making the transition to agriculture in general and raising wheat in particular.

In the early 1870s, north of the Pembina River and west of Pembina, Charles Bottineau, the Métis/Chippewa brother of Pierre, became one of the first wheat farmers in the territory.[34] He cultivated ten acres of wheat and claimed yields as high as forty to fifty bushels per acre. As with those residents who purchased flour, he had to freight his wheat harvest to Selkirk to be milled. That probably made a significant dent in his profit margin. Still, such a small success story illustrated that as with most transitional economic endeavors in the Red River region, the Métis showed the way toward commercial success. Despite frequently adverse environmental conditions, combined with scarcity of capital and infrastructure, the long-time inhabitants did not exist in an economic backwater. Instead, they provided invaluable experience that paved the way for the subsequent success of the European American bonanza farmers later in the 1870s.

Yet no successful precedent in eastern North Dakota for the risky venture of large-scale wheat farming existed. That changed in 1874 when a homesteader yielded 1,600 bushels of wheat from forty acres of land for the amazing annual return of $1,900.[35] So by 1875, wealthy railroad stockholders and many others became excited about bonanza wheat farming and ranching on the northern plains. After gobbling up all the best Red River land, this profitable phenomenon lured more and more European Americans to settle farther west in North Dakota and within unceded Turtle Mountain Chippewa territory. This land and wheat boom continued for the remainder of the 1870s and the 1880s. The redistribution of huge parcels (3,000 to 65,000 acres) of the Northern Pacific's ten-million-acre railroad land grants to railroad presidents, directors, bank presidents, iron ore barons, merchant princes, and land speculators brought industrial-scale commercial agriculture to the Great Plains.[36]

North Dakota and other areas of the West became owned increasingly by a small number of rich landlords, along with a great many tenants and landless agricultural laborers. Historian Paul W. Gates found that "the federal disposal of cheap lands encouraged the development of a landed aristocracy on the frontier, encouraged speculation, and demonstrated that the accumulation of real estate was a major way to wealth."[37] This constituted the post-Civil War reality of western landholding, which differed significantly from Jefferson's yeoman farmer dream for America. North Dakota became dependent on access to external markets controlled by the "owners and managers of the railroads, flour mills, grain elevators, and banks." Large-scale farming dominates North Dakota to this day.[38]

Many smaller farmers (with tracts of 450 to 640 acres) followed in the wake of the huge bonanza enterprises. Railroad advertisements publicized free homesteads and promising townsites. The "news spread like prairie fire—we must all go farming."[39] Since most of the Red River Valley lands became occupied quickly and drove up area land prices, some farmers pushed farther north and westward along the Great Northern Railway and the ever-growing number of short-line railways into the unceded territory of the Turtle Mountain Chippewa west of the 1863 treaty cession. In 1873, their domain became the aptly named Buffalo County in north-central Dakota Territory.[40] This southern extent of Turtle Mountain on the edge of the prairie consisted of fine agricultural, grazing, and timber lands.[41] Because of these resources, the United States expropriated tens of thousands of acres of Native American country into public domain and military reserve (e.g., Fort Totten timber) lands without acquiring the band's consent or compensating them for their loss. The federal government conveyed them to non-farming interests, such as land speculators, timber companies, and cattle companies. Driven by the cumulative impact of these encroaching economic endeavors, the pressures on Turtle Mountain Chippewa sovereignty coincided closely with the construction of the Great Northern Railway after 1879, and the completion of the Northern Pacific to Montana in 1881.

Neither claims of unextinguished title—acknowledged and recognized by the BIA—nor pleas for a protected homeland reservation from the Turtle Mountain people could stem the tide of bonanza wheat farms and the immigrants that pushed farther west in their wake. The large yields and profits of commercial agriculture generated enormous regional, national, and international publicity, leading to exaggerated claims, such as labeling the northern wooded and brush-covered Turtle Mountain as "the Garden of the Northwest." Such claims ignored the fact that significant environmental differences precluded the profitable duplication of eastern family farmsteads on the Great Plains.[42] A short-lived cycle of above average rainfall created an irrational exuberance that unleashed a smaller-scale homestead wheat farmer land rush west of the huge bonanza farms and the 1863–1864 Old Crossing Treaty cession.

Emboldened by the federal government's hasty sale of public domain land, squatters, townsite speculators, surveyors, and entrepreneurs all encroached on unceded Turtle Mountain territory. The railroads—with their land grants, land departments, and publicists—lured European Americans onto the northern Plains stretching from the Red River to the Missouri River. Railroad networks became the conduits for a transcontinental U.S. economy.[43] They imported immigrant laborers, tenants, and homesteaders, along with the new technologies that made

farming both possible and profitable. In turn, they exported the fruits of
their labor to various industrial processing centers and markets in other
regions. This system fueled the settlement and unbalanced economic
development of North Dakota. It also began the process of illegally
dispossessing the Turtle Mountain Chippewa of their lands in North
Dakota.

The economic development of the Red River region also led to
related Native dispossession farther north in the future province of
Manitoba. The westward expansion of Canada led to the transfer of
Rupert's Land from the Hudson's Bay Company in 1868. In response,
the Métis Red River Resistance of 1869–1870 contested the Hudson's
Bay Company's sellout of territory and sovereignty to the Dominion
of Canada without the consent of the Native inhabitants.[44] Under the
leadership of the charismatic and eloquent Louis Riel, the dominant
Métis population established its own provisional government in opposition to the imposition of the Dominion of Canada's authority. Riel
declared that "we may be a small community and a Half-breed community at that—but we are men, free and spirited men and we will not
allow even the Dominion of Canada to trample on our rights."[45] After
having struggled for decades to wrench greater economic opportunities and a voice in the governing councils from the domineering HBC,
the Métis of Red River resolved to preserve their hard-won autonomy
and have a say in determining their own future.[46]

The Red River Resistance of 1869–1870 had a significant impact on the future of the Pembina and Turtle Mountain Chippewa and
their Métis relations.[47] Parallel and convergent developments involving cultures, politics, economics, and the law ignored and superseded
porous borders perceived as alien by the region's Native inhabitants.
The international boundary, whether denoted as the astronomically
based forty-ninth parallel or the informal "medicine line" between the
United States and Canada, could not separate the fates of mixed-race
and mixed-nation Indigenous peoples. Their co-evolution derived
from the family ties and historical development of the Métis and the

Pembina and Turtle Mountain Chippewa bands from the fur trade in the Red River borderland.[48] The majority Métis population resisted this infringement by the Dominion of Canada on their political and land rights unsuccessfully.[49] The failure of their resistance led to a dispersion of the Red River population. Most migrated to Saskatchewan, while many fled to relations at Turtle Mountain. Their bitter experiences over autonomy and land in Manitoba foreshadowed similar negative developments faced by the Turtle Mountain Chippewa in neighboring North Dakota.

While the new Dominion government attempted to impose greater control over the First Nations peoples of western Canada to open the region to European Canadian settlement, the U.S. government wanted to change tribal-federal legal relations to foster the same ends. The actions of one key politician sheds some light on the connections between U.S. policy formulation, railroad company influence peddling, and the end of treaty making. Because he became known as a "friend of the Indian," some historians have almost canonized Henry L. Dawes for his benevolence and honesty.[50] Yet as a congressman, he took part in the most notorious political scandal of the 1870s.

The railroad corporations constituted the most powerful special interest and political lobby in the United States. Dawes and many other prominent Republican legislators became involved in the infamous Crédit Mobilier scandal. Stock from a dummy holding company controlled by the Union Pacific was distributed to influential legislators to avoid investigations into the enormous cost overruns in building the federally subsidized railroad.

This aggressive pursuit of power and wealth unleashed by the post–Civil War economy facilitated what policymakers had been seeking for two decades. After his failed endeavors on behalf of the unratified Pembina Treaty of 1851, Alexander Ramsey raised the key question of why "the government should place itself on an equal footing in treating with hordes of savages."[51] By 1863, a few months before the

Old Crossing council, a Minnesota agent reported to the commissioner of Indian Affairs that "the government should at once abandon the
treaty system."[52] These sentiments became so prevalent among various
Indian Affairs officials, that it is surprising that the U.S. pursued a treaty
with the Red Lake and Pembina Chippewa in 1863. It seems that the
imperative of obtaining the prized Red River Valley compelled the
U.S. to continue with the expediency of treaty-making.

Federal policymakers believed that treaties interfered with their
mandate to "compel the Indians to submit to the authority of the government."[53] As chairman of the powerful House Ways and Means
committee, Dawes held sway over all federal legislative appropriations.
He had considerable influence on Native American affairs. According
to Wilcomb Washburn, Dawes "almost single-handedly forced the
Senate to do away with the [Native American] treaty system as the
price for obtaining appropriations from the House for carrying out the
government's commitments to the Indian."[54] Reacting against the liberal concessions in the Fort Laramie Treaty of 1868, Dawes asserted his
power to prohibit anymore treaties with Native tribes.

But the formal end to treaty-making with Native peoples, did not
just stem from an internal debate between the legislative branches and
the executive branch of the federal government over who would control federal policy. "Dawes consistently asserted in congressional de-
bates that his real concern was to break up the treaty system as the first
step toward general allotment of Indian lands." Washburn concluded
that "Dawes's ability to compromise, even with principle, was true to
his character."[55] In the case of Native allotment, the railroads and other
non-benevolent special interests saw that they did not need to expend
much political capital to achieve their ends, so they let reformers like
Dawes take the lead and saved their resources for more urgently needed lobbying efforts. These circumstances show that Dawes acted to reduce the semi-sovereign legal status of Native Americans and curtail
their land rights long before the "friends of the Indian" embraced him
as their political champion for allotment.[56]

All of these converging interests demonstrated an inherent conflict of interest in federal policy formulation that contradicted its benevolent rhetoric. The unilateral alteration in the federal relationship with Native tribes—semi-sovereigns to "wards of the nation"—became the rationalization for a more aggressive assertion of various elements from the federal policy grab-bag to solve the professed "Indian problem." Although the United States continued to impose "agreements" on various tribes (including the Turtle Mountain Chippewa) up until 1914, this act of Congress signaled the more forceful exercise of federal power against the Native Americans. In 1872, the commissioner of Indian Affairs asserted that:

> No one certainly will rejoice more heartily than the present
> Commissioner when the Indians of this country cease to
> be in a position to dictate, in any form or degree, to the
> Government . . . If they stand up against the progress of
> civilization and industry, they must be relentlessly crushed.
> The westward course of population is neither to be denied
> nor delayed for the sake of all the Indians that ever called this
> country their home.[57]

These developments came at a bad time for the Turtle Mountain band. Just when they needed a treaty for protection and security before European American intrusion became irreversible, Congress made mutual accommodation less likely.

Two prominent realities of Native American existence always impeded the grab-bag strategies of federal policy in the Trans-Mississippi West. First, many Native American tribes still exercised varying degrees of sovereignty. Second, they possessed large amounts of territory. Their sovereignty and occupancy of valuable land constituted the real "Indian problem" as perceived by policymakers. The goal and practice of federal policy always attempted to undermine one or both conditions. Of the various courses of action adopted from the federal policy grab-bag, treaties no longer provided any tactical advantage for the United States. In 1872, the Secretary of the Interior asserted that:

> In our intercourse with the Indians it must always be borne
> in mind that we are the most powerful party . . . We . . .
> claim the right to control the soil which they occupy, and we
> assume that it is our duty to coerce them, if necessary, into the
> adoption and practice of our habits and customs.[58]

The pretext for coercion accorded with the views of prominent officials like General Sherman. He touted railroads as the key instrument that would "settle forever the Indian question" because they acted ostensibly as "agents of expanding civilization." In 1872, Commissioner Walker commented tersely that "the interests of the Indians are, or may be, affected," by railroads like the Northern Pacific. He also asserted that "the Northern Pacific Railroad will of itself completely solve the great Sioux problem."[59]

Of course, the Northern Pacific Railroad and various special interests had less high-minded motives. Their goal endeavored to bring Native land and resources into the expanding national industrial economy. For the Lakota and other tribes in Dakota Territory, this development threatened their seasonal migratory subsistence system. The Indians feared rightly that the advent of the railroads meant the end of the buffalo. Turtle Mountain chief Kah-ishpa Gourneau stated, "our land is our support, and when the Great Father takes away our land, he takes away our support." Another chief named Kakenowash (Flying Eagle) concurred by affirming, "we want to make a living on our land."[60] They knew that if a community lost control over its resources, their autonomy, culture, and socio-political structure would be undermined. The railroads also diminished the lucrative Métis cart freighting business, which had linked much of the trade of the upper West to the Red River. Both the Chippewa and the Métis at Turtle Mountain feared that their self-sufficiency would be transformed into economic and political dependency, along with cultural disintegration.

These intersecting forces intruded on the Turtle Mountain Chippewa in negative ways. In 1871–1872, the Northern Pacific Railroad reached the Red River at Fargo, and the first telegraph in the region linked Fargo to Winnipeg. This infrastructure verified the viability of settlement, despite Clement Lounsberry's observation that "practically all of North Dakota until 1873 was vacant." After the Northern Pacific reached the Missouri River at Bismarck in 1873, Lounsberry founded the *Bismarck Tribune* newspaper. By 1872, 105 preemptions, 55 homesteads, and six Sioux scrip land claim filings had been made in North Dakota. The first Dakota land boom commenced. [61]

Despite some decline in their numbers and the westward migration of the buffalo herds caused by railroad encroachment, the lifeways of the Plains-Ojibwe bands remained largely intact. Archbishop Tache remarked in 1868 that "all of them . . . retain their social customs."[62] Social, cultural, and political stability prevailed, yet continuity did not preclude change. Dissolution had not set in yet as a result of the band's treaty relationship with the U.S. Their treaty entitlement had not resulted in dependency. The first post-Old Crossing treaty annuity roll in 1864 indicated that a little over $5,000 had been distributed to 674 Pembina Chippewa. Chief Little Shell II received a "regular share" and a "chief's share."[63] These small per capita stipends augmented the band's economic endeavors. As long as they could still hunt buffalo and utilize them for sustenance, trade, and spiritual purposes, the Turtle Mountain Chippewa would remain self-sufficient and autonomous.

Yet declining and more distant bison herds combined with greater European American infringement caused most of the full-bloods and mixed-bloods who had coalesced around Chief Little Shell II to renew their efforts and better secure legal recognition and protection for a homeland. The CIA acknowledged belatedly that the lack of a reservation for the Pembina and Turtle Mountain Chippewa might have been an unfortunate oversight.[64] He warned that "unless the Department [of the Interior] shall recognize the Turtle Mountain band of Pembinas" formally, any federal efforts to secure a reservation for them would be thwarted. The commissioner conceded that at the time of the treaty they lived west of the line of the Old Crossing cession, "and would seem to retain all the natural rights which Indians ever acquire to territory" (i.e., "Indian title"). Now "they ask that this Tur-

tle Mountain country shall be acknowledged to them as their reservation."[65] Ironically, as external influences impinged upon their territory,
the Turtle Mountain Chippewa began to receive greater validation for
their unceded land claim from the federal policy echelon.

Unfortunately, the proximity to the Canadian border of any
reservation at Turtle Mountain impaired its likelihood. Since its inception, the U.S. feared that borderlands with foreign powers like
Spain, France, or Britain harbored hostile to say Native Americans.
The development of an increasingly boundaryless economic region
of cross-border trade and the traffic involving Native peoples and European Canadians after 1870 coincided with renewed efforts to secure
the international boundary. To begin this process, the United States
and the new Dominion of Canada endeavored to clarify the 1818 international boundary line along the forty-ninth parallel from the Red
River to the Rocky Mountains. Concerns over the Red River Métis
Resistance and the subsequent creation of the province of Manitoba
became exacerbated by an auxiliary event. In 1871, a raid by some
Irish Fenian filibusters on the HBC post at Pembina brought to the
attention of the U.S. War Department and Congress the lack of a well-
drawn international boundary along the forty-ninth parallel west of
the Red River.

Although the U.S. Army caught the Fenians engaged in the
armed raid, they avoided criminal conviction due to lack of proof over
clear national jurisdiction. During the trial of the Fenians, U.S. officials
admitted that they encountered neither British nor U.S. flags in the
area and conceded that "there is some dispute about the jurisdiction of
the territory."[66] While this incident remained peripheral to the Métis
resistance in Manitoba, its relevance to this study revolves around the
fact that no clearly posted U.S.-Canadian border existed between 1818
and 1876. This lack of a definitive boundary between the United States
and the British Possessions (i.e., Canada after 1870), illustrates the unrealistic and impractical nature of the attempts by U.S. policymakers to
delineate accurately between "American" and "Canadian" Indigenous
peoples and Métis.

Such arbitrary distinctions would become deployed increasingly against the Turtle Mountain Chippewa in attempts to divide the band. In response to the confusing international border situation, a joint British and U.S. Boundary Survey Commission conducted a definitive survey from 1872 to 1874. As was usually the case in this region, the Métis, many of them from Turtle Mountain, provided almost all the local knowledge and labor needed to complete this task. They acted as scouts, guides, security detail (e.g., the Forty-Ninth Rangers), and hunters, while utilizing their Red River carts for transporting the baggage and scientific equipment. The densely wooded Turtle Mountains proved to be one of the most difficult border sectors through which to cut an accurate demarcation "line."[67]

Of course, these undertakings commenced without regard to the legal claims of the Turtle Mountain Chippewa. The governing power structure prioritized the interests of its European American constituents well above the interests of the Native Americans. With the commissioner of Indian Affairs proclaiming that "the westward course of [European American] population is neither to be denied nor delayed," the federal and local pressure for Pembina Chippewa removal put the band's membership in greater flux.[68] Even in the eastern-most extent of Dakota Territory, "Indian title had not been extinguished at the time . . . to the lands about Fargo, though they had been surveyed in 1867, anticipating such extinguishment, and settlement was allowed upon them."[69] As usual, the presence of Native peoples constituted a "problem" in the eyes of federal policymakers.

As often happened, Washington, D.C., bureaucrats made such pronouncements in lieu of accurate information. The annual reports of the CIA failed to acknowledge that any Plains-Ojibwe bands even lived in Dakota Territory. The Pembina band had been misidentified as "Minnesota Chippewa."[70] But these omissions or errors did not concern the policy echelon. They preached that "the true and permanent Indian policy of the Government" centered on the fact that Native peoples must "work or starve." No other options could be considered.

The reservation system would provide the necessary "legalized reformatory control" over Native peoples west of the Mississippi River.[71] "If they stand up against the progress of civilization and industry, they must be relentlessly crushed." Legal formalities like "Indian title" would not be allowed to impede advancing European American settlement "for the sake of all the Indians that ever called this country their home." The commissioner justified the "unquestioned" right and duty of the United States to implement this policy on the grounds of "self-protection," "self-interest," "common sense principles," and of course, "considerations of justice."[72]

Despite obtaining nearly ten million acres of valuable land for a pittance, Alexander Ramsey had failed to fulfill the commissioner's primary goal of Native peoples' removal from the 1863–1864 Old Crossing treaties. In 1868 the Inspector General of Dakota Territory reported to the Secretary of War that "although the Chippewa have sold their lands upon the Pembina River below St. Joseph, they continue to claim it, and will not allow the whites to settle upon it."[73] Until enough European Americans came in to push them out, most of the Pembina Chippewa remained on their ceded territory. In support of his dubious claim that European American settlers would not even want these lands for a long time, Ramsey had assured the Pembina Chippewa that they could continue to live in the ceded area. Yet because the treaty did not set aside a reservation, the tribe had no recognized boundaries or entitlement to federal protection. Contrary to Ramsey's prediction and promise—and spurred by the actual or anticipated completion of various rail lines—settlers moved quickly to homestead the lands west of the Red River in Dakota Territory after 1868.

In conjunction with the end of the ten-year annuity period stipulated in the Old Crossing treaty, a memorial from the Dakota Assembly to Congress requested a mandate for the removal of the Pembina band from Dakota Territory. The legislature considered the Chippewa to be "a great nuisance" to existing European American settlement, and an impediment to future ones.[74] This initiative coincided with the federal bureaucracy's declaration that "the true [Native American] policy of the Government should be one of concentration." Commissioner of Indian Affairs E. P. Smith agreed and passed his recommendation on to Congress. The national legislature appropriated $10,000 to purchase a township on the White Earth (Minnesota) reservation, "seventeen miles northwest of the agency" on the Wild Rice River. It also arranged for the removal of an estimated four hundred "Pembina Indians" to that location. The allocation procured the township, but it proved insufficient to the other task at hand.[75] While some Pembina moved to the Red Lake or White Earth Chippewa reservations in Minnesota, other band members and some Métis relocated to Turtle Mountain or Montana for greater access to the buffalo. In violation of the Old Crossing treaty, the local Indian Affairs office ordered local agents to coerce compliance.

To overcome resistance to removal, the Indian Affairs office resorted to an isolate-and-separate strategy pulled from the federal policy grab-bag. In violation of the spirit, if not the letter, of the treaty, they decided that the next annual annuity would only be made at the White Earth agency. This inducement, or bribe, did not achieve the desired result. Only a few of the band complied with repeated requests that they abandon their homeland and uproot themselves to the White Earth Chippewa reservation in Minnesota. Aside from the fact that most of the Pembina band did not want to relocate, they lived two hundred to three hundred miles away. Chief Little Shell III protested that their destitute and near starving circumstances precluded such lengthy travel because the costs of the trek exceeded the meager payout. He wanted to believe that the "Great Father" meant to "treat them justly," but accused the local agent of not "doing what is right to us."[76] Moreover, the European American "Indian ring" in Dakota, who reaped much of the benefit from the prior annual payments, did everything they could to dissuade them from going. As a result, the White Earth agency rescinded its original orders. Most of the band's members received *le Pay* at Pembina as Little Shell III insisted upon, and in accordance with their treaty.

Contrary to the agent's report, the Turtle Mountain band's attorney, J. B. Bottineau, refuted the assertion that they had "virtually abandoned" their distant homeland to the Sioux.[77] The CIA confirmed that the Turtle Mountain band of Pembina lived west of the 1864 cession line and continued to press their legal claims.[78] This affirmation indicated that despite all the misinformation about them, the Turtle Mountain band began to receive more official attention. The fact that the Old Crossing treaty had not allocated a reservation for the Pembina and Turtle Mountain Chippewa finally began to dawn on the Indian Affairs echelon as a mistake. While federal administrators and local agents reasserted that "the true policy of the Government should be one of concentration," repeated Native and territorial "Indian ring" resistance to removal made this solution unworkable.[79] If the Pembina band would not go east to an established reservation in Minnesota, perhaps the Interior Department could find a place for them farther west with their Chippewa relations in "Turtle Mountain country." A reservation could be created there if the United States recognized "the claim of the Turtle Mountain band of Pembina, who at the time of the [1863/1864] treaty, were living west of the line of the ceded territory." The CIA admitted that they "would seem to retain all the natural rights which Indians ever acquire to territory."[80]

Even so, it came as a surprise to federal officials that the annual inspection tour by the Board of Visitors (BOV), stipulated by Article Six of the Old Crossing treaty, reported to the CIA that "they cling with tenacity to their old homes." Because of this attachment to a homeland they considered to be sacred, the Pembina Natives in Dakota Territory requested a reservation at Turtle Mountain, as opposed to removal to White Earth.[81] The BOV found that "the Turtle Mountain Indians regard these mountains as their own and express a strong desire to have a reservation definitely located for them in that region, before white settlers shall further encroach upon them." They recognized "the justice of their request."[82] Agent E. P. Smith conveyed the desire of the Turtle Mountain Chippewa when he reported that "they ask that their rights in this unceded country may be recognized." The CIA confirmed that they wanted to have "Turtle Mountain country" acknowledged to them as a reservation.[83]

This plan accorded with the wishes of the "full-blood" Chippewa and the "half-breed" relations of both the Pembina and Turtle Mountain bands. Yet federal policymakers attempted to denigrate affiliated mixed-bloods. They could not disregard their notable existence. Commissioner Walker wrote in the *North American Review* that, "half-breeds bearing the names of French, English and American employees of fur and trading companies . . . are to be found in almost every tribe and band."[84] He noted their talents and substantial influence on Native relations. Nevertheless, all of their positive qualities neither satisfied Walker nor his colleagues' racial assumptions. Anthropologist Jack Forbes has noted that, "in the nineteenth-century, and especially after the U.S. Civil War, a greater emphasis was placed upon wholly biological or 'racial' categorization and differentiation in North America." The federal government's pseudo-scientific racial categorization became the basis for marginalization, not assimilation. The precepts of the age ordained that "successful exploitation . . . could only be obtained by exclusion." This underlying double standard justified the policy where the "legal-judicial property rights" of European Americans superseded "Indian title." "Racism and settler-colonial domination" became the unspoken rationale behind federal "assimilationist politics."[85] Walker conveyed this overall attitude of the federal policy echelon. He considered "half-breeds" as "incapable of leading the savages in better courses."[86]

Because they might impede federal assimilation policy or lead their Native cousins to resist it, U.S. officials attempted to separate mixed-bloods from tribes or bands. The agent for the Chippewa, E. P. Smith, attempted to cut off the "half-breeds" from any land claims and the tribal rolls of the full-blood Native Americans. The reduced number of authorized band members from 547 in 1872 to 396 in 1873, resulted from Smith's dropping of 151 "half-breed Pembinas from the annuity roll" without the band's consent.[87] These types of unilateral actions by local agents established a dangerous precedent that would be deployed against the Turtle Mountain band twenty years later. It certainly represented an intrusion into the most fundamental attribute of tribal sovereignty: the right to determine their membership. Yet, as Smith noted in the context of the end of U.S. treaty-making with Native tribes, Native Americans would no longer be considered as "independent and sovereign people." Instead, they would be dealt with as "wards of the nation" with no political rights.[88] These presumptions set off a downward spiral in tribal-federal relations. "Wardship" and "pupilage" became the clichés of a more assertive policy of assimilation in the late nineteenth century

Smith's immediate actions stemmed from his membership on an 1871 Interior Department commission created to investigate the eligibility provisions for "half-breed" land scrip under the 1854, 1863, and 1864 Chippewa pacts. Allotting the Pembina Chippewa and the Métis in the Old Crossing treaties served a purposeful design of federal policymakers. Allocating a reservation for the Native Americans, or a large tract of land for the "half-breeds" would have interfered with European American land selection and the subsequent development of the region. The shift from the 1863 treaty's Article Eight allotment provision to the 1864 treaty's scrip stipulation under Article Seven had consequences not intended to benefit the Métis. The Office of Indian Affairs conceded that the issuance of scrip served as a "practicable method of disposing of the half-breed claims."[89]

By the end of 1871, the commission found, and CIA Smith reported, "frauds connected with the issuance of Chippewa half-breed scrip." Massive fraud had been committed by speculators, brokers, and "the principal banks of St. Paul [Minnesota]." After the 1854 and 1864 compacts, "Chippewa scrip began to be considered desirable property," despite treaty provisions that declared that scrip could not be assigned, transferred, or alienated legally.[90] These mercenary entities made applications on behalf of illegitimate claimants or intervened with legitimate applicants, charging finders fees or securing power of attorney without the informed consent of the signatories. Each of these bogus transactions came with a fee of $10, $25, or $50, and only a "promise" that the mixed-bloods would eventually receive their cash or land entitlement.[91]

Despite being non-transferable, this scrip became an "assignable" article of trade "kept on sale by brokers and at the principal banks of St. Paul."[92] This turned scrip land grants into cash grants that could be bought, sold, and alienated. Scrip buyers, locators, brokers, and speculators foreswore settlement for themselves. They desired to turn land over quickly for profit. One agent made a gain of $2.50 per acre on 199 certificates at 160 acres each! [93] To accomplish this, they took advantage of unsuspecting and unprepared half-breeds, many of whom signed legal documents with an easily forged X.

With the incursion of European Americans into any newly surveyed lands resulting from a Native American treaty cession, high demand meant a booming land market, rising land values, and easy profits with virtually no labor. Scrip also had a high resale value because it conveyed a quick land patent without the fees and requirements of homesteading. Not surprisingly, Norman W. Kittson became one of the leading scrip speculators. By using his own notary, interpreters, witnesses, and finders, he managed to procure 415 applications at a fee of $50 each, to acquire 105 pieces of scrip from his old friend, ex-Commissioner of Indian Affairs William Dole.[94] Only two applicants ever received any money or scrip from Kittson. He held onto the remaining 315 applications and received scrip for all of them even though none of the claimants proved to be legitimate. To make matters worse, the commissioner re-endorsed the certificates so they could be located on more lucrative lands.[95]

Scrip speculation was neither small-time nor haphazard. It became a big business, providing huge infusions of capital into local banks and real estate firms. Speculators bought scrip for next to nothing and sold it at face value or assembled large tracts of land for future resale. Some local and federal officials objected to these sharp practices.

Since the unscrupulous practitioners claimed that they followed the letter of the law, most Métis had no legal recourse to being swindled out of their land.[96]

No law enforcement efforts attempted to curtail the activities of the commercial scrip dealers. Thus, through a combination of ignorance, fraud, and apathy, the Métis treaty beneficiaries found themselves "cut off from further receipt of scrip" or 160 acres of land and prevented from "participat[ing] in the benefits of the treaty made expressly for them." CIA Smith acknowledged that "it seems a hardship that they should thus be made to suffer through the crime of others."[97] Yet he felt no compunction about pruning them from the Pembina tribal roll. So, the Pembina and Turtle Mountain Chippewa, and their Métis kin, had to live with violations of their treaty, denial of sanctioned scrip, interference with tribal enrollment, threats, and bribes to coerce removal, and no action by the federal government to secure a tract of land set apart and withheld for them in their unceded territory.

The issue of "half-breed" scrip in the United States is fascinating and under explored. "Half-breed" scrip provisions in treaties have been largely overlooked by most of American historians, even to those working on Native-related issues. Some North American Indigenous peoples history scholarship has studied how this worked in Canada or has explored the few instances where some Métis received specific U.S. treaty allotments or tracts.[98] It should be pointed out that the term "half-breed" was a misnomer. The term was intended to include all those having an admixture of European and Native blood. Legally, they remained Native American, even those with a preponderance of European blood. "Half-breeds," mixed bloods, or Métis remained unrecognized under U.S. law as having "Indian title" or constituting a tribe or nation, in the legal sense of those terms. They had no distinct legal standing to treat with the U.S. government.[99] In the wider historical context of applications of "mixed-bloods" for land or scrip under treaties with various bands of Chippewa in Wisconsin and Minnesota, the Pembina and Turtle Mountain Chippewa experience with "half-breed" scrip constitutes one of the most important findings of this study.

Failing to secure any legal land title, and faced with an influx of European Americans seeking cultivatable farmland, most of the Native Americans in and around Pembina moved west to live with their kin-folk at Turtle Mountain.[100] Others went even farther west into Montana, or up into Saskatchewan. They all hoped to continue making a living from the dwindling fur trade, buffalo hunting and provisioning, and carting commerce. Meanwhile, the CIA confessed "that country [was] now opening to settlers," but failed to note the illegality of such settlement.[101] On top of encroaching railroads, European American settlement, and diminishing political status, two other occurrences made the Turtle Mountain Chippewa's situation much more precarious.

The beginning of the end for the northern plains bison constituted the single most crippling development that threatened their community structure, survival, and way of life. By the early 1870s, the diminished range of the herds stood well beyond Pembina, St. Joseph, and even west of Turtle Mountain. No sizeable groups of buffalo roamed east of the Missouri River. The leading Métis provisioner at St. Joseph, Antoine Gingras, could no longer procure buffalo meat (or pemmican). Instead, he had to sell pork to the international boundary commission.[102]

Due to the growing precariousness of their physical existence, with its potentially dire consequences, the band arranged for a delegation to visit Washington, D.C., in November 1874. Unfortunately, the death of beloved hereditary chief, Little Shell II (Weesh-e-damo), hampered their effort to respond in a timely and forceful enough manner to the various federal plans to dispose of them and their legal claims. Up until his demise, Little Shell II insisted correctly that the Pembina and Turtle Mountain lands west of the Old Crossing cession remained unceded Chippewa territory. This material fact had been recognized by the United States, the Territory of Dakota, the Dakota bands, and the Métis. He also opposed removal to White Earth and consolidation with Minnesota Chippewa bands.

Saddened by his death, yet determined to push their claims, the remaining band representatives journeyed eastward despite being afflicted with head colds. They expressed a desire to cede some of their occupied lands. In return, the band's spokesmen had two major demands. They wanted federal recognition of their land claim and "proper recompense" for any cession.[103] As a result of this conference, government representatives assured the delegation that the United States recognized the validity of Turtle Mountain Chippewa land "ownership" in the sense of "Indian title." Yet in the absence of their head chief, no formal negotiations about any reservation or removal proposal could be conducted. In 1875, Little Shell II's son, Ayabe-way-we-tung (He Who Rests on His Way), became the new "first chief." In honor of his grandfather and signifying the continuity of the band's hereditary chieftainship, he became known as Little Shell III. He and the other sub-chiefs notified Washington, D.C., that they wanted to return with another delegation to conduct formal negotiations for a comprehensive land cession treaty.[104]

As a symbol of Chief Little Shell III's leadership for the entire band during his visit to Washington, he wore the Abraham Lincoln peace medal given to his father at the 1863 Old Crossing treaty. The band's sub-chiefs Kaishpa (The Elevated One) Gourneau, Mis-to-ya-be (Little Bull), and Ke-woe-sais-we-ro (The Hunter) accompanied him (see Image 10).[105] They protested pending proposals for their removal to either White Earth, Minnesota, or farther west. Preferring to remain at their beloved Turtle Mountain, they pressed for a reservation within their unceded Indigenous lands and a treaty-based settlement recognizing their territorial claim and compensating them for any land cession. But the end of official treaty making conducted exclusively by the Executive branch of the federal government in 1871, meant that such overtures now fell under the plenary authority of the national legislature or executive orders.

On February 23, 1876, the tribal leaders sent a memorial to Congress. It restated their land claim in the strongest possible terms. The Turtle Mountain band of Chippewa and their forefathers for many generations, inhabited and possessed, "as fully and completely as any

**Image 10. Studio portrait of the Pembina Chippewa delegation of 1874.** Seated, left to right: unidentified (possibly Louis Lenoir), unidentified, Little Shell III, Kaishpa (Something Blown Up by the Wind). Back row, left to right: unidentified, Ke-Woe-Sais-We-Ro (The Man Who Knows How to Hunt), Mis-To-Ya-Be (Little Bull). The men wear a combination of European-style and traditional dress. Little Shell III wears his father's peace medal around his neck. *National Museum of the American Indian photo.*

nation of Indians on this continent have ever possessed any region of country," a well-defined tract. They detailed their territorial boundaries and reiterated that "their possession of this country has never been successfully disputed by any of the neighboring nations or tribes of Indians, but has at all times been recognized as the country of the Turtle Mountain band of the Great Chippewa Nation."[106]

To remove any doubts concerning the continuity of their tribal government, they reminded Congress that three successive generations of Little Shells acted as hereditary principal chief. This had been confirmed by Little Shell II during the 1863 treaty proceedings when he asserted that "he had a right to talk about the Pembina Country, as his father owned all that country."[107] It should be noted that during this visit to Washington, Little Shell III stated incorrectly that the Old Crossing treaty cession never received the sanction of the Turtle Mountain band. His father had signed the 1863 treaty as a Pembina chief. Nevertheless, the band's representatives sharply accused the United States of encroaching on their domain by setting aside the Fort Totten reservation for the Dakota Natives at Devils Lake without any compensation. They questioned the legality of such a taking, since "no one has or can justly question" their possessory rights or land claim.[108]

This claim encompassed fifteen thousand square miles.[109] The Turtle Mountain leaders knew that this ancestral legacy represented their only hope for a viable future in a rapidly changing world. With the railroads, bonanza farms, and settlers crowding in, along with the demise of the buffalo, they wished to "abandon their present mode of life." With the days of large-scale subsistence hunting at an end, they asked "for instruction that they may be able to follow pastoral and agricultural pursuits."[110] They petitioned Congress to pass a bill for their relief, authorizing the president to create a reservation to be set apart and confirmed to them, the full-bloods and half-bloods of the Turtle Mountain band of Chippewa, and their descendants in perpetuity.

These delegates wanted to retain their band's unity and guard against division by arbitrary federal blood quantum ratios that would hurt their community and diminish their land claim. The main objective focused on reserving an adequate portion of their homeland. Just as his father recounted for Alexander Ramsey at the Old Crossing council in 1863, Little Shell III described the exact same area.[111] He asked for a reservation extending fifty miles north and south, and sixty miles east and west (with the northern border being the international boundary with Canada).

To help them make the transition to "pastoral and agricultural pursuits," they requested an agency with an agent, doctor, farmer, blacksmith, wagon-maker, and two teachers. In terms of compensation for their ceded lands, they made a reasonable and creative long-term development request that would help provide for their "descendants in perpetuity." The delegation asked for an annuity of twenty-thousand dollars per year for twenty years, plus U.S.–issued land scrip for six hundred sections of land anywhere within the reservation. Five hundred sections would be sold by the United States "at not less than fifty cents per acre," with the proceeds to be invested into 5 percent bonds to create a school fund, and the proceeds for the remaining one hundred sections to be allocated to the tribal council.[112] Such a sophisticated plan hardly qualified the Turtle Mountain Chippewa for relegation to wardship status. The plan confirmed that they could act in their own best interests and stave off dependency, with some technical and financial assistance from the United States. Even while fighting for their survival, the band's generosity prevailed. They offered some of their reservation to "the Assiniboine tribe or any other Indians" in the region who remained landless.[113] Such foresight and magnanimity verified that they remained committed to strengthening Native ties and the trust relationship with the government, while federal officials continued to undermine both.

Their compelling message seemed to have made its mark. A Joint Resolution of Congress on April 6, 1876 "recognized the Turtle Mountain Band with Little Shell as its chief," and reaffirmed their undisputed territorial possession and bona fide "Indian title."[114] Although such acknowledgement had been implicit since the Old Crossing Treaty of 1863, this explicit vindication met the tougher test for common law recognition of a Native tribe by being a united community under one leadership.[115] The report confirmed that "the Turtle Mountain band of Chippewa Indians, and their forefathers for many generations, have inhabited and possessed, as fully and completely as any nation of Indians on this continent have ever possessed any region of country."[116] As a result, the Senate Select Committee on Indian Affairs authorized the Secretary of the Interior to establish a reservation in northern Dakota for the Turtle Mountain band of Chippewa Indians from their Indigenous territory. It seemed that their prayers, memorials, and lobbying might pay off. Certainly, the Senate committee respected their devotion. Unfortunately, others within the federal Indian Affairs bureaucracy with countervailing influence saw things differently.

This chapter examined how national post–Civil War developments set the stage for a series of diverse but mutually reinforcing regional crises for the Turtle Mountain Chippewa. The advent of bonanza wheat farming in the Red River Valley of the North propelled European American settlement into the unceded Turtle Mountain region. Beginning in the 1870s European Americans pushed west beyond the Old Crossing treaty line set back in 1863. Foreseeing the dire consequences of rapid and illegal encroachment after beginning to absorb their dispersed Pembina band relations, the Turtle Mountain Chippewa sought the protection of a reservation. Although the validity of their exclusive land claim vis-à-vis any other tribes was recognized by commissioners of Indian Affairs, various local, territorial, and national non–Native economic and political interests forestalled any satisfactory legal settlement, while the wheat boom spurred increased immigration into the region. These encroachments represented illegal trespass because the Turtle Mountain Chippewa still retained, occupied, and used their unceded territory.

In response to the demographic burdens of European American settlement, the band initiated a diplomatic dialogue with federal officials to preserve their land base and autonomy. They sought to secure enough of their Indigenous territory for a reservation to insure the preservation of the current and future generations. In exchange for an exclusive use reservation of adequate size with federal protection, they would cede the balance of their territory to the United States for a fair price that could sustain them through and beyond the economic transition from buffalo hunting to farming and stock raising. Yet as noted by historian Angie Debo, "when the land was acquired by white men, it came under legal protection. As long as it was owned by Indians, no

**Image 11. Turtle Mountain Band of Pembina Chippewa delegation to Washington, D.C. (1876). Left to right: Bemosageshig, Little Shell III, Little Cloud, Animosung (or Auimosung), and Midewinind (One Called from a Distance).** *Smithsonian Institution National Anthropological Archives, Negative No. 51,107. By Charles M. Bell, Washington, D.C. Image colorization for book cover by Kade M. Ferris, Turtle Mountain Chippewa/Métis, Dibaajimowin.com.*

laws or courts or the plighted faith of the government could keep it free of intruders."[117]

Other factors also undermined any negotiated settlement. The Red River Métis resistance movements over land rights and self-governance across the border in Canada made the Métis-dominated Turtle Mountain community suspect in the eyes of federal policymakers, who worried about independent bands on the international boundary not under the control of either the United States or Canada. This perceived need or ability to achieve greater control also led to the formal and unilateral end of treaty making by the United States in 1871. Thus, the federal government refused to negotiate in good faith with the Turtle Mountain Chippewa. As a result, the Turtle Mountain band could not retain a reservation during the so-called "reservation era" of federal policy. Instead, the Indian Affairs apparatus attempted to deploy the grab-bag policy of removal over and over again. This counter-productive approach only stiffened the resolve of the Turtle Mountain Chippewa to stand fast in their homeland in the face of increasing poverty, hunger, and violation of their rights. Amidst one attempt to comply with Turtle Mountain Chippewa memorials for an adequate reservation, most federal officials still wished the tribe would relocate themselves to Minnesota or hoped that they would just disperse across the northern plains into Montana, Manitoba, or Saskatchewan.

## CHAPTER 5
## The Legal Struggle for Federal Recognition, 1877–1882

*These Indians have all the original rights in an unceded territory.*[1]
—Commissioner of Indian Affairs, Hiram Price, 1882

By the late 1870s, policy "reformers" increasingly favored Anglo-American law to solve the "Indian problem." As stated by Commissioner of Indian Affairs Ezra Hayt in 1879, "[I]t is the bounden duty of the government to provide *laws suited to the dependent condition of the Indians.*" An "increasing pressure arose for *law as a necessary means to bring about the Indian reform and civilization the humanitarians wanted.*"[2] Unfortunately for the Turtle Mountain Chippewa, these attitudes coincided with the advent of the first Dakota land boom. Between 1879 and 1886, one hundred thousand people immigrated into Dakota Territory. This demographic deluge, combined with the maneuvers of federal policymakers and local officials, led to the reduction of the nine- or ten-million-acre Turtle Mountain Chippewa homeland to two townships (46,000 acres).

Within six months of efforts in the U.S. Senate to set aside a reservation to preserve Turtle Mountain Chippewa autonomy, the new commissioner of Indian Affairs, John Q. Smith, mocked any concept of Native self-governance as "rude regulations of petty, ignorant tribes."[3] He concluded his annual report by conceding that "we have despoiled the Indians of their rich hunting-grounds, thereby depriving them of their means of support."[4] This candid assessment mirrored the stark reality faced by the Native peoples at Turtle Mountain, despite some Congressional support for an adequate reservation and financial compensation for lost land. Without a hint of embarrassment, the CIA believed that dispossession was a "cheap" price for them to pay in return for the "priceless benefit of just and equitable laws." The commissioner promised that they "will be protected, by the authority and power of the Government," in their "life, liberty, property, and character" just as if they were European Americans. As with prior pledges, this plan to further extend U. S. law over Natives and "give them at least a secure home" would have dire consequences for the Turtle Mountain Chippewa.[5]

The death of Antoine Gingras in 1877 coincided with the thinning out of the Métis community in Pembina and St. Joseph. Throughout the decade, the Red River Métis on both sides of the international boundary drifted westward to be closer to the last remaining northern plains buffalo range in north-central Montana. As they shifted from Turtle Mountain towards the Milk River, their numbers in and around Pembina and St. Joseph dropped from two thousand to two hundred. At the same time an influx of almost one thousand predominantly Scandinavian immigrants supplanted them. The extent of this demographic shift resulted in the local postmaster renaming St. Joseph to Walhalla.[6]

Still in exile from Canada because of the 1869–1870 Red River Resistance, Métis leader Louis Riel visited Pembina in 1878. He then came to live with Antoine Gingras's son Norman at St. Joseph in 1879. Although these locales put him in proximity to some old Red River contacts and allies remaining in the region, Riel soon followed most of his displaced Métis countrymen to Montana.[7] By 1878 the last Canadian buffalo herd on the northern plains had been depleted. The very real threat of starvation existed for the Indigenous inhabitants. This dire situation compelled some of the Cree, Assiniboine, Blackfoot, and Dakota tribes in Canada to also hunt the dwindling Montana range. The Native-Métis convergence provoked some anxiety in American and Canadian governing circles over border transit security issues. While these concerns proved to be unsubstantiated, in the interim, Riel believed they provided an opportunity to leverage concessions for the Métis from both governments.

During the winter of 1879–1880 he attempted to forge an alliance with the various tribes. They declined because of suspicions about his motives and leadership abilities. These tribes knew from their long-standing relations that in spite of some residual kinship affinity, the cultures and economic aspirations of many Natives and Métis had diverged significantly. This rift became more manifest after 1870 when Canadian policy defined the Métis as legally distinct from First Nations peoples without the option of settling on "status Indian" reserves.[8] The tribes decided that their best chance to resolve land claim grievances with both governments would be to honor their treaty commitments. At least this approach entitled them to some desperately needed rations and supplies in the short term. Perhaps if they remained peaceful and loyal, they could stave off starvation and re-negotiate for better conditions and terms in the future.[9]

As a result of this rebuff, in the summer of 1880 Riel appealed for a contiguous land base in the United States. He asked the U.S. government if it would "set apart a portion of land as a special reservation . . . for the half-breeds," along with a short-term monetary appropriation. He sent a formal petition with one hundred Métis signatures to the local American military commander in Montana, Nelson A. Miles. Unlike in Canada, Riel did not base this request on any inherent mixed-blood right of "Aboriginal title." Federal policy did not recognize such separate interests. As happened at Turtle Mountain, mixed-bloods could join full-blood kinfolk on their reservations. Riel hoped in vain that the United States would have pity or compassion for his people, as they faced greater competition from Native Americans and European immigrants for diminishing land and resources. He still believed that the "half-breeds" could act as intermediaries between the European Americans and Native peoples on behalf of the U.S. government's assimilation campaign. But Riel remained deluded about his influence amongst the region's tribes. He also did not seem to realize that despite General Miles's favorable recommendation, the War Department, Interior Department, and B.I.A. considered his request too extraordinary to be taken seriously.[10]

Ever since 1871, when the United States tried to end the policy of treaty-making with Native American tribes, the federal government's emphasis on the "dependent condition" of Native peoples diminished them to a status of "wardship," without any "pretensions of sovereignty."[11] The few remaining tribes or bands not situated permanently on reservations, like the Pembina and Turtle Mountain Chippewa, would be under federal guardianship sooner rather than later, especially after the demise of the last buffalo herd in 1883. This less-than-benevolent policy coincided with the post-Reconstruction Era rise of social Darwinism in the 1880s. Limited faith in the effectiveness of assimilation accompanied the racial, political, and economic exclusion of non-European groups in the United States. During an era of Jim Crow segregation for African Americans and a national Chinese Exclusion Act, policymakers wanted to disband tribes via allotment to solve the "Indian problem." Within this "survival of the fittest" setting, the federal government refused to recognize the "half-breeds" as a distinct collective entity with any unique legal status or land rights. This circumstance explains why the agent's report characterized Riel's request as "extraordinary." The request remained beyond the comprehension of the current Indian Affairs' ideological consensus.

With the end of treaty-making and the advent of allotment, the United States did not need any help from "half-breeds" they considered less "civilized" than the Native Americans. The agent from the Crow reservation in Montana, which Riel had proposed as a possible site for their reserve, wrote the formal letter rejecting the petition. The agent applied many of the derogatory characterizations used against Native Americans to the "half-breeds," denigrating them for their "nomadic" subsistence mode and "little practice in agriculture." Furthermore, their Catholic faith and propensity toward trading alcohol and guns offended Protestant missionaries and U.S. military officials. The agent even held their intelligence; rudimentary education; competence in Native and European languages and dialects; skill with weapons; fondness for drinking; adeptness at trading, carting, trapping, hunting, and fishing; and amicable relations amongst all the Northwest tribes against them.[12] All of these attributes made the Métis seem more cunning and dangerous than the Natives and a potentially disruptive or corrupting influence with the tribes.

Despite the submissiveness of Riel's petition, federal officials feared correctly, based on their resistance at Red River in 1869–1870, that the Métis would contest the downward push toward wardship status, and perhaps influence some tribes to do likewise. Ignoring the broad admixture of Native descent among the Métis, especially the predominance of Pembina Chippewa intermarriage at Red River earlier in the century, the agent considered them all to be descended from the Cree, and therefore British or Canadian subjects. This opportune rationale absolved the United States from any responsibility to recognize their "Aboriginal title" or legal rights. From the perspective of American policymakers, the "half-breeds" had only two options. They could stay in the United States, become naturalized citizens like Riel, and then homestead and assimilate into the dominant European American society. Or they could head north and pursue their Indigenous rights claims in Canada.

While the agent accused the Métis of "masquerading . . . to and fro between the United States and Canada," U.S. policymakers indulged in the real masquerade.[13] They ignored the Indigenous origins of the Red River Métis population that came into demographic prominence before the United States or Canada established any nominal sovereignty in the region or settled upon the exact location of the international boundary. The Métis communities in the Red River Valley, from St. Francois Xavier (Winnipeg) down to Pembina and St. Joseph in North Dakota, constituted an identifiable geopolitical borderland known as Assiniboia within the HBC's Rupert's Land. The best evidence supporting the existence of an extensive cross-border Métis and Native community comes from the well-documented convergence of their annual hunts down in the Turtle Mountain Chippewa's buffalo grounds and the Pembina and Turtle Mountain Chippewa rolls collected by John B. Bottineau and his uncle, Charles Bottineau.[14]

As a blood relation and member of the band, who traced his family's heritage back for five generations, the younger Bottineau would come to play a prominent role in the legal struggles of the Turtle Mountain Chippewa as their "attorney in fact and at law."[15] He resided at St. Joseph, Dakota Territory, for many years as a trader. People described him as "a very intelligent mixed-blood of the Pembina band." Through "repeated visits" to the greater Pembina region, he "kept up an intimate acquaintance with the families and almost all the individual members of the families of the mixed-bloods" connected with the Pembina and Turtle Mountain bands (e.g., John Baptiste Wilkie and Antoine Azure, "two reliable mixed-bloods" of St. Joseph).[16]

As noted by historian Thomas Flanagan, "for a largely illiterate people, the Métis are astonishingly well documented for genealogical purposes."[17] His own analysis of the geographic and community affiliations of the mixed-blood signers of Riel's petition showed that 80 percent of the predominantly French Métis came from Red River (40 percent) and Pembina (43 percent). These families (Bottineaus, Renvilles, Bellegardes, Montreuilles, Grants, Vennes, Gardners, LaRoques, Brunelles, Delormes, Poitras) still organized themselves in accordance with the patrilineal clan system derived from the Pembina Chippewa and other Plains-Ojibwe.[18] Flanagan pointed out that some of the petitioners had also been included in the 1850 Pembina census for Minnesota Territory. Charles Bottineau's genealogical collection dated back to the 1830s, meaning that certain families had lived in the United States for three to five decades. Flanagan concluded that "to call them British subjects was clearly misleading."[19]

In conjunction with the less-than-accommodating developments noted above, the Senate bill authorizing a Turtle Mountain reservation

**Image 12. Chief Little Shell III and Attorney John B. Bottineau.** At left: Ayabe-Way-We-Tung, Chief Little Shell III. Photo taken during a delegation visit to Washington, D.C. (1896). At right: John B. Bottineau (1896), Turtle Mountain Métis member and band attorney from 1878 to 1911. Bottineau compiled a 178-page account of the band's history and legal claims. *See "Turtle Mountain Band of Chippewa Indians: Papers Relative to an Agreement with the Turtle Mountain Band of Chippewa Indians in North Dakota," 56th Congress, 1st Session, June 6, 1900, Senate Document 444, Serial set 3878,7. Little Shell III photo (Negative No. 550-A) and Bottineau photo (Negative 556-A), both by William Dinwiddie of the B.A.E., Washington, D.C.*

in Dakota Territory did not pass. As a result, Little Shell III and the tribal council engaged tribal member and solicitor, J. B. Bottineau, to be their official representative and lobbyist in Washington, D.C. This positioning indicated that the Chippewa had not lost confidence in their mixed-blood relatives. Bottineau was the oldest son of the prominent scout, hunter, trapper, boatman, and land/townsite entrepreneur Pierre Bottineau. His father had firsthand knowledge of Chippewa tribal politics and relations with the United States in his capacities as guide, interpreter, and witness to the 1851 Pembina treaty and the 1864 Old Crossing treaty. Although he lived most of his life in Minnesota, both the town and county of Bottineau, North Dakota, just west of Turtle Mountain, were named after him and his brother Charles.[20]

On February 16, 1878, Bottineau submitted an eloquent fif-
teen-page appeal to Secretary of the Interior Carl Schurz on behalf of
the "Chippewa Indians of Northern Dakota Territory." Bottineau categorized their case as a "matter of marked justice to a wronged people."[21]
The terse sub-title asked whether the government would recognize
their claim and provide for them. Since 1878 would be the last annual
Le Pay from the 1863 Old Crossing treaty, each passing year without
a legal settlement made the Pembina and Turtle Mountain bands' existence more precarious. European American trespassers increasingly
drove the game—on which the bands depended—out of their country,
leaving them in dire straits. Bottineau lamented their "deplorable" and
"almost hopeless" condition of "suffering and destitution."[22] Even in such
a needy condition, most of the bands' people refused to be removed to
the White Earth reservation in Minnesota, or to "adopt the habits and
pursuits of civilized life" (i.e., become farmers).[23] "Prompt recognition
of their plain rights and a just settlement" had to come first. Then they
would relinquish most of their unceded territory to the United States in
exchange for much needed agricultural assistance, but only if the government guaranteed a reserve for them as a permanent homeland.[24]

Bottineau also sought federal re-acknowledgment of the legal fact
that "these Indians have never relinquished to the United States that
part of their country which lies west of the tract ceded by them to the
United States under the treaty of 1863." He appealed to the agent at
White Earth (the BIA agency responsible for the Pembina and Turtle
Mountain bands) for assistance in compelling the U.S. government to
"recognize their right to their remaining land and properly treat with
them for its acquisition."[25] Yet instead of recognizing this "just claim,"
as had been proposed in the Senate bill, the Interior Department insisted on removal to White Earth. The bands refused this option and
resisted subsequent attempts of coercion, because "such removal would
be construed as an abandonment of their remaining territory, and that
they would thus be unable ever after to maintain their rights to their
remaining lands." [26] As a result, Bottineau observed that they "cling

with tenacity to the hope that the government will at some time recognize their claims and pay them a sufficient sum for a release of their
remaining lands." Clearly, the bands wanted to stay, although they recognized that their hope was becoming increasingly unrealistic. They
remained adamant about receiving fair market value for their lands if
displacement could not be precluded. Meanwhile, "they linger about
the vicinity of the Turtle Mountain and adjacent country unwilling to
remove therefrom until their claims have been so recognized by the
United States and properly adjusted."[27]

Bottineau's memorial confirmed the bands' shrewd understanding of market relations. It also raised some doubts and questions about
the Pembina's unity of leadership. In making his case for all the "Chippewa Indians of Northern Dakota Territory," he felt compelled to assert the primacy of the Little Shell lineage, while demeaning Red Bear's
legitimacy. Bottineau reiterated that Little Shell's hereditary principal
chieftainship "descended from father to son in a regular succession."
Perhaps because he had only recently assumed the mantle of leadership
after his father's demise in 1874, Bottineau claimed that Little Shell III's
"right and title was recognized by all the Chippewa tribe, as well as by
all other Indian nations." In contrast, Bottineau identified Red Bear as
a "source of trouble . . . among these bands of the Chippewas."[28]

Apparently, this discord dated back to the Old Crossing treaty
negotiations in 1863. The lawyer asserted that Red Bear "had never been recognized as a chief" until "induced to assume that title" by
traders in the hopes of furthering their interests during treaty negotiations. As noted in the previous chapter, it remains uncertain why both
chiefs signed the treaty at the Old Crossing, but only Red Bear went to
Washington, D.C., and signed the supplemental 1864 pact. Some have
claimed incorrectly that Little Shell died in 1864. Bottineau leveled
the serious charge that "Red Bear was induced to go to Washington
against the will of Little Shell."[29] The solicitor probably received information to draw this conclusion from his Uncle Charles, who accompanied Red Bear and the Pembina delegation and signed the treaty as

a witness. As a result of the supplemental treaty, Red Bear received a 640-acre reserve, most likely as the inducement referred to by Bottineau. Yet it could not provide for "his family and a few of his friends" comprising perhaps 200 to 250 of the 550- to 600-member band.[30]

This sub-group of full-blood Pembina Chippewa, who "clung with tenacity to their old homes" in their ceded lands around Fort Pembina, St. Joseph, and the Pembina Mountains, are the ones referred to in the various agents', commissioners', and Board of Visitors' reports as poor, straggling, destitute, wretched, deplorable, and hopeless enough to be a "constant annoyance to settlers."[31] The bands began dissolving, with some staying near Pembina, a few leaving for Red Lake or White Earth, Minnesota, and most heading west to Turtle Mountain. The 1878 memorial represented more than a list of claims or complaints. Overall unity still prevailed, with Bottineau fighting hard for the Pembina and Turtle Mountain Chippewa. It framed their collective grievances "as a matter of marked justice to a wronged people." Yet the revelations about Red Bear as a "source of dissatisfaction" foreshadowed intra-tribal dissension that could be exploited by the United States in future negotiations.[32]

In the interim, the political leadership of the Pembina and Turtle Mountain Chippewa remained consistently persuasive with some federal officials. The impact of Bottineau's appeal had the same positive effect on Secretary Schurz, as the bands' delegations had in Washington, D.C., a few years before.[33] Yet there never seemed to be enough collective political will within the federal bureaucracy or the Congress to deal with the Turtle Mountain Chippewa as a community entitled to full—rather than grudging—recognition of their rights and a settlement of their land claim. The inability of policymakers to take care of this relatively simple matter baffled Little Shell, Kaishpau, and Bottineau. Bottineau charged that the government's "arbitrary proceedings threatened to jeopardize our claim."[34] The bands' leaders could not discern any rational structure or definable set of principles from their bewildering experiences with the federal government.

Since its inception in 1849, the Interior Department exercised administrative responsibility for land policy, Indian Affairs, education, railroads, geological surveys, the census, and territorial governments. The possibility of a coherent perception of the "Indian problem" was skewed by an inherent conflict of interest between the Bureau of Indian Affairs, and all of the other administrative agencies of the department.[35] In addition, the BIA was rife with incompetence, corruption, fraud, and mismanagement. The commissioners of Indian Affairs in the late 1870s and early 1880s—E. P. Smith, J. Q. Smith, and E. A. Hayt—were all dismissed under a cloud of official corruption, along with Secretary of the Interior Delano. The official counterweight to this corruption was supposed to be the Board of Indian Commissioners (BIC). But they were opposed by western politicians, like Colorado Senator and Secretary of the Interior Henry M. Teller, who resented losing their political patronage and retaliated by cutting the funding of the BIC.

The Turtle Mountain Chippewa grew frustrated after hearing repeatedly the acknowledgement of their case, the legitimacy of their claim, and the reasonableness of their proposed solution, only to have the process break down somewhere prior to a definitive resolution. Then they had to go back to square one again, often from a resulting change in presidential administrations or other personnel shifts within the federal bureaucracy. In terms of organizational theory, this recurring pattern of incoherence and irresolution illustrated that federal policy operated at the opposite end of the continuum from the "rational choice" model and helps explain the inconsistent, chaotic, and dysfunctional nature of federal policy.[36] There appeared to be no process or mechanism to turn the Turtle Mountain band's "just and reasonable" grievances into any kind of equitable solution. Without a clear set of principles, precedents, or norms, inconsistent policies produced corresponding unjust results. Indian Affairs failed consistently to reflect either rationality or the "rule of law." Federal policymakers continued to try and impose social, economic, and political control upon Native Americans under "the guise of law."[37]

In late 1879, a Pembina Chippewa delegation led by Kaishpau visited Agent James McLaughlin at the Fort Totten Devils Lake agency. They alleged a band count of 518 families totaling 2,115 people "scattered throughout Dakota and Montana." They wished to secure a reservation at Turtle Mountain, and "commence an agricultural life" before European American encroachment precluded the possibility for such an arrangement.[38] But by 1880, time was running out. The European American population in what became North Dakota hit 37,000. A year later, a U.S. Land Office opened at Devils Lake. Without a reservation, the unceded Turtle Mountain Indian north and northwest of Devils Lake was accessible for preemption, homestead, and timber claims.[39]

Commissioner of Indian Affairs Hiram Price's annual report for 1881 reflected the reality of this boom. As the European American populace increasingly settled in Native country, Price stated the premise for the future direction of federal policy bluntly. Native Americans faced only two options: "either civilization or extermination." "We are fifty millions of people, and they are only one-fourth one million. The few must yield to the many."[40] As before, new railroad branches brought more settlers to unsettled areas, while connecting the fruits of their labors with expanding national and international markets. In February of 1882, the Bismarck, Mouse River, Turtle Mountain and Manitoba Railroad Company came into being. It had $2,000,000 in capital to run a line north from Bismarck to Minot (at the "big bend" of the Souris [Mouse] River) and beyond up into Canada.[41] The first squatter's claim occurred at Minot in 1885. By this date, the European American population in Dakota Territory stood at 152,000. In 1887 the Great Northern Railway reached Minot, and a "mushroom-like" tent city of five thousand appeared.[42] All of these rail lines and boom towns west of the 1863 treaty cession line made unauthorized and uncompensated use of unceded Turtle Mountain Chippewa territory.

Despite this unstoppable overstepping of their boundaries, the Turtle Mountain band still refused to relocate. Although local Pembina real estate agent H. R. Vaughan made his living selling real estate to incoming European Americans, he felt outraged enough by their incursions and maltreatment of the Natives to complain to the commissioner of Indian Affairs. Vaughan protested about many white settlers "fast occupying" and "locating on lands" belonging to the Turtle Mountain Chippewa. He observed that the Indians complained about these incursions after a tribal delegation visited Washington, D.C., and had been advised that "when their lands were settled upon by the whites, they would be protected." If nothing happened soon to satisfy their desire for a reservation at or near Turtle Mountain, Vaughan feared troubles and depredations. The area federal agent, on the other hand, remained unaware of any "ill feeling." The Chippewa dreaded that "they may soon be driven from that country as they have been from" Pembina.[43] They feared that any abandonment of their territory would be seen by the federal government as an abdication of their rights.

The commissioner of Indian Affairs replied to Vaughan that "it is impossible to afford them relief without Congressional action." Previous bills mandating the removal of the Chippewa from Dakota Territory had failed. Therefore, the Turtle Mountain people "should be counseled to wait with patience and forbearance" and "trust the Government for their final protection."[44] Shortly after that advice, however, a petition from "the [European American] people of Pembina" complained about how the Chippewa contributed to the "great annoyance of the citizens." In an attempt to revive federal removal efforts, they requested that the Interior Department purchase the "lands claimed by the Pembina bands of Indians," and then relocate them to the White Earth agency in Minnesota.[45] Such requests put pressure on the Indian Affairs office to act accordingly.

A week later the Chippewa offered a counterproposal. Representatives of the "Turtle Mountain band of Chippewas and Mixed-bloods" petitioned Agent James McLaughlin at the Fort Totten Devils Lake agency. The delegation revealed the leadership and subdivisions within the band. Nine "Chippewa delegates" signed first. The mixed-

bloods signed in two groups: a Pembina/St. Joseph assemblage of sixteen, and a Turtle Mountain delegation of eleven. Little Shell III was
acknowledged as chief. His band numbered "about 550 lodges," most
of whom lived out "west in the prairie" (i.e., near Turtle Mountain),
while "forty lodges still lived in the vicinity of St. Joseph. The St. Joseph and Pembina mixed-bloods claimed to represent "250 families at
Pembina and St. Joseph," while another 500 lived out west with the
Turtle Mountain Métis.[46] They asked McLaughlin to use his influence
and pass along their request to the Secretary of the Interior and the
commissioner of Indian Affairs. Reflecting the consensual nature of
their tribal council, they made an appeal "after consulting each other in this our assembly." They defined their territorial boundaries by
citing prominent geographic markers, noting other tribes' agreement
with their demarcation.[47] The delegation asserted that they wanted
to retain "a certain portion of this Country for a reserve in which to
make our homes," making it clear that they would choose the reserved
tract, not the U.S. government.[48] Such an assertion exemplified tribal
sovereignty in action.

The reason for this request and its urgency derived from their
complaint that "the white people are trespassing on our lands."[49] The
delegation protested about European Americans cutting down two
thousand cords of wood per year along the north shore of Devils Lake,
entitling the Native peoples to perhaps $150,000 in compensatory
damages. Thirteen white families had already trespassed and settled in
this area. The same type of illegal incursion and harvesting also occurred at Turtle Mountain and Pembina Mountain. European Canadian interlopers had trespassed and begun hauling timber for building
back into Canada. Meanwhile, the tax assessors of Pembina County began harassing the Chippewa for payments from which they considered
themselves exempt and could not afford. As a consequence, the band
representatives stated emphatically that they "lived miserably" because
"all the game is gone" and "our country is being ruined.' They estimated that "perhaps in a year or two we may be driven out of our country."

If the government continued to ignore their plight, "what then will become of us? Where are we to seek a home?" They still believed that a "good and just" "Great Father" would protect and help them.[50]

In a subsequent letter to McLaughlin nine months later, they filed the same complaints, adding the despairing note that "we are helpless to protect our own rights."[51] Once again they appealed to the United States to live up to its trust responsibilities. While most of the Indian policy echelon seemed to acknowledge the Turtle Mountain Chippewa claim and sympathize with their awful situation, it failed to prod the federal government into responsible action. This lack of any satisfactory resolution illustrated the arbitrary nature of federal policy. Instead of a timely and direct resolution of long-standing problems, government decision-makers avoided or suppressed difficult issues until a major crisis erupted.[52]

, While federal policymakers seemed paralyzed, western politicians assuming offices of national political prominence acted aggressively against the Chippewa band's interests. Richard Franklin Pettigrew had started out in Dakota Territory as a surveyor. He exploited the vital knowledge learned from his trade into real estate and land speculation interests. The acquisition of properties soon led him into railroad boosterism and territorial Republican politics. In 1880, he won election as the territorial delegate to Congress. From this powerful position, he used his influence to control political patronage and create new opportunities for personal gain through railroad development and land speculation.[53]

Pettigrew served as the Dakota Territory delegate to Congress from 1881 to 1883, critical years in the political fate of the Turtle Mountain Chippewa and Métis. He began lobbying against the band's interests immediately. In May 1881, Pettigrew wrote to the CIA about the unresolved status of their land claim. His letter acknowledged that their territory comprised nine million acres "of the finest wheat lands in the world." Yet, as Alexander Ramsey had done at the Old Crossing treaty council back in 1863, Pettigrew denigrated their ownership rights because "they did not cultivate the soil." Pettigrew asserted incorrectly that the Chippewa had only inhabited this area "part of the time since 1863." Based on these two baseless allegations, he declared that "these Indians never owned this country." Instead, it belonged to the Red Lake and Pembina Chippewa, and they had ceded it to the United States in the Old Crossing treaties. Although he claimed that the "spirit of the treaty had been carried out," Pettigrew ignored that the actual extent of the treaty cession extended no farther west than St. Joseph, and no reservation had been created for the Pembina band.[54] Just as most of the Pembina and Turtle Mountain Chippewa had feared, Pettigrew used the removal of some band members to the White Earth, Minnesota, reservation as a pretext for dismissing the entire band's land claim.

Without any reliable information, such as that gathered by Agent McLaughlin at Devils Lake, Pettigrew alleged that the Turtle Mountain band only amounted to "250 Indians led by a few adventurous half-breeds." Such "wandering vagabonds" could not lay a rightful claim to any lands because, as he assumed, "this vast country has never been the home of any tribe of Indians." It had always been a "common hunting ground" for a variety of northern plains tribes, and if any had a superior claim, it would be the Assiniboine. One can only wonder if Pettigrew thought anyone would believe all of these contradictory allegations. He probably did not care. As a Dakota Territory politician in Congress, who in the nation's capital could or would challenge him? He maintained that "250 Indians should not be recognized" because "they have no title to these nine million acres." Pettigrew's bottom line embodied two precepts. First, the Turtle Mountain Chippewa should be removed to White Earth in Minnesota, and second, "a separate reservation should not be established for these Indian under any circumstances."[55]

Pettigrew's deceptions stemmed from the fact that plenty of potential voters waited eagerly to access this unceded territory. Foregoing the need for any legal instrument, like a treaty, to achieve his desired end, Pettigrew declared that "this empire . . . ought to be opened up to settlement immediately." He acknowledged that the Turtle Mountain Chippewa had protested about "a large number of [non-Native] people . . . now residing upon these lands," and predicted that "several thousand people" would move in as soon as the lands had been surveyed and opened for settlement by the General Land Office. According to Pettigrew, obviously representing other like-minded petitioners in northern Dakota Territory, nothing should "stop the progress and development of that great country because of the pretended claim of a few thieving vagabonds."[56] Unfortunately for the Turtle Mountain Chippewa, powerful individual politicians had significant influence on federal policymakers. Pettigrew helped set the agenda, frame the debate, control the discourse, and provide the data. His influence illustrates how federal policy was shaped by local politicians to better serve their own personal priorities and the interests of their European American constituents, rather than Native peoples.[57]

In response to Pettigrew's charges, the commissioner of the GLO asked the commissioner of Indian Affairs to look into whether any other tribe claimed, or if the United States had acquired title to, the Turtle Mountain region in northern Rolette and Bottineau Counties in Dakota Territory. The essential question remained whether the "Indian title" to the area north and northwest of Devils Lake had ever been extinguished legally. The CIA concluded that the "Indian title to the lands in question has never been extinguished by treaty or otherwise."[58]

Supporting evidence derived from the Old Crossing treaty of 1863 when Alexander Ramsey confirmed the Pembina Chippewa's retention of lands west of the Red River cession. As noted previously, subsequent Commissioners of Indian Affairs confirmed this understanding. But the acting commissioner acknowledged plans for a renewed federal government effort to consolidate via legislation eight Minnesota Chippewa tribes and the Turtle Mountain Chippewa upon the White Earth reservation.[59] With each group ceding their lands to the United States, substantial tracts in Minnesota and Dakota Territory could then be opened to legal European American settlement.

The impetus for the inclusion of the Chippewa bands of Dakota Territory in this consolidation effort came from Pettigrew.[60] By selecting some information from Ramsey's 1863 treaty report out of context, he repeated the conventional wisdom that the Red River comprised the western extent of "Chippewa country." According to Pettigrew, no Plains-Ojibwe or Chippewa lived in Dakota Territory. They acted only as nomadic hunters in contention with other tribes over lucrative buffalo grounds. Since the 1863 treaty, they only "pretend to claim" ownership "of this great country."[61] All Chippewa bands with any legitimacy to claims of "Indian title" resided in Minnesota, Wisconsin, and Michigan. But, Ramsey's negotiations in 1851 and 1863 with the Pembina Chippewa for territory west of the Red River and refuted Pettigrew's ahistorical allegation. Although previously Pettigrew had claimed that the Assiniboine had the best claim on northern Dakota, he now alleged that "it is a well known fact that this country belonged to the Sioux for ages."[62] When in doubt, it seemed that any other northern plains tribe would serve his purpose to marginalize the Chippewa out of existence.

Pettigrew also derided all subsequent Pembina and Turtle Mountain Chippewa land rights as invalid because of the predominance of "half-bloods" among them. Often if mixed-bloods lived with Native tribes, they shared any treaty-derived reserves or benefits. Yet if they distinguished themselves from their tribal relations, half-bloods could not be recognized as having "Indian title" under U.S. law. Even concessions of land or scrip did not convey recognition of Indigenous rights. Pettigrew attempted to define Turtle Mountain mixed-bloods as non–Native "citizens" who could only make their land claims as individuals in accordance with the provisions of homestead and pre-emption laws.[63] Such self-serving blood quantum categorizations became part of a pattern to divide and diminish the Turtle Mountain Chippewa in an attempt to uncouple their Métis members with "no rights to be respected."[64]

Pettigrew not only ignored Ramsey's 1863 report about Chippewa land retention west of the thirty-mile Red River cession. He stated falsely that Ramsey reported "the Chippewa ceded *all* their lands west of the Red River by the treaty of 1863."[65] Pettigrew's conclusions cannot be reconciled with the material facts cited. He manipulated contradictory information to discredit the valid land claim of the Turtle Mountain Chippewa. Pettigrew made his case on behalf of "several hundred" American citizens who had already settled on these unceded lands. The denial of Native land rights served to bolster the economic and political advantages of himself, his European American constituents, and various land-associated speculation and railroad interests.

The Turtle Mountain band not only faced the vagaries of federal policy or the disinformation of territorial politicians. Equally dangerous involvement from other concerns arose to pressure the federal policy apparatus into serving private interests. In 1880, Lt. H. M. Creel, an officer in the 7th Cavalry, undertook an assignment from Ft. Totten to survey a portion of the nearby Devils Lake region known as Graham's Island.[66] Both the governor of Dakota Territory and the Secretary of the Interior wanted to expand the military reservation at Fort Totten further north and west from Devils Lake to incorporate the valuable timber lands of Graham's Island, and keep them out of the hands of encroaching squatters.[67] Apparently neither official had any concern that such an enlargement would intrude illegally on unceded Turtle Mountain Chippewa land. While on this assignment, Creel noted the "fine agricultural lands lying north and west" of Devils Lake. He stated that these lands "attracted my attention." When he asked why they had not been settled, he was told "it was Chippewa land."[68]

Yet it seems that Creel was not an ordinary cavalry lieutenant involved in a minor surveying detail. He was an ambitious young man playing a leading role in a townsite speculation syndicate. He used his family's political connections to arrange military postings so he could be involved in "trying to open up for settlement" a "tract of land" near Devils Lake, Dakota Territory. He envisioned that the Turtle

Mountain and Mouse (Souris) River country farther north and west would contribute significantly to the commerce of Devils Lake in the very near future. As a result of his surveying expedition, he made an inquiry to George W. Manypenny, who had been CIA from 1853 to 1857. Conveniently, Manypenny was his father's first cousin. During his tenure as CIA, Manypenny had communicated and met with Father G. A. Belcourt. The priest conveyed the "griefs and demands" of thousands of "half-breeds and Indians of Pembina County" when it was still part of Minnesota Territory, and extended as far west as the White Earth River, which coincided with the western periphery of the Turtle Mountain Chippewa territory.[69]

Although Creel did not record Manypenny's response to his query, the ex-commissioner would have known from his communications with Belcourt that his nephew's allegation that no Indigenous people had a "valid claim" over this territory was untrue. The priest had consistently informed various federal policy officials that the Pembina and Turtle Mountain Chippewa had desired a land cession treaty with the federal government to secure land title and protection from encroachment since 1851.[70] Perhaps this led Creel to also contact Senator William Windom of Minnesota, chairman of the Indian Affairs Committee, and F. R. Pettigrew, Dakota Territory delegate to the House of Representatives. Windom had been a big booster of bonanza farming and its high profit margin. He also supported authorization for the Northern Pacific Railroad to secure its construction bonds—at the inflated rate of $2.50 per acre—by mortgages on half of its land grant.[71] Creel identified Pettigrew correctly as a potential ally. The territorial representative had been a surveyor, land speculator, railroad booster, and "a witness before both Houses of Congress on the proposition to open up this land for settlement."[72]

Like Pettigrew, Creel contended that the Turtle Mountain Chippewa band had "no valid claim" to the lands "north and west of Devils Lake." He misrepresented the extent of the Pembina Chippewa band's land cession in the Old Crossing treaty of 1863–1864. Creel claimed

incorrectly that the western boundary of the cession, as defined specifically in Article Two, "by inference," meant "the western boundary of
*all* lands to which they made claim."[73] Such an inference conveniently included the remaining 9.5 million acres of unceded Pembina and
Turtle Mountain Chippewa territory under dispute.

Creel used a newspaper editorial by Joseph A. Wheelock from
the *St. Paul Pioneer Press* to "prosecute his claims." Because Wheelock
had been the secretary for Governor Ramsey's treaty commission back
in 1863, Creel tried to turn his anecdotal eighteen-year-old reminis-
cence into a material fact that would supersede the actual treaty language. Wheelock claimed that during the Old Crossing negotiations,
Little Shell II ceded all the Chippewa lands "west to the setting sun."
In addition, Wheelock asserted that Ramsey's opposite recollection,
which confirmed federal recognition of the legitimacy and unceded
nature of Chippewa territory west of the treaty cession, "was mistak-
en due to lapse of time."[74] Yet the treaty journal and the treaty itself
invalidated Wheelock's memory and verified Ramsey's remembrance
and Little Shell's position.

To further his own economic agenda, Creel attempted to further
discredit the claim. He stated that Little Shell II, who had signed the
treaty, lived with his band in Pembina County, Dakota Territory, at
the date of signing. Because this region embodied part of the ceded
territory, Creel assumed that somehow Little Shell forfeited all Pembina and Turtle Mountain Chippewa lands. Whether Creel pinpointed
the location of Little Shell's band accurately or not, at the time of the
treaty signing it remained irrelevant to what Article Two defined as
the land cession. In addition to Ramsey, others in the federal policy echelon disagreed with Creel's statement that "in my opinion the
[Chippewa's Indian] title was not 'imperfect,' but absolutely void."[75]

Perhaps realizing that he was pushing too far beyond the precedents and practices of federal policy, Lt. Creel changed course in a
subsequent letter from his total denigration of the Turtle Mountain
land tenure claim. At least he now conceded that the "Indian title" for

the country to the north and west of Fort Totten to the international boundary had not been "extinguished." He stated accurately that these "almost starving" Indians "want a small reservation in Rolette County." In line with the policy that Natives would pay for their own "civilization," despite a large federal budget surplus, Creel deployed a more palatable proposal to a stingy Congress. The proceeds from any Turtle Mountain Chippewa land cession "would aid in their conversion to civilized agricultural pursuits."[76]

Like Creel, the incoming European American settlers persisted in petitioning Pettigrew and Congress to open the Turtle Mountain tract for settlement. They acknowledged that "settlers have already entered upon said lands," while evading the illegal nature of such activities. Knowing the unlawful nature of their enterprise, Creel inquired into "the nature of the unceded Chippewa lands." Without acknowledging his personal involvement, he stated that "various soldiers and settlers claimed that no Chippewas ever lived on portions of land north of Devils Lake, or desired to do so."[77] Although Creel continued to assert that the Chippewa had no claim on this area, he still made the contradictory appeal to the government for a treaty to extinguish their "Indian title." He knew that without such a legal instrument, his company's land titles for Creel City and its environs could not be secured, and they might lose their claim and investment. Creel's syndicate continued to justify their actions in two ways. First, this land was too "valuable for agricultural purposes" to "forbid settlement." And second, "a very limited number of Indians are in possession of said tract."[78] Claims of imperfect title, superior land use, and demographic superiority often trumped the rule of law regarding federal policy.

Agent McLaughlin at Devils Lake (Fort Totten) remained the sounding board for both sides. The Turtle Mountain chief Kaishpau wrote to McLaughlin regarding "rumors" that a "government agent visited Pembina and told the Indians that [their] territory would be bought by the Great Father." This "agent" also told them that McLaughlin "had nothing to do with the Indians at Turtle Mountain."

The so-called "agent" was probably Creel, since these erroneous understandings match closely with his other documented misstatements. Kaishpau asked for an official refutation, fearing "that my people may be misled."[79] It was likely that Creel was one of the "whites continually troubling me with inquiries regarding anticipated action of the [Interior] Department" mentioned by McLaughlin. Fortunately for the Turtle Mountain band, McLaughlin served them well in his role as an honest broker of competing interests.

Often Turtle Mountain Chippewa delegations made the ninety-mile trek to visit McLaughlin to pass along their grievances to higher level federal officials. They had "great confidence" in his fairness and desire to protect them and their interests. The agent complained to the Indian Office that numerous and hostile "squatters" had converged on Devils Lake, making unsubstantiated land claims and cutting down valuable timber, as the Turtle Mountain band had charged. Major J. S. Conrad, the post commander at Fort Totten, confirmed the agent's assessment of the situation. Although more concerned with the fort's timber reserve than Native rights, Conrad confirmed to his superiors that an organized effort existed "to hold . . . the timber land in that locality for speculative purposes."[80] McLaughlin added that all these actions encroached illegally on "Indian country" since the "Indian title" had never been extinguished.[81]

Yet more than one way to abrogate unceded Native land prevailed without resorting to a negotiated legal agreement. Turtle Mountain Chippewa solicitor J. B. Bottineau dreaded that nobody within the federal government would "protect our interest against designing men [with] selfish motives."[82] Senator Windom responded to Creel's inquiry, not by requesting any further investigation into the validity of the lieutenant's contention, but by asking the Interior Department what legislation "would be expedient" to access the territory in question for settlement. Creel and his cronies anticipated the pending appointment of Senator Henry M. Teller of Colorado as the new Secretary of the Interior.[83] They recognized Teller as a powerful western politician sympathetic to their interests.

It seems that Creel, Pettigrew, and Windom wanted to short circuit any process that might investigate the material facts or legal issues of the Turtle Mountain Chippewa land claim. They used their influence to pressure federal officials into expediting the desired outcome of opening unceded lands to settlement. As a result, Commissioner of Indian Affairs Hiram Price passed along Creel's contentions to the Secretary of the Interior. Price concluded, correctly, that "the object of Lieutenant Creel appears to be to secure legislation looking to the extinguishment of the Indian title to a vast area of country lying in the northern part of the Territory of Dakota."[84]

Price also provided his new boss, Secretary Teller, with a response to Lt. Creel's inquiry, along with an update on his 1881 report on the "Turtle Mountain Band of Chippewas in Dakota."[85] He clarified the heart of the legal struggle by acknowledging the Turtle Mountain band's petitions, memorials, and delegations. Their actions demonstrated that the "unsettled condition of affairs with these Indian[s] has long been a matter of deep concern . . . to the Indian[s] themselves."[86] While the commissioner claimed that the BIA shared their concerns, the outcome desired by each party diverged significantly. The federal government had vacillated for eighteen years between 1864 and 1882. Only the "fast flowing" influx of European Americans now made it a pressing concern for the Interior Department.[87]

The commissioner also mentioned the BIA's on-going efforts to remove the Turtle Mountain Chippewa to White Earth, Minnesota. He did not mention his own role in attempting to withhold treaty-promised rations or arranging for their exclusive distribution to be located inconveniently at White Earth, in an attempt to compel removal. At least Price conceded that most of the Pembina and Turtle Mountain Chippewa "steadfastly resisted such removal, lest the abandonment of the country claimed by them might be looked upon as a willing relinquishment of their title."[88] With this observation, the commissioner honed-in on the main problem. "Prominent among their troubles is the uncertainty on their part as to the view held by the government relative to the status of the lands claimed by them, and the purposes of the department in the matter of their ultimate disposal." As the band kept asserting, their unextinguished Indigenous domain consisted of "the tract of country inhabited and claimed by them . . . north and northwest of Devils Lake" totaling roughly 9,500,000 acres.[89]

In response to the stratagems of Creel, Dakota Territory Governor Ordway, a political rival of Pettigrew, telegraphed Secretary of the Interior Teller. Ordway stated that Pettigrew and Lt. Creel acted as "land sharks" engaged in fraudulent scrip purchases, while paying monthly wages to dummy entry men or "squatters" to secure unceded land illegally. These phony claimants looking for quick profit also sought to keep the valuable timber and lands on the north side of Devils Lake out of the hands of "honest settlers" looking for a home. The governor called for an investigation of this "unlawful combination."[90] A subsequent report by Devils Lake agent John W. Cramsie noted that the squatters in the employ of the speculators "violently drive away real settlers" by damaging or destroying their houses and improvements.[91] This conflict demonstrated that territorial development also pitted different groups of European Americans against each other politically and economically.

From this example we can better grasp the political context of policy formulation and implementation. We cannot understand the politics of tribal-federal relations unless we know what the struggle was about.[92] The increased lobbying to remove the Turtle Mountain Chippewa did not constitute a new policy, nor should it be seen as a policy at all. Removal was just another federal solution looking for an "Indian problem." The real problem in Dakota Territory during the 1880s centered on the fact that it was not the Native American who was vanishing, but the frontier. Because the Turtle Mountain Chippewa laid claim to nine million acres in north-central Dakota, many competing non-Native interests wanted them out of the way. The Native population had declined, but so had the supply of desirable "free land." This created serious problems for speculators, other economic concerns, territorial politicians, and the Interior Department. Their in-fighting helps us better understand the dysfunctional nature of federal policy.

Within this context, Pettigrew wrote to Teller asking that Secretary Schurz's 1880 Interior Department order "withdrawing this country from settlement be revoked."[93] Secretary Teller responded by ordering the GLO to investigate the status of northern Dakota Territory lands regarding whether they should be made available or withdrawn from European American settlement. Such a prompt reply to Pettigrew contrasted sharply with the department's delayed responses toward similar appeals from the Turtle Mountain Chippewa. Yet, at least one positive development acknowledged the validity of the band's land claim. The GLO confirmed that in August and September of 1880 they had informed their Grand Forks and Bismarck offices and the Surveyor General in Dakota Territory, that non-Natives should not be allowed to acquire unceded and unsurveyed lands in northern Dakota. This action somewhat acknowledged the "alleged rights" of the Turtle Mountain band. Thus, no legal homestead or preemption entries had been made during the intervening two years.[94]

All of these developments forced Teller to confer with his commissioner of Indian Affairs. With all the federal authority vested in him, Price refuted Creel's misstatements, and made the most explicit acknowledgement of Chippewa rights on record. He affirmed that:

> These lands have never been ceded to the United States, and the claim of the Turtle Mountain band to ownership, is based upon continuous occupation by them and their ancestors for many generations. That the Indian title to the country in question has never been extinguished or successfully disputed cannot be denied, and according to the theory that has been adopted by the government it would seem that *these Indians have all the original rights in an unceded territory*.[95]

Finally, after a decade of Turtle Mountain Chippewa political engagement in the face of halfhearted federal responses, the head of the Bureau of Indian Affairs recognized the rights of the band and the merits of their case. Price went on to emphasize "that these Indians are justly entitled to recognition of their claim on the part of the government to the lands in question, *and the files and records abound in evidence showing that this office has long recognized such claim.*[96] The commissioner's recognition of material facts confirmed by sources of unquestioned accuracy constituted a major breakthrough. Although he did not reveal the origins of these sources, much credit should go to the various Chippewa and Métis chiefs, headmen, councilors, warriors, delegates, and their solicitor for creating a substantial public record on their own behalf. Collectively they demonstrated the importance of Native insistence on original possession as the root of "Indian title." In this high-level official report to the Secretary of the Interior, Price acknowledged the essential legal criteria for federal recognition of the Turtle Mountain Chippewa's legitimate land tenure.

This conclusive determination should have settled any current or future controversies. Even in the post-treaty era after 1871, both precedent and practice dictated the course of action recommended by Price. The United States should send commissioners to negotiate "with the Pembina band of Chippewas and such other Indians [the Turtle Mountain band] as should properly take part in such negotiations" for a land cession agreement. The band's representatives could consent to relinquish their unceded lands and the "Indian title" to them. In return the government would authorize them to "retain in a compact body" an approximately 500,000-acre portion of their Indigenous territory for a "tract sufficiently large to secure to them allotments in severalty for their permanent settlement."[97]

But these terms did not align with what the Turtle Mountain band wanted. Five years before the General Allotment (Dawes) Act of 1887, the Interior Department, BIA, and Congress attempted to impose the panacea of allotment to forestall the creation of any new sizeable reservations or break up existing ones. At least a reservation, held in trust for the Turtle Mountain band, provided "some provision . . . for their protection" by the federal government.[98] In addition to negotiating the exact size and location of the reservation, the Natives counted on a "share in the benefits arising from such sale" of their lands. A written agreement, signed by the negotiators and witnesses from both sides, would confirm the pact. If Congress ratified the agreement, the formal legal process could have ended satisfactorily for both sides. The Turtle Mountain band's nearly 500,000-acre reservation, comprising over twenty townships, would have been large enough for current and future generations of the small number of "full-bloods" and the much larger number of Métis.

As usual, the federal government desired to profit as much as possible. To get to the bottom line for Congress and the Secretary of the Interior, Price presented a few cost calculations. The range of "suitable compensation" ranged from twenty-five cents to $1.25 per acre.[99] His estimates focused not on the costs incurred from purchasing Native land, but the potential proceeds from reselling it. The commissioner based his figures on a cession of 8,500,000 acres, accounting for a 500,000-acre reservation, and the 500,000 acres already appropriated for the Fort Totten reservation, without delving into the legalities of such an appropriation. The bills before Congress considered "suitable compensation" for 8,500,000 acres to be the annual sum of $50,000 for twenty years, or almost twelve cents per acre (or less if considering the deferred payments and the inevitable increase in land values in a seller's market).

Instead of the promised "just and equitable" terms and conditions, the federal government proposed a lucrative scheme to "reimburse itself out of the proceeds of the sale of the ceded lands."[100] Considering the various interest-bearing calculations made by Commissioner Price, ranging from a low of twenty-five cents per acre to the minimum price for public lands of $1.25 per acre, the twelve-cent proposal bore no relationship to fair market values. Another unmentioned factor made the deal even sweeter for the government. Based on the high-end estimated population figure of 2,500 for the Turtle Mountain band, allotting 500,000 acres into 160-acre tracts would leave one-third of their land as "surplus," which would revert to the public domain for government resale. No wonder Price concluded confidently that the modest amount of "assistance" extended to the Turtle Mountain band "could be afforded in the manner suggested."[101]

At the fair, yet still low, market price of fifty cents an acre, the Turtle Mountain band would have received $4,250,000. Earning 3 percent interest, it would yield $127,500 annually. At the lower and far-below-market price of twenty-five cents an acre, the band would have been compensated with $2,125,000, bearing a 3 percent annual return of $63,750, which matched the projected annual administrative costs.[102] To put the above figures in perspective, Price pointed out the unlikely maximum payout based upon the minimum sale price of public lands at $1.25 per acre, resulting in the "very great" total amount of $10,625,000, or $318,750 in interest per year. Given the government's estimates of the Turtle Mountain band's population from 300 to 2,500, any payment between seventy-five cents and $1.25 per acre would have been able to provide adequate annuities and rations to those who could not adapt to the new economic realities and those who wanted to attempt the transition to farming and ranching. In an era of a large budget surplus, the federal government could have lived with this simple, low-cost, and equitable solution, while fulfilling its national economic development goals in the region. Eight and one-half million acres of ceded Native land just beyond the vicinity of the bonanza farming "boom" would have entered the public domain. Although already encroached upon illegally, these lands would have been surveyed and opened to homesteading, settlement, and wheat farming during a time of dwindling new frontiers with prime agricultural lands.

But this plausible scenario, as outlined by some in the BIA, fell victim to the biases, lack of political will, and irrational chaos inherent in federal policy. Price's assessment became the paramount issue of contention within the federal bureaucracy instead of working toward a fair settlement with the Turtle Mountain Chippewa. This misplaced focus proved that the arbitrary nature of federal policy decision-making did "not resolve problems well."[103] Despite the consistent recognition by BIA officials of the legality of the Turtle Mountain band's claim and promises of a "just and equitable" resolution, the bureau really wanted these Native peoples to disappear.

Instead of upholding federal law, and fulfilling its self-proclaimed guardianship responsibilities, the BIA contrived to undermine the legal rights of the Turtle Mountain Chippewa. Perhaps influenced by lobbying from Creel and Pettigrew, the federal bureaucracy persisted in its preference for removal. Inadequate compensation offers and threats of allotment tried to compel the Turtle Mountain band to remove itself to White Earth despite the complete inadequacy of the one township set aside for them.[104] This proposal ignored the fact that the band had no desire to relocate, rightly fearing that any sign of abandonment would be seized upon as a pretext for extinguishing all their legal claims. Since the government acknowledged the facts and legalities that upheld the position of the Turtle Mountain Chippewa, some other contrivance had to be selected from the federal policy grab-bag.

Discussions continued between the BIA and Congress over the specific wording in the pending relinquishment bill. Commissioner Price acknowledged the absolute authority of Congress over Native affairs by noting that "the consent of the [Turtle Mountain] Indians" was not a "prerequisite condition" for the "opening and settlement" of their lands.[105] This declaration coincided with Secretary Teller's dismissal of any need for tribal consent on the grounds that Natives must submit to federal authority. To evade the questionable legalities inherent in the exercise of plenary power, Price felt obliged to offer Congress some "potent reasons that may be properly urged to justify [such a] proposed action."[106]

Price utilized one of the most timeworn federal policy excuses. By noting that "a large immigration, attracted by the profits of wheat-raising [had] poured into Northeastern Dakota," the commissioner resorted to the demographic deluge justification.[107] Price mentioned specifically the counties of Pembina, Cavalier, Ramsey, and Grand Forks. Pembina and Grand Forks lay along the Red River and within the Old Crossing treaty cession of 1863. While Pembina and Grand Forks qualified legally for government surveys and non-Native settlement, Cavalier and Ramsey Counties remained west of that cession, and within the unceded territory of the Pembina and Turtle Mountain Chippewa. Their location within "Indian country" should have precluded any non-Native immigration or settlement. The CIA failed to make this crucial legal distinction. Moreover, he justified the fact that portions of these counties had been "overrun with settlers" on the unlawful grounds that these squatters comprised "a worthy class eager to cultivate the soil."[108] The racial bias of federal policy could not have been stated more boldly.

The legality of "settlement" did not matter if it secured "the largest returns at a minimum cost."[109] Price reiterated that the "Indian title" of the Pembina and Turtle Mountain Chippewa "has long been recognized" by the BIA "on the ground of original Indian rights," and that these lands "have never been ceded to the United States." Nevertheless, he also acknowledged that "numerous petitions and appeals have been received from settlers." Like Pettigrew, who represented their interests in Congress, they held that "the Indians have no real title, and that their claim should not be respected." Popular anti-Native attitudes provided federal policymakers with a convenient excuse to displace Native communities. As summarized by Price, "the Indians themselves have never of late years made any good use of these lands" since hunters working for, or conveyed by, the railroads killed off the last of the Dakota buffalo herds in 1881 and 1882.[110]

Even this calamity did not deter the ever-resourceful people at Turtle Mountain. The advent of the railroads into the northern plains, which escalated the slaughter of the bison and curtailed their Red River cart commerce, also created a new low-end economic niche for some of the Plains-Ojibwe and Métis. They entered the buffalo bone scavenger trade. Eyewitness accounts remarked upon the "white pastures" of sun-bleached bison skeletal remains, and many photographs captured the mountains of bones awaiting shipment at various rail-heads.[111] Once thought of as a useless waste product left behind in the procurement of buffalo hides and meat, the heavy freight hauling capability of railroads linked to eastern processing factories turned it into a marketable commodity (fertilizer, glue, or charcoal). The extraction of this resource brought much-needed early profits to the railroads. At $6.00 to $8.00 per ton, it also created a competitive money-making opportunity for Natives and newcomers on the northern plains.[112]

Originally lying within Turtle Mountain Chippewa territory, the St. Paul, Minneapolis, and Manitoba railheads at both Devils Lake (southeastern corner) and Minot (southwestern corner), northern Dakota Territory became became regional buffalo bone depots. Harvesting and carting buffalo bones to these nearby railroad towns enabled many Turtle Mountain Métis and Chippewa to earn a living. As they had during the buffalo hunts, they organized themselves into informal bands of up to fifty families to gather bones during extended excursions. The economic motives behind this proto-capitalist commerce remained linked with their culture's customary non-economic motives. The bone trade prolonged their bison-based lifestyle, subsistence, culture, and self-sufficiency for a brief period from 1881–1891. By the time the Panic of 1893 curtailed the market, this non-renewable resource had been depleted, and the profitable large-scale commerce in buffalo bones in northern North Dakota ended. European American settlers collected bones on their land claims while denying access to Native gatherers. Yet, even after the bottom dropped out of this market, local newspaper reports confirmed that some Natives and "half-breeds" from the Turtle Mountain country still gathered and transported bones to try and make ends meet in the face of near or actual starvation.[113]

This economic adaptability and persistence created much consternation among federal policy officials. Although Commissioner Price stated repeatedly throughout various reports that the Chippewa refused to abandon their territory and conceded that their steadfastness "entitled them to some respect," his mischaracterization of their land use attempted to convey the false impression that these Native Americans had abandoned their country.[114] However rational this assessment may have seemed in a capitalist context, lack of "good use" did not preclude the legality of "Indian title" or authorize non-Native squatting in "Indian country." The Supreme Court decision of *Mitchel v. United States* in 1835 rejected the validity of the "useful occupancy" legal argument. The Court ruled that Native "hunting grounds were as much in their actual possession as the cleared fields of the whites."[115] Although the BIA recognized "the ground of original Indian rights," unlike the courts it privileged European American assertions of proper use rights and occupancy (i.e., squatting) at the expense of legal "Indian title."

Pulling out one of the oldest and most inaccurate negative stereotypes about Indigenous peoples, Price reverted to the worn-out assertion about the "vastness of the area claimed by these wandering people."[116] This litany of allegations led the CIA to contradict his previous statements and go beyond the material facts of the case. As another rationalization for disregarding their claim, he alleged that the Pembina and Turtle Mountain Chippewa lacked "any definite knowledge respecting their original rights against various other tribes" in the region.[117] Such a deliberate misrepresentation ignored the Prairie du Chien and first Sweet Corn treaties of 1825, the follow-up Fond du Lac treaty of 1826, the second Sweet Corn treaty of 1858, the Pembina and Red Lake treaty of 1863, and the Sisseton-Wahpeton Sioux treaty of 1867. All of these compacts acknowledged repeated and consistent Native territorial demarcation and U.S. legal recognition of a clearly defined Turtle Mountain band of Pembina Chippewa domain.

To validate their claims of adverse possession at these treaty councils, they often recounted how they had defended their territorial integrity against other tribes. Yet Price stated that "no attempt has been made [by the Natives] to keep settlers from occupying" their territory.[118] In a reversal of the usual "savagery" accusation, the CIA now blamed the Turtle Mountain Chippewa for being too peaceful. The lack of "strictest surveillance . . . in respect to encroachments upon their lands" became the fault of their "shiftless [and] aimless" lifeways.[119] The federal government, with its ring of forts in Dakota Territory, absolved itself from any responsibility for allowing European immigrants to trespass on unceded Native lands. Allegedly, all of these considerations "lessen[ed] the respect that, under other conditions, might have been entertained in regard to their claim to title to the lands in question."[120] Obviously any "other conditions" would have been dismissed by the Indian Affairs bureaucracy with the same enthusiasm as that deployed by Commissioner Price.

While federal policymaking remained rigid and uninventive, it was neither unitary nor monolithic. Its lack of consistency created some spaces for the memorials, petitions, and delegations from Turtle Mountain to be heard and considered. Yet, it also forestalled any equitable settlement, while aiding even greater European American encroachment at the expense of the valid legal claims of the Turtle Mountain Chippewa. The BIA characterized tribal-federal conditions in north-central Dakota Territory as "unsettled." This dishonest understatement ignored the federal government's responsibility for allowing events on the ground to evade the law. The band's representatives correctly perceived that "the arbitrary will of the government's agents" failed to provide the "protection, peace, and tranquility" desired by the tribe.[121]

# CHAPTER 6

## Dispossession under the Cover of Law, 1882–1889

*There is ample evidence showing the merits of the claim*
*of the Turtle Mountain Indians.*[1]
—John B. Bottineau, Attorney, Turtle Mountain Indians

Given the preceding assertions by Commissioner of Indian Affairs Hiram Price, the anxieties of the Pembina and Turtle Mountain bands over their legal rights and chances of a just and equitable agreement seemed well founded. In the end, legal precedent lost out. The rationale for Commissioner Price's harmful interpretation of events on the ground epitomized the untrustworthy BIA policy towards the land claim and legal status of the Turtle Mountain Chippewa. Flawed understandings of federal law relating to Native title converged with incorrect statements of fact. Tribal attorney J. B. Bottineau protested about the "unfairness," inconsistency, and lack of evidence for Price's conclusions.[2]

The increased contention between the Turtle Mountain band (led by Chief Little Shell III, his council, and attorney Bottineau), against Dakota Territory and federal authorities led to the unilateral extinguishing of the tribe's "Aboriginal title" in exchange for a reservation. But no monetary compensation for the cession of over nine million lucrative acres was forthcoming. Despite the promise of an ample reservation by the BIA, the Secretary of the Interior decided otherwise. To expedite and attempt to legalize European American settlement, the Secretary acquiesced to the demands of Dakota Territory politicians and land speculators. They threw open Turtle Mountain Chippewa territory for non-Native settlement, leaving only a two-township reservation, inadequate for the band's existing population of 2,100, let alone future generations.[3] Tribal representatives rejected the federal government's actions as illegal and unjust.

From the perspective of the Turtle Mountain Chippewa, Price's 1882 report set this protracted process in motion. The BIA remained "strongly inclined to favor" pending legislation "in the interest of the very large immigration now seeking that country and the settlers already there."[4] The only minor concession stipulated that if any Natives had made improvements upon their lands, they could select an allotment and avoid dispossession. But the commissioner doubted that this stipulation would apply to anyone. He supposed that the Natives would "not be exacting" and "gladly accept any reasonable terms that may be offered them." The BIA still hoped for the removal of the Turtle Mountain band to existing Chippewa reservations in Minnesota. This attitude provided the policy framework for all subsequent legislation, Executive Orders, or tribal-federal agreements with the Turtle Mountain Chippewa for the next two decades. The BIA rummaged around the grab-bag of federal Indian policy until it found a way by which non-Natives could acquire land under the cover of law.

On April 28, 1882, Congress issued a report titled Turtle Mountain Band of Chippewa Indians to accompany bill H.R. 1885. The federal government attempted to induce the removal of the full-blood Chippewa to the White Earth reservation in Minnesota. Despite being destitute, the Natives refused to relocate. The proposed legislation endeavored "to provide for the support and civilization of the Turtle Mountain band of Pembina Chippewa Indians." It intended "to extinguish their title to lands claimed by them in the Territory of Dakota for *suitable compensation*."[5] The report's author, Congressman Nathaniel C. Deering, recommended passage of the bill with amendments. In reference to the 1863 Old Crossing treaty, his summary confirmed that the Pembina and Turtle Mountain Chippewa "ceded their lands in the Red River Valley."[6]

In contrast to Creel's misrepresentation, the summary confirmed that "they reserved the lands north and west of Devils Lake, in Dakota Territory" and "claimed title to about 9,000,000 acres of land." Yet with the demise of the buffalo, the local agent reported that the remaining "portion of the Pembina band" were "roaming over the territory" as "destitute vagabonds."[7] Unfortunately, "this vast country is now being occupied by hundreds of settlers, many of whom settled upon these lands before the Indian title was recognized by the Interior Department."[8] On this last point the report contradicted itself. The Old Crossing treaty recognized their Indian title, and as a result so did the BIA.

The proposed legislation failed to pass because it was "too low down on the calendar." According to Creel, "some fool member from North Carolina tacked on a rider," which further delayed consideration of the bill.[9] Creel had strong enough political connections via family ties to achieve the same goal of removing Native peoples by different political means. He accompanied Senators Plumb and Cockrell and Representative "Sunset" Cox, whom he identified as "a classmate of my father's," to a luncheon with President Arthur at the White House. Creel was so well connected that the president had extended his leave of absence, "over the head of the General of the Army," for twenty days to further his stay in Washington, D.C., to secure this statute. Failing to accomplish his goal via legislation, Creel presented Arthur with a legal brief. The brief contained the erroneous allegations noted above concerning "the status of the land claimed by Little Shell's Band of Turtle Mountain Indians." Creel reiterated that the band had "no valid claim," and proposed "that the land could be opened up for settlement by Executive Order."[10]

Failed legislation and rapid European America incursion, along with the diplomatic initiatives of Little Shell and J. B. Bottineau, mandated a thorough review of the Pembina and Turtle Mountain Chippewa/Métis situation by the Indian Affairs office. Congressional and CIA reports agreed on this fundamental need and the pivotal problem facing them. The Pembina and Turtle Mountain Chippewa inhabited and claimed "Indian title" to approximately nine and a half million acres of unceded territory north and northwest of Devils Lake.[11] No other Native American tribes had any contending or overlapping claims. The Chippewa bands and the United States agreed on these truths. The source of contention stemmed from the fact that "this vast country is now being occupied by hundreds of settlers, many of whom settled upon these lands before the Indian title" was extinguished by the federal government.[12]

Although Commissioner Price's convoluted assessment acknowledged that the Turtle Mountain Chippewa had a legitimate land claim and that the bureau should address their concerns, other federal officials remained indifferent. As a consequence, Bottineau railed against the deployment of the federal policy grab-bag against his peoples' rightful claim. He protested to the House Committee on Indian Affairs that "they have . . . been subjected to . . . half a dozen or more policies or regimes, under different administrations and agents, each having a policy . . . of his own."[13] The high turnover at all levels of the Indian Affairs bureaucracy left the Turtle Mountain Chippewa bewildered about their current status and future security. A newly appointed agent, commissioner of Indian Affairs, or Secretary of the Interior often had contrary opinions and took different actions than their predecessor. The federal government had deployed threats of removal to the White Earth reservation in Minnesota, hopes for a reservation within their unceded territory, or assurances that they would be better off with individual allotments within a reservation or on public domain land. The Turtle Mountain band of Chippewa resisted these government proposals "lest the abandonment of the country claimed by them might be looked upon as a willing relinquishment of their title" without a settlement or payment.[14] These observations illustrated the fallacy of trying to understand nineteenth century tribal-federal relations in terms of distinct policy eras. The Turtle Mountain Chippewa experienced the chaotic nature of federal policy and suffered the consequences.

The Department of the Interior and the BIA initiated actions before analysis and then sought the best rationale for the measures taken.[15] From the tribe's perspective, no consistent policies could be comprehended, let alone contended with successfully. Confronted by this confusing array of policy proposals to solve the "Indian problem," the Turtle Mountain Chippewa simultaneously faced increasing European American intrusion. While Dakota petitioners and more influential individuals like Creel and Pettigrew pressed Congress and the Interior Department to open the unceded territory of the Turtle Mountain Chippewa for European American settlement, continuing illegal incursions escalated tensions and threats of violence. A few months before Secretary Teller complied with their demands, a party of European Canadians crossed the international border and settled just east of the Turtle Mountains.[16] In a telling contrast to their protests concerning Canadian First Nations peoples or Métis, Indian Affairs officials, European American settlers, and local newspapers welcomed the European Canadians into Dakota Territory, stating that they should not be discouraged from squatting or homesteading.[17] The term "Canadian" only became a distinguishing and negative connotation when joined together with the words Chippewa, Cree, or "half-breed." This bias stemmed from the shared perception of federal policymakers that privileged settlers as "a worthy class" with an assumed superior entitlement over a "worthless set" of "Indians and breeds."[18] As a result, attorney Bottineau noted ironically that the "Indians had been driven out of their homes by the operation of the settlement laws."[19]

In lieu of a federally protected reservation, Chiefs Little Shell and Kaishpau decided to exercise effective sovereignty on behalf of their people. They assembled the tribal council, which declared that the Canadians had trespassed on their land. The chiefs and council, along with two hundred band members, met with the Canadians and told them to move out. They declared their land claim boldly by asserting a definable "Turtle Mountain Dakota Territory" and posting warning signs stating:

It is here forbidden to any white man to encroach upon this Indian land by settling on it before a treaty being made with the American government.[20]

The interlopers complied and went back across the border into Canada. Complications arose because their party included two U.S. citizens. Aggrieved by the audacity of such a declaration of Native entitlement and their involuntary departure, they and other incensed local European Americans threatened violence and petitioned the U.S. government.[21] They demanded federal government protection and that the unceded Turtle Mountain Chippewa lands be opened for settlement.

This minor confrontation occurred during a period when federal authorities had other Native-related priorities in the region. They concerned themselves mostly with unregulated Native border crossings. As they had long before 1872, when a physical demarcation denoted the international boundary, the Chippewa and Métis band members crossed back and forth on a regular basis. After all, the Turtle Mountains straddled the forty-ninth parallel. New tensions arose not just because they had expelled some European American and Canadian settlers in the area. They refused to pay any customs duties levied by the collector stationed at Pembina. Deputy Collector McCullum met with Chief Little Shell III and "200 half-breeds." The Customs officer claimed that only ten of seventy half-breeds who crossed the border had paid the required duty. Noting some disagreement within the band's leadership over this issue, the inspector reported that "Kaishpau favored obeying the law." Little Shell III objected to its imposition and refused to comply. He told the collector:

> these are all my lands and these are all my people. They shall pay no duties and respect no Customs officers. I have many more children across the line, and I shall bring them all over. We recognize no boundary line, and shall pass as we please."[22]

This incident heralded more than further European American encroachment and the intrusion of federal law into Turtle Mountain Indian territory. It demonstrated dissension within the leadership of the Turtle Mountain band between Little Shell III and Kaishpau over how to respond to such incursions. These fissures existed ten years before similar disunity would split the band apart during the maneuverings of federal agents in support of the McCumber Commission and the imposition of its "obnoxious agreement."[23]

As a result of these peaceful attempts by the Turtle Mountain Chippewa to exercise sovereignty and protect territorial integrity by ejecting trespassers, local and federal officials called out the army. They dispatched Major Conrad, along with forty to fifty soldiers from Fort Totten, to read Little Shell III the riot act. Apparently, the Major "rode up to Little Shell and told him that he would kill him if he attempted any injury to the white men."[24] A few days later, the expelled European American squatters returned without incident. At the same time the federal government relented in expanding the Fort Totten military reservation. Although it wanted to secure much-needed timber lands along the north shore of Devils Lake, it could not because of Creel's syndicate and other interlopers. "Most of the land proposed to be added to the said reservation was already occupied by squatters."[25] These related events illustrated the priorities of federal policy. Settler incursions received the protection of the military, while executive branch departments acquiesced to violations of federal land law.

In his study of Dakota Territory, historian Howard Lamar concluded that "speculators, developers and citizens all agreed that the federal government should subsidize frontier settlement."[26] Yet these sanctioned illegalities on behalf of squatters could no longer be hidden beneath the cover of law if the New York Times and regional newspapers continued to provide increased coverage to such minor affairs that usually went unnoticed by the press. They also increased the likelihood for some sort of violent clash, which would generate unwanted attention to federal policy neglect. Such mismanagement called for a quick fix. Secretary Teller was just the man to break all the rules to overcome this irresolution, while protecting European American interests in Dakota Territory at the expense of the Turtle Mountain Chippewa's appeals and well-being. It should be noted that his brother, James H. Teller, had been chosen as territorial Secretary in 1883.[27] Ignoring federal law, the Secretary of the Interior acquiesced to demands opening unceded country to European American settlement, without any negotiations with the Turtle Mountain band to secure a homeland or to extinguish legal title to their territory by consent. He also did not pass along Commissioner Price's somewhat favorable report to Congress. Teller's concealment of findings that contradicted his own views suggests a deliberate attempt to pursue undisclosed political objectives contrary to federal law. Without Price's report, Congress would exercise its plenary authority based upon the lobbying and disinformation of Pettigrew and Creel, rather than the differing and more authoritative assessments of the BIA.[28]

As a U.S. Senator from Colorado and Secretary of the Interior from 1882 to 1885, Teller's policies generally favored the political and economic interests of men like Pettigrew and Creel. Nevertheless, Teller held contradictory views on policy. Because he is often cited as a critic of the 1887 Dawes Act and its tribal land allotment provisions, some scholars have concluded incorrectly that he was more supportive of Native land rights than the eastern self-proclaimed "friends of the Indian." A closer look at his political career indicates that Teller remained as eager as allotment proponents to have tribal lands pass into non-Native hands. He advocated different means to the same end. On May 1, 1882, Pettigrew wrote to Teller and asked "that the order of your department withdrawing [Turtle Mountain] country from settlement be revoked."[29]

In response, on October 4, 1882, Teller directed the General Land Office (the federal agency that administered public domain lands) to:

> revoke the action "by which this land had been withheld from the practical operation of the settlement laws, and to restore the same to the public domain," but "subject to the restriction" of the Turtle Mountain Chippewa making any "*improvements*" or "attempt[ing] to make *permanent location* on any of said lands," and that "such Indians shall be *protected* by having their lands withheld from white settlement until they could have an *opportunity to secure title.*"[30]

The federal government failed to keep its promises to protect improvements or secure legal title to tribal lands. Instead, the commissioner of the General Land Office informed the Surveyor of Dakota about Secretary Teller's decision "throwing open" to settlement under the homestead and preemption laws "the lands in Dakota Territory lying north and west of Devils Lake, *better known as Turtle Mountain lands*."[31] The Turtle Mountain Chippewa protested that their unceded lands "were not withdrawn from white settlement to *protect* them." "It was *all* thrown open to settlers without any . . . restriction or regard to these Indian occupants, [and these] tracts have nearly all been taken away from them by white settlers."[32] This bewildering unilateral action by the Interior Department threw open to European American settlement over nine million acres of "good wheat land," "without any consideration to these Indians" or "payment of any kind."[33] Such a maneuver violated "the ground of original Indian rights" and all customary and legal practices by which the federal government secured title to tribal land through negotiations or purchase by consent, not by decree.[34]

Most blatantly, it violated the "Indian disclaimer" provision in the Dakota Territory enabling act of Congress. This proviso stated that "*nothing*" could "impair the rights of persons or *property*" of the Natives within the territory, "so long as such rights shall remain unextinguished by treaty" with the United States.[35] Unceded Native country constituted "no part of the territory of Dakota." For such Indigenous lands to be included within the "territorial limits or jurisdiction" required "the consent of said tribe."[36] This requirement could not be more explicit.

As noted by political scientists David Wilkins and Tsianina Lomawaima, "disclaimer clauses confirm[ed] the tribal nation-to-federal nation relationship."[37] These provisos illustrated how occasionally the assertion of the plenary authority of Congress over Indian Affairs, at the expense of local jurisdictions, recognized the inherent legal standing of Native peoples. No local (e.g., taxes) or national (e.g., GLO land laws or BIA allotment policies) "regulations" regarding Native "lands, property or other rights" could go into effect without tribal "assent."

After Teller made his one-sided decision, the Secretary of the Interior granted Little Shell III's demand to head a delegation to Washington, D.C., resulting in a contentious meeting. Based on his vague promise to reexamine the Turtle Mountain band's land claim after opening their territory to settlement, Teller's position seemed to remain unchanged. He reiterated that "after a careful examination . . . they had no valid claim." Little Shell III disagreed. Similar to statements made by Little Rock at the Old Crossing treaty council in 1863, the chief asserted that "this land was given to him by God." With no capacity to discern Native people's spiritual relationship to lands regarded as sacred, Teller retorted that "God only gave land to those who made it useful."[38] While at cross-purposes over the law relating to "Indian title," it seemed that Teller would once and for all refuse the Turtle Mountain Chippewa's request for an adequate reservation chosen by them from their Indigenous territory. Surprisingly, Teller relented, at least temporarily. Without acknowledging that "these lands in question *have never been ceded to the United States*," the Secretary conceded that because "they lived a long time in that section of the country," a reservation would be set aside for them.[39]

As a result of the Turtle Mountain delegation's efforts, the Interior Department "initiated action before analysis" in accordance with its grab-bag policy.[40] Teller countermanded part of his October 4, 1882, order to the General Land Office. On December 21, 1882, two days after the session with the Turtle Mountain delegation, he convinced President Chester A. Arthur to issue an Executive Order providing the Turtle Mountain Chippewa with their reservation. This required removing nearly 500,000 acres from the public domain opened just two months before. It provided for a large reservation running thirty-two miles north and south, and twenty-four miles east and west. With the international boundary as its northern extent, it encompassed almost all of Turtle Mountain, along with some prairie lands to the south. This seemed to be a last-minute solution that might be satisfactory to all parties involved. For Teller, Pettigrew, Creel, and many other acquisitive

European Americans, such a reservation still left 8,500,000 acres in their hands. It looked like the 1,300 to 2,000 Turtle Mountain Chippewa would secure a large enough land base "severally located either upon tracts already improved by individual Indians, or upon lands to be allotted," and encompassing good farmland and the southern part of the Turtle Mountains below the Canadian border (see map on back cover, particularly the section labeled "Turtle Mountain Reservation, 1882").[41]

The tribe must have been quite relieved, but several factors intervened to dispel their optimism. The terms of allotment led to factionalism within the band. Some of the minority full-bloods (350–500 persons) did not want individual allotments. If necessary, they would take a smaller non-allotted reservation held in common. Many of the Métis majority preferred their own 160-acre homesteads.[42] In addition, external interests fumed about this modest concession to the Turtle Mountain Chippewa. The CIA acknowledged that "a large [white] immigration, attracted by the profits of wheat raising, has . . . been pouring into . . . lands claimed by the said Indians."[43] Special Indian Agent Cyrus Beede investigated the conditions within and neighboring the proposed reservation. He filed a deceptive report under-counting the number of full-bloods, misrepresenting their views about securing a permanent reservation, and denigrating their land use practices.[44] As part of an often-repeated strategy of dispossession that minimized the numbers of "real" (i.e., full-blood) Natives with legitimate legal requirements, while dismissing the claims of mixed-bloods as not being "real" Natives, Beede's census deliberately excluded them. Official counts made before and after 1883 reflected much higher figures. Yet this one detrimental conjecture became the rationale for federal authorities to reduce the original twenty-two township Turtle Mountain reservation to a mere two townships.

The tribe recognized such ploys. Although it had often been expedient for the United States to set aside a few "half-breed reserves" in order to procure full-blood Native land cessions in the Old Northwest and the lower Missouri River region in the 1820s and 1830s, af-

**Image 13. A western North Dakota Scene in 1883,** Metis family and Red River Ox Cart. *Photo courtesy of the State Historical Society of North Dakota, A4365.*

ter 1870 neither the United States nor Canada recognized the Métis as a tribe or nation with Indigenous rights.[45] In the United States, if mixed-bloods associated with tribes, then they became Native Americans. Yet they resented being classified as "wards" under the strict control of BIA agents, Protestant missionaries, local sheriffs, and the army. Most of them remained unwilling to redefine their identity and align themselves with the culturally dominant northern European Protestants who discriminated against them. Attorney Bottineau protested that this reduce-and-divide strategy "greatly wronged" all of the Turtle Mountain Chippewa, but especially the mixed-bloods.[46] He noted that "the unfortunate half-breed Indian has never had his position or status fixed by the United States. He is one thing to the Government today, and tomorrow he is metamorphosed into an entirely different person." Aside from deploying this tactic during treaty negotiations, it also became expedient in electoral politics and disputes over land claims. Bottineau complained that "when his vote in an election is wanted, he is a white man; but should he have taken up a homestead upon the public lands, and the tract happens to be coveted by a white man, then the half-breed is an Indian and as such he cannot hold against the white man." The tribal solicitor noted that "nine-tenths of the farms occupied by the white settlers within the boundaries of the reservation were the homes of the mixed blood Indians, selected by them as their future allotments in pursuance of said Executive Order."[47]

The special agent's findings and a report from Commissioner of Indian Affairs Price confirmed the settler incursions on Turtle Mountain Chippewa land. While recognizing the band's exclusive right to their unceded territory, the BIA justified settler encroachment with the rationale that "the whites have held that the Indians have no real title and that their claim should not be respected." The Turtle Mountain Chippewa's attorney objected to this mischaracterization and its negative implications for their "Indian rights."[48] As Bottineau pointed out, the commissioner reported falsely that the Turtle Mountain Chippewa had abandoned their territory and ignored agent reports about *why* the Turtle Mountain Chippewa could not make adequate use of their lands. The tribe refused to file their claims or make any improvements because European Americans had already filed claims on land they occupied. This led to "much bad feeling between them and the whites."[49] Although the Bureau of Indian Affairs continued to recognize "the ground of original Indian rights," that meant nothing when "numerous petitions and appeals" from European American settlers asserted that their "proper" use rights and occupancy (i.e., squatting) had greater legal standing than "Indian title."[50]

These reports had devastating consequences for the Turtle Mountain Chippewa. Teller lived up to the expectations of his western constituents who had been "sure of reasonable rulings on questions affecting public lands" when he took over the Interior Department.[51] Although the December 21, 1882, Executive Order looked straightforward enough to the Turtle Mountain delegation, the Indian Affairs bureaucracy considered it a temporary expedient "until a suitable smaller tract within its lines could be selected."[52] The tribe remained unaware of this undisclosed agenda. In March 1884, Secretary Teller and Commissioner Price convinced President Arthur to issue another Executive Order reducing the 491,520-acre reserve from two years prior to a minuscule two townships (46,080 acres) of "hilly and stony land cut up by patches of timber and lakes." As a consequence, "tracts that the Turtle Mountain Chippewa occup[ied] and improv[ed]" were illegally taken away from them and "restored" to the public domain. This misrepresentation constituted a legal fiction because the unceded territory in question had never been part of the public domain.[53]

In response to Turtle Mountain Chippewa protests against the in-equity, inadequacy, and non-consensual nature of this two-township reservation, Commissioner Price assured everyone that "they have all the land they need or will ever make use of." These circumstances pre-cluded enlarging the reservation because the Native Americans were technically "at liberty to take homesteads on the public domain."[54] Al-though head of the BIA, Price claimed that any redress had to come from Congress, not his office. While Congress had plenary authority over Indian Affairs, such a claim mischaracterized the way federal pol-icy really worked in the creation of this reservation. Price's boss, Sec-retary of the Interior Teller, had talked President Arthur into issuing the reduced reservation Executive Order. Such an action, while legal, deliberately avoided soliciting the "advice and consent" of Congress or the Turtle Mountain Chippewa.

From this shocking retraction, the Turtle Mountain Chippewa came under the tutelage of the highly touted solution of assimilation and allotment. This federal policy re-emerged as a reaction against the much maligned and corrupt reservation system. It intended to break up tribal governance and social structure by dividing communally held tribal lands into individual parcels of private property. Teller's succes-sor as head of the Interior Department confirmed that the proposals for allotment were "dictated less by a regard for the interests of the Indian than for those of the white people who want his lands."[55] Non-allotted "surplus" land would be appropriated by the federal government for European American settlement. As private property owners, Native Americans would supposedly become farmers and citizens of the United States, subject to state and local jurisdiction and taxation like non-Natives. Nevertheless, the procurement of some farming tools, draft animals, and a farming teacher could not overcome the futility of farming for the Turtle Mountain Chippewa. They complained that "we have no seed grain to sow this spring."[56] With their most arable prairie lands taken away, they knew that the federal government had no intention to help them become independent farmers.[57]

Little Shell III complained that "what seed the Government gave us is only to bother and weary the time away."[58] Instead of being encouraged to become self-sufficient in a new market economy, the lack of a "just settlement" impeded their productive power. Neighboring European Americans moved in illegally and began cutting timber while denying the Native Americans' right to chop wood or threatening to tax the wood they cut. The tribal council complained that "they don't want us to chop . . . while the whites are all going in the woods to chop all the wood there is and sell it." Meanwhile, enterprising Turtle Mountain Chippewa "cannot sell anything [i.e., hay and wood] . . . we cannot find buyers, because the whites are chopping themselves, have taken arms against us, and [are] taking wood from Indian lands."[59] This testimony described the inequitable consequences of federal policy.

In contradiction to the benevolent claims made by federal policymakers like Commissioner Price, the agent for the Turtle Mountain Chippewa reported that their reduced reservation was "not large enough for the number of people claiming residence; there is not land enough to ever make them self-supporting either by means of farming or stock-raising."[60] The special agent's erroneous estimate of only twenty-five full-blood families remained the justification for a diminished reservation. The incorporation of the "vanishing Indian" myth into the rationale for assimilation and allotment policy calls into question its benevolent intent. Did late-nineteenth-century federal policy really want to save the Native Americans from extinction? Or, as historian Brian Dippie noted, did this "convenient extinction doctrine" have ulterior motives?[61] The cultural and economic fate of tribes like the Turtle Mountain Chippewa became defined by reformers and policymakers in minimalist terms. CIA Officer Francis Walker declared that "Indian blood . . . has tended decidedly towards extinction."[62]

The doctrine also became associated with poverty, dependency, and criminality. Allegedly, Native Americans had too much land, too much time on their hands for socializing and ceremonial life, and too much freedom. So, they must give up their under-utilized "surplus" lands, tribal autonomy, modes of subsistence, and religious practices. In return, they should adopt the "benefits of civilization." Yet the actions of the Turtle Mountain Chippewa rejected these paternalistic notions. Reports by agents and visiting clergymen insisted that any "improvement toward civilization" was "directly due to the credit of their own efforts" and not "meager annual appropriations" that were "far from being sufficient to furnish them with seeds and other assistance in farming, to say nothing of food."[63] Such a clear statement reflected the dynamism of the Turtle Mountain Chippewa. Adjusting to new circumstances did not diminish their insistence on self-determination.

But the band's dire situation became even more precarious after the Canadian government "laid its hands on the land of the Métis [in Saskatchewan] as if it were its own" in 1885. According to their leader, Louis Riel, "by this one act" Canada "showed its plan to defraud" the Métis of their future.[64] As a result of Canada's repressive military response to unresolved Métis grievances over land titles and self-governance, many allied First Nations Cree and Métis in Saskatchewan sought refuge with kinfolk living near their old buffalo grounds south of the international boundary in Montana and Dakota Territories.[65] This diaspora had a negative effect on the Turtle Mountain Chippewa/Métis community. Anti-Native and anti-Métis sentiment among many European Americans immigrants to the region already existed.

The failure of the Northwest Métis rebellion, combined with decreased access to good and cheap land, further aggravated ethnic tensions. The increased deprivation of the Métis and Cree made them appear less sympathetic than ever. Along the "magical cage line" between Canada and the United States, neither European American residents nor federal and territorial governments wanted these undesirables to congregate near towns, reservations, grazing lands, mining areas, timber lots, or railroad and telegraph lines.[66]

Existing reservations had already proved less than adequate for the local Indigenous population. Yet various regional economic interests wanted reserves decreased in size or allotted. Nobody contemplated creating any new ones. They hoped that such inhospitable inclinations would convince any Cree or Métis from north of the border to go back to Canada. When they persisted in staying, fearing further reprisals from the R.C.M.P. if they returned, U.S. Cavalry detachments rounded up and deported groups of Métis and bands of Cree. Still, such a vast border could not be secured. Many Métis, such as their military leader Gabriel Dumont, sought refuge in various isolated river valleys in Montana Territory and around the Turtle Mountain reservation in Dakota Territory. Dumont and his family and relations fled to Lewistown, Montana. Others settled along the Milk River or further east in the Judith Basin. At least one son, Isidore, settled at Turtle Mountain and appears on the tribal roll. This diaspora intensified the already overcrowded conditions at Turtle Mountain.[67]

The 1884 two-township Executive Order reservation reduction did not provide enough land for all the band's members. It dumped many tribal members on the public domain to fend for themselves against the onslaught of new Canadian, Norwegian, and Germans from Russia immigrants eager to file claims for "the black rich loam" in one of the "best parts of the great hard wheat belt."[68] The generally hostile environment confronting the Métis influx also changed their attitudes and dealings with Native relations, as well as their own self-identity. Many attempted to distance themselves from their Native origins or kin to gain greater socio-economic status and acceptance into European American society.[69]

Increased competition for scarcer resources, combined with a more hostile cultural environment towards anything associated with Indigenous people, confronted the Turtle Mountain Chippewa with a stark reality that jeopardized their future. Agent John Cramsie blamed their extreme poverty on the demise of the buffalo. He estimated that even $50,000 worth of stock and farm equipment would not be enough to meet their needs.[70] Yet some people had adapted rather successfully to these less than favorable conditions. Many Métis who relocated in western Dakota or Montana Territories retained close kinship ties with relations at Turtle Mountain. Others took up allotments on the public domain in these areas, only to sell them off for some ready cash. These funds enabled some of them to move back near Turtle Mountain and stake a new claim or share land with relatives.[71] Despite some increase in Chippewa/Métis ethnic tensions over land and resources, kinship connections often overcame ethnic boundaries by extending social affinities and providing economic niches. Yet the virtual extermination of the last of the northern plains buffalo herds by 1883, along with railroad expansion and European American immigration, threatened to eradicate the subsistence of the Turtle Mountain community.

In 1887, a member of the Board of Indian Commissioners, Episcopal Bishop William Walker of St. Paul, Minnesota, and Fargo, Dakota Territory, confirmed the lamentable conditions at Turtle Mountain. He pointed out the "untillable land" of the diminished reservation, the obliteration of game by encroaching whites, and the fact that many of the Turtle Mountain Chippewa lived

> on the ragged edge of starvation. They have managed to keep body and soul together by subsisting upon rabbits and digging roots in summer. During the winter, some of these poor people devoured carrion, dead dogs, and dead mules.[72]

For the Turtle Mountain Chippewa, the critical issue was starvation, not "civilization." The "free land" ideology underlying the dream of European American homesteading in the Trans-Mississippi West had disastrous consequences for Native Americans. "Go West" and "free West" boosters got it wrong, especially regarding Native peoples. Boosters assured fellow European Americans that those desirous of freehold farms would neither crowd nor starve anybody. The bitter experience of the Turtle Mountain Chippewa proved otherwise. Recovery from such a tragedy remained painful and protracted. The threat of starvation provided the context for all relations between the band and the federal government over the next two decades. As Bishop Walker had pointed out, the Native people lacked game to hunt, tillable land, and agricultural implements. Only 500 of the 1,930 tribal members received government rations regularly. Each of these individuals received only two to four pounds of pork and ten to fifteen pounds of flour to live on for a month. The bishop observed, "Many families had not tasted food for upwards of six days!"[73] Although local and visiting clergy reported on and condemned such a situation, federal officials (with the exception of Agent Cramsie) failed to acknowledge or take action to remedy these terrible conditions.

While Native peoples starved or froze to death during the bitter winter, the Secretary of War ordered that any destitute European American settler in Rolette and four nearby counties could apply for and receive food for their stock and six cords of wood. All the wood came from the Fort Totten reservation. Since this reserve had been taken from the Turtle Mountain Chippewa by the U.S. government without compensation, the resources of impoverished Natives subsidized hard-up European Americans who settled on their lands illegally, aided and abetted by the federal government.[74] Increasingly frustrated with these inequities, and wanting to avoid another winter of extreme privation, some Chippewa and Métis threatened that they would take what they needed from their agency storehouse, by force if necessary, to avoid starvation.[75] The imminent collapse of their Indigenous subsistence and the advent of economic dependency demonstrated the direct link between the band's wretched material conditions and the precarious position of their legal claims.

Bishop Walker noted that "if a white man was reduced to such a condition, life would have few charms for him."[76] The bishop recognized the gap between the professed benevolence of policymakers and the destructive reality of such policies for Native peoples. He reported that "large tracts of land have been taken from them and settled by white men." While the proceeds from the sale of these lands "poured into the United States Treasury," the Turtle Mountain band "received nothing but this beggarly pittance." The bishop wondered if "this is the benevolent position of the United States Government for its wards?" He informed the Board of Indian Commissioners, the oversight body which Teller had weakened by cutting its funding, that

> this band of Indians have been greatly wronged. It is the duty
> of the Government to make a just settlement of their claim
> to large tracts of land taken from them, for which they have
> received no compensation whatever.[77]

Local clergy in both the Catholic and Episcopal dioceses similarly exhorted federal policymakers to live up to their promises, but to no avail.

Policy critiques also came from within the Indian Affairs bureaucracy. To address the increasingly deplorable living conditions of the Turtle Mountain Chippewa, and to avoid a humanitarian disaster, Agent John Cramsie requested additional funds. The gratuitous annual appropriations from Congress ranged from $5,000 in 1885 to $10,000 in 1883.[78] Such sparse amounts provided some farm equipment and household implements, almost no animals, and a scanty ration of pork and flour. The availability of flour became even worse after the gristmill at Devils Lake broke and could not be fixed in a timely manner.[79] Crop yields remained minimal due to the lack of arable land (approximately 13,000 acres on the 46,080-acre reservation), along with killing frosts, long dry spells, intense heat, hailstorms, crop-destroying insects and gophers, prairie fires, blizzards, severe winds, cyclones, and tornadoes.[80] Faced with these realities, Cramsie challenged the "windy" rhetoric from the "ignorant" Indian Affairs echelon. He rebuked a circular letter sent out to agents mandating imposition of a "work or starve" regime. "If the Indian is to become civilized and support himself by agriculture, must he not first be furnished with the necessary animals and implements before you can tell him to work or starve?"[81] The agent's question exposed the incoherence behind the self-proclaimed civilizing mission of federal policy.

Cramsie also scolded his superiors for talking about civilizing Natives, but not funding the proposed programs. He declared that if policymakers wanted to fulfill their goal of transforming the band into independent farmers, it would require $64,000.[82] This figure represented less money than was spent on feeding the Sioux. Such an amount could be obtained easily. The United States owed the Turtle Mountain Chippewa compensation for taking a portion of their unceded territory when establishing the Fort Berthold reservation in western Dakota Territory. If the government wanted to "pass this one act of simple justice," it could cover the cost for the tribe's needed improvements by paying $1.00 an acre for the 64,000 acres taken.[83] Without such a bold initiative, "the Indians on the Turtle Mountain Reservation cannot work and support themselves for lack of means." Seizure of any cattle or horses by the local sheriff in lieu of taxes would push them further into destitution. Cramsie warned his superiors about the potential for "serious trouble." The Chippewa and Métis would not let their families starve "while there are large herds of fat cattle now grazing upon lands to which they have as good a title as any Indians ever had to lands in the United States, but which were thrown open to settlement without their knowledge or consent."[84]

Such sincere and practical advocacy on behalf of the Turtle Mountain Chippewa by their agent contrasted sharply with continued calls by the local press for their removal. Bishop Walker and Attorney Bottineau pushed for a "just settlement." They challenged the legality of the diminished reservation from the second Executive Order of 1884. "The question may arise as to whether this reservation which was allotted to these Indians by an Executive order, which they were occupying and improving, could be legally taken away from them."[85] Bottineau asserted that the grounds for President Arthur's and Secretary Teller's revocation of the original reservation, based solely on special agent Beede's erroneous report, would not be sustained as lawful in a court of justice.[86] The Turtle Mountain Chippewa had not asked for an unreasonable portion of north-central Dakota Territory. They offered a compromise "provided a reservation of sufficient quantity of land is allotted to enable each individual to take his allotment."[87] Even this modest proposal proved to be too generous for most federal policymakers and neighboring European Americans.

In the election of 1884, Grover Cleveland became the first post–Civil War Democrat president. He appointed southern Democrats to handle affairs. Such a party shift did not signify any real changes in federal policy. The new CIA still wanted to remove the Turtle Mountain Chippewa to the White Earth reservation in Minnesota. Yet these new office holders could not avoid the problems created by their predecessors. In early 1886, almost three and a half years after Secretary Teller ordered the unceded Turtle Mountain Indian country opened to European American settlement, GLO Commissioner Sparks made a "startling discovery" about the unlawful nature of this situation. Approximately twenty thousand European Americans had settled within fourteen or fifteen counties in the Devils Lake, Turtle Mountain, and Souris River land districts and portions of the Grand Forks and Bismarck sections. Sparks cited CIA Price's detailed 1882 report to Secretary Teller, which substantiated the unceded territorial claim of the Turtle Mountain Chippewa. The land commissioner also recounted Teller's opinion "that this claim was not well grounded," and the Secretary of the Interior's subsequent directive to the GLO to proceed with surveying and opening land districts to oversee settlement. As a result of this finding, Sparks ordered the Surveyor General to suspend all surveying contracts. He also refused to allow a survey proposed by railroad magnate James J. Hill through the Turtle Mountain reservation, which angered the local European American residents.[88]

The GLO's inquiry to the Secretary of the Interior came to the new CIA for review and recommendations. John D. C. Atkins reviewed the 1882 reports of his predecessor, Hiram Price, and not surprisingly reached similar contradictory conclusions. First, Atkins affirmed what Sparks had uncovered. The Turtle Mountain band's territory constituted "unceded Indian country" to which they had "some claim thereto." But then he asserted that only Congress could make a final determination, because "no action . . . taken by the Executive branch can finally settle this matter."[89] Such an assertion overlooked the fact that the unilateral actions of the Executive branch's Interior Department under Henry Teller had violated federal law and policy precedents. Administrative decrees unleashed a demographic deluge that "settled this matter" on the ground without any regard for the rule of law.[90]

As Agent John Cramsie noted to the CIA, "our laws" were made for Native Americans' "restraint," but "not for their protection."[91] Atkins acknowledged that fact, stating "that country is very valuable," and a "large emigration is constantly seeking a home there." Without waiting for Congress as he recommended, Atkins asserted that the claim of the Turtle Mountain Chippewa should not "be a bar to further settlement and development." Reverting to the old saying that possession is nine-tenths of the law, the CIA believed that the "most feasible way of disposing of the [legal] question" entailed removing "all restrictions" to settlement by resuming surveys and permitting entries.[92] So while the GLO acknowledged the validity of the Turtle Mountain Chippewa's land claim, the BIA contrived another illegal yet "feasible" outcome from the policy grab-bag to benefit European American interests.[93]

The new Secretary of the Interior also wanted the opinion of the Assistant Attorney General (AAG) concerning the legal issues raised by Sparks's discovery. He reviewed the CIA's findings, and easily recognized their contradictions. The AAG found it "difficult to reconcile the facts thus conceded with the conclusion reached."[94] If the federal government acknowledged that a recognized tribal claimant possessed unquestioned "Indian title" to unceded land they occupied, then it could not authorize any non-Native surveys, entries, or settlement in that territory. Such activities could only be construed as illegal trespass. The Assistant Attorney General cited *Cherokee Nation v. Georgia* (1831) and *Worcester v. Georgia* (1832) as legal authority from the Supreme Court in support of his conclusion.[95] He also invoked the key legal prerequisite that Teller, Pettigrew, Price, Atkins, and others had overlooked or dismissed. The United States could not take unceded lands or title without tribal consent. Therefore, the Interior Department had no "legal authority" to implement the CIA's recommendations permitting settlement.[96]

Yet impending North Dakota statehood coincided with increased competition for wheat lands and grasslands during the late 1880s. The pressure of farmers and cattlemen upon the public domain and Native reservations escalated. This situation prompted the Turtle Mountain Natives to protest against the encroachment of European American dairymen who proposed to build a creamery and cheese factory on the reservation, while "our people suffer from hunger."[97] Physical privation became so acute that some famished Native Americans threatened to throw the farmer-in-charge off the reservation if greater quantities and more equitable distribution of rations did not occur.[98] Unfortunately, Agent Cramsie's and Bishop Walker's terrible predictions about the consequences of sustained malnutrition finally became a reality.

From 1886 to 1888, two successive brutal winters followed by summer droughts devastated the Turtle Mountain Chippewa. The unusually frigid weather limited the gathering of roots or hunting and trapping small game, while the out-of-commission mill at Devils Lake reduced their meager flour ration. These environmental circumstances only compounded the bureaucratic causes of this humanitarian crisis. James Howard mentioned that "shortly after the Plains-Ojibwa had been placed on reservations on both sides of the international boundary, the Canadian Mounted Police killed all the buffalo found near the line to keep the U.S. Indians from crossing into Canada and vice-versa."[99] Reduced to trying to dig out gophers from their dens through the frozen ground, they fell from the "ragged edge of starvation" into the precipice of mass deprivation and death. In a chillingly personal yet succinct account, Father J. B. Genin confirmed that "in the winter of 1887 to 1888 there were counted 151 persons, big and small," who died [at Turtle Mountain] of starvation. I buried a number of them myself."[100] So, why did the U.S. government ignore the pleas, proposals, and problems reported by Cramsie? Why did higher level federal policymakers fail to provide a "benevolent provision" or "just settlement"?

Meanwhile, European Americans continued to take up residence on Turtle Mountain Chippewa lands because it remained difficult to evict or convict trespassers. Local officials ignored these violations of the law. Some Turtle Mountain Natives captured a mining entrepreneur, identified as a "prominent and wealthy citizen" named Michael Ohmer from Dayton, Ohio. But Ohmer turned out to be no simple prospector. The *New York Times* described him as one of many "colonists now settled about the mountain" among the "capitalists who have secured title to the rich silver and coal mines of Dunseith, where they have laid out a town."[101] The town of Dunseith, hyped in Great Northern railroad advertisements as the "Little Chicago of the North," lay only a few miles west from the Turtle Mountain reservation as amended by the 1884 Executive Orders.

Agent Cramsie made a significant disclosure about this development. Recall that J. B. Bottineau could find "no other ground" for the 1884 Executive Order reservation reduction other than Special Agent Beede's erroneous report, which undercounted the full-blood Chippewa and disregarded the mixed-blood Métis.[102] Cramsie revealed that:

> soon after the settlement of these people on the [original large] reservation it was discovered or supposed that extensive mines of good coal existed within its boundaries. A syndicate was immediately formed [which] seem[ed] to have had influence with the administration at that time. It resulted in getting

the reservation reduced to two townships so as to throw the supposed coal field outside the reservation which was taken possession of by the syndicate.[103]

This "supposed" area centered on the town of Dunseith, located due west of the southwestern corner of the reservation. The Natives threatened not to free Ohmer until the removal of "all the machinery and men he took with him with a view to mining." They tried unsuccessfully to ransom him. The newspapers made inaccurate claims about "every evidence indicat[ing] a general rising among the redskins."[104] After being released, Ohmer blamed his predicament on the refusal of Little Shell's band to stay on their reservation, rather than his own trespass. It should be noted that no silver strike occurred. Miners exploited some sizeable lignite coal outcroppings around Turtle Mountain, but the mining output never equaled the commercial quantities anticipated by early prospectors like Ohmer. Most of the lignite coal discoveries in North Dakota occurred further west of the Missouri River. Although a profitable coal mining industry failed to develop, various discoveries of lignite coal powered the town's brickyard and lime kiln.[105] The speculation about its greater profitability seems to have influenced Beede's erroneous report and Teller's unilateral taking.

Not surprisingly, the town's newspaper referred to this same causal factor when the Turtle Mountain Chippewa turned up the pressure to reinstate their land claim a few years later. In reporting that J. B. Bottineau had returned to the reservation from his office in Washington, D.C., to "look after the interests" of the Turtle Mountain Indians, an article alleged explicitly yet briefly that the original threat to their ten-million-acre land claim stemmed from its being "opened up for mining purposes" by Secretary Teller.[106] One month later, Joseph Rolette wrote to the CIA on behalf of Little Shell's council and reiterated that mining interests had been involved in influencing the federal government to radically reduce their original reservation.[107]

Four independent sources, including the *New York Times* stories about Ohmer, Cramsie's letter, the *Dunseith Herald* article, and Rolette's letter, corroborated that coal mining interests played some role in the reduction of the Turtle Mountain reservation.[108] The sources correlate with a preponderance of other evidence indicating that substantial European American settlement during the "great Dakota boom" from 1879 to 1886 converged with various economic interests. Railroad, land speculation, and lignite coal companies promoted regional settlement by sustaining enough political pressure on sympathetic federal officials to condense the Turtle Mountain reservation. Each non-Native entity benefited from Native land appropriation and had little or no concern for the illegalities involved in such an undertaking.

The increasing frequency of these types of incursions contributed to Native American and European American misunderstandings. Local officials continued to exceed their authority and harass the Turtle Mountain Chippewa. The agent reported that "they are constantly in trouble by fighting against the civil authorities of that county, in their attempt to collect taxes from them."[109] The issue of local property taxes became another in a long line of harmful consequences for not being able to secure an adequate reservation.[110] Ironically, local tax rolls excluded the lands of homesteaders until they received fee simple title via a Land Office patent. All of the benefits touted by federal policy officials about securing allotments or homesteads on the public domain failed to acknowledge this stumbling block. Secretary Teller supported county and state efforts to tax Natives and their land. Little Shell felt obliged to inform the current Secretary of the Interior that such views or practices had no basis in federal law or policy.[111]

Not all of the Native American and European American conflict resulted from intrusive local officials. On July 4, 1889, an Independence Day celebration in nearby Rolla, North Dakota, turned into a Native American versus European American street brawl. Historian John Hesketh recounted that "the whole crowd was engaged in a hand-to-hand encounter, fighting with clubs, bats, wagon spokes, or anything else they could get hold of." During the melee, a Chippewa was killed when he was struck over the head by a plow.[112] Although few such incidents occurred, they signified that violent eruptions could flare up at any time, often to the detriment of the outnumbered Chippewa and Métis. Despite rising tensions, Little Shell and his premier Red Thunder did all they could do to avoid another episode where "our blood has been shed by a white man."[113]

These violent incidents raised the question of how, in the midst of trying to survive physically by hunting, haying, foraging, wood cutting, collecting buffalo bones, threshing wheat, or working on the railroad, could Chippewa and Métis families (many of them quite large) secure enough money to buy seed, stock, or equipment, let alone pay taxes? Hewing and hauling wood to nearby towns should have rendered them a price of seventy-five cents per cord. Yet the merchants of Rolla would only barter twenty cents worth of provisions for a cord of wood.[114] A severe drought during the summer of 1889 brought about a general crop failure in central-northern Dakota Territory. Band members living outside of the reservation feared utter ruin and the loss of their only marketable asset, other than their labor.

Unable to do anything about the weather, Little Shell remained focused on important legal issues. The chief argued to the Secretary of the Interior that since most property taxes went to support local public schools, Turtle Mountain band members should be exempt since they did not send their children to these schools. The federal government and various Catholic and Episcopalian groups established five schools for the exclusive benefit of the band's children. Little Shell believed in school education as a way of maintaining tribal rights and integrity in an increasingly European American world.[115]

The chief focused on the central legal issue ignored by local authorities. The Turtle Mountain Chippewa still retained their "Indian title" as recognized by the commissioner of Indian Affairs. This undisputed fact exempted them from all local jurisdiction and any taxation. No civil law could be applied to Natives living in unceded Indigenous territory.[116] To protect themselves from losing their parcels of land if they even filed claims, the band had insisted upon and procured what they thought amounted to immunity from local taxes. After Inspector Gardner completed a tribal census in 1885, those beyond the reservation secured certificates of exemption from him.[117]

Yet local officials disregarded these federal exemptions. Seemingly oblivious to the band's continued destitution and want of food, the sheriff of Rolette County, within which their two-township tract resided, decided to force the collection of taxes on those living outside of the reservation near the town of St. John. The sheriff attempted to eject "the breeds from valuable lands which they occupy, and upon which they refuse to make filings or pay taxes."[118] In response to newspaper accounts of "breed trouble," Father Genin received a letter from principal chief Little Shell, head warrior Red Thunder, and Henri Poitras "the half-breed chief" asking for the priest's intervention on their behalf.

In defense of their resistance to the questionable actions of the sheriff, Genin commented, "I know well personally Little Shell and Red Thunder, both honourable men, and Henri Poitras, a true and faithful Christian man, whose life has been one of heroic deeds of charity in behalf, not merely of his own people but of all white men as well."[119] Father Genin's significant influence with the Chippewa and Métis helped to convince them that any resort to violence would jeopardize their legal claims. Because he urged his Native adherents to continue with their letters, petitions, and delegations to federal authorities for the redress of their grievances, the priest's relations with the agents at Devils Lake remained strained.

During another disputed tax incident in 1889, the Rolette County sheriff confiscated cattle and other personal property of the Turtle Mountain Chippewa under the pretext that the Natives had refused to pay any property taxes. The sheriff ignored the fact that they had not purchased the cattle. The cattle had been given to them by the federal government, which exempted them from state or local taxes. When the Turtle Mountain Chippewa refused to comply, the sheriff appealed to the North Dakota National Guard to intervene. A troop assembled and set out toward Turtle Mountain. Fortunately for them and the sheriff, the Indian agency farmer and Reverend Wellington Salt intercepted them with a telegram from the governor calling off the maneuver. According to historian John Hesketh, the prompt intervention of the governor and the agent saved the lives of the soldiers "from a certain death," as they had all been targeted by the well-armed "rebels," all identified as "half-breeds." Hesketh concluded that "in this affair the Indians or half-breeds were not in the wrong. It was the rashness of the county officers."[120]

Another potentially violent incident arose from over-reaching local European American officials. The expediency of typing mixed-bloods interchangeably as Native non-citizens, "white" citizens, or "British half-breeds" often resulted in ejection; tax battles; loss of homes, lands, and improvements; and election fraud.[121] An "insurrection" almost broke out again near St. John in 1891. Some Turtle Mountain Natives refused to pay a poll tax. When attempts were made by a local officer to collect them, the Indians broke into stores, stole guns and ammunition, and fortified themselves in an old log house under the leadership of Little Shell's chief warrior, Red Thunder. Seeing the superior numbers of white men arrayed against them, they surrendered to the authorities.[122]

In a letter to the *Duluth Journal*, Father Genin refuted the most outrageous claims about the "Indian troubles" at Turtle Mountain. He exposed false accounts alleging how it took six young deputies to capture and restrain Red Thunder. Genin pointed out that the tribe's *premier* was "an infirmed 83-year-old man doubled over with age and afflicted with pleurisy." He also testified to the longstanding composite nature of the band, by identifying Red Thunder as "a Cree Indian born in the Pembina Mountains," who had "spent his entire life there and in the Turtle Mountains." Although ailing, Red Thunder's spirit remained unyielding. When asked by his jailer if he would like to accompany him for a little exercise, the chief refused on the grounds that "he would not leave the jail as a prisoner, but would walk out only as a free man."[123] Such strength and dignity in the face of adversity demonstrated Turtle Mountain Chippewa resistance to local authority whose civil jurisdiction they refused to recognize.

The federal government created the legal chaos that precipitated these local tensions and violence. Yet it failed to redress the major grievances or stop local officials from attempting to manipulate legal technicalities to their advantage. At the same time the Turtle Mountain Chippewa edged closer to the brink of despair. While they faced "the ragged edge of starvation," European American's cattle grew fat on their land. Although the Chippewa had some success with farming the little arable land available, repeated crop failures led Little Shell to conclude that "from destitution and want of food . . . a great number are determined to feed themselves upon the white people's cattle."[124] Worst of all, unknown assailants engaged in a form of late nineteenth-century chemical warfare aimed at what little remained of the Chippewa's subsistence base. The tribal council informed Attorney Bottineau that "a great number of the white people are distributing strychnine (poison) all over our reservation to purposely destroy all the small wild animals, as well as ducks, geese, and every dog they can give a bait to."[125] An agent's report stated that "instead of making any improvement in their efforts towards civilization and self-support, they have been disintegrating." This circumstance stemmed not from indolence, but "because of the constant friction with their European American neighbors, attributed mainly to complications arising from their unsettled condition."[126]

The Turtle Mountain Chippewa living on the reduced reservation or out on the public domain failed to receive the physical and legal protection promised by the U.S. government. Either they could not keep European American squatters off their lands, or they were unable to make the necessary improvements to sustain a legal claim. Their agent called attention to this predicament by asserting that "their greatest trouble is caused from being strictly forbidden by the federal authorities to take any of the timber (which rightfully belongs to them) necessarily required for their use in making improvements."

How could they make improvements if they could not harvest timber for fences, sheds, corrals, and cabins? These circumstances "resulted in very serious complications and nearly bloodshed." They almost caused "an uprising and Indian war."[127] The agent's report illustrated that without federal protection, promises to Native Americans about settlement on "public lands" could not be realized. The Turtle Mountain Chippewa members who could not secure adequate land on the reservation had to fight against the civil authorities of Rolette County.

Perhaps a quicker resolution would have occurred if the Chippewa had not been so peaceful and had instead turned to serious violence. Bishop Walker remarked that despite numerous provocations, the Turtle Mountain Chippewa avoided armed conflict. He also noted the irony of the situation where fiercer tribes (e.g., the Dakota and Lakota) received more favorable treatment from the federal government than the nonviolent Turtle Mountain Chippewa. "The marvel is that if they had shown their teeth somewhat, I wonder if their condition would not be materially better today?"[128] Another decade of dysfunctional federal policy failed consistently to take the tribe's legal protests seriously. This refusal to engage in the process of negotiating an equitable solution demonstrated that the grab-bag nature of federal policy failed to resolve problems.[129]

The Turtle Mountain Chippewa suffered a painful lesson about the "rule of law" and the benevolence of the "Great Father." What can be granted by one Executive Order may be rescinded by another. The radical reservation reduction opened up eighteen more townships to European American settlement. This left most of the band with no place to call home on or near the diminished reservation. When some Métis tried to file claims under the Homestead Act (1862), local land district officials declared them to be ineligible as Native Americans, and if they tried to obtain land via the Indian Homestead Act (1875), they became ruled out as white citizens. Even the local agent lacked enough understanding about the eligibility requirements to advise them.[130] In this legal purgatory, European American immigrants encroached, secured their titles, and left many landless Métis to fend for themselves in Dakota Territory or emigrate to Montana. So, they scattered across the shrinking public domain after all the best land had already been claimed.

As Teller and Commissioner Price knew, "Indian title" could not be extinguished legally by the establishment of an Executive Order reservation created by the president. The creation of a reservation did not necessarily extinguish tribal title unless Congress indicated clearly such an intent.[131] Congress expressed no such intent in the 1880s. Since all subsequent bills related to the land tenure of the Turtle Mountain Chippewa from 1864 to 1904 failed to pass, the Indian disclaimer in the acts that enabled Dakota Territory in 1861, and the state of North Dakota in 1889, remained the law of the land. It should have precluded the October 4, 1882, directive by Secretary Teller, which opened unceded Turtle Mountain Chippewa territory to GLO administration and European American settlement, along with the March 29 and June 3, 1884, reservation reduction Executive Orders from President Arthur. This imposition of federal policy by administrative decree reflected the post-1871 shift in Native American and European American relations. The security of "Indian title" and recognition of tribal sovereignty had ended, along with treaty-making. With Native Americans transformed legally into being "wards of the nation," the Turtle Mountain Chippewa lawyer J. B. Bottineau pleaded with federal policymakers for the "efficient and speedy execution" of a "rational code of laws" to protect the legal rights of his tribe. They could not fend for themselves without federal protection on public domain lands, because "the white man wins every time."[132]

The band's lawyer challenged the legal basis of the 1884 Executive Orders on these grounds. Bottineau stated that "the question may arise as to whether this reservation, which was allotted to these Indians by an Executive Order, which they were occupying and improving, could be legally taken away from them?"[133] Falsifying a tribal census, and then using it as the pretext to reduce the size of a reservation could not be interpreted as an abandonment of their claims to their land.

Contrary to the arguments of Teller, Pettigrew, and Creel, European American infringement on unceded land did *not* extinguish "Indian title." If an Executive Order proved insufficient to extinguish Indigenous claims, then so did the actions of businesses or citizens. Such encroachment had to be authorized explicitly by Congress granting fee-simple patents in accordance with federal land laws.[134]

Federal policies frustrated the Turtle Mountain Chippewa as much as, or more, than European American land-grabbers. The indifference of the president and Congress allowed the Secretary of the Interior to engage in an arbitrary taking that dispossessed the Turtle Mountain Chippewa under the cover of law. These illegal actions by federal authorities provoked Bottineau to "submit that there is ample evidence showing the merits of the claim of the Turtle Mountain Indians, and the great wrongs and injustice in their treatment by this Government."[135] Meanwhile, most of the Turtle Mountain band found themselves unable to secure homes in their homeland. Almost a year after the winter of mass starvation, Agent Cramsie reiterated that the lack of food persisted. The agent requested additional appropriations to try and prevent another humanitarian disaster. Along with the Turtle Mountain Chippewa's destitution, tensions remained high because local officials persevered in their efforts to confiscate their meager possessions in lieu of taxes.[136] These events initiated twenty more years of U.S. disregard for the legal rights and very survival of the Native community at Turtle Mountain.

# CHAPTER 7
## The "Ten Cent" Treaty and Its Aftermath, 1889–1905

*We ask justice upon the merit of this claim.*[1]
—John B. Bottineau, Attorney, Turtle Mountain Indians

Between 1879 and 1886, over one hundred thousand immigrants entered northern Dakota Territory. Only one year after North Dakota statehood, between February 22 and November 2 of 1889, the European American population reached 191,000. This trend contrasted sharply with the estimated Turtle Mountain Chippewa population ranging from 1,245 to 2,496. As North Dakota shifted from a frontier territory to a settled state, it still remained, in the words of historian Elwyn B. Robinson, a "colonial hinterland."[2]

As a result of this demographic deluge, federal policymakers forced a final agreement on a non-authorized tribal council faction influenced unduly by BIA agents and adverse material circumstances. From the perspective of the legitimate chiefs, council, and their lawyer, this "defective agreement" exemplified the "mopping up" nature of federal policy.[3] The government imposed a set of discredited remedies that failed to resolve the Turtle Mountain Chippewa's land claim. Contention over the McCumber Agreement from 1892 to 1905 further marginalized the tribe by appropriating their land and resources for a trifling compensation (i.e., ten cents per acre), while undermining the tribe's autonomy, culture, and ability to make a living.

By 1889, the lack of any fair settlement to reserve an adequate reservation became more intolerable because of increased European Amer-

ican encroachment, persistent harassment by local officials, and the intrusion of outside economic interests. Responding to this deteriorating
situation, the Turtle Mountain community sent a delegation to Washington, D.C., in early 1889 to confer with Commissioner of Indian Affairs John H. Oberly. The three delegates included sub-chief Kaishpau,
Maxime Marion, and Joseph Rolette, who also acted as interpreter and
persistent leg-puller.[4] Kaishpau spoke of the urgent need of his people
to negotiate a settlement that would preserve an adequate land base. He
noted with frustration that this was his fifth trip to the nation's capital.
Each time he had been told to be "quiet" (i.e., patient), but he insisted
that he would keep coming until "the Great Father . . . recognized my
rights on Turtle Mountain." When asked what rights his people claimed,
the chief reiterated the well-documented boundaries of their territory. A
Bureau of Indian Affairs clerk assured Oberly that "this office has recognized their claim and has tried to get Congress to recognize it, but the
Secretary of the Interior . . . says they have no claim."[5]

Differences between federal policymakers left the Turtle Mountain Chippewa without a reliable negotiating partner. This meeting
confirmed the inconsistencies between the Secretary of the Interior, the
Commissioner of Indian Affairs, and Congress. The national legislature
remained uninterested in fulfilling their trust responsibilities. They regarded the legal quagmire engulfing the Turtle Mountain Chippewa
as a peripheral problem. So, the matter became the sole province of
the Interior Secretary, whose higher authority countermanded any
commissioner's findings that deviated from his own views. Given this
situation, the new commissioner could not understand why the tribal
delegation had come, or what issues remained unresolved.

Kaishpau responded that they first required re-recognition of
their title. Then they wanted it extinguished legally by a negotiated treaty. Rolette added that with adequate compensation from such
a substantial land cession treaty, they could fund their schools, stock
their farms, and achieve self-sufficiency in ten years.[6] Ironically, these
outcomes aligned with the assimilation policies touted by federal poli-

cymakers. Yet as happened in many of these types of meetings, federal officials got bogged down in the numbers. Along with the reservation's farmer-in-charge E. W. Brenner, they wanted to know how many "Indians proper" could claim potential treaty benefits, versus how many interlopers "putting the government to large and useless expenses" intruded?[7] Commissioner Oberly asked Rolette to conduct another census. Given the intra-tribal tensions and disputes with agents and commissions over membership, he made light of this serious situation by joking that he did not want to get his "head broken" during such an endeavor.[8]

On a more serious note, he pointed out the contradiction between benign U.S. attitudes toward European Canadian immigration into Turtle Mountain territory versus federal government hostility toward Canadian Métis, Chippewa, or Crees. He joked that unlike federal officials, the Turtle Mountain band concerned themselves as much with the encroachments of "white Canadians from Ontario" as any unwanted First Nation Canadians or "half-breeds."[9] The CIA deflected responsibility to address the band's concerns by urging the Turtle Mountain delegates to take up their case with Senator Dawes, head of the Senate Indian Affairs Committee. Sensing the usual bureaucratic shuffle, in a parting jibe Rolette interjected a veiled threat that if the United States did not sign a treaty with them, then perhaps it could give them an appropriation for three hundred or four hundred rifles. Then the band would settle their affairs accordingly.[10] His comment reflected the growing frustration of the Turtle Mountain Chippewa over finding anyone in the federal policy echelon with whom they could negotiate.

Once again, the Turtle Mountain tribe's precious few resources went to waste as the federal government remained apathetic to their difficulty. In early 1890, Agent Cramsie continued to press his superiors in the BIA for adequate relief appropriations (i.e., $25,000 instead of $7,000). He reported that the band lived in a state of "abject poverty." Cramsie also reiterated an unpleasant truth related to the source of their dire situation. It all stemmed from when Secretary Teller set aside the twenty-four-by-thirty-two-miles reservation in 1882. As a result, "these people came and settled at Turtle Mountain in good faith." Since then, they have been "left to starve . . . owing to the long years of waiting and delay until the government gets ready to pass upon their title to the lands claimed by them and to which lands, they have never relinquished their title."[11] This admonishment verified many similar statements from tribal attorney Bottineau. The corroboration between the view from the ground by various Turtle Mountain Chippewa representatives and their agent validated the reasonableness of their claims. This convergence stood in stark contrast to the intransigence of remote and higher-level officials in the federal policy echelon. The disconnect continued to frustrate the Turtle Mountain Chippewa. In early 1890, the Turtle Mountain Chippewa sent another delegation to Washington, D.C., to once again negotiate a reasonable settlement. They still hoped that working within the U.S. legal system would avert violence and produce an equitable resolution. Little Shell III and the tribal council resisted relocation and insisted on expansion of their reservation back to its twenty-township December 21, 1882, borders.[12] In response, another three-man commission came to Turtle Mountain during the summer of 1890. The commission rejected Little Shell's solution because it "would not be possible to remove enough [white] settlers to expand the reserve" back to its larger extent.[13]

The U.S. delegation wanted to conduct a census, convince the Turtle Mountain Chippewa to cede all their land rights in North Dakota, and relocate them to the White Earth Chippewa reservation in Minnesota. The tribal council rejected these objectives for not being in their best interests.[14] Little Shell repeated his demand for the restoration of the original large reservation set aside for them in 1882. Acting Commissioner R. V. Belt confirmed that "none of the objects for which the commission was established was accomplished by it." Although he suggested that the local agent "obtain any propositions they may desire to make in regard to their affairs," Belt rejected Little

Shell's proposal on the grounds that such a request "would be in opposition to the policy of the government to reduce, as far as practicable, and not to enlarge the area occupied by Indian reservations."[15]

While the BIA Commission failed, the Government Land Office blundered into the same tense situation stirred up by the local sheriff and tax collector. Government Land Office agents attempted to assess the properties of off-reservation band members. The Métis members warned them off with guns. As a result of this interference, on August 3, 1890, Little Shell assembled the tribal council and issued a declaration of independence and solidarity. The council reaffirmed Little Shell's leadership by declaring loyalty to him as the only legitimate authority representing their ten-million-acre land claim and the other compensatory interests of the entire band. They rejected the authority of any BIA agent, especially Farmer-in-Charge E. W. Brenner, and refused to obey his orders or tolerate further meddling in their affairs. These actions precipitated a subsequent call by the sub-agent for U.S. troops to be sent from Fort Totten. But since no violence erupted, the commander did not dispatch any troops.[16]

The band's proclamation precipitated a process whereby the BIA sought to incapacitate the authority of Little Shell and the tribal council as a prelude to imposing a unilateral settlement upon the Turtle Mountain Chippewa. In contrast to former agent Cramsie's eloquent pleas on behalf of the legitimate claims and needs of the band, Agents Brenner and John H. Waugh attempted to undermine the legitimacy and governmental organization of Little Shell and the tribal council. Brenner alleged falsely that non-member Canadian Métis agitators manipulated and controlled the head and representative men.[17] In response, Congress authorized the Mahone Commission to reassess and resolve this situation.[18]

The backdrop for this sudden shift from federal apathy to a hasty settlement derived from widespread reports about the "Messiah craze." This prophet-inspired spiritual revitalization movement swept across the northern plains among various tribes (i.e., most prominently with the Lakota bands, but also the Gros Ventre and the Crow) and became known as the Ghost Dance. The Turtle Mountain Chippewa remained aloof from the movement.[19] Their non-involvement stemmed from a traditional antipathy toward the Lakota and Dakota. In addition, the traditional Midewiwin practices and Episcopalian affiliations of the Chippewa, along with the long-standing and staunch Catholicism of the Métis, weakened this Native prophetic movement's appeal to either group. Unfortunately for the Turtle Mountain Chippewa, European American overreaction to the Ghost Dance in 1890 produced a generalized and negative anti-Native American backlash similar to that evoked by the Dakota War of 1862. Local newspapers still accused them falsely of participating in the Minnesota massacres.[20] Each of these nearby but unrelated incidents came at a pivotal moment in the Turtle Mountain band's diplomatic negotiations with the U.S. government. In both instances, local European American attitudes hardened against all agreements that left any Native tribes in close proximity.

The final report of the Mahone Commission claimed that the lack of "sufficient room" on the White Earth, Minnesota, reservation accounted for its failure to convince the Turtle Mountain Chippewa to relocate themselves.[21] This was not true. While lack of space constituted a problem, focusing on it as a deal-breaker endangered the land claim settlement and adequate reservation for which the band wanted to negotiate. The commission failed in part because it resurrected the removal solution out of the federal policy grab-bag. As they had done previously, the Turtle Mountain band rejected both initiatives forcefully. The New York Times reported the "ferment" of the Natives of Turtle Mountain over another federal commission that accomplished nothing.[22] Any further negotiations became impossible because the band believed that the United States had acted in bad faith. "The Indians reiterated . . . their attachment to Turtle Mountain and preference to remain where they are."[23] The federal government persisted in doing everything except addressing the key issues raised consistently by Turtle Mountain leaders and delegations. Parallel efforts by the Interior Department looked into the feasibility of moving the band to the Fort Totten (Devils Lake) or Fort Berthold reservations in North Dakota. Although later deemed unfeasible by the department, such proposals made the band even more suspicious and dismissive of any federal initiatives.

In response to one more failed federal commission, the tribal council held a grand council on January 7, 1891. They declared that "we propose to remain here at home," because "we, the Turtle Mountain Band of Chippewa Indians, are justly entitled to the recognition of our claim." They complained that "repeated appeals and petitions" had caused them a "great deal of trouble and expense." Moreover, after all their trips to Washington, D.C., and accommodation to various visiting federal commissions, "nothing has as yet resulted toward a settlement of our claims," while "the whites are still invading our country."[24] Frustrated with the BIA, Congress, and its obstructive commissions, Attorney Bottineau recommended bypassing them all and filing a lawsuit against the Mahone Commission "for the purpose of examining the status and merits of said claim."[25]

After six more months of irresolution, the resolve of the band to remain at Turtle Mountain waned significantly. In contrast to previous tribal council affirmations, Little Shell III acknowledged that "most of my tribe are not contented to live at Turtle Mountain." Continual encroachment, episodic conflict, and the U.S. government's persistent removal talk began having its intended effect. The chief confided that he could "never live at Turtle Mountain . . . under the circumstances."[26] On August 28, 1891, Little Shell wrote to the CIA from Wolf Point, Montana, while visiting Chief Red Stones of the Assiniboine tribe. The Turtle Mountain leader recounted how the Mahone commission had suggested the possibility of a land exchange. If he and his people would relinquish their reservation and unceded territorial claim in North Dakota, could they choose another suitable location for a reservation, and be compensated for any difference in value? Little Shell III decided to explore this option, and his search brought him to Wolf Point.

Plains-Ojibwe bands like those at Pembina and Turtle Mountain had long been trading partners and allies with the Assiniboine. Little Shell obviously respected Red Stones by referring to him as "Uncle." The Turtle Mountain chief also liked the lay of the land north of the Fort Peck reservation. Based on his survey, Little Shell III asked the CIA for "a strip of land on the Missouri River above the mouth of the Milk River" (near Glasgow, Montana). Little Shell reiterated that, like the dimensions of the original 1882 Turtle Mountain reservation, the dimensions of the reservation needed to be thirty miles long and twenty-five miles wide.[27] Because "the land at Turtle Mountain [was] much more valuable to the White Man than the land on which I wish to be located, and of larger domain," the chief insisted on being compensated financially for the difference (i.e., approximately nine million acres with a higher market value). Little Shell hoped that this reasonable offer would resolve the impasse with federal authorities and "settle this matter for all time to come."[28] While Little Shell traveled out to Montana's Milk River Valley to scout for a possible new reserve large enough for the entire band, his chief warrior, Red Thunder, assumed leadership for the band and tribal council. During the chief's absence, the negotiating positions within the band and the BIA began to change in order to break the stalemate. In response to Farmer-in-Charge Brenner's 1891 report to the CIA conceding that the deplorable conditions at Turtle Mountain had been aggravated by the lack of a legal settlement in the eyes of the band, Commissioner T. J. Morgan responded untruthfully that his office had always been willing to render them a helping hand. Morgan ordered Brenner and Agent Waugh, stationed at Devils Lake, to get a definitive proposal for a settlement from the Turtle Mountain band.[29]

Based on the agents' actions, it appears their superiors had concluded that Little Shell III stood as the primary impediment to the final settlement federal officials wanted to impose. Consequently, Waugh and Brenner began undermining the principal chief's authority at Turtle Mountain. During Little Shell's absence, and in response to CIA Morgan's directives for a new census and settlement proposal, the agents engaged in a less-than-transparent process resulting in the creation of a "committee composed of sixteen half and sixteen full-blood Indians . . . trained to do [the agents'] bidding."[30] This body consisted of sixteen full bloods and sixteen mixed bloods, all "American born." They claimed "to represent the interest of their people in *any* transaction with the government in the *adjustment* of their claims."[31] This statement showed their intention to not confine themselves to acting as an ad hoc body and a willingness to scale back the band's settlement terms. They intended to supplant the authority of the principal chief and tribal council.

Questions remain about who elected this committee. No record exists of any authorization or delegation by Little Shell or the tribal council. The fact that the formation of this committee occurred during Little Shell's absence, without the inclusion of his designated deputy, Red Thunder, or other leading members of the tribal council, indicates some intrigue. While the "lack of any further action" from federal authorities had been the norm for twenty years, the increased threats of starvation and destitution most certainly made the band's dire circumstances that much worse, but not new. In terms of intra-tribal politics, Kaishpau and Little Shell had clashed before over how best to deal with European American encroachment, while J. B. Wilkie's father and Joseph Rolette had shown and affirmed their strong support for Little Shell's leadership. Yet under new pressures, prior opinions about people or personal relationships can change. The chief's trip to Montana should not have raised undue concern within the band about lack of attention to their legal claim or any sign of abandonment. Little Shell made such excursions frequently. When he did, Red Thunder and the tribal council remained authorized and in position to deal with their agents and any other federal or local officials. Meanwhile, Solicitor Bottineau remained in Washington to lobby Congress and the federal bureaucracy while pursuing the band's legal claims and lawsuit.

Agent Waugh represented the only new player in this mix. Could he have been the source for the "reports from friends in Washington" that alarmed the committee members? The reports certainly did not come from J. B. Bottineau. He remained a steadfast supporter of Little Shell's leadership. Bottineau pledged to use his Pakamagan, or "war club," "to be used in the prosecution [of] our case against the government."[32] The band's most reliable source of information from the nation's capital about their lawsuit and legal claims continued to come from their attorney. Yet this committee made no mention of their solicitor, despite the fact that he had been pressing their case forward as directed by the grand council in January 1891.

Close scrutiny of the available evidence indicates that while some genuine political dissent existed within the Turtle Mountain band and may have been exacerbated by some (but not primarily) younger Métis interlopers, no hard and fast political factions developed along blood, ethnic, geographic, religious, or ideological lines.[32] As had been the case traditionally, the fragmentary nature of Chippewa politics centered usually on family and kinship relations. As author and band member Louise Erdrich observed, "families ranged on either side of the question of money settlement."[33] Of course twenty years of frustration over coming close to any equitable settlement with the federal government led to dissent over how to proceed. Time had not been on the side of the Turtle Mountain band. The reduction of their nine-and-a-half-million-acre unceded territory to an inadequate two-township reservation became more intolerable. The aggravation of European American encroachment in the forms of cutting their timber, killing off their game, grazing cattle on their land, and harassment by local tax and law enforcement officials had exacerbated tensions to a level just shy of outright violence. All of these complications, on top of the persistence of near starvation, undermined some band members' (and nonmembers') confidence in Little Shell's and Bottineau's "great earnestness" in negotiating with the federal government.[34] Perhaps in order to survive and better their lives slightly, some felt they should pull back from previous demands for the restoration of their original 1882 reservation and accede to considerably less restitution for the cession of their homeland.

Waugh followed Morgan's directive and "called together" 167 tribal members "for the purpose of making a proposition to the United States."[35] The agent included very few of the band's representative men. Instead, he chose a sizeable segment of younger-generation mixed-bloods, many of whom had longstanding family ties within the band dating back at least twenty years.[36] This stand-in body seemed dissatisfied with the lack of progress by tribal elders like Little Shell, Red Thunder, and Bottineau toward any final agreement. They welcomed this opportunity to settle the band's claims and create the conditions necessary for them to become "self-supporting."[37] Motivated by immovable European American settlement and the persistent threat of starvation, they proposed a conceivable compromise that seems not to have been influenced unduly by Agent Waugh.

The council still wanted a reservation at Turtle Mountain. It had to be of sufficient size to accommodate the entire band based on the minimum 80-acre (or 160 acres if possible) allotment per head of household provisions of the Dawes General Allotment Act of 1887. They proposed to add an adjacent seven townships to the immediate north, west, and south of their existing two-township reservation for this purpose.[38] This creative middle course solution sought to reserve nine contiguous townships within Rolette County. It recognized the facts on the ground as reported by the various commissions that most of the easternmost townships within their original territory had already been taken by European American squatters. Only an estimated 256 immigrants had settled within the area under consideration for an adequate reservation.

This new reservation configuration—adding three southern and one western township—would give the tribe much-needed prairie lands, rich in native grasses. It provided better potential for making the transition to farming and stock raising.[39] The three additional north/northwestern townships remained unsurveyed and unsettled by European Americans. This increased the likelihood of their inclusion in the proposed reservation. These three upland townships would also provide band members with unimpeded access to timber, game, water, and fish. While this proposal fell far short of Little Shell's previous insistence on the restoration of the 1882 twenty-township reservation, they felt that more than quadrupling their current reserve to nine townships would provide them with a secure domain of "sufficient size" to accommodate all the band's household heads with adequate allotments. If accepted by the government, the band could obtain enough federally protected land without being forced to fend for themselves out on the public domain as proposed originally by Secretary Teller in 1884.

To settle the membership controversies, the ad hoc caucus asked the government to prescribe rules of evidence to determine definitively who was, and was not, an "American" Turtle Mountain Indian. This had never been an issue within the band since its inception in the greater Pembina "Hair Hills" district of Assiniboia, long before any nation-state (i.e., the United States or Canada) exerted its jurisdiction in the region.

The consanguine ties, kindred relations, geographic mobility, and cultural attributes of the Métis trumped any state identity, while both the United States and Canada denied the rights of citizenship to Natives.[40] The special council recognized that this contentious topic remained a problem for federal authorities. One can infer the council suspected, based on past experience, that officials in Washington, D.C., could never come up with any kind of fair or accurate criteria for determining U.S. versus Canadian band members. At least the council's diplomatic request put the onus for dealing with this uncertainty back on the government where it belonged.

In contrast to prior memorials, the new council's proposal omitted the usual delineation of their domain and did not mention the extent of their unceded territory. Although at least this segment of the band now seemed willing to downsize from a twenty-township to a nine-township reservation, they still insisted on equitable compensation for relinquishing such a vast portion of their homeland. Their request for $30,000 cash per annum payment as compensation for ceding

Wonequot
Chippewa

**Image 14. Wonequot and his wife dress in a way that shows how they have blended both Chippewa traditions and European American traditions.** The studded leather belt, beaded necklace, and beaded collar on the woman's dress are based in traditions acquired in the 18th century. Her blouse and skirt are typical dress of European American women at the end of the 19th century. His neck scarf and shell pin are traditional, while his shirt and trousers are modern. *State Historical Society of North Dakota, A0149.*

the rest of their Indigenous territory, plus an extensive list of articles, stock, implements, provisions, supplies, and services needed to engage in farming and to become self-sufficient, indicated that they would not settle cheaply.[41] Commissioner of Indian Affairs Morgan forwarded this new proposition from Agent Waugh to the Secretary of the Interior. The commissioner estimated its total cost to be $2,250,000.[42]

While acknowledging that "these demands may be regarded as exorbitant," he conceded that they at least "furnish a basis for a satisfactory adjustment of their alleged claims against the government." After all, the CIA asked for, and received, a "definitive proposal."[43] The entire compensation should not have been considered "exorbitant," or in need of "satisfactory adjustment" for a community facing the persistent threat of starvation. The total cost aligned closely with prior estimates from Commissioner Price and Agent Cramsie.[44] If the categorization of the Turtle Mountain Chippewa's claims as "alleged" still persisted, why did the BIA send commissions to Turtle Mountain or request a claims settlement proposition from them? Challenging the legitimacy of the band's claims after twenty years of recognition and vacillation confirmed what various Turtle Mountain representatives always complained about. They had just cause to question the good faith of the federal government to reach a fair settlement.

The real problem came down to the fact that the Turtle Mountain band's definitive proposition for a comprehensive settlement of their land claim—creation of an adequate reservation, and provision for the transition to farming and self-support—asked for too much in the eyes of their federal guardians. Federal policymakers such as Senator Dawes or T. J. Morgan, or reformers like Alice Fletcher, liked to tout the benefits Native Americans would receive from assimilation and allotment policies. Fletcher believed in the efficacy of these endeavors to "lead the natives to abandon the hunter stage and depend for their subsistence on agriculture."[45] The Turtle Mountain Chippewa's proposition indicated their willingness to embrace this approach. Yet Morgan's refusal to add the three southern townships to the existing reservation denied the area's best arable land to the band's agricultural use. Neither Congress nor the federal bureaucracy ever wanted to expend sufficient resources or funds to ensure the success of such a major transition, even when at least part of a Native community like the Turtle Mountain Chippewa wanted to undertake the transformation.

The CIA tried to explain away any consideration of the band's proposition by reverting to three old and discredited excuses. First, he asserted that federal policy precluded the creation of any new reservations except in "extreme cases." This assumed incorrectly that any consistent policy governed Indian Affairs. Since 1851, the Turtle Mountain band had held out against contrary federal policies. In 1885, President Grover Cleveland had insisted that any viable federal policy must regard each tribe's "variation of wants."[46] Second, while the government objected to "any" reservation located near the international boundary, the Turtle Mountain Chippewa reservation already existed near the border.[47] And, the addition of seven townships could not be considered a "new" reservation since legally they remained within the band's unceded territory. Third, the CIA conjectured that it would be too "expensive, difficult and impractical" to purchase the improvements of 256 European American settlers. No doubt such an undertaking would have been "difficult." Morgan's $3.75 per acre price for a 160-acre quarter section plus fixed improvements aligned with the 1890 census of wealth, debt, and taxation. The per capita value of property in Rolette County equaled $675, the highest of any of the northern two tiers of counties in North Dakota. These facts explained the actual reason why federal authorities balked.[48]

While neither a common nor popular practice from the federal government's perspective, recent precedent within Dakota Territory existed for the removal of European American squatters. In 1885, President Cleveland nullified an Executive Order by his predecessor, President Arthur. Recall that in 1884 Arthur, at the behest of Secretary of the Interior Teller, downsized the Turtle Mountain reservation by Executive Order. Arthur and Teller enacted a similar measure divesting the Lower Yankton band at Crow Creek of their treaty protected lands without tribal consent.[49] Because Cleveland believed this action caused too "much distress and suffering to peaceable Indians," he restored these tracts and ordered European American squatters evicted.[50] The close parallels in time, location, and circumstances between the Sioux and Chippewa situations and their different outcomes confirmed Cleveland's observation about the "lack of a fixed purpose or policy" within federal affairs.[51] The CIA deployed these rationalizations to cloud the real issues involving the legal claims of the Turtle Mountain Chippewa, rather than resolve them justly.

One last chance to avoid legal oblivion appeared in the summer and fall of 1892. The government relented to enter into a land cession pact and pay compensation for ceded land. It authorized the McCumber Commission to forge a final agreement with the Turtle Mountain Chippewa. McCumber claimed correctly that the purpose of his Congressional authorization sought to impose two conditions on the band: the relinquishment of all land in North Dakota, including their two-township reservation, and subsequent removal to some other reservation.[52] Yet the commission never divulged these goals to the band's representatives. This omission followed a pattern of misrepresentation and concealment. To make matters worse, upon their September arrival at the Turtle Mountain agency in Belcourt, North Dakota, the commission claimed that they encountered "two factions" representing the interests of the tribe.[53]

But the term "faction" did not reflect the state of intra-tribal turmoil. Three persistent Plains-Ojibwe cultural attributes had become more pronounced and corrosive under the pressures of near starvation and inability to secure an adequate land base. As anthropologist James Howard observed, bands like the Turtle Mountain Chippewa "usually had several chiefs," often with one becoming hereditary principal chief. This arrangement had been the case throughout the nineteenth century with the three successive generations of leaders called Little Shell. Yet, as Howard noted, "the powers of the head chief were very limited." This structure made the longevity of the majority of the band's adherence to the Little Shells even more noteworthy. Secondary chiefs (e.g., Black Duck, Red Bear, Green Setting Feather, Kaishpau) always had "followings of relatives and friends."[54] Yet consensual tribal politics usually created a prevailing super-majority that insured coherence in matters of subsistence, trade, war, or diplomacy.

By 1892, the consensual modes of Turtle Mountain Chippewa politics had become strained. Little Shell III's limited powers had eroded even further. Some scholars have alluded to greater cultural, economic, and political divergences between the Chippewa and the Métis as the major source of intra-tribal dissension.[55] Contradictory anecdotal testimony confirms and denies this state of affairs. Any conclusive inferences remain difficult to substantiate from the historical record. Another causal factor can be derived from the fact that any chief's authority would have been impaired by the convergence of adverse circumstances. By 1892, a Turtle Mountain chief faced reduced capability to organize and manage a buffalo hunt, feed his people adequately, lead the tribe in war, expend gifts and redistribute wealth, protect his people from European American encroachment and harassment by federal and local officials, or intercede with traders or agents to acquire better goods and services. A chief could still mediate some internal disputes, perform ceremonial duties if they had not been banned by the BIA, and treat with the U.S. representatives if they would deal with him. This restricted reality undermined the leadership of Little Shell III and the future of the band's cohesiveness.

Both intra-tribal groups encountered by the McCumber Commission wanted better arrangements and beneficent outcomes for their community. Chiefs Little Shell, Red Thunder, and the tribal council represented the tribally authorized and federally recognized legitimate governance of the band. They disputed the committee of thirty-two's claim to have been "elected." Most likely Agents Waugh and Brenner enticed most of them with the incentive of being "maintained and supported out of the government's rations," while Red Thunder hoped "you will relieve us from starvation, for we have nothing to eat." Claims by the commission that the group represented a "larger faction" within the band than Little Shell's following also cannot be substantiated.[56] Although the evidence indicates that they did not represent a majority of the band, McCumber decided that his commission would only negotiate with the committee of thirty-two, rather than Little Shell and the tribal council. As a result, the first flash of contention between the two groups originated from the federal government's latest attempt to create a tribal membership roll.

Anticipating a land cession settlement requiring compensation, the McCumber Commission first focused on the results of a tribal census determining how many persons would be entitled to share in any final agreement's payment. In a gross violation of tribal sovereignty, Agent Waugh attempted to dictate who belonged to the tribe. Using a sub-committee from the committee of thirty-two, the agent purged over five hundred people from the band's estimated total population of 2,284.[57] The pretext for such actions derived from arbitrary and unsubstantiated allegations that certain Native or Métis interlopers from Canada should be excluded. Because of the failed 1885 Northwest Rebellion led by Louis Riel and Gabriel Dumont in Saskatchewan, many Métis had sought refuge at Turtle Mountain. Yet knowledgeable regional observers like Father Genin disputed the persistent allegations from various BIA agents and officials about disturbances from Canadian agitators that exaggerated their numbers and influence for expedient political reasons. The priest refuted assertions that the Riel rebellion refugees flocked to Turtle Mountain and committed depredations. He claimed to have "personal knowledge that all the Indians and half-breeds now at Turtle Mountain have a perfect tribal and native right to be there."[58]

The tribe's authorized leadership reiterated the priest's position. Chief Little Shell's Cree *premier* and *chef soldat*, Red Thunder, addressed the two most critical issues facing his people: the tribe's sovereign right to determine its own membership, and the threat of starvation to their

Image 15. Red Thunder was important in the history of the Turtle Mountain Chippewa. He was a secondary chief to Little Shell III and instrumental in dealing with the McCumber Commission. *State Historical Society of North Dakota.*

physical existence. First, he recounted to the commissioners the band's mixed-blood history and hybrid collective identity. "When you [the white man] first put your foot upon this land of ours you found no one but the red man and the Indian woman, by whom you have begotten a large family." Pointing to the half-breeds present he said that "these are the children and descendants of that woman, and they must be recognized as members of this tribe."

During a meeting in January 1892, the tribal council made it clear that the band would not be separated by the federal government's intentional or haphazard efforts to determine who was, or was not, a Turtle Mountain Chippewa. The council "resolved that all the mixed blood descendants of our tribe belonging to our said band are hereby recognized to be Indians for all intents and purposes and are fully entitled to the benefits hereof the same as any of the full bloods of our said tribe and band."[59] Red Thunder went on to state that their current deplorable material circumstances derived from the lack of a legal land claim settlement with the United States. Many had gone hungry or died from starvation. To forestall this dire situation various band members "dispersed themselves over the land and across the line into Canada in quest of something to live upon pending the settlement for their lands." They would return to Turtle Mountain if a concord could be reached. Until then "those of us who are here assembled to meet you are starving . . . and we hope you [the McCumber Commission] will relieve us from starvation."[60] But these urgent pleas went unheeded. The commission refused to meet with or feed the band's general population.

The absurdity of downsizing the tribal roll based on blood quantum or unspecified "American" versus "Canadian" criterion, excluding the latter as an undesirable "foreign element," had been noted previously. Former agent John Cramsie criticized the inaccurate counts of Turtle Mountain Chippewa members based on blood quantum, and the futility of discerning distinct countries of origin for a mobile Plains-Ojibwe/Métis borderlands community. Whether someone was born in the United States or Canada ignored their historical origins. Cramsie declared that they are *all* descendants of the "Selkirk Settlement" and, when the international boundary line was run between the United States and Canada, "some were made American and some Canadian subjects. I am of the opinion that these people have rights on both sides of the line."[61]

In 1885, Robert S. Gardner, the Indian Inspector to the Secretary of the Interior, had been charged with the same pointless task. He had attempted to get band members to distinguish between "native born Indians" and "foreign born Indians," full-bloods and mixed-bloods. The tribal council responded that such distinctions represented "almost an impossibility" to discern. Gardner, like Cramsie but unlike Waugh or McCumber, conceded that the question of blood quantum remained mostly irrelevant in the Turtle Mountain community. He concluded "they are all more or less related by consanguinity and intermarriage." The tribal council informed the inspector that they and their fathers had been born and had lived in this part of the country for generations. Their origins and territorial sovereignty predated the agreed-upon international boundary line between the United States and Canada demarcated from 1872–1876. U.S.-issued certificates declaring them to be American Indians "not subject to any foreign country" confused them, since few if any knew the exact location of their birth. They considered the incoming "whites" from Canada and the United States to be the foreigners, not themselves.[62]

Some of those removed from the rolls by the committee of thirty-two, Waugh, and McCumber still possessed their certificates issued by Gardner. Little Shell and the tribal council "insisted" on the restoration of those 112 families or 512–525 individual members struck off the tribal roll by what they termed as the "pretended" business committee.[63] While McCumber claimed that his commission remained open to any valid membership appeals, in fact they refused to reinstate any of the members who had been taken off the roll. The census undertaken by the sub-committee under the tutelage of Waugh and

Brenner did not abide by any evidentiary rules or valid criteria to determine who was, or was not, entitled to be a member of the Turtle
Mountain Chippewa. Evidence from subsequent membership reduc-
tions designated the exclusion of persons born in Canada or holding
Canadian land scrip. Those born within the original nine-million-acre
Turtle Mountain tract of what became North Dakota (e.g., Pembina,
Devils Lake, Stump Lake, St. Joseph, Towner) with paternal or maternal relations within the tribe received recognition.[64] The commission
accepted unquestionably the decisions of the committee of thirty-two
by placing the burden of proof for "satisfactory evidence" of membership on those who had been removed, rather than the committee. No
evidentiary burden fell upon the committee because Agent Waugh
assured the commission that he had chosen the census sub-committee
based on their knowledge of family histories within the band. Without knowing the identities of these individuals, the agent's claim can
neither be verified nor denied.

Waugh's reassurance overlooked the fact that he blocked the participation of the tribal member with the most extensive knowledge of
family genealogy within the band: J. B. Bottineau.[65] The agent re-
neged on his promises to permit Chief Little Shell and Solicitor Bottineau to participate in the process and to review the results before
being finalized. Waugh struck tribal members off the roll despite the
fact that "the majority are holders of certificates from U.S. Indian inspector" Gardner, and thirty-five of them "occupy tracts of land upon
the reservation."[66] On September 24, 1892, the agent posted the irre-
vocable final roll on the reservation's mission church doors. It stipulated in a rather draconian manner that anyone not on this register must
leave the reservation immediately or be arrested. In response, Bottineau asserted the most vital element of sovereignty: self-determination
of tribal membership. On behalf of Little Shell and the tribal council
their attorney asserted:

> There can be no one who is more competent to judge as to
> who are and who are not members of their tribe than the chief

and his *Loge Soldat*, which, according to their laws, customs, and traditions, is the council or legislative body of said Turtle Mountain Indians, and the only representative and authority with whom business may be transacted.[67]

With this statement, the legitimate leadership of the Turtle Mountain Chippewa rejected the plenary power wielded by the commissioners and agents of the federal bureaucracy.

Bottineau alluded to his "appreciations as an Indian" for a "system" or "rational code of laws," rather than the federal government's contradictory policies. He complained about the lack of consistency faced by his people "through half a dozen or more policies and regimes under different administrations and agents."[68] Local agents and superintendents often made policy decisions on their own authority and in contravention of official directives from Washington, D.C. Two rulings on the issue of control over tribal membership by the Assistant Attorney General of the United States came too late to change the legal fate of several hundred band members who had been excluded arbitrarily from the tribal census rolls by local federal representatives. The Attorney General upheld the right of the Turtle Mountain Chippewa to determine their own membership, "without discrimination and irrespective of the source or amount of Indian blood," or whether any members had previously accepted any benefits or guarantees from the government of Canada.[69]

Bottineau protested the entire proceeding's lack of transparency and arbitrary results that separated husbands from wives and children from parents. In response, Waugh ordered Bottineau to "withdraw from the limits of the reservation" under threat of removal by the agency police. The BIA and the commission would not recognize an attorney acting on their tribe's behalf. These federal officials claimed disingenuously that they had been instructed "to deal directly with the [Turtle Mountain] people."[70] McCumber acknowledged that the "ill feeling that existed before" from the dissension of intra-tribal politics had intensified as a result of federal interference in the band's internal affairs. He alleged that threats had been made against the agency police and the committee of thirty-two. Although the commissioner did not think that any threat of "serious troubles" or imminent violence existed, he deferred to the "advise" of Waugh, Brenner, and the committee of thirty-two.[71] They requested that a company of U.S. Army troops be dispatched to the reservation without delay. Fear of illegitimacy, failure, or active resistance led the agents to almost consider a military coup d'état. But the army perceived no imminent threat and did not comply with the agent's request. Bottineau, Little Shell, and his adherents continued their protests by lawful means.

With no threat of violence and its census mandate fulfilled, the McCumber Commission began the process toward a final settlement. As with the tribal roll, McCumber refused to deal with Chief Little Shell, the tribal council, and Attorney Bottineau. Although they constituted "the only authority recognized by them, and invariably sanctioned by the United States, in the transaction of business of such matters with the Indians," Agent Waugh once again insisted that the commission would deal exclusively with the committee of thirty-two. Bottineau objected since it had not been "designated, named, or countenanced by any council of the tribe, and against their expressed wishes."[72]

After being excluded from conducting or verifying the tribal census, denied rations from the agency storehouse during the meetings with the commission, and blocked from negotiating any terms of the take-it-or-leave-it "agreement," Little Shell and the tribal council protested by leaving the sessions and the reservation. They stayed nearby and camped on Belcourt Creek hoping for a resumption of the talks.[73] Without enough food, the chief and his family—along with 140 other families—left to hunt and find support with friends and relations along the Milk River in Montana. This impasse pressured the committee of thirty-two into compliance with the McCumber Commission's settlement. With Little Shell's departure and Bottineau's removal under threat of arrest, the agents and the commission knew that they could impose the prescribed terms and conditions without any further objections. Waugh appointed Kakenowash as the new principal chief.

With Little Shell, the tribal council, and their attorney out of the way, McCumber delivered the *coup de grace*. An interpreter informed Kakenowash that "today you will have to sign for that million dollars. If you don't sign this document I brought for a million dollars, you will never get anything. Uncle Sam will take everything away from you for nothing."[74] The commission repeated this ultimatum for two days. No actual negotiations occurred. Federal officials settled the Turtle Mountain Chippewa's legal claims against the government for a pittance. While the government's offer of one million dollars ($50,000 per year for twenty years) may have sounded generous, Little Shell and his council objected to this "beggarly consideration" and the terms of distribution.[75]

The contrived negotiations concluded on October 22, 1892, with an agreement of dubious legitimacy. On behalf of—although not authorized by the recognized political representatives of—the Turtle Mountain Chippewa, 259 signatories followed the lead of Joseph Rolette and sub-Chiefs Kakenowash and Kanik. Little Shell and the tribal council accused their agents and "his adherents among the tribe" of "deception, undue influence, and intimidation." While the agents purported that the agreement had been signed by a majority of the tribe, only "one-fourth of the representative men of the tribe" participated.[76] Little Shell, Red Thunder, the tribal council, and J. B. Bottineau never signed the pact. The McCumber Agreement reaffirmed and instituted permanently the March and June 1884 Executive Orders that reduced the Turtle Mountain reservation to two townships. The McCumber Agreement became the final settlement despite eight years of persistent and compelling Turtle Mountain Chippewa protests.

Bureau of Indian Affairs agents and commissioners, plus various church officials, confirmed that such a paltry tract of land could not begin to support a majority of the band's members if federal policymakers wanted them to attain self-sufficiency. No other parts of the original and larger 1882 reservation, or any other land in North Dakota, would be reserved for them as a collective tribal entity. Instead, they had to renounce "all claims, estate, right, title, and interest" in "all lands" within the state except for the twelve-mile by six-mile two-township reservation. Even this tract did not really belong to the band. It constituted trust land "held at the pleasure of the United States." As a result of the Dawes General Allotment Act of 1887, the meager reservation would be surveyed and allotted into individual head-of-household homesteads with any surplus opened for European American settlement. If any members of the band could not secure acreage on the reservation, they could "take" free homesteads on unclaimed public domain land. For ceding all "right, title and interest" to approximately nine million acres of north-central North Dakota, the United States agreed to pay the Turtle Mountain Chippewa one million dollars in cash or annual payments as the Secretary of the Interior saw fit (see map on back cover, section labeled 1884).[77]

Questions about this "alleged agreement" remain. Did a majority of the Turtle Mountain Chippewa enter into the compact knowingly and freely? Was the bargain struck "for the best interests of the said Indians"? Clearly, Solicitor Bottineau, Chief Little Shell, and the legitimate tribal council answered no to both questions. It would seem that a majority of the band agreed, while the approximately 25 percent of the adult tribal members who consented to this pact did not constitute a certifiable majority. An analysis of the ever-changing tribal rolls, subjected to political manipulation, makes it impossible to determine this definitively. Yet the preponderance of evidence confirms that the lack of majority assent constituted one of the grounds why Chief Little Shell, the tribal council, and Attorney Bottineau considered the agreement to be "defective."[78]

The ad hoc committee's acceptance of the McCumber Commission's agreement left Little Shell, the tribal council, and Bottineau with a fait accompli. After being forced to withdraw from the meetings and the reservation due to coercion and lack of food, they reconvened the tribal council with "other representative men of the tribe" at the courthouse in nearby Rolla on October 24, 1892. They vowed to protest against the "obnoxious" agreement's ratification by Congress. The most prominent local political official, Judge John Burke, assisted them in creating this forum and acted as an advisor and witness to these proceedings. The beloved local Catholic priest, Father John Malo, also presided. At this session the chief and council of the recognized tribal government sent a formal protest to the commissioner of Indian Affairs against the ratification by Congress of the "alleged" agreement.[79]

They reiterated their adherence to Pembina and Turtle Mountain Chippewa "custom, practice, and tradition" in recognizing Little Shell as their hereditary chief. The detailed information on each tribal council member's age, rank, and years of service affirmed them as a group of respected elder councilmen and braves with long-standing ties to the Little Shell lineage and significant kinship ties and community service within the bands. The empowerment of Chief Little Shell and *La Loge Soldat* (tribal council) accorded with "the laws of said Indians," and "represented the only authority recognized by the tribe for the transaction of any business of the tribe with the Government, or with any other nation or tribe." These self-governing entities had "always been recognized by all Indian tribes or nations, as well as by the Government of the United States." They contrasted themselves pointedly with Agent Waugh's unauthorized committee of thirty-two and categorized "Little Joe Rolette" as "an incompetent and prejudiced interpreter" with no official tribal sanction.[80]

The formal protest from the lawful representatives of the Turtle Mountain Chippewa rested upon the following eight grounds. First, as hereditary chief, Little Shell and his tribal council constituted the only legitimate government of the Turtle Mountain band. They demanded re-recognition of their authorized status as a necessary prelude for any talks with the commissioners. The self-constituted committee council "was never selected, appointed, or recognized by the tribe," and therefore had no authority to transact any official business on the band's behalf.[81] Second, while Waugh had originally sent out invitations for the entire tribe to meet with the McCumber Commission, he and Brenner used the inadequate agency storehouse for the band's meetings with the commissioners. Because of its structural limitations and inventory, most of the people inside could neither see nor hear the proceedings. Waugh packed the place with the committee of thirty-two and their adherents to weaken the authority of Little Shell, the tribal council, and their attorney. This forum only represented one-fourth of the tribe's members and not a legitimate majority as mandated by the commission's instructions from Congress.

Third, in addition to the lack of space for a full tribal assembly, those tribal members who participated were not given sufficient time, freedom, or opportunity to deliberate on the commissioner's proposals. Band representatives still objected to the two-township Executive Order reservation of 1884. Little Shell and tribal council wanted the 1882 twenty-township reservation restored to the Turtle Mountain Chippewa. But the commission decreed a non-negotiable settlement. The band had to relinquish all their land claims within North Dakota (except for the two-township reservation, which technically had become federal trust land) for one million dollars. Tribal representatives deemed this paltry compensation for their ceded lands as wholly inadequate, and not in line with local market values or awards to neighboring tribes. Since the territory of the Turtle Mountain Chippewa approximated ten million acres of land, Attorney Bottineau dubbed the McCumber agreement as the "ten-cent treaty."[82]

Fourth, Agent Waugh unduly influenced the unauthorized committee of thirty-two's decision by making sure that they and their families received food, while threatening to remove any dissenters from their land. At the same time, he withheld the distribution of any rations to Little Shell and his followers. This duress produced the desired result. The chief and tribal council left the proceedings in protest. The BIA agents and the McCumber Commission refused to allow Native "wards" to have any legal representation of their own choosing. As directed by Little Shell and the tribal council, J. B. Bottineau did his best to assist the agents with the crucial and controversial tribal census and represent the band's interests in negotiations with the commission. Instead, Agent Waugh broke his promise to let Bottineau review the tribal roll before the BIA finalized it. The agent then ordered Bottineau removed from the commission meetings and the reservation under threat by the agency police.

Fifth, Bottineau had submitted a legal brief outlining the band's legal claims to John W. Noble, the Secretary of the Interior, before the arrival of the McCumber Commission.[83] While the band's representatives wanted desperately to negotiate a good faith settlement with someone in authority from the federal government, neither Noble nor McCumber would do so. The McCumber Commission did not come to Turtle Mountain to negotiate a settlement. Instead, it imposed a non-negotiable pact. The Secretary's pending review and decision should have precluded any other federal initiatives, especially the finality of the commission's edict.

Sixth, the heart of Little Shell and Bottineau's protest derived from their outrage over the federal government's paltry land cession compensation, which they characterized derisively as the "ten-cent treaty." After its longstanding loyalty and peaceful relations with the United States, the tribe felt insulted and betrayed. Recently they had assisted federal officials in stopping Canadian smugglers along the international boundary through Turtle Mountain. The real inequity stemmed from the much larger payments given to other regional tribes, some of whom had engaged in hostilities with the United States. In 1889, Minnesota Chippewa and Dakota bands in Dakota Territory received $1.25 to $2.50 an acre for agricultural lands, and fifty cents to seventy-five cents per acre for pine lands. The $2.50 per acre amount compensated the neighboring Sisseton-Wahpeton bands, whose lands constituted a similar type and quality of soil, climate, and value. These disparities stunned the Turtle Mountain Chippewa representatives into wondering why they had been discriminated against and unable to receive comparable compensation.[84]

They did not limit their objection to the miserly and far-below-market-value payout of $50,000 per year for twenty years. Rather than the per capita cash annuity option in the agreement, the Secretary of the Interior "saw fit" to instead designate $45,000 of each year's appropriation for farming equipment and products. The tribe's representatives knew from "past experience" that this "invariably prove[d] more profitable to the commission or middle men, transportation and other agents, than to themselves."[85] Without going into specifics, Bottineau referred to the well-known convergence of self-interest among groups of local merchants, politicians, bureaucrats, and federal agents who skimmed profits from the sale of government-supplied equipment, tools, stock, rations, clothing, and other goods allocated for reservation Natives. The agreement's allocation of every year's payment guaranteed that the cash amount for each tribal member would only equal $1.50 or $1.60. Instead of ceding their birthright for a sustainable future, such a pittance would only perpetuate the band's hardship and increase their dependency.

Seventh, one-third of the tribe's members lived within the original twenty-township reservation but resided outside of the reduced two-township tract. The McCumber Agreement left them unprotected by the federal government, subject to the hostile jurisdiction of local county authorities, and cut off from Native schools. As a result of all these grievances, Little Shell and the tribal council felt compelled to act quickly. Rather than accede to the McCumber Agreement or await the Secretary of the Interior's pending review of Bottineau's proposal, the chief and his council insisted on sending a delegation to Washington, D.C., to meet with the House Committee on Indian Affairs. If Congress could not determine the validity of the Turtle Mountain Chippewa request, the band would seek approval for their petition to be referred to the Court of Claims.

For their eighth proposal the tribe wished to "finally settle this perplexing and protracted claim," "adjust all differences and objections," and "negotiate . . . for an equitable settlement of their claim by treaty or agreement."[86]

The entire McCumber Commission episode represented an egregious example of federal officials using food as a weapon to coerce a starving people into relinquishing their birthright for a pittance. Since the authorized leader and representatives of the tribe refused to sign the agreement, opposed its execution, and protested against its ratification, it could be construed as not legally binding.[87] The agent's undue influence and the commission's arbitrary proceedings "vexed the Turtle Mountain Indians" and created legal grounds for nullifying the agreement.

Attorney Bottineau stated that ratification by Congress of this "alleged agreement . . . would not only perpetrate the grossest injustice," but also "lay the government open to the charge of being inconsistent with its dignity or not honorable to its humanity."[88] By any standards of justice or equity, such dealings were neither "fair" nor "honorable," compounded by the "grossly inadequate and unconscionable" compensation.[89]

Resisting attempts by unscrupulous agents to usurp their limited tribal sovereignty and delegitimize their governance, Attorney Bottineau insisted that they remained capable of self-determination. He asserted that they "are as well qualified today to judge for themselves as to what may be needed for their best interest as any other class of people."[90] They wanted a fair market price for their land. Because nearby railroads and other Native tribes received $1.00 to $2.50 per acre for farmland, and $3.00 or more per acre for timber land, the Turtle Mountain Chippewa rejected the government's ten cents an acre settlement as a "gross discrimination" and "monstrous injustice."[91] The commission conceded that it sought the $1,000,000 remuneration as "the lowest sum it could secure." While admitting that the government had "paid other tribes quite liberally for their claims," they seemed obliged to rationalize the amount as "exceedingly favorable to the government."[92] That understatement cannot be disputed.

The band also objected to how treaty funds would be distributed. They asserted that an annual $5,000 per capita payment for approximately 2,500 Chippewa would have been meaningless. The other proposed annual payment of $45,000 would be used for seed, farm equipment, and other goods and services. The Turtle Mountain Chippewa saw through this sleight of hand. With such a ploy, 90 percent of their compensation would go to non-Native agents, contractors, and businesses. Attorney Bottineau had nothing but contempt for agents "who, after having failed to make an honorable living for themselves in their civilized communities, have sought an Indian agency" not for the salary but the "prerequisites."[93] Since the actions and proposals of the agents went "against the wishes of the Chief Little Shell and his council, said treaty agreement was not signed," and the Turtle Mountain Chippewa "protest[ed] against the ratification of the same by Congress."[94]

Little Shell, Red Thunder, and Bottineau always regarded Kakenowash and the adherents of the former committee of thirty-two as unauthorized to represent the band's interests in part because they remained under the sway of BIA officials. In 1893, the commissioner of Indian Affairs confirmed their partial collaboration. He stated that this working group "labored faithfully to help the recent commission to make the agreement for the settlement of their affairs . . . in line with the views of the department."[95] Yet this body's protests to federal authorities proved them not to be complete tools of the BIA. Frustrated by the unratified status of the McCumber Agreement they had signed three and a half years before, they sent a formal memorial to Congress. They reiterated their rights of "occupancy and possession" as the "rightful owners" of at least 9,000,000 acres in Turtle Mountain country. Since many federal officials had recognized this question of fact, they asked how the government had taken possession of and sold lands without their consent, "and allowed its white children to occupy" them "without compensation to us." They not only pushed for speedy ratification, but also made other demands. Their desperate need for money led them to propose a dramatic alteration of the payment terms. Instead of extending over twenty years, their memorial called for $200,000 cash remuneration for the first two years, and a $100,000 payment the third year. The initial $1,000,000 fund and the $500,000 remainder would receive 5 percent interest annually.

The band's representatives argued that only with these larger infusions of cash could they "establish permanent homes" and "do more than eke out a scanty existence." Since lack of land still comprised the major problem, they asked for an additional four townships to be added to their two-township reservation. This request represented another step-down attempt at a compromise similar to, but smaller than, their 1891 proposition. New demands included compensatory claims arising from the incorrect determination of the southern boundary of their domain, the government's cutting of 100,000 cords of wood on their land at the Fort Totten reservation near Devils Lake, and lands taken but not paid for by the Great Northern Railway.[96]

But another European American demographic wave, combined with "a perpetuation of a long line of minimal interest" by the U.S. government, finally stymied the legal struggle of the Turtle Mountain Chippewa.[97] Tenant farmers from Pennsylvania, Ohio, Virginia, Indiana, Illinois, and Michigan moved into the burgeoning wheat belt of North Dakota by the trainload to secure a freehold. The Great Northern Railway sponsored special "moving party" trains of fifty passengers and eighty freight cars carrying as many as 1,500 farmers and their families from Chicago to the Devils Lake, Turtle Mountain, and the Souris (Mouse) River districts.[98] The "expected young Oklahoma boom" happened finally, and prior settlers anticipated that increased immigration would raise their property values.[99]

To make matters worse for the Turtle Mountain Chippewa, a "serious outbreak" of smallpox, accompanied by calls for quarantine, vaccine, and "full rations" cast a further pall over their community, which had grown to 3,410 by 1900.[100] As had happened before, the non-implementation of the pending 1892 settlement exacerbated the tribe's dire circumstance. Aware of the negative consequences this imposed on the band's welfare, Bottineau continued to lobby against the McCumber Agreement. He lodged one more formal protest with the Secretary of the Interior citing four major grievances: 1) the land cession compensation's "beggarly consideration" only "netted each indi-

vidual about $1.50 or $1.60 in cash" per year; 2) the agreement fell far
short of the money needed for education, especially for the one-third
of the band comprised of Natives; 3) it failed "to protect the persons
and property" of the Chippewa and the Métis; and 4) the execution
of the agreement remained unlawful without the consent or approval
of the chief or council of the tribe "according to the laws, regulations, customs, and traditions of the Indians."[101] Bottineau succeeded
in getting his alternatives to the McCumber Agreement, including
restoration of the original twenty-township reservation, through the
Committee on Indian Affairs for consideration by the House of Representatives. Although modeled on recent agreements made with the
Minnesota Chippewa and the Sioux in Dakota, the acting commissioner of Indian Affairs belittled these proposals as "fanciful" and "ridiculous," thus killing their slim chance for enactment.[102]

While the extraordinary efforts of Bottineau in Washington,
D.C., failed to improve the band's legal situation, the combined actions of Agents Waugh and Brenner, the McCumber Commission,
and the committee of thirty-two had weakened and eroded the authority of Little Shell's chieftainship and the tribal council since 1892.
The aging chief admitted to his attorney that "my greatest fatigue is
to see my people so poor and going so hungry." Frustration over the
inability to protect his people from disease, hunger, poverty, and injustice caused Chief Little Shell III to "die unhappy for his people" in
1900. Red Thunder died in 1902.[103] The spark of the Turtle Mountain
band's political resistance faded considerably, but it did not die.

Kakenowash became principal chief, while others from the committee of thirty-two joined the tribal council. J. B. Bottineau continued the fight against ratification of the McCumber Agreement on behalf of the new chief and council from his office in Washington, D.C.
He lobbied U.S. Attorney General George H. Shiels for his opinion on
the findings of the McCumber Commission and the status of the Turtle Mountain band's "Indian title." The executive branch's chief legal
officer criticized McCumber's title investigation because it exceeded

the commission's authorization by Congress. In addition, Shiels stated that no Native land cession agreement could be ratified prior to his investigation and approval. Without this sanction, Bottineau stood on solid legal ground by referring consistently to the agreement as "alleged" and "being inconsistent" with the honor of the government.[104]

But the band's latest agent, W. O. Getchell, reiterated the same racist rationalizations as his immediate predecessors. He believed their "claim to be a just one, if any Indian claim was ever a just claim." The commission's title search had concluded "that the Turtle Mountain Band of Chippewa Indians have as valid an original title to [their] entire [8,000,000 to 10,000,000 acre] tract of land [north and west of Devils Lake] as any Indian tribe had to any" Indigenous territory.[105] Yet the agent alleged that "the Turtle Mountain band of Chippewa should never be considered as a band of Indians" because "they are half-breeds, quarter breeds, etc." In Getchell's opinion, such circumstances precluded their entitlement to any reservation. He also ignored that they had been self-supporting and independent prior to 1892. Believing in the assimilationist myth of a level playing field that guaranteed success, the agent recommended that they should be "paid off" and then left to "sink or swim in the same boat as their white competitors."[106]

The agent implied that the Chippewa and Métis people of Turtle Mountain could not adapt to the new market economy of the late nineteenth century. Yet they were never given a fair chance to "swim" after the destruction of their traditional subsistence practices by external forces. Government policy and European American attitudes and behaviors excluded them from sustainable economic endeavors and forced them to "sink" into dependency. Despite all the rhetoric about assimilation into European American society, neither federal policies nor their North Dakota neighbors welcomed the Turtle Mountain Chippewa into their communities or bestowed the "benefits of civilization" upon them. Instead, "arrogant provincialism" prevailed.[107] The local *Dunseith Herald* continued to reflect the reality of anti-Native and anti-Métis racism through its constant references to Turtle

Mountain "breeds" and "half-breeds" as "dirty" and "lazy" "vagabond bucks" whom they would like to see removed to make room for "worthy" European American or Canadian farmers in the "Garden of the Northwest." The paper updated "an old saying that 'no Indian is so good as a dead Indian,' but we venture the opinion that no Indian at all is better."[108] At the bidding of powerful local and national interests, federal policy directed at Native Americans continued to be "a process of economic destruction" imposing formulas that ignored their sovereignty, land and timber claims, legal rights, treaties, and customs.[109] The injustice of the federal government toward his people mystified J. B. Bottineau. Yet he remained confident that a future review of the facts in their case by judges and historians might render a disposition that would "do substantial justice."[110]

Getchell's recommendation on behalf of the band's "white competitors," rather than equity, began taking its final form. The Senate Committee on Indian Affairs, chaired by Senator McCumber of North Dakota, confirmed the 1892 agreement with the Turtle Mountain band on January 25, 1904.[111] On March 21, 1904, the U.S. Senate engaged in a brief debate before making minor amendments and finally ratified the McCumber Agreement.[112] Senator McCumber and Senator Henry Teller dominated the discussion. Teller reviewed how he had vacated Secretary of the Interior Schurz's 1881 Order, withdrawing unceded Turtle Mountain Chippewa territory from survey and opening it to settlement. He based this dubious legal action on his unsubstantiated characterization of the Turtle Mountain Chippewa's "Indian title" as "somewhat uncertain." At the same time, the U.S. House of Representatives had passed a bill to pay the band $4,000,000 in compensation for this federal "taking." But Teller asked the Senate to "withhold action" on the bill, which the Senate did as a courtesy to one of its former members. Not surprisingly, in 1904, he opposed proposals from other senators for an $8,000,000 or $10,000,000 recompense and recommended that they should stick to the original $1,000,000 sum. In a revealing statement possibly indicating Teller's unease, the senator told his colleagues that "the best thing to do is get rid of the controversy by the passage of this bill."[113]

At least Senator McCumber reviewed some of the questions of fact in the Turtle Mountain claim. He reiterated that the Turtle Mountain Chippewa's "vast tract" of nine to ten million acres of land occupied "some of the very best portions of the State of North Dakota." Land in this region ranged in value from less than $10 to more than $30 per acre, averaging $15 to $25 per acre. McCumber countenanced Teller's actions as Secretary of the Interior and the subsequent Executive Orders. He rationalized that "whatever might be the result of an investigation as to their title, there was no *necessity* of holding this vast tract of land from settlement."[114] According to Teller and McCumber, "Indian title" did not exist as a matter of law, judicial precedent, or question of fact. If a federal official in a position of power discerned its "uncertainty," while another felt no "necessity" to honor its legal significance and act accordingly, then no tribe's unceded lands could ever be protected from being extinguished by the U.S. government. As Solicitor Bottineau lamented, "the authorities of the Government have really done nothing for these Indians, only to consume time and expense during the period of nearly 30 years in endeavoring to remove them from their home on Turtle Mountain."[115]

McCumber claimed that Congress appointed his commission to determine the questions of Turtle Mountain Chippewa title and tribal membership. While questions remained as to the exact number and the precise extent of their domain, the commission confirmed Turtle Mountain Chippewa title to the nine or ten million acres in question based upon their continuous occupation of the Turtle Mountain district under the leadership of three successive generations of chiefs named Little Shell. These lands had never been ceded to the United States by the band. During the attenuated negotiations in 1892, the band's attorney had proposed a $1.25 per acre basis for a total compensation of $12,500,000 to settle their claim. McCumber asserted that his take-it-or-leave-it offer of $1,000,000, or $.10 per acre, derived from

the Senate Committee on Indian Affairs determination that this represented an "equitable and fair" settlement. Reconciling this final figure
with his prior statements, noting the less than $10 to more than $30
per acre market value of these lands, remains difficult.

McCumber expressed the urgent need for a final settlement to
avert violence and bloodshed because European American settlers had
secured almost all of the Turtle Mountain Chippewa land. The senator
noted how "every quarter section is taken right up to the reservation,"
creating contentious circumstances where "you will find the claim
shanty on the same quarter section that you find the Indian shanty."
McCumber provided a dramatic episode to underscore his concerns:

> An Indian full blood had cleared up to forty acres, moved the
> stone from it, broke it, and cropped it. A [European American]
> settler came in last year, filed a homestead on it, and put in
> his crop. He raised a crop, and harvested, cut and shocked
> it. Every full-blooded Indian in that section of the country
> came over one Sunday with their teams and wagons and
> hauled away every shock on that place, as they did on several
> others.[116]

McCumber quoted an unspecified Turtle Mountain band member,
after being arrested and taken before a magistrate, as saying:

> Here we have been docile. We have never been at war with
> the United States. We have been their scouts when they had
> wars with the Sioux. We have always been friendly to the
> [United States]. On the other hand, the moment the Sioux
> raised [their] arms against the whites, the Government went
> down in its pockets and paid them $2.50 to $3.00 per acre for
> their land.[117]

This testimony substantiated Bottineau's charge of federal policy discrimination against the Turtle Mountain Chippewa.[118]

Despite the letter and spirit of the McCumber Agreement, one
constant problem confronted by the Turtle Mountain Chippewa centered on their inability to secure legal title on allotted Native or public
domain lands. The lack of land on the two-township reservation had
been a persistent problem since its creation by Executive Order in

1884. Even at that time—let alone twenty years later—neither current adult members nor their born or unborn children could secure enough land to live on. The Land Office case of *William Morgan v. Andrew Vandal et.al.,* in 1910 illustrated the legal problems over land faced by countless tribal claimants forced to compete with non-Native immigrants. William Morgan, a Welsh coal miner, emigrated to Montana via Canada and North Dakota. In 1908, he filed for a homestead on allotted Native land selected previously by Turtle Mountain Band of Chippewa members Andrew Vandal and his two sons-in-law, Frank and Gregory Grant.

Vandal lived at Graham's Island, off the reservation, near Devils Lake. The Grants lived on the reservation at Belcourt. Because almost all the land on or near the reservation had long been taken, members like Vandal and the Grants tried to secure property on the public domain near Glasgow, Montana. They probably had relations among nearby members of the Little Shell band. Yet the land acquisition process turned out to be cumbersome, expensive, and less than secure. First, they had to pay perhaps a quarter of their meager per capita payment from the McCumber Agreement to a non-Native "locator" to find an available plot. Then they had to file their "squatting papers." During this process, Morgan filed a homestead claim on the same piece of land. Vandal and the Grants had to hire a lawyer to try and protect their rights. In this case, their lawyer demonstrated during cross examination that Morgan testified falsely to the dates and duration of being on his illegal homestead. His alleged "improvements" consisted only of a ten-by-twelve-foot sod shack and a furrow around the claim, which failed to meet the minimal requirements for securing a homestead. Witnesses placed him elsewhere in Montana and North Dakota working at various coal mines to make a living.

Although Vandal and the Grants won their case against Morgan, such an outcome remained atypical. Very few Turtle Mountain families had the resources, tenacity, or faith in the equity of the U.S. legal system to pursue and win challenges to their land claims from European Americans. This case provides a glimpse into some of the legal nightmares of land allotment. Overlapping and conflicting categories and entitlements collided. "Ward, or trust patent Indians" had their land held in trust by the federal government. "Patent in fee Indians" had fee-simple title to their land. "Non-enrolled Indians" had no entitlement to land and were subject to the same land laws as non-Natives.[119] This unmanageable situation deteriorated further into complete legal chaos when the children of these various classifications intermarried and created innumerable fractionated heirship allotments resulting in tiny plots of land unable to sustain anyone.

Because most of the dispersed Little Shell band fell into the "non-enrolled Indians" classification, they could not secure land tenure under any treaty, agreement, or federal allotment laws. Instead, they had to fend for themselves on the public domain subject to homestead laws. A far more representative example of this scenario, in contrast to the legal victory of Vandal and the Grants, involved Joseph Dussome.[120] The most significant sites of his early life illustrated the broad geographic range of the Turtle Mountain Chippewa across the northern plains. His mixed-blood parents had been born into the Pembina Chippewa band in the Red River Valley of northeastern North Dakota. Dussome was born at Malta, Montana, in 1879, and baptized in Leroy, North Dakota, on the Pembina River (east of St. Joseph and west of Pembina). Since the predominant mixed-blood aspect of the band always raised questions about whether they should be considered "real" Natives, Dussome asserted, "I am Indian, sure, you bet. I belong to the Chippewa tribe. I am a mixed blood." His first language was the unique blend of French, Cree, and Chippewa known as Michif. He claimed that all the differently named groups—Turtle Mountain Chippewa, Pembina Chippewa, or Little Shell's band—"spoke the same language."[121]

To help clarify the overlapping nature of these groups, Dussome identified his parents as members of the Turtle Mountain band until 1892. Then they "pulled out" with Little Shell III after his refusal to comply with the dictates of agent Waugh and the McCumber Commission. Dussome's mother received some rations but no allotment of land from the "alleged agreement." Many ex-Turtle Mountain Chippewa in Montana became known as the separate Little Shell band. Members of both groups applied for land allotments on the public domain of Montana.

Dussome's mother "filed" and "paid the dues" to secure land tenure. Yet after living on their allotments from two to six years, they were "cancelled" on the grounds that the Little Shell were not affiliated with any recognized tribe. As a consequence, the breakaway Little Shell Band became known as the "landless" Natives of Montana.[122]

Dussome's testimony and personal experience illustrated the difficulties faced by mixed-blood Native Americans to secure any land tenure. He acquired a 160-acre homestead "close to Malta" and then acquired an additional 320 acres. He lost the 320 acres to a European American who took it up as a homestead. As a Native American, Dussome was told that he could not "hold" (i.e., acquire a patent in fee title) land. As a result, he felt compelled to "give up" his original 160-acre homestead. "There was no use trying to hold it. I just as well might borrow money on it and quit the country." He turned it over to a local bank.[123] This became a frequent scenario for many Turtle Mountain people who tried to obtain an allotment or a homestead on the public domain of North Dakota or Montana.

The promises of the 1863 Old Crossing Treaty, the Executive Order of 1884, and the 1892 McCumber Agreement to "fair and reasonable" access to "adequate" non-reservation public domain land remained unfulfilled by the federal government. As envisioned by Secretary of the Interior Henry M. Teller in 1882, federal land and policies divided and scattered the Turtle Mountain Chippewa across the northern plains.[124] The Native Americans faced surges of aggressive European American settlers lured to North Dakota and Montana by promises of "free land" advertised by railroad land departments, land speculation companies, bonanza farm publicity, and boosterish local newspapers. Because government solutions to the alleged "Indian problem" remained so divorced from reality, none of them—especially allotment on the public domain—ever worked to benefit Native people.

Since the McCumber Agreement affirmed the two-township reservation of the 1884 Executive Orders, by 1904 European American encroachment and the growing population of the band made the land scarcity situation that much worse. The senator conceded that 90 percent of the Chippewa and Métis would have to secure land elsewhere. Yet the experiences of Vandal and Dussome showed the emptiness of such vague assurances. The agreement stipulated that all Turtle Mountain band members unable to secure land on the reservation could take a homestead upon any vacant land on the public domain, with the General Land Office waiving the $14 entry and any other fee. The federal policy echelon's goal of displacement had been realized. Henry Teller's solution of scattering the band across the public domain had been implemented. As McCumber summarized approvingly, "the result will be to destroy the tribal relations of the Turtle Mountain tribe, because the Indians will have to be scattered. The land is not there for them."[125] The goals of federal policy toward the Native population had rarely been stated so candidly.

After Congress ratified the McCumber Agreement on April 21, 1904, one last legal formality had to be performed before it went into effect. A majority of the adult males from the Turtle Mountain band had to sanction the amended agreement.[126] As with the McCumber Commission in 1892, when Agent Waugh allowed no interference or dissent in getting the requisite compliance from enough band members, Agent Charles Davis rode roughshod over his "Indian wards" when the McCumber Agreement came up for final ratification in February 1905.

At the ratification meetings, Davis reminded the band members assembled that for them to finally get the $1,000,000 (i.e., the forced recompense from 1892, which remained conveniently free of any accrued interest), they had to relinquish "all of their rights and every claim that you have against the U.S. government."[127] As McCumber had told them twelve years before, Davis reiterated that if they did not sign, they would receive no money. In the subsequent casting of votes, whose procedures deviated from those stipulated in the agreement, far less than a majority of the adult members on the Davis Roll of 2,094 persons (201 full-bloods and 1,893 mixed-bloods) voted. Davis conceded the incompleteness of his census and admitted that "scores of eligibles" should have been included.[128]

According to tribal historian Charlie White-Weasel, the rush to finalize the agreement precluded any further delay.[129] The voting results demonstrated the irregular nature of the process. Glossing over the coercive tactics employed by U.S. officials, Davis telegraphed the band's ratification vote to the Interior Department on February 18, 1905. The tally read 280 votes for and zero against.[130] J. B. Bottineau protested the "arbitrary proceedings in securing the acceptance and ratification," including the insufficient notice given prior to signing the amended treaty and the fact that many band members were absent from the reservation at the time of the vote.[131] This charade of consent belied the "rule of law" pronouncements of federal policymakers. Bottineau remonstrated that "there can be no practical civilization with the Indians, or any other people, until a rational code of laws is established and adequate means provided for their efficient and speedy execution."[132]

In 1905, as in 1892, how did these pressure tactics by U.S. representatives work so effectively? During the intervening thirteen years, the physical security of the Turtle Mountain Chippewa became more tenuous. Actual and potential European American settler encroachments gave the federal government a political potency it could not have achieved otherwise. John Summer confirmed that when the agreement became final in 1905, "there was no land here to be taken, all taken up, so we were shoved toward Montana where there was vacant land."[133] Mathias LaFromboise corroborated that "the whites filed on Indian homesteads and booted them out of their homes and off their land."[134] These dire circumstances convinced some in the band to take the necessary desperate measures of removing their tribe's legitimate representatives, and settle for something rather than risk losing everything. In the end, starvation and its pervasive threat cowed the Turtle Mountain Chippewa into acquiescence. The deaths of 150 people in the winter of 1887 haunted the band for generations. In 1905, Chief Kakenowash confirmed that the band's appalling circumstances leveraged his vote in favor of the "ten-cent treaty." He confessed to be starving when he made his mark. He believed sincerely that "with a million dollars they would be well fed."[135] Even that logical assumption turned into more bitter disappointments, as most of the money went to non-Natives.

By 1905, after decades of legal wrangling with the federal government, incursions by neighboring European Americans, and harassment by local authorities, the Turtle Mountain Chippewa were forced to accept the two-township reservation mandated by the 1884 Executive Order and the "obnoxious agreement" of 1892. But they still contested this outcome by reiterating that "there is ample evidence showing the merits of the claim of the Turtle Mountain Indians, and the great wrongs and injustice in their treatment by this Government." Yet the "monstrous injustice" of the "ten-cent treaty" became the law of the land.[136] Despite all the rhetoric about assimilation into European American society, their North Dakota neighbors did not absorb the Turtle Mountain Chippewa into the European American community or bestow the "benefits of civilization" upon them.

Further evidence for the lack of factionalism, and confirmation that the signing of the McCumber Agreement occurred under the duress of starvation, can be inferred from the subsequent about-face in Kakenowash's political stance vis-à-vis the federal government. After 1905, Kakenowash pursued the same claims as his predecessor, Little Shell. The new chief declared that "our claim against the Government is for land we did not sell, and for land sold to the white people that should have been paid to us, and for putting railroads on our land [that] we didn't get any money for it." Tribal delegates and deponents continued to persist that the U.S. government took possession of Turtle Mountain Chippewa lands "forty years before they gave us anything."[137]

The United States permitted the Great Northern railroad company to establish their rights-of-way, stations, tracks, and other facilities in 1889, before consummating the McCumber Agreement in 1892. The Turtle Mountain band contended that they should be compensated by one-fourth of the profits that the government derived from this illegal taking of their land. But the Department of the Interior and the BIA denied the legitimacy of these claims and resorted to undermining the legal implications of the December 21, 1882, Executive Order that created the original large reservation. Because Congress had no role in the Executive Order process, an assistant commissioner alleged that Congress had never recognized the Turtle Mountain land claim or their initial reservation.[138] This allegation implied that the president had the unquestioned right to change the size and location of the reservation and to restore the remaining lands to the public domain, as he did on March 29, 1884. Since these changes occurred prior to granting a right-of-way to the Great Northern railroad, the government insisted that it did not constitute a "taking" and precluded any additional compensation for the Turtle Mountain band.

These legal interpretations followed neither the letter nor the spirit of the law. Such rulings ignored the Native disclaimer clause in the Dakota Territory and North Dakota state enabling acts. They also violated the spirit of what the Turtle Mountain Chippewa thought they had secured. How could they have been expected to understand the technical differences between an Executive Order reservation versus one ratified by Congress? This duplicity represented one example of what tribal Solicitor J. B. Bottineau categorized as part of the "damages and wrongs perpetrated upon our people under the guise of law."[139]

For generations, this Native community had heard a variety of treaty commissioners, agents, visitors, and other federal officials tell them how the "Great Father" had unbounded amounts of power, wealth, and compassion at his disposal. Treaty councils and delegation meetings in Washington, D.C., informed them that he would protect the interests of his Native "children." Now, after more than thirty years of litigation, a minor official within the federal policy bureaucracy asserted that a president of the United States can give with one hand and take away with the other. Since Congress chose not to take any corresponding legislative action from 1882 to 1892, which at the time would have been redundant and unnecessary, the Turtle Mountain Chippewa's claim fell victim to the consequences of such "arbitrary proceedings."[140] The urgency and importance of their case remained a "painful fact" and "matter of life and death" because, as Kakenowash reiterated, "we did not sell the Turtle Mountains."[141] Long after the ratification of the McCumber Agreement, none of the band's political representatives believed that their claim with the federal government had been settled justly. Shortly before his death in 1911, J. B. Bottineau reaffirmed the political determination of the Turtle Mountain Chippewa by declaring that "we shall proceed and succeed in redeeming, if not all, the greater part of our long practical cause."[142]

# CONCLUSION

*Too bad the Indians are not the lineal and direct descendants of Methuselah and inherit his longevity coupled with the patience of Job, that they might live to see some of the just obligations, established by precedent and treaty stipulations, fulfilled by the government.*[1]
—John W. Cramsie, U.S. Agent for the Turtle Mountain Indians (1886)

By focusing on the Turtle Mountain Chippewa's history, we can gain a new outlook on tribal-federal relations from a Native American perspective. The tribe consistently based their nineteenth-century legal claims on the grounds of "rights," "settlement," and "payment for the land we rightfully own."[2] In addition to providing strong proof for the validity of their case, they documented their struggle "to secure the recognition of, and a settlement with the United States Government, for our unceded lands."[3] They challenged the "injuries, wrongs and damages to our rights and property which we as a tribe and as individuals have suffered" at the hands of federal authorities that attempted to force the Turtle Mountain band from their homeland. Policymakers refused to create an adequate reservation and reach a just settlement with the Turtle Mountain Chippewa. Such governmental misdeeds left most of the band "outside of their reduced reservation, unprotected from being driven out of their individual locations and homes by white settlers." Yet, even under duress, the Turtle Mountain Chippewa remained gracious enough to want "protection, peace and tranquility" for themselves "as well as their white neighbors."[4]

This case study shows that during the nineteenth-century, the Turtle Mountain Chippewa suffered from the institutionalized bad faith imposed by "the arbitrary will of the Government's agents" from "half a dozen or more policies or regimes," rather than "the merits of the claim," "a system of law," or "the ground of original Indian rights."[5] The stronger federal guardian imposed its plenary power on its weaker Native "wards" to undermine "an independence for which we have been fighting incessantly for its recognition and settlement during the past 47 years" (i.e., since the Old Crossing Treaty of 1863). Although federal policy subverted the legal status and self-governance of the band, the positive historical legacy of the Turtle Mountain Chippewa's persistence lives on. Native legal scholar Kevin Washburn reminds us that "persistence is the single most important trait of any tribal nation in the United States. I have always told my law students that persistence is the most important trait of American Indians. If our ancestors had lacked that, we would have been wiped from the earth long ago." As celebrated by enrolled tribal member Louise Erdrich, "there's a sense of history in Chippewa culture. There's a long-running sense of loss and of extreme pride in ancestry."[6] This testimony upholds the finding that through the effective exercise of tribal sovereignty the pursuit of justice can be sustained.

The band took important political initiatives in the face of a confusing array of BIA pronouncements, local agent dictates, Executive Orders, rulings by the Interior Department, and the general disregard of Congress. Spurred by local, regional, and national non-Native interests, the federal government's actions excluded Turtle Mountain people from due process under the law, and the consent of the governed.

In 1910, Solicitor Bottineau noted the "thirty years of litigation to have our claim recognized for settlement . . . to protect our interest against official acts of inadvertency and covetous and designing men with selfish motives." Neither constitutional checks and balances nor any legally binding concept of the inherent rights of Indigenous peoples limited the coercive power behind those "official acts" of the federal government in Indian Affairs. The grab-bag of arbitrary policies arrayed against them showed that the strategies of U.S. federal policy existed to serve economic interests with political influence.[7] Officers of the federal government acted primarily as the enablers of European American expropriation of Native American land and resources.

The existence of distinct "federal Indian policy eras" has gained wide acceptance in legal, political science, and historical scholarship. Historians' stock in trade of explaining change over time lends itself to this model. Yet the experience of the Turtle Mountain Chippewa refutes this paradigm. When the legal struggles of the Turtle Mountain Chippewa occupy the center of the historical stage, existing nineteenth-century federal policy periods do not fit the tribe's legal relations with the government of the United States. The bad faith and disruptive tactics of federal policy remained far more pronounced than the discontinuity implied by the policy era model. The political history of the Turtle Mountain Chippewa provides a deeper understanding of the dysfunctional nature of federal policy and its shattering effects on a peaceful community that deserved a better fate.

The responses of the Turtle Mountain band demonstrated that they soundly rejected the pretensions and disorder of federal policy. Their narrative demonstrated that they desired to stay on their reserved tribal lands and receive fair compensation for the lands they ceded to the United States. They asserted sovereign rights to govern themselves and control their own tribal membership. The band's representatives insisted that the federal government live up to its trust responsibility and protect Native peoples from unlawful injury to their property and rights. The United States government had a self-proclaimed legal obligation to uphold the trust relationship it imposed on Native Americans.

This unique political arrangement represented an on-going partnership designed to ensure that in exchange for their valuable lands, Native American tribes had the tools and resources needed for future survival. The federal government's recognition of their legitimate right to a reservation large enough to accommodate the Turtle Mountain Chippewa would have resolved almost all of the remaining issues of tribal autonomy, adequate subsistence, and economic sustainability. Instead, Native peoples' modest needs conflicted directly with the money-driven desires of European American development. Tribal members decried the negative attributes of the trust relationship. Yet the crucial element remained the relationship itself. Despite the heavy-handedness and false promises of the federal government, the Turtle Mountain community believed that adherence to the tribal-federal relationship provided a slim legal avenue for negotiation, settlement, and betterment.[8]

The Turtle Mountain Chippewa tried to work within the U.S. system of law to preserve their tribal autonomy and retain their tribal lands. In response to their agreeable approach, solicitor Bottineau complained that "the authorities of the Government have really done nothing for these Indians, only to consume time and expense for nearly thirty years in endeavoring to remove them from their home on Turtle Mountain."[9] The Turtle Mountain Chippewa believed that by adhering to peaceful relations and the rule of law, their sovereign legal status and land title would be upheld by the United States. Nevertheless, their modest needs to secure 500,000 acres of land for two thousand members conflicted directly with the expansionist agenda of European American settlement. As observed by Lakota scholar and jurist Frank Pommersheim, "the land must hold the people, and give direction to their aspirations and yearnings."[10] For Native peoples, the crucial importance of a sacred homeland cannot be overstated.

Review of the documentary record of the Turtle Mountain Chippewa's political relationship with the United States for over a century reveals the persistence of the Turtle Mountain Chippewa throughout the nineteenth century. Under three generations of Little Shell leadership and Attorney Bottineau, the Turtle Mountain Chippewa asserted their determination to protect their tribal lands and to preserve their tribal autonomy. They endeavored to manage or contest the turbulent consequences of illegal European American encroachment by attempting to make their own decisions and solve their own problems.

A majority of the community believed that preserving their lands and their communal integrity as one autonomous entity provided the key to Turtle Mountain Chippewa survival. These objectives of self-determination remained rooted in the band's cultures and politics. In the hope of obtaining a just and equitable accommodation of their rights, the letters, prayers, memorials, briefs, and delegations of the Turtle Mountain Chippewa gave voice to their "aspirations and yearnings."

In its relations with the band during the first half of the twentieth century, the United States continued to act indifferently toward the rights and welfare of the tribe. The descendants of the Turtle Mountain Chippewa at the heart of this story lived on to fight their legal battles another day. In 1981, the Indian Claims Commission (ICC) awarded the Turtle Mountain Band of Chippewa Indians $52,277,337.97, "the second largest Indian judgment award."[11] The award represented a long-delayed attempt by the United States to rectify the McCumber Agreement's appropriation of unceded Turtle Mountain territory for what the Commission found to be an "unconscionable consideration."[12] The monetary award for the "ten cent" treaty's grossly inadequate remuneration provided the seed money to build the late twentieth-century tribal institutions needed to regenerate their road to self-determination. In that sense, the ICC resolution of the Turtle Mountain Chippewa case at last recognized the merit of their claim and granted some small measure of compensation and belated justice. Tribal Chairman Richard J. LaFromboise declared it as "a moral victory to a principle well taken by the Turtle Mountain Band for the distribution of something long waited for." This "object of hope" vindicated Bottineau's longstanding assertion that "a court of justice would not sustain the actions" of various federal policy officials.[13]

The tortuous path to such vindication illustrates that effective tribal sovereignty will continue to exist as long as Native and non-Native peoples fight the battles necessary to uphold the fundamental legal relationship between tribes and the federal government. As we move forward into the twenty-first century, it remains uncertain whether hopes for multiculturalism and legal pluralism can be enriched by a greater appreciation of the sovereign endeavors of Native American peoples.[14] The historical record shows that the Turtle Mountain Chippewa believed that by adhering to peaceful relations and the rule of law, their sovereign status would be upheld by the United States.

The Turtle Mountain people had one objective: "[W]e ask justice upon the merit of [our] claim."[15] Yet federal policy did not adhere to the rule of law or seek justice. Instead, it operated under "the semblance of legal right" that has the "apparent authority of law but is actually contrary to law."[16] The legal struggles of the Turtle Mountain Chippewa throughout the nineteenth century demonstrated the culpability of the federal government. The U.S. government did not pursue an equitable course of extinguishing Turtle Mountain "Indian title." Federal authorities ignored the band's just claim to remain in the possession and enjoyment of their lands until they chose to part with them.[17]

Late twentieth-century movies like *Smoke Signals* (1998) depicted Native peoples asserting their own voices increasingly in the American cultural mainstream. The same trend has been happening within the genre of scholarship known as federal Indian law and policy. One of the main characters of *Smoke Signals*—the visionary storyteller Thomas Builds-the-Fire—has once again come up against the U.S. legal system. After order is restored following a minor courtroom disturbance, the judge wonders if, "now, we can go about the administration of justice?" But Thomas asks, "Is that real justice, or the idea of justice?[18]

Thomas's skepticism summarizes the feelings of many Native Americans whose historical relations with state and federal government authorities have been at odds with the governmental authorities' professed adherence to the rule of law. In many ways, justice amounts to telling stories that reveal overlooked or long-buried truths. Responding to the U.S. government's illegal taking of ten million acres of Turtle Mountain band of Pembina Chippewa land in 1892, tribal member and Solicitor John B. Bottineau asserted that *"in order that justice may be done,"* the United States must live up to the Preamble's declaration that the Constitution is meant to establish justice and the "undertakings for the furtherance of justice."[19]

# APPENDIX:
## TRIBAL NAMING CONVENTIONS AND STANDARDS

As noted in chapter one, effective communication requires naming conventions even though they change over time and often remain contested, mirroring controversies within specific historical contexts. *In Order That Justice May Be Done* employs naming standards chosen with respect, along with a desire to enhance readability while recognizing that self-identification is more important than external labeling.

*Anishinabeg (Anisinaubaek)* The Ojibwe call themselves collectively *Anishinabeg/Anishinaubaek/Aunishenaubaig* (nish-NAH-bek), and singularly *Anishinaabe/Anishinaubae/Aunishenaubay* (nish-NAH-bay), meaning "the good beings." There is no standard English spelling. See *Anishinabe: 6 Studies of Modern Chippewa*, ed. by J. Anthony Paredes (Tallahassee: University Press of Florida, 1996), and Basil Johnston, *Ojibwe Peoples Dictionary* https://ojibwe. lib.umn.edu/.

*Algonquian/Algonkian/Algonquin* Language grouping; Ojibwe is classified as a Central Algonquian language since it is believed to have originated in northern Michigan. See *Aboriginal Migrations: A History of Movements in Southern Manitoba*, by Leo Pettipas; *The Proto Central Algonquian Kinship System*, by Charles F. Hockett. Alexander Henry (the younger) stated that the English referred to the "Ojibway" as Algonquians, but he referred to them as "Saulteurs" (see below).

*Ojibwe/Ojibwa/Ojibway* Term used in the historic record and the anthropological literature; term used by linguists to denote the Native language; legal term employed by the Canadian government. Fur company geographer David Thompson recorded the use of the appellation *Oochepoys* in the journal of his 1798 exploration. The famous white captive John Tanner referred to *Ojibbeway* in his 1830 autobiography. The earliest published tribal historian, William Warren, used the designation *Ojibway* in his 1851 history. Today, Ojibwe is the current preference.

    A great deal of uncertainty and confusion remains over the derivation and original meaning of the word. A plausible explanation by historian Theresa M. Schenck (of the Blackfeet Nation), that makes sense logically and accords with some of the most significant primary source material and modern anthropological interpretations, posits that *Ojibwe* derived from the Algonquian word for crane. She noted that this derivation accords with the "animal-name designations" of other Indigenous peoples in the Great Lakes region. See Schenck's *The Voice of the Crane Echoes Afar: The Sociopolitcal Organization of the Lake Superior Ojibwa, 1640–1855*, p. 23. In addition, its foremost clan status (the crane, or "echo maker," clan being the source of tribal leaders) in the Ojibwe totemic system, as documented by tribal member William Warren, associated the "clear and far-reaching cry of the crane . . . with the acknowledged orators of the tribe." See Warren, *History of the Ojibway People*, p. 47. Hence the first part of the title of Schenck's book— taken from a War of 1812 speech by a Lac du Flambeau band headman— concluded that the word *Ojibwe* meant the people called together by the "voice of the crane." See Schenck, p. 23.

***Chippewa*** Legal term employed by the U.S. federal government. In addition, most of the historical record uses the identifier of Chippewa. The self-constituted community and federally recognized tribe at the core of this study is known as the "Turtle Mountain Band of Chippewa Indians" under Article 1 of their Constitution and Bylaws. Tribal historian Charlie White-Weasel provided the following explanation for the shift from *Ojibwe* to *Chippewa* in the United States. "In the course of time, American officialdom dropped the 'O,' took the 'chip' from the [1840s Slovenian Catholic missionary] Baraga dictionary [i.e., *Otchipwe*], and then gave it a French twist from the French spelling *O-ge-bois*, giving the ending a 'wauh' sound. The American government then made Chippewa the officially correct pronunciation and spelling." See White-Weasel, *Pembina and Turtle Mountain Ojibway (Chippewa) History*, p. 92.

***Plains-Ojibwa/Bungi/Southwestern Ojibwe*** Interchangeable labels for those Ojibwe/Chippewa/Saulteaux who transformed culturally into Plains Indians and settled in northwestern Minnesota, the Pembina and Turtle Mountain regions of North Dakota, northeastern Montana, and southern Manitoba. In the 1830s, George Catlin referred to these people as "Ojibbeways," related to but distinct from the "Chippeways" south and west of Lake Superior. Canadian Anthropologist Alanson Skinner coined the first term in 1914 after conducting field worked at the Long Plain Reserve in 1913. The term *Bungi* or *Bungee* was used by eighteenth-century Hudson's Bay traders, as noted by Alexander Henry. It means "a little bit," and may have indicated their mixed Woodland and Plains characteristics. The terms were also applied to their unique Cree-influenced dialect of Ojibway. Both expressions have been adopted by anthropologists A. Irving Hallowell and James H. Howard. Isaac Stevens employed the term "Prairie Chippewa," which he probably picked up from the Minnesota Ojibwe, in his 1854 report. Ethnohistorian Harold Hickerson employed the Ojibwe designation.

*Saulteurs/Saulteaux* The first European term applied to these Indigenous people. Derived by the French name for the Anishinaabe due to their "contact" location in the Great Lakes area of Upper Michigan near Sault Ste. Marie. Term employed by Montreal traders like Alexander Henry for "his Indians," i.e., the Chippewa with whom he worked and traded in the Red River and Pembina regions. Today the term is both applied and self-applied (e.g., the actor Adam Beach) to tribal descendants in the Red River of the North and the Winnipeg, Manitoba, Canada area.

*Métis/Michif/Métifs/Métchif/Méchif/Métsif* The Oxford English Dictionary etymology for *Métis*: 1) from the post-classical Latin *misticius*, also the root of the Spanish *mestizo*; 2) in Old French, Middle French as *mestis* or *metice* meaning "hybrid," "of mixed blood"; 3) from the French *métif* for a person with parents of different races; *mestif, métif, mestis*. The North American version for a French Métis person of mixed European and American Indian originated from around 1740. Mixed-blood women were often referred to as *Métisse*. For the origins and cultural components of the Métis (pronounced *may-tee*), which, while literally translated from French to English as mixed-blood, refers to people of mixed French or French Canadian and Chippewa or Cree descent, from the fur trade regions of the Great Lakes, Western Canada (Manitoba, Saskatchewan, and Alberta), and the North-Central Western United States (North Dakota and Montana), and the culturally ambivalent attitudes toward them held by Anglo-Canadians and Anglo-Americans. See Verne Dusenberry, "Waiting for a Day That Never Comes: The Dispossessed *Metis* of Montana," in Peterson and Brown's *The New Peoples: Being and Becoming Metis in North America*, pp. 119–23.

\*\*\*

Lucy Murphy stated that "although they were not Indigenous in the same sense that Indian peoples were, they were residents with a culture that was specific to the region, and strongly related to Indian culture," and "pre-dated

U.S. [or Canadian] hegemony." See her article, "Public Mothers: Native American and *Metis* Women as Creole Mediators in the Nineteenth Century Midwest." *In Order That Justice May Be Done* aligns with the significant (but not unanimous) anthropological, historical, and legal scholarship that denotes the Métis as an Indigenous people entitled to Indigenous land rights under U.S. and Canadian law.

The Turtle Mountain Chippewa are multilingual (Cree, Ojibwe, French, and English). Some members speak a unique language of Cree and French called *Michif.* See John C. Crawford, "What is *Michif?*" in Peterson and Brown's *The New Peoples*, pp. 231–40; *The Michif Dictionary: Turtle Mountain Chippewa Cree*, edited by John C. Crawford; and "Speaking *Michif* in Four *Metis* Communities," *The Canadian Journal of Native Studies* III, no. I (1985): 47–55. Peter Bakker performed an even more extensive study of *Michif* in his book, *A Language of Our Own: The Genesis of Michif, the Mixed Cree-French Language of the Canadian Metis.*

As with many North American Indian communities that ended up within the legal dominion of the United States or Canada, there has been a great deal of confusion and controversy over the names attached to Native peoples and the diverse components of their cultural identity. Historical sources and contemporary interpretations often reflect this confusion.

The Turtle Mountain Band of Chippewa Indians of North Dakota comprise the largest of the western bands of Plains-Ojibwe (or Chippewa) with a preponderance of Métis mixed-blood relations residing in the United States and Canada. In the United States, there are three federally recognized bands of Plains-Ojibwe: Turtle Mountain Band of Chippewa Indians, Chippewa Cree Tribe of the Rocky Boy's Reservation, and the Little Shell Tribe of Chippewa Indians of Montana.

The Turtle Mountain band consisted primarily of "individuals of mixed Chippewa blood" and "the Pembinas (i.e., the Pembina Band of Chippewa Indians) and other mixed bloods and their descendants," who resided primarily west of Pembina, along the Pembina River, and in the Pembina and Turtle Mountain areas. See J. B. Bottineau's genealogy, from a letter dated November 4, 1910: 7–8, Bureau of Indian Affairs, Record Group 75, Records of the Turtle Mountain Agency, ND, National Archives, Central Plains Region, Kansas City, Missouri.

Contemporary Turtle Mountain tribal members refer to themselves as Chippewa or Michif (as per White-Weasel). Outside scholars like

Dusenberry, Crawford, and Bakker only refer to *Michif* as a language, spoken by some *Métis* people. According to Les LaFountain at the Turtle Mountain Community College, "I would prefer Michif for the spelling, because that is how it is spelled on the Michif Dictionary by local elders (Ida Rose Allard and Pauline Laverdure) and by the Gabriel Dumont Institute." I have honored this preference unless used in a quote.

Other Méchif/Méchif/Métchif communities exist in Montana and the western Canadian provinces. In *In Order That Justice May Be Done*, all other American or Canadian mixed bloods not associated with the Turtle Mountain band are labeled Métis.

Three successive generations of principal chiefs named Little Shell became the hereditary chiefs of the Turtle Mountain band. See Nancy O. Lurie, "Little Shell Genealogy," ICC, Docket 113/ Petitioner's Exhibit 215. They remained leaders of the Pembina band until it dwindled from the lack of a reservation, becoming absorbed primarily into the Turtle Mountain band, and as a result of the coerced removal to the White Earth reservation in Minnesota during the 1870s. Some band members also sought refuge with the Red Lake Chippewa. Sometimes the Turtle Mountain group was referred to as the Little Shell band. Such overlapping and imprecise designations did not become a contentious issue from outside or within the band until 1892 (see chapter seven). Ultimately, the Indian Claims Commission designated them legally as the "American Pembina Chippewa group (full and mixed bloods), including the subgroups of the Turtle Mountain Band, the Pembina Band, and the Little Shell Bands."

The chief designated as Little Shell I was the only Pembina and Turtle Mountain Chippewa leader actually named Little Shell (Aisance or Aise-Anse). "After the death of Little Shell I, the white man persisted in naming two lineal descendants according to the Caucasian surname system. In actuality, Little Shell II's name was Weesh-e-damo. See Warren, *Ojibway History*, 47. Little Shell III's name was Ayabe-way-we-tung. See White-Weasel, *History*, 336.

Regarding the anthropological designations derived from the concept of "cultural ecology," James H. Howard cautions that "culture areas" are generalizations that should not be adhered to rigidly because they undervalue the array of diversity within each one. "Groups like the Plains-Ojibwa, because they are culturally in between two classic culture areas, and share complexes of both, have been systematically ignored" or "misidentified." See Howard, *Plains-Ojibwa*, 5–6. In accordance with the anthropological schema of "culture areas," the natural environment (i.e., the climate and the types and abundance of plants and animals) configured subsistence (i.e., the way you make a living, what you eat, what you wear, and what you live in, how you get around), and subsistence shaped human culture (i.e., social arrangements, political organization, material culture, beliefs, and behaviors). The culture and society of the Chippewa developed from the lands where they lived. The Plains-Ojibwe groups, like the Turtle Mountain band, were positioned geographically to retain and adopt the cultural attributes of both the Eastern Woodlands and Great Plains regions. See Howard, *Plains-Ojibwa*, 8–9. It is one of the few maps that depict accurately the location of the Plains-Ojibwe (neither the Royce nor the Prucha maps are correct in this regard). In an 1882 report, Commissioner of Indian Affairs Hiram P. Price consulted maps of the United States published by H. S. Tanner from 1832 to 1839, "on which the Indians of the Western country are noted." He found "that the territory west of the Red River and north and northwest of Devils Lake is given to the Chippewas." See House Report No. 1144, to accompany bill H.R. 1885.

# ENDNOTES

## INTRODUCTION ENDNOTES

[1] Louise Erdrich, *Tracks* (New York: Harper & Row, 1988), 34–35. Ms. Erdrich is an enrolled member of the Turtle Mountain Chippewa. She is a descendant of sub-Chief Kaishpau Gorneau. Many of her fictional works reflect the harsh historical realities endured by various band members near or on the Turtle Mountain reservation in North Dakota.

[2] John B. Bottineau, *The Turtle Mountain Band of the Pembina Chippewa Indians: Brief and Points in Support of H.R. Bill No. 3541 Now Pending,* 1895 (Historical Society of Wisconsin, Microfilm 621 I 1002): 24. Hereafter referred to as *Brief*. Bottineau descended from a prominent family (his father, Pierre, and his uncle Charles) long associated with the Pembina and Turtle Mountain Chippewa. Bottineau was a lawyer and an enrolled member of the tribe. He acted as legal counsel for Chief Little Shell III and the tribal council from 1878 until his death in 1911.

[3] *Annual Report of the Commissioner of Indian Affairs* to the Secretary of the Interior, National Cash Register Microfiche Edition, 1969. Hereafter referred to as *ARCIA*. *ARCIA* 1879: 44.

[4] Nell Jessup Newton, "Introduction," *Arizona Law Review* 31, no. 2 (1989): 193.

[5] James H. Howard, *The Plains-Ojibwa or Bungi: Hunters and Warriors of the Northern Prairies with special reference to the Turtle Mountain Band* (University of South Dakota Reprints in Anthropology 7. Lincoln, NE: J. & L. Reprint Company, 1977); Patrick Gourneau, *History of the Turtle Mountain Band of Chippewa Indians,* 7th ed. (Belcourt: North Dakota, 1980); Charlie White-Weasel, *Pembina and Turtle Mountain Ojibway (Chippewa) History* (Belcourt, North Dakota, 1995).

[6] Mary Jane Schneider, "An Adaptive Strategy and Ethnic Persistence of the Méchif of North Dakota," unpublished Ph.D. dissertation, University of Missouri, 1974. According to my colleague Les LaFountain at Turtle Mountain Community College, "I would prefer Michif for the spelling, because that is how it is spelt on the Michif Dictionary by local elders (Ida Rose Allard and Pauline Laverdure) and by the Gabriel Dumont Institute."

I have honored this preference unless citing a direct quote indicating otherwise.

[7] Gregory S. Camp, "The Turtle Mountain Plains-Chippewas and Métis, 1797–1935," unpublished Ph.D. dissertation, University of New Mexico, 1987; "The Chippewa Transition from Woodland to Prairie, 1790–1820," *North Dakota History* 51, no. 3 (Summer 1984): 39–47; "The Chippewa Fur Trade in the Red River Valley of the North, 1790–1830," in *The Fur Trade in North Dakota*, ed. Virginia L. Heidenreich, 33–46 (Bismarck: State Historical Society of North Dakota, 1990); "Commerce and Conflict: A History of Pembina, 1797–1895," *North Dakota History* 60, no. 4 (1993): 22–33; "Working Out Their Own Salvation: The Allotment of Land in Severalty and the Turtle Mountain Chippewa Band, 1870–1920," *American Indian Culture and Research Journal* 14 (1990): 19–38; David P. Delorme, "History of the Turtle Mountain Band of Chippewa Indians," *North Dakota History* 22 (1955): 121–34; James H. Howard, "The Turtle Mountain 'Chippewa," *North Dakota Quarterly* 26, no. 2 (1958): 37–46; Stanley N. Murray, "The Turtle Mountain Chippewa, 1882–1905," *North Dakota History* 51, no. 1 (1984): 14–37; John Hesketh, "History of the Turtle Mountain Chippewa," *Collections of the State Historical Society of North Dakota* 5 (1923): 85–124; Harold Hickerson, "The Genesis of a Trading Post Band: The Pembina Chippewa," *Ethnohistory* 3 (1956): 289–345.

[8] This case study is based mainly on the following primary sources: microfilmed government documents from various collections at the University of Arizona's Main, Special Collections (Serial Set), and Law libraries; archival RG 75 Office of Indian Affairs and RG 279 Indian Claims Commission materials from the National Archives in Washington, D.C.; RG 75 Turtle Mountain Agency records from the National Archive regional center in Kansas City, MO; microfilmed local newspapers from the North Dakota Historical Society in Bismarck, ND; and national newspapers from University of Arizona online databases. Given the geographic origins of the band, a lot of relevant material resides in North Dakota and Minnesota. I obtained most of this material via invaluable interlibrary loan resources. I realize that documents may never tell the entire story, especially when trying to convey the Indigenous side of a story. But many of the documents crucial for this analysis were written by tribal members (e.g., Attorney John B. Bottineau, Tribal Chairman Patrick Gorneau, Tribal Historian Charlie-White-Weasel), interpreted for tribal

members (e.g., Little Shell II and Little Shell III, Red Thunder), come from family genealogies (in *St. Ann's Centennial*), or recorded oral testimony (e.g., Delorme's interviews with eighty-seven tribal members in the 1950s).

[9] *ARCIA* 1906, "Reports Concerning Indians in North Dakota": 293.

[10] *Brief*, 13.

[11] Harold Lasswell, *Politics: Who Gets What, When, How* (Cleveland: Meridian Books, 1958).

[12] Edward Said, *Culture and Imperialism* (New York: Vintage Books/ Random House, 1993), xii–xiii.

[13] A recent Royal Commission on Aboriginal Peoples delineated succinctly these characteristics of Indian nationhood. See "Restructuring the Relationship," Vol. 2 Part 1 (Ottawa: Canada Communication Group, 1996), 182.

[14] Richard White, "Indian Histories," in *The New American History*, ed., Eric Foner (Philadelphia: Temple University Press, 1997), 208.

[15] Robert A. Williams, Jr., "The People of the States Where They Are Found Are Often Their Deadliest Enemies": The Indian Side of the Story of Indian Rights and Federalism," *Arizona Law Review* 38, no. 3 (Fall 1996): 985.

[16] Daniel K. Richter, *Facing East from Indian Country: A Native History of Early America* (Cambridge, MA: Harvard University Press, 2001).

[17] Jill Norgren, *The Cherokee Cases: The Confrontation Between Law and Politics* (New York: McGraw Hill, 1996). Norgren noted that even the educated and legally savvy Cherokees in the 1830s had "no Cherokee attorneys trained to litigate" in U.S. courts and "had to rely on foreign members of that profession," 53.

[18] Robert K. Thomas, "Afterword," in *The New Peoples: Being and Becoming Métis in North America*, eds. Jacqueline Peterson and Jennifer S. H. Brown (Winnipeg: University of Manitoba Press, 1985), 243–49.

[19] I owe my dissertation director Roger Nichols a big thanks for making me more aware of the historiographical significance of Métis scrip in U.S. Indian history and policy studies. See a brief discussion of how this federal policy anomaly impacted the Pembina and Turtle Mountain Chippewa in chapter four.

[20] Prucha's *The Great Father*, Priest's *Uncle Sam's Stepchildren: The Reformation of United States Indian Policy, 1865–1887* (Lincoln: University of Nebraska Press, 1975); Fritz's *The Movement for Indian Assimilation, 1860–1890* (Philadelphia: University of Pennsylvania Press, 1963), and Frederick E. Hoxie, *A Final Promise: The Campaign to Assimilate the Indians, 1880–1920* (Cambridge: Cambridge University Press, 1984).

[21] Patricia Nelson Limerick, *The Legacy of Conquest: The Unbroken Past of the American West* (New York: W.W. Norton & Company, 1987), 195.

[22] Nell Jessup Newton, "Introduction," *Arizona Law Review* 31, no. 2 (1989): 194, citing Vine Deloria, Jr.

[23] Vine Deloria, Jr., "Laws Founded in Justice and Humanity: Reflections on the Content and Character of Federal Indian Law," *Arizona Law Review* 31, no. 2 (1989): 203.

[24] Robert F. Berkhofer, "The Political Context of a New Indian History," *Pacific Historical Review* 40, no. 3 (August 1971): 368. Berkhofer called on historians to explore "the nature of political organization in a . . . tribe and the role it plays in Indian-Indian and Indian-white relations."

[25] Randall B. Ripley and Grace A. Franklin, *Congress, the Bureaucracy, and Public Policy* (Homewood, IL: Dorsey Press, 1980), 1; H. K. Colebatch, *Policy* (Buckingham, UK: Open University Press, 1998).

[26] I am indebted to Tom Holm for the applicability of the grab-bag metaphor to federal Indian policy. The related social science organizational "garbage-can" theory comes from the following sources: Dennis J. Palumbo, *Public Policy in America: Government Action* (New York: Harcourt Brace Jovanovich, Publishers, 1988), 26, 87, 150–51; and Michael D. Cohen, James G. March, and Johan P. Olsen, "A Garbage Can Model of Organizational Choice," *Administrative Science Quarterly* 17, no. 1, (March 1972): 16.

[27] *Prayer*: 7–8.

[28] *Brief*: 31–32.

[29] Letter from Commissioner of Indian Affairs Hiram Price to the Secretary of the Interior, Office of Indian Affairs, Washington, D.C., February 14, 1882.

[30] Palumbo, *Public Policy*, 87, 150. Palumbo illustrated what he termed the "reverse decision cycle" with the aphorism that "if the only tool in your

toolbox is a hammer, then all your problems are going to look like nails." This provides a droll insight into how the grab-bag model applies to the machinations of nineteenth-century federal policy.

[31] Cohen, March, and Olsen, *Garbage Can Model*, 16.

[32] Ripley and Franklin, *Public Policy*, discusses the role of feedback loops in public policy formulation.

[33] Francis Paul Prucha, "The Challenge of Indian History," *Journal of the West* (January 1995): 3–4.

[34] Peter Nabokov, *A Forest of Time: American Indian Ways of History* (Cambridge, UK: Cambridge University Press, 2002), 5.

[35] Philip J. Deloria, "Historiography," in Philip J. Deloria and Neal Salisbury, eds., *A Companion to American Indian History* (Malden, MA: Blackwell Publishers, 2002), 21.

[36] Gregory S. Camp, "Working Out Their Own Salvation: The Allotment of Land in Severalty and the Turtle Mountain Chippewa Band, 1870–1920," *American Indian Culture and Research Journal* 14 (1990): 19–38; David P. Delorme, "History of the Turtle Mountain Band of Chippewa Indians," *North Dakota History* 22 (1955): 121–34; Stanley N. Murray, "The Turtle Mountain Chippewa, 1882–1905," *North Dakota History* 51, no. 1 (1984): 14–37.

[37] *Brief*, 18.

[38] Robert F. Berkhofer, *The White Man's Indian: Images of the American Indian from Columbus to the Present* (New York: Vintage Books, 1978), 135.

[39] Harold Hickerson, "The Genesis of a Trading Post Band: The Pembina Chippewa," *Ethnohistory* 3 (1956): 289–345; Gregory S. Camp, "The Chippewa Transition from Woodland to Prairie, 1790–1820," *North Dakota History* 51, no. 3 (Summer 1984): 39–47; Gerhard J. Ens, "Métis Agriculture in Red River During the Transition from Peasant Society to Industrial Capitalism: The Example of St. Francois Xavier, 1835 to 1870," in *Swords and Ploughshares: War and Agriculture in Western Canada*, ed., R. C. Macleod, 239–62 (Edmonton: University of Alberta Press, 1993).

[40] Letter from Commissioner of Indian Affairs Hiram Price to the Secretary of the Interior, Office of Indian Affairs, Washington, D.C., March 11, 1882.

[41] Richard White, *The Middle Ground: Indians, Empires, and Republics in the Great Lakes Region, 1650–1815* (Cambridge University Press, 1991), ix.

[42] J. B. Bottineau, *Chippewa Indians of Northern Dakota Territory: Will the Government Recognize Their Claim and Provide for Them?* (Washington, D.C.: United States Department of the Interior, Thos. J. Brashears, 1878), 10, 12.

[43] *Brief*, 8.

[44] St. Ann's Centennial Committee, *St. Ann's Centennial: 100 Years of Faith, 1885–1985; Turtle Mountain Indian Reservation, Belcourt, North Dakota* (Rolla, ND: Star Printing, 1985), next to last page, unpaginated. Hereafter referred to as *St. Ann's*.

[45] *Brief*, 31.

## CHAPTER 1 ENDNOTES

[1] Erdrich, *Tracks*, 32.

[2] Stephen Cornell, *The Return of the Native: American Indian Political Resurgence* (New York: Oxford University Press, 1988), 33.

[3] Wilcomb Washburn, *Red Man's Land, White Man's Law* (Norman: University of Oklahoma Press, 1971), 143.

[4] Cornell, *Return of the Native*, 225 n7.

[5] Edwin S. Gaustad, *Liberty of Conscience: Roger Williams in America* (Grand Rapids, MI: William B. Eerdsmans Publishing Company, 1991), 29.

[6] *Johnson v. McIntosh*, 21 U.S. (8 Wheat) 543 (1823). Tribal opponents to the imposed McCumber Agreement of October 22, 1892, denigrated its $1,000,000 in compensation for a land cession of 10,000,000 acres as the "ten-cent treaty." Turtle Mountain Métis member and band attorney from 1878 to 1911, J. B. Bottineau, compiled a 178-page account of the band's history and legal claims. See U.S. Congress, Senate, *Turtle Mountain Band of Chippewa Indians: Papers Relative to an Agreement with the Turtle Mountain Band of Chippewa Indians in North Dakota*, 56th Congress, 1st Session, June 6, 1900, Senate Document 444, Serial set 3878, 7. Hereafter referred to as Senate Doc. 444. According to the Oxford English Dictionary, the word Indigenous is derived from the Late Latin construction of indigen-us or indigen-a, which means "born in a country," "native," or "a native."

The primary definition emphasizes someone (a person) or something (a plant or animal) that is born, produced, or belongs naturally to a region of land. The use of the adverb naturally in the definition implies an organic relationship between the person or thing and the land. Thus, the word Indigenous is most often used in the context of "aboriginal inhabitants" or "natural products." Interestingly enough, the first cited use of the root word indigene is attributed to the late sixteenth-century promoter of English colonization, Richard Hakluyt (the geographer). In 1598, he wrote, "They were Indigene, or people bred upon that very soyle." The first known use of the word *Indigenous* is ascribed to Sir T. Browne, who commented in 1646 that the Black slaves in the American Spanish colonies "were all transported from Africa . . . and are not Indigenous or proper natives of America." The best definition may come from the Ahnishinahbae-Ojibwe historian Wubekeniew, *We Have a Right to Exist* (New York: Black Thistle Press, 1995), 246, who says that Indigenous means "those who have sprung from the land itself." Thomas Jefferson first used the phrase "empire of liberty" for his vision of the future development of the United States in a December 25, 1780, letter to fellow Virginia expansionist George Rogers Clark. See *The Papers of Thomas Jefferson*, ed., Julian P. Boyd (Princeton: Princeton University Press, 1950), Vol. IV, 237. The "guise of law" charge came from Solicitor Bottineau in a letter to Chief Kanick and the Standing Committee of the Tribe, September 15, 1910, Bureau of Indian Affairs, Record Group 75.19.121, Records of the Turtle Mountain Agency, ND, National Archives, Central Plains Region, Kansas City, Missouri, 4.

[7] Red Lake orator Little Rock, in *Journal of the Proceedings Connected with the Negotiation of a Treaty with the Red Lake and Pembina Bands of Chippewas—Concluded at the Old Crossing of Red Lake River on the Second of October, 1863*, Treaty File, Records of the Bureau of Indian Affairs, National Archives, Washington, D.C., 1863, 11. Hereafter referred to as Old Crossing *Treaty Journal*. Pembina comes from the Métis take on the Ojibwe/Cree word ni-pimina-na, which referred to the abundance of bush cranberry (*viburnum trilobum*) vegetation in northeastern North Dakota (i.e., Pembina, Pembina River, Pembina Mountains). Charlie White-Weasel claimed that because of the "the curvature of the [highbush cranberry] stem, looking somewhat like a bird's neck, is said to have given rise to the name 'crane-berry,' which was later changed to cranberry." Tanner called the Pembina River nebeninnah-ne-sebee. This name is not related to the Ojibwe/Cree word pimihkan or pemmican.

[8] William W. Warren, "Answers to Inquiries Regarding Chippewas," *Minnesota Pioneer*, December 5, 12, 19, 26, 1849, Reprinted in *Minnesota Archaeologist* 13 (January 1947): 20; "Sioux and Chippewa Wars," *Minnesota Chronicle & Register*, June 3 and 10, 1850, Reprinted in *Minnesota Archaeologist* 12 (October 1946): 95; "History of the Ojibways, Based Upon Traditions and Oral Statements," *Collections of the Minnesota Historical Society* 5 (1885): 127. The widespread Native American use of the term "Long Knife" referred specifically to U.S. soldiers with bayoneted rifles, but also generally to any U.S. representative, usually accompanied by soldiers in encounters with American Indians.

[9] The full text of this passage from the Northwest Ordinance, U.S. 1 Stat., 50 (1787), reads: "The utmost good faith shall always be observed toward the Indians; their land and property shall never be taken away from them without their consent; and their property, rights, and liberty shall never be invaded by Congress; but laws founded in justice and humanity shall from time to time be made for preventing wrongs to them, and for preserving peace and friendship with them."

[10] *Brief*, 8.

[11] The legal test for proving "Indian title" to land imposed by the United States on Native Americans rested upon the Supreme Court decision in *United States v. Santa Fe Pacific Railroad Company*, 314 U.S. 339, 345 (1941). The Court ruled that the "occupancy necessary to establish aboriginal possession is a question of fact to be determined as any other question of fact." The historical events outlined in this chapter establish the facts supporting the "Aboriginal title" of the Turtle Mountain Band of Pembina Chippewa.

[12] This "arc" included southern Ontario, Manitoba, and Saskatchewan in Canada, and northern Michigan, Wisconsin, Minnesota, North Dakota, and Montana in the United States. Image 1, The Migratory Path of the Ojibwe People, by Cassie Theurer, adapted from Benton-Benai, Land of the Ojibwe, Minnesota Historical Society, 1973, State Historical Society of North Dakota. Effective communication requires naming conventions, even as they change over time, often remain contested, and mirror controversies within specific historical contexts. This work employs naming standards chosen with respect, along with a desire to enhance readability. See Appendix: Tribal Naming Conventions and Standards for examples.

[13] Plains-Ojibwe or Plains Chippewa is a modern anthropologist label coined by Alanson Skinner, "The Cultural Position of the Plains-Ojibway." *Anthropological Papers of the American Museum of Natural History* 16 (1914): 314–18. The label was adapted and expanded upon by anthropologist James H. Howard. Howard noted that the designation "is reflected in the native name which these people give to themselves, which is Nakawiniuk." The term means "those of another speech. It refers to the particular dialect of the Ojibway language which is spoken by the Plains-Ojibwa as distinguished from Ojibway proper." The Ojibwe language (Ojibwemowin) is part of the "Algonquian language family," with various regional dialects. Howard's oral testimony before the Indian Claims Commission is at ICC, Docket 113, Transcript, September 18, 1962, 86. Also see Howard, *Plains-Ojibwa*, 6. Image 2 is from Leo Pettipas, *Aboriginal Migrations: A History of Movements in Southern Manitoba*. Winnipeg: Manitoba Museum of Man and Nature, 1996, 162. MAP 5: Indian Tribes before 1850 map, *State Maps on File* (North Dakota), New York: Facts on File, 1984, Figure 5.14.

[14] Image 3 shows the region known as the "Red River Basin," which formerly constituted the southern tip of Rupert's Land below the 49th parallel. The original homeland of the Turtle Mountain Band of Pembina Chippewa was situated within the western portion of the cession (west of the Minnesota-North Dakota border formed by the Red River of the North). https://upload.wikimedia.org/wikipedia/commons/9/94/U.S._Territorial_Acquisitions.png

[15] Binnema, Ens, and MacLeod (eds.), *From Rupert's Land to Canada*. This territorial entity lasted until 1867, when the British government forced the HBC to sell its interests (while retaining valuable posts and properties) and turn over governance to the newly constituted Dominion of Canada.

[16] Warren, *Ojibway History*, 132–35.

[17] Ibid., 195. Also see Cornelius Jaenen, "French Sovereignty and Native Nationhood during the French Regime" In J. R. Miller, ed., *Sweet Promises: A Reader on Indian-White Relations in Canada* (1991), 38.

[18] Howard, *Plains-Ojibwa*, 3.

[19] Although the Plains-Ojibwa adopted the Sun Dance as their principal ceremony (which also often served as a Rain Dance), it never superseded the older Woodlands Midewiwin practices completely. See Howard, *Plains-Ojibwa*, 107; Howard, "Sun Dance," 251–52.

The Plains-Ojibwa bands, like the eastern woodland Ojibwe, prospered as go-betweens in the trade between the French or British, and the tribes farther to the west. The more western and northern Cree and Assiniboine wanted better weapons in their wars with the Dakota. The Plains-Ojibwa obtained horses from their Cree and Assiniboine allies by trading for them with the metal weapons and tools procured in the fur trade. The Cree and Assiniboine engaged in a similar pattern of horse acquisition via trade with the Blackfoot. This period of acquisition occurred between 1732 and 1754. By the 1770s the Plains-Cree and the Plains-Ojibwa possessed herds of horses.

Alexander Henry the elder's journal provided a 1765 fur trade price list as follows:

| Item | # beaver skins |
|------|----------------|
| gun | = 20 |
| lb of powder | = 2 lb of shot |
| an axe or knife | = 1 |

Alexander Henry (the elder), *Travels and Adventures in Canada and the Indian Territories* (Toronto: Vermont Tuttle Co. Inc., 1809, reprinted in 1969).

The price list indicates that metal weapons and tools were obtainable by Native Americans. So, by the middle of the eighteenth-century, horses and guns became plentiful on the northern plains and transformed the lifeways of the Native peoples when they became the primary means to hunt buffalo. John S. Milloy, *The Plains Cree: Trade, Diplomacy and War, 1790 to 1870* (Winnipeg: University of Manitoba Press, 1988), 24. Because Howard did not indicate when or how the Plains-Ojibwe obtained horses, I have relied extensively on Milloy's research into the similar and often intertwined cultural evolution of the Plains-Cree. Milloy also made many specific references to the Plains-Ojibwe in his study.

[20] George Catlin, *Letters and Notes on the North American Indians* (New York: Penguin Paperback Edition, 1995; original edition 1832), "Letter—No. 8 from the Mouth of the Yellowstone, Upper Missouri," 52–55; Skinner, *The Cultural Position of the Plains-Ojibway*, 318; Howard, *The Plains-Ojibwa*, 23; John Tanner, *A Narrative of the Captivity and Adventures of John Tanner* (Reprint of the G. & C. & H. Carvill 1830 edition, New York: Penguin Books, 1994), 141; Catlin, *Letters*, 52–55; Hesketh, "History of the Turtle Mountain Chippewa," 85; Alexander Henry the Elder, *Journal*, 413; *Dunseith Herald: The Pioneer Journal of the Turtle Mountain Region* 6 (35), March 6, 1890, 1, labeled Turtle Mountain as both "the Garden of the

Northwest" and a "hunter's paradise." "Turtle Mountain oral history [also] tells us that Native elders and medicine people used natural landforms to mark the seasons. Literally hundreds of stone forms and mud mounds dot the landscape in and around Turtle Mountain, and even the hills themselves are incorporated into the patterns." http://exhibits.turtlemountain.org/mythandhistory/astronomy

[21] Alexander Henry the Elder, *Journal*, 44; Warren, *Ojibway History*, 218–19, 196.

[22] Howard, *Plains-Ojibwa*, 3, 45.

[23] Warren, *Ojibway History*, 356; Tanner, *Narrative*, 132–42; Elwyn B. Robinson, *History of North Dakota* (University of Nebraska Press, 1966), 24; Kiowa writer N. Scott Momaday defined oral tradition as "that process by which the myths, legends, tales and lore of a people are formulated, communicated, and preserved in language by word of mouth, as opposed to writing." See "The Man Made of Words," 87.

[24] Interview with James McKenzie, *North Dakota Quarterly* 59, no. 4 (Fall 1991): 101. Mr. Cree is a descendant of Oshkiniwaence, who was a member of Little Shell III's council in the 1890s, according to Charlie White-Weasel, *History*, 274. Mutual coexistence in terms of reciprocal hunting rights among these three tribes was confirmed by Howard's ICC, Docket 113, Transcript, September 18, 1962, 72.

[25] As noted by historian Eric Hindraker, "the Northwest Ordinance undermined the presumption of Indian sovereignty, and at the same time granted implicit legitimacy to the expansionist impulses of the [European American] settler population." See *Elusive Empires: Constructing Colonialism in the Ohio Valley, 1673–1800* (Cambridge: Cambridge University Press, 1997), 236.

[26] Kappler (ed.), *Indian Affairs: Laws and Treaties*, Vol. 2, 8–11.

[27] Prucha, *Documents of United States Indian Policy*, August 7, 1786, 8.

[28] Ibid., Secretary of War Henry Knox's *Report on the Northwestern Indians* in 1789, 13; Washington's 1783 letter to James Duane, 2.

[29] John MacLeod, "Diary of Chief Trader John MacLeod, Senior of Hudson's Bay Company, Red River Settlement, 1811," *Collections of the State Historical Society of North Dakota*, Vol. II (1908): 123, fn 1. Hereafter referred to as MacLeod *Diary*.

[30] Senate Doc. 444, 46.

[31] Alexander Henry and David Thompson, Elliot Coues ed., *New Light on the Early History of the Greater Northwest: The Manuscript Journals of Alexander Henry and David Thompson, 1799–1814* (New York: F.P. Harper, 1897), 81, fn 3. Hereafter referred to as Coues, *New Light*. This Alexander Henry was the nephew of Alexander Henry the Elder and is often referred to as Alexander Henry the Younger. He based his fur trade business at Pembina from 1800–1808. Quote is from Warren, *Ojibway History*, 40. William Whipple Warren's (1825–1853) *History of the Ojibway Nation* is the best early nineteenth-century source on the Chippewa. As the son of a European American trader, Lyman Warren II, and a French-Ojibwe Métis mother, Mary Cadotte, William Whipple Warren gained significant first-hand knowledge from his Ojibwe relatives, while learning the fur trade business from his father, and being sent away to receive a formal education. He functioned uniquely in the European American, American Indian, and Métis worlds, and acted as a cultural broker between all three. The North Dakota map (Image 6) is from the book leaf of Robert P. Wilkins and Wynona H. Wilkins, *North Dakota: A Bicentennial History* (New York: W.W. Norton, 1977).

[32] Coues, *New Light*, 118–19, 422–31; Tanner, Narrative, 120–23, 181; Senate Doc. 444, Exhibits IV–VIII; J. B. Tyrell, ed., *David Thompson's Narrative of His Explorations in Western America, 1784–1812* (Toronto: The Champlain Society, 1916), 251. David Thompson's achievements deserve much more than this footnote. He was the greatest nineteenth-century surveyor and cartographer in North America. His explorations covered vast areas that later became part of Western Canada and the northwestern United States. The Blackfoot Indians, who were well known for thwarting or killing many European American fur traders in their region, called Thompson koo-koo-sint, or "You who Look at the Stars," due to the constant use of his sextant, which the Native Americans considered possessed of special powers. In 1796, he blazed a new route from York Factory to Lake Athabaska for the HBC. "After he joined the Northwest Company in 1797, Thompson surveyed (1797–98) the Mississippi's head waters, crossed (1807) the Rocky Mountains by the Howse Pass to the source of the Columbia, explored (1808–10) the present states of Washington, Idaho, and Montana, and became the first European American to travel (1811) the Columbia's entire length. All of these

explorations and observations resulted in a map (1813–14) that became the basis for all subsequent maps of western Canada" into the twentieth century. Because of Thompson's remarkable achievements, historian J. B. Tyrell (who uncovered his field notes, journals, maps, and *Narrative*) called David Thompson "the greatest land geographer who ever lived." For more information see: http://www.davidthompsonthings.com.

[33] Howard, *Plains-Ojibwa*, 20; *Journals of Alexander Henry*, 53–54; Senate Doc. 444, Exhibits IV–VII.

[34] Image 7 is from ICC, Docket 113/Petitioner's Exhibits 3, 58, 112, 166, p. 104, "Collection of Interpretive Maps . . . Prepared by Nancy O. Lurie." Lurie's map correlates to a more detailed map provided in James Howard's ICC, Docket 113, Transcript, September 18, 1962. Howard verified these sites with documentary, ethnological, and archeological evidence. St. Joseph and the Pembina Mountains are on Howard's map but not Lurie's. Dog Den is marked as Anamoose, which means dog in Ojibwe. Cottonwood Lake (not indicated on the map) was just beyond the western extent of the "buffalo grounds," north of the Knife and Missouri river juncture. Unfortunately, Howard's map did not reflect all of the particular sites he testified about. The map's caption reference to the "Little Shell Memorial of 1876" is actually: "Memorial of the Chippewa Indians of Turtle Mountain, Dakota Territory, praying for the segregation and confirmation of a certain tract of their land to them, and that certain provisions be made for their protection," February 23, 1876. S. Misc. Doc. No. 63, 44th Cong., 1st Sess. (1876).

[35] White-Weasel, *History*, 336; *Journals of Alexander Henry* (the Younger), 226; J. B. Bottineau, family genealogy, November 25, 1910.

[36] Sylvia Van Kirk, *Many Tender Ties: Women in Fur Trade Society, 1670–1870* (Norman: University of Oklahoma Press, 1983), 4. Jennifer S. H. Brown, *Strangers in Blood: Fur Trade Company Families in Indian Country* (Norman: University of Oklahoma Press, 1980), 76. Gary B. Nash, "The Hidden History of Mestizo America," *The American Journal of History* (1995): 947. As noted by Gary Nash in his observations about American frontiers as both "battlegrounds" and "marrying grounds," U.S. history has downplayed the pervasiveness of "race-mixing" for far too long. For the ubiquity of "métissage" in North America since the colonial contact era, see James Axtell, "The White Indians of Colonial America," *William and Mary Quarterly* 37 (January 1975): 55–88. John Tanner made significant

contributions to the history of the Canadian plains. Although usually dubbed as merely a "hunter," his extensive travels and writings provided ethnographic and linguistic information on the Saulteaux and Cree, as well as geographic knowledge of the Assiniboine and Red River watersheds. His Métis progeny also played significant roles in Canadian prairie history. Reverend James Tanner was the half-brother of Picheito, the powerful Saulteaux-Cree chief of the Assiniboine, in the Red and Pembina River regions of Manitoba.

[37] Gender constructions and relations provide crucial intersections within the broader context of power and resistance that encompasses inter-cultural accommodation and conflict. Van Kirk, *Many Tender Ties*, 28, 73. "The norm for sexual relationships in fur-trade society was not casual, promiscuous encounters but the development of marital unions which gave rise to distinct family units . . . The fur-trade society developed its own marriage rite, marriage '*a la facon du pays*,' which combined both Indian and European marriage customs. In this, the fur-trade society of Western Canada appears to have been exceptional . . . In the Canadian West, alliances with Indian women were the central social aspect of the fur traders progress across the country," 4.

[38] Senate Doc. 444, 5, where Cottonwood is referred to by his French name, *Le Liard*, by Henry; Warren briefly described the nature of Chippewa band leadership succession, *Ojibway History*, 316–19; Coues, *New Light*, 71–73, 163, 169.

[39] Frances Densmore, "Chippewa Customs," *Bureau of American Ethnology*, Bulletin 45 (Washington, D.C. 1929), 9; Warren, *Ojibway History*, 34–35; Sister M. Inez Hilger, "Some Customs of the Chippewa," *North Dakota History* 26, no. 3 (Summer 1959): 125. Also see Howard, *Plains–Ojibwa*, 86, for an anthropological graph of the Plains-Ojibwe kinship system.

[40] Warren, *Ojibway History*, 47; Henry in Senate Doc. 444, No, VII; Tanner, *Narrative*, 170; White-Weasel, *History*, 91. On the particular qualities of Ojibwe leadership, see Basil Johnston, *Ojibway Heritage* (Toronto: McClelland & Stewart, 1976), 61–62. Also see Ruth Landes, *Ojibwa Religion and the Midewiwin* (Madison: University of Wisconsin Press, 1968), on the Ojibwe connection between "power" and "medicine," 42, and *The Ojibwa Woman* (New York: W.W. Norton, 1938), 133–34 for political influence of spiritual leaders. Little Shell belonged to the Grand Medicine

Society. The "crane" totem literally meant "Echo-maker," in reference to the "far reaching cry of the crane." See Theresa Schenck, *"The Voice of the Crane Echoes Afar": The Sociopolitical Organization of the Lake Superior Ojibwa, 1640–1855* (New York: Garland Publishing Inc., 1997), 49, for a pictograph illustrating the Ojibwe clan hierarchy. Schenck notes that "the animals represent the Ojibwe clans (dodaim)," led by the Crane, with the connecting lines between hearts and minds being "symbolic of the group's unity of purpose." Also see Tom Holm, "Indian Concepts of Authority and the Crisis in Tribal Governments," *The Social Science Journal* 19, no. 3 (July 1982): 60. The testimony on the origination of personal names from dreams comes from a Turtle Mountain Chippewa informant named Standing Chief, as told to Sister M. Inez Hilger in 1940.

41 *ARCIA* 1887, 117.

42 Warren, *Ojibway History*, 135; A. Irving Hallowell, *The Ojibwa of Berens River, Manitoba*, ed. Jennifer S. H. Brown (Fort Worth: Harcourt Brace Jovanovich, 1992), 50–53.

43 Howard, *Plains-Ojibwa*, 79–80.

44 James G. E. Smith, *Leadership among the Southwestern Ojibwa* (Ottawa: National Museum of Canada, 1973), 16.

45 Maurice G. Smith, *Political Organization of the Plains Indians, with Special Reference to the Council* (Lincoln: University of Nebraska, 1924), 73.

46 *Brief*, 43.

47 Verne Dusenberry, "The Dispossed Métis of Montana," in *The New Peoples: Being and Becoming Métis in North America*, 122.

48 Although they did not follow the Chippewa clan system, the Métis organized themselves politically and for their hunts in a parallel fashion with Plains-Ojibwe bands. For details on the Red River Métis hunts, see Alexander Ross, *Red River Settlement: Its Rise, Progress, and Present State; with Some Account of the Native Races and Its General History to the Present Day* (London: Smith, Elder and Co., 1856), 248.

49 Skinner, "Political Organization," 485–87. A corresponding women's okitcitakwe also existed under the direction of a head woman warrior. Anthropologist Alanson Skinner noted the example of an okitcita woman from the Pembina band named Ka-gi-ge-mai-ya-o-sek. Within patrilineal

Chippewa society, while woman did not have equality with men, such evidence confirms that woman exercised at least some share in the consensual management of tribal affairs.

⁵⁰ *ARCIA*, 1873, 4–5.

⁵¹ Michael Coyle, "Traditional Indian Justice in Ontario: A Role for the Present," *Osgoode Hall Law Journal* 24, no. 3 (1986): 606, 627; A. C. Hamilton and C. M. Sinclair, "'Justice Systems' and Manitoba's Aboriginal People: An Historical Survey," in Gerald Friesen, ed., *The Canadian Prairies: A History* (Toronto: University of Toronto Press, 1984), 51, lists eight "rules of the hunt" citing Alexander Ross, *Red River*, 249–50.

⁵² Hamilton and Sinclair, "Justice Systems," 74, fn 2. The "contemporary informants" include John Tanner, William Warren, Alexander Ross, Alexander Begg, Father G. A. Belcourt, and Bishop A. A. Taché.

⁵³ Warren, *Ojibway History*, 316.

⁵⁴ Ibid., 354–56, for the general account and the quotes. The "push" and "pull" factors impinging on the Ojibwe and the Dakota, their clashes, and the creation of new communities like Turtle Mountain, North Dakota, are summarized by Anton Treuer, ed. *Living Our Language: Ojibwe Tales & Oral Histories* (St. Paul: Minnesota Historical Society Press, 2001), 6.

⁵⁵ D.W. Menig, *The Shaping of America: A Geographical Perspective on 500 Years of History*, Vol. 2, *Continental America 1800–1867* (New Haven: Yale University Press, 1993): 37. See area labeled Red River Basin.

⁵⁶ Warren, *Ojibway History*, 349; James P. Ronda, *Lewis and Clark among the Indians* (Lincoln: University of Nebraska Press, 1984), 133. It should be noted, but not to denigrate Lewis and Clark's acclaimed achievements, that the first European American to cross North America (north of Mexico) was not Lewis or Clark, but the Scots-Canadian Alexander Mackenzie. In 1793, he explored far more of the geography of western North America, with far fewer resources, a decade before the journey of the Corps of Discovery. In fact, Thomas Jefferson purchased Mackenzie's published maps and journals, and Lewis and Clark took them on their expedition. See Derek Hayes, *First Crossing: Alexander Mackenzie, His Expedition Across North America, and the Opening of the Continent* (Seattle: Sasquatch Books, 2001). The experiences of Zebulon Pike stand in stark contrast to these great explorers. One of Pike's biographers, John Upton Terrell, summarized Pike's fruitless 1805

expedition as follows: "From almost every standpoint, the expedition was a failure. He drove no British trader from the North. He won no Indian allies for the United States. In scientific fields, he accomplished nothing. He discovered nothing. The lakes he identified as the source of the Mississippi were not that at all," 48.

[57] In addition to Gregory E. Dowd's exemplary work, *A Spirited Resistance: The North American Indian Struggle for Unity, 1745–1815* (Johns Hopkins University Press, 1992), more information about Tenskwatawa can be found in R. David Edmunds's *The Shawnee Prophet* (University of Nebraska Press, 1983). For a historical analysis based on the discipline of comparative religion, consult Joel W. Martin's *Sacred Revolt: The Muskogees' Struggle for a New World* (Boston: Beacon Press, 1991), which examines the Creek "Redstick" Rebellion of 1813–1814. The classic work on American Indian religious revitalization movements, which utilized history, anthropology, and psychology, is Anthony F. C. Wallace's *The Death and Rebirth of the Seneca* (New York: Vintage Books, 1969).

[58] Warren, *Ojibway History*, 67. Warren claimed that the "great rules of life" of the "Me-da-we" "bear a strong likeness to the ten commandments." White-Weasel, *History*, 276.

[59] Tanner, *Narrative*, 169–70.

[60] Howard, ICC, Docket 113, Transcript, September 18, 1962. Howard identified Graham's Island as the "seat" of Little Shell I and the "site of a strong Plains-Ojibwa village," 70. See Howard, ICC, Docket 113, Map, site #5.

[61] Tanner, *Narrative*, 170–71. Sources vary as to the date of Little Shell I's demise, ranging from 1804–1810. The consensus for his date of death is 1808. Howard believed that sub-chief Black Duck succeeded Little Shell I as head chief of the Turtle Mountain band until Little Shell II matured enough to become head chief, ICC, Docket 113, Transcript, September 18, 1962, 79. Black Duck's village at Stump Lake was just southeast of Devils Lake and is marked as site #4 on Howard's ICC map. According to Warren, Black Duck's fame as a warrior derived from an 1805 battle with the Yankton Dakota led by Wa-nah-ta. The battle took place near where the Goose River entered the Red River. See Warren, *Ojibway History*, 364. It should be noted that the son of Little Shell I, hereafter referred to as Little Shell II, was named Weesh-e-damo, not Aisance, or Little Shell.

See Warren, *Ojibway History*, 47. Nevertheless, it seems that since Little Shell I was held in such high regard by band members, other Indians, and European Americans, when his son and grandson succeeded to the hereditary head chieftainship of the Turtle Mountain band, they assumed the name of Little Shell in his honor. The Turtle Mountain Chippewa were blessed with effective and continuous leadership from three generations of Little Shells from 1800 to 1900.

[62] Harold Hickerson, "The Genesis of a Trading Post Band: The Pembina Chippewa," *Ethnohistory* 3 (1956): 315–23, settled on that date, and Howard concurred: ICC, Docket 113, Transcript, September 18, 1962, 106.

[63] Baraga's dictionary published in 1878 translated the male gendered Ojibwe word wissakodewinini (female = wissakodewikwe) as "half-burnt-wood-man," which became "half-breed man" in English. J. B. Bottineau's genealogy, from a letter dated November 4, 1910, 7–8. Charles Joseph Bottineau was J. B. Bottineau's grandfather.

[64] Howard, ICC, Docket 113, Transcript, September 18, 1962: 136; Mrs. Belgarde in St. Ann's Centennial Committee, *St. Ann's Centennial: 100 Years of Faith, 1885–1985; Turtle Mountain Indian Reservation. Belcourt, North Dakota* (Rolla, ND: Star Printing, 1985), 236; Warren, *Ojibway History*, 91.

[65] *St. Ann's Centennial*, 236.

[66] Tom Holm, "Politics Came First: A Reflection on Robert K. Thomas and Cherokee History," in *A Good Cherokee, A Good Anthropologist: Papers in Honor of Robert K. Thomas*, ed., Steve Pavlik (Los Angeles: University of California American Indian Studies Center, 1998), 42–45; Tom Holm, J. Diane Pearson, and Ben Chavis, "Peoplehood: A Model for the Extension of Sovereignty in American Indian Studies," *Wicazo Sa Review* 18, no. 1 (Spring 2003): 11–16. The Turtle Mountain Band of Chippewa exhibited the five major unifying forces comprising the American Indian identity of an "enduring people" or "peoplehood" as 1) sense of a particular territory, place or sacred land; 2) cultural heritage rooted in the past (i.e., a sacred history); 3) kinship; 4) common world view and system of values (reinforced through spiritual ceremonies and rituals); and 5) a distinct language. In addition, they governed themselves loosely, yet effectively enough to maintain a cohesive autonomy in relation to other Indian and non-Indian groups. Also see, A. Irving Hallowell, "Northern Ojibwa Ecological Adaptation and Social Organization," in *Contributions to Anthropology:*

*Selected Papers of A. Irving Hallowell*, ed., Raymond D. Fogelson (Chicago: University of Chicago Press, 1976), 340–41. In terms of international law regarding Indigenous peoples, "they comprise a distinct community with a continuity of existence and identity that links them to the communities, tribes, or nations of their ancestral past." See S. James Anaya, *Indigenous Peoples in International Law* (New York: Oxford University Press, 1996), 3. In regard to the validity and longevity of Ojibwe "sacred history, mid-nineteenth-century tribal historian and mixed-blood member William Warren claimed an unbroken oral history covering eight or nine generations. His primary informants were "the old men of the tribe," *Ojibway History*, 15.

[67] *St. Ann's Centennial*, 237; James H. Howard, "The Sun Dance of the Turtle Mountain Ojibwa," *North Dakota History* 19, no. 4 (1952): 250.

[68] Tanner, *Narrative*, 29–36, 40–49; White-Weasel, *History*, 336.

[69] *St. Ann's Centennial*, 236; Also see Emerise LaVallie, 300.

[70] Howard, *Plains-Ojibwa*, 8–9. In his ICC, Docket 113, Transcript, September 18, 1962 testimony, 139, Howard stated: "Whether one identifies more with the half-breed way of life or with the Indian way of life is very often a matter of personal choice. It is my understanding this has always been the case." Turtle Mountain Chippewa historian Charlie White-Weasel recalled that "his maternal grandmother was Métis with French as her first language." Although "very dark and Indian in features" she attempted to "pass for French" to deflect anti-Indian prejudice—it being "the smart thing to do" during the 1930s, *History*, 8.

[71] John C. Crawford, "What Is Michif? Language in the Métis Tradition," in *The New Peoples: Being and Becoming Métis in North America*, eds., Jacqueline Peterson and Jennifer S. H. Brown (Minneapolis: Minnesota Historical Society Press, 1985), 235, emphasis added. Modern linguists like Crawford and Peter Bakker assert that Michif is a bona fide language and cannot be marginalized or dismissed as only a dialect, jargon, pidgin, slang, or creole. This unique language amalgamation was noted in the "Journal of Trip to Red River, August and September 1861," kept by Bishop of St. Paul Thomas L. Grace when he visited Pembina. "They [the Métis of Pembina and St. Joseph] speak the Cree and Chippewa languages and also a corruption of French." *Acta et Dicta* 1 (1908): 176–79.

[72] William Sturtevant, "Anthropology, History and Ethnohistory," *Ethnohistory* 13, nos. 1–2 (Winter–Spring 1966): 37; *St. Ann's Centennial*, 316.

[73] Richard White, *The Middle Ground: Indians, Empires, and Republics in the Great Lakes Region, 1650–1815* (Cambridge University Press, 1991), for White's concept of a "middle ground" as a "joint Indian-white creation," ix–xiv. "Transculturation" is a term coined by anthropologist Irving Hallowell, by which he meant mutual acculturation. Charlie White-Weasel laments that despite the efforts of some college and home-study courses, Michif is "fast dying out. My generation will probably be the last" for conversational Michif, *History*, 93.

[74] s. 35(2) of the Constitution Act, 1982, being Schedule B to the Canada Act 1982 (U.K.), 1982, c. 11, recognized and affirmed the existence of the Métis as an "Aboriginal people." However, they have not been granted "Aboriginal rights" as defined in Section 35(1). For details on the debate over what this means for their future legal status in Canada, see Catherine Bell's "*Métis* Constitutional Rights in Section 35(1)." Manitoba Scrip for $160 or 160 acres was offered to all residents (i.e., Métis or "half-breeds," and all original European Canadian settlers and their children) living in Manitoba when it was founded in 1870. Application for the land scrip began in 1875 and continued until the early 1880s. See Gail Morin, ed., *Manitoba Scrip* (Pawtucket, Rhode Island: Quinton Publications, 1996).

[75] The educated son of Chief Peguis expressed his father's dismay in "Letter from Peguis, Chief of the Saulteaux Tribe at the Red River Settlement, to the Aboriginal Protection Society, London," Appendix No. 16, "Report of the Select Committee on the Hudson's Bay Company," 1857 in Russell Smandych and Rick Linden, "Co-existing forms of Aboriginal and Private Justice: An Historical Study of the Canadian West," in *Legal Pluralism and the Colonial Legacy: Indigenous Experiences of Justice in Canada, Australia, and New Zealand*, ed., Kayleen M. Hazlehurst (Brookfield, VT: Ashgate Publishing Company, 1995), 24. Regarding the "half-breeds," see Ross, *Red River Settlement*, 10–11, 242; Marjorie Wilkins Campbell, *McGillivray, Lord of the Northwest* (Toronto: Clark, Irwin, 1962).

[76] The quoted text is from MacLeod *Diary*. There are many versions biased towards the HBC perspective on this bloody incident (e.g., Alexander Begg's account) whereby Grant and his NWC Métis were depicted as the wanton murderers of HBC Governor Semple and his party. However, it is

interesting that a chief HBC trader like MacLeod (who was "elsewhere" at the time and displayed other pro-HBC prejudices in his accounts) conceded that "much had occurred to rouse the N.W. party to desperate measures," 128. The armed hostility at Seven Oaks constituted the culmination of the "Pemmican War." This conflict began when the HBC attempted to cut off the staple pemmican foodstuff supply of the NWC posts in 1814. Mere trade rivalry escalated into the retaliatory seizure of goods or supplies, and the destruction of posts (e.g., HBC's Brandon House, NWC's La Souris) near the vital Turtle Mountain region, and at Red River.

[77] For the anti-British trader legislation, see Prucha, *Documents*, 28–29. Two years later, the act had to be amended because even American fur companies had to rely on non-citizen Natives, Métis, and European Canadians as guides, boatmen, and interpreters. Jay's Treaty is known formally as the *Treaty of Amity, Commerce, and Navigation, Between His Britannick Majesty;– and the United States of America, By Their President, with the Advice and Consent of Their Senate*, Nov. 19, 1794, U.S.-U.K., T.S. No. 105. For British Indian policy during the War of 1812, see Calloway, *Crown and Calumet*, 240. The Treaty of Greenville ceded all of southern and eastern Ohio to the United States as a result of their victory over the regional Indian confederacy at the Battle of Fallen Timbers in 1794. For the British to try and roll back the ensuing twenty years of U.S. westward expansion was an absurd proposal and rejected as such by the U.S. negotiators.

[78] The Pembina River generally parallels and undulates back and forth across the international boundary from its source on the northeastern slope of Turtle Mountain, which lies 120 miles west of the Pembina Mountains, to its mouth into the Red River. Alexander Henry referred to the Pembina Mountains as the "Hair hills," 81, fn 3. This appellation apparently derived from the abundance of buffalo wool that rubbed off onto the bushes and tree bark.

[79] MacLeod *Diary*, 129. The Great Walker family living on the Turtle Mountain reservation are direct descendants from Black Duck, per Howard's ICC, Docket 113, Transcript, 136. In *Culture and Experience*, Hallowell categorized Chippewa social structure as "atomistic," 349.

[80] "Early History of the Turtle Mountain Indians and Their Trails" (unattributed), Bureau of Indian Affairs, Record Group 75.19.121, Records of the Turtle Mountain Agency, ND, National Archives, Central Plains Region, Kansas City, Missouri, 2; David P. Delorme, "History of the Turtle

Mountain Band of Chippewa Indians," *North Dakota History* 22, no. 3 (1955): 122–23; Stanley N. Murray, "The Turtle Mountain Chippewa, 1882–1905," *North Dakota History* 51, no. 1 (Winter 1984): 15–16; Dusenberry, 123. The colloquial quotations are from the oral histories of Turtle Mountain Chippewa members Matilda and Frank Poitra and Francis Davis, as recounted in Nicholas C. P. Vrooman's "Buffalo Voices," *North Dakota Quarterly* 59, no. 4 (Fall 1991): 118. As used from the eighteenth century to present and across the United States and Canada, the term "half-breed" is usually an offensive and demeaning term and intended as such. But in this instance, it has a more specific and non-pejorative usage. The quote also included the term "Métchif," which is not used anymore (see Endnote 12 above).

[81] Patricia F. Poitra and Karen L. Poitra, *The History and Culture of the Turtle Mountain Band of Chippewa*. Howard's ethnography confirmed that other nearby Chippewa bands recognized a unique Turtle Mountain band. Red Lake Chippewa informants referred to the Turtle Mountain people as Mashkodenininiwak, while Manitoba Chippewa called them Mikinakwatshuininwak. Howard, ICC, Docket 113, Transcript, 124–25. Perhaps fittingly, an estimated 60 percent of Native lands within the Turtle Mountains are covered by water (lakes, ponds, swamps, and marshes) to this day. See C. M. Harrer's 1961 Bureau of Mines report to the Department of Interior, 2. My colleague Dr. Denise K. Lajimodiere informed me about the preferred term in Ojibwe, Mikinaak Wajiw.

[82] Edmund C. Bray and Martha C. Bray, eds., *Joseph N. Nicollet on the Plains and Prairies: The Expedition of 1838–39 with Journals, Letters, and Notes on the Dakota Indians* (St. Paul: Minnesota Historical Society Press, 1976), 187; Lise McCloud, "Heart of the Turtle," *North Dakota Quarterly* 59, no. 4 (Fall 1991): 90. From *The Dunseith Herald: The Pioneer Journal of the Turtle Mountain Region*, 6, no. 35 (March 6, 1890): 1, "the name is derived from the turtle-shape-like appearance." Copway, *Life, History, and Travels*, documented over two hundred figures used in Ojibwe picture writing, 134–36. Interestingly, the pictograph representing "land" was a turtle. In requesting assistance in locating twenty-two stray horses, the Turtle Mountain sub-chief Kaishpau Gourneau referred to the "tail of the Mountain" in his April 19, 1881, letter to Agent McLaughlin at Fort Totten. See Charlie White-Weasel, *History*, 141. White-Weasel, *History*, also recounted the varying Turtle Mountain oral accounts as told to him by his

father regarding how Turtle Mountain (Mekinock Wujiw in Ojibwe) got its name, 13.

[83] Coues, *New Light*, 409, during an 1806 expedition. The categorization of the North Dakota prairies as "semi-arid" stems from the long-term average annual precipitation of approximately seventeen inches for the state. See Harrer, Report, 3. Because the cited descriptions of Turtle Mountain derived mainly from hunters, trappers, traders, and gatherers who had little or no interest in farming, their reports rarely mention the quality of the soils. Since the land surface of the region derived from glacial drift, the silt, clay, sand, and gravel glacial debris created a generally poor-quality soil, with meager prospects for successful agriculture. The virtual extinction of the bison herds and subsequent confinement to this geological anomaly threatened the Turtle Mountain Chippewa with starvation in the 1880s and beyond. See chapter six for details.

[84] NWC geographer and cartographer David Thompson, always a stickler for detailed accuracy, referred to these unique uplands as "Turtle Hill" during his travels in the region in 1797 and 1798. *David Thompson's Narrative*: 185, 212, 214–15, 217, 218, 241; Howard, ICC, Docket 113, Transcript, 129; and *Plains-Ojibwa*, 109.

[85] O. A. Stevens, "Turtle Mountains of North Dakota," *The American Botanist* 28, no. 1 (February 1922):10; White-Weasel, *History*, 6.

[86] Alfred C. Farrell, "A Calendar of Principal Events of the French and Indians of Early Dakota," *Collections of the State Historical Society of North Dakota*, Vol. 1 (1906): 293. J. M. Gillette, "Advent of the American Indian Into North Dakota," *North Dakota Quarterly* VI, no. 3 (April 1932): 215.

[87] J. B. Bottineau's genealogy, from a letter dated November 4, 1910:7–8; Warren, *Ojibway History*, 355–56; Howard cites the continuity in many "full-blood" and "mixed-blood" Turtle Mountain Chippewa family surnames over the past two hundred years, as does Bottineau. Raymond J. DeMallie and many other scholars confirm that "kinship is fundamental to every aspect of Native American studies," DeMallie, "Kinship: The Foundation for Native American Society," in *Studying Native America: Problems and Prospects*, ed., Russell Thornton (Madison: University of Wisconsin Press, 1998), 350.

[88] Clifford Geertz, *The Interpretation of Cultures* (New York: Basic Books, 1973), 52, 89. One definition of cultural identity is "an historically

transmitted pattern of meanings embodied in symbols which give order, direction, and meaning to life." Most of the existing scholarship on the Turtle Mountain Chippewa comes from the fields of cultural anthropology (ethnology) or ethnohistory. This literature focuses on three convergent cultural and historical developments in the late eighteenth and early nineteenth centuries:

1) the cultural migration and transformation of the Plains-Ojibwe from an Eastern Woodlands to a Great Plains Indian culture (Skinner, Howard);

2) the emergence ("ethnogenesis") of the Turtle Mountain band (Howard, Hickerson, Delorme, Camp) in relation to the evolution of the British and French-Canadian fur trade in the region of the Red River of the North, and intertribal rivalry with the Dakota Indians;

3) A kin-related but increasingly distinct "half-breed" or *Metis* culture emerged from the long-term Ojibwe/Chippewa involvement with the European fur trade and intermarriage with European Canadian fur traders (Brown, Peterson, Bakker).

[89] See endnote 11 above. The situation of the Turtle Mountain Chippewa circa 1818 exemplified Chief Justice John Marshall's U.S. Supreme Court decision in *Worcester v. Georgia*, 6 Pet. 511 (1832), 542–543. Marshall characterized American Indians as "distinct people, divided into separate nations, independent of each other, having institutions of their own, and governing themselves by their own laws." The modern *McClanahan* decision confirmed that "it must always be remembered that the various Indian tribes were once independent and sovereign nations, and that their claim to sovereignty long predates that of our own Government." *McClanahan v. State Tax Comm'n of Ariz.*, 411 U.S. 164, 173 (1973). Also see *Talton v. Mayes*, 163 U.S. 376 (1896). The legal actions involving the Turtle Mountain Chippewa before the Indian Claims Commission will be discussed in the Conclusion. The Indian Claims Commission established in 1946 (25 U.S.C. 70-70v) enabled tribes to seek legal redress for prior detrimental land cessions. To this court the Turtle Mountain Chippewa had to prove their existence as an "identifiable group" with "possessory occupation" of a "definable territory" for a long period of time. This required sufficient ethnohistorical evidence to establish these "questions of fact," and convince the commissioners, who sat as both the "fact finders" and as the "triers of law," of the band's factual contentions, which accorded with the material presented in this chapter.

[90] *Note Regarding Article 2.* The Avalon Project at Yale Law School, http://www.yale.edu/lawweb/avalon/diplomacy/britian/conv1818.htm. It should be noted that the forty-ninth parallel international boundary line from Maine to the Rocky Mountains, including its location on the Red River, was not established legally until the 1842 Webster-Ashburton Treaty, and was not fixed permanently until United States and British boundary commissions made a final determination in 1872. Therefore, it took almost ninety years (1783–1872) for the United States and British Canada to determine their border. Such contention and lack of precision belied their claims of superior sovereignty over Indian and Métis peoples, whom they accused falsely of lacking a sense of definable territory.

[91] Ibid., Articles III and V. See Felix S. Cohen, "Original Indian Title," *Minnesota Law Review* 28 (1947): 34–35. The Louisiana Purchase provided the classic example of how the European doctrine of discovery doctrine impacted the "aboriginal title" of American Indian groups. France claimed paramount title to the Louisiana Territory as a result of its discovery and exploration. When the United States purchased that title from France in 1803, it only acquired the right to negotiate for future land purchases from the Indians. Cohen stated that while the United States paid France fifteen million dollars for title to the Louisiana Territory, it eventually paid the Indian inhabitants twenty times that amount for the same land.

[92] Prucha, *Documents*, 32; Secretary of War Calhoun on Indian Trade, December 5, 1818: *American State Papers: Indian Affairs*, 2, 183.

[93] Until 1837, the United States recognized through treaties the "Chippewa Nation" as a single legal group, although in fact, such a cohesive or monolithic entity never existed.

[94] *Johnson v. McIntosh*, 21 U.S. (8 Wheat.) 543, 1823. Chief Justice Marshall justified his mandate for conquest by stating that: "However extravagant the pretension of converting discovery of an inhabited country into conquest may appear; if a country has been acquired and held under it; if the property of the great mass of the community originates in it, it becomes the law of the land, and cannot be questioned" (591). The first officer of the Supreme Court overlooked the fact that thirty-four years before, the federal executive officer in charge of Indian affairs, Secretary of War Henry Knox, stated that such a rationalization constituted "a gross violation of the fundamental laws of nature, and of that distributive justice which is the glory of a nation." See Prucha, *Documents*, 12–13. Knowing that his assertion about the sovereign

prerogatives of the United States being derived from Britain contradicted the "natural rights" ideals of the American Revolution, Marshall could only posit weakly the legitimacy for a doctrine that denied "natural rights" to Indians by writing that: "So, too, with respect to the concomitant principle, that the Indian inhabitants are to be considered merely as occupants . . . However, this restriction [i.e., their inability to transfer their title to anyone except the federal government] may be opposed to natural right, yet, if it be indispensable to that system under which the country has been settled, it may, perhaps, be supported by reason, and certainly cannot be rejected by Courts of justice"(592).

The Chief Justice reformulated the colonial European "doctrine of discovery" and created a very useful legal fiction to rationalize the appropriation of Indian land by the U.S. government. He knew that the application of the doctrine of conquest to the American Indian situation in the U.S. was not accurate historically or in accord with international law. Almost all Indian lands in the United States had been acquired by purchase (i.e., by consent), and not by conquest. Henry Knox recognized that in accordance with international law dating back to the sixteenth century (which derived from earlier medieval canon law), "conquest" resulting in the taking of Indian lands without their consent could only be lawful if implemented by a "just war." See Prucha, *Documents*, 12. A "just war" could not be waged by a European or European-derived sovereign against Indigenous peoples unless any of three basic conditions were not met: 1) they rejected Christian missionaries; 2) they refused to engage in trade; or 3) they engaged in unprovoked attacks. Over centuries, none of these conditions ever applied to more than a few Native tribes among the several hundred living in North America. They certainly never applied to the Turtle Mountain Chippewa, who accepted Roman Catholic and Episcopalian missionaries, became the mainstays of the Red River and northern plains fur trade, and always maintained peaceful relations with the United States. Marshall and other early federal policymakers believed that the Indians would continue to willingly cede their land, as they had for the most part since 1778. However, by the 1820s this was no longer the case. Unfortunately, the decision in *Johnson* encouraged Georgia to claim that its assertion of jurisdiction over the Cherokees was legal. This assertion led to the constitutional crisis over federalism, which Marshall attempted to resolve in two subsequent landmark cases (*Cherokee Nation v. Georgia* [1831] and *Worcester v. Georgia* [1832]). These two cases, along with *Johnson*, became known as the "Marshall trilogy." Of course, in the eyes of the Indians and many subsequent scholars, each ruling derived from the expediency of national politics rather than being "supported by reason." These decisions are considered by legal scholars to be *the* foundational Indian law cases. Three of the four major principles of federal Indian law were derived from *Johnson*: 1) the plenary power of Congress over Indian affairs; 2) diminished tribal sovereignty; and 3) "Indian title." The fourth principle, known as the "trust relationship," derived from the Cherokee Nation decision. It defined Indian tribes as "domestic dependent nations . . . in a state of pupilage," and that "their relation to the United States resembles that of a ward to his guardian . . . look[ing] to our government for protection" (30 U.S. [5 Peters], 1, 17. 1831).

[95] The basis for this legal claim as it relates to the Turtle Mountain Chippewa hearkened back to the 1670 royal charter bestowed by King Charles II of England on the HBC and its territorial right to Rupert's Land.

[96] *Johnson v. McIntosh*, 21 U.S. (8 Wheat.) 543, 1823, at 588.

[97] Ibid., at 573–74.

[98] See Richard A. Epstein, "Property and Necessity," *Harvard Journal of Law & Public Policy* 13, no. 1 (Winter 1990): 2–3 for an analysis of the concept of property as a "bundle of rights," i.e., the rights of use, possession, and disposition.

[99] Stpehen H. Long and William H. Keating, eds., *Narrative of an Expedition to the Source of St. Peter's River* (London: Geo. B. Whittaker, 1825), 43. Major Samuel Woods found the post "rotted away" in 1849. See U.S. Congress. House, *Report of Major Woods, Relative to His Expedition to Pembina Settlement*, 31st Congress, 1st Session, 1850, House Executive Document 51, Serial set 577, 19.

[100] Keating, *Long Expedition Narrative*, 38–43, *Collections of the State Historical Society of North Dakota*, Volume I (1906): 217. In 1823 the Red River settlement up in the British Possessions that later evolved into Winnipeg, were called either Fort Douglas or St. Boniface. Father Severe Dumoulin had established the first Catholic mission in the territory at Pembina in 1818, to minister to the Métis inhabitants.

[101] Keating, *Long Expedition Narrative*, 41.

[102] Van Kirk, *Many Tender Ties*, 170–72; Robert E. Bieder, "Scientific Attitudes Toward Indian Mixed-Bloods in Early Nineteenth Century

America." *Journal of Ethnic Studies*, 8, 1980: 17–30; Reginald Horsman, "Science, Racism and the American Indian in the Mid-Nineteenth Century," *American Quarterly* 27, no. 2 (May 1975): 152–68. Berkhofer, *White Man's Indian*, warns against making modern distinctions between ethnocentrism and racism. He says these distinctions have no historical validity "before the early decades of [the twentieth] century when culture and biology were still fused and therefore confused categories"(55).

[103] Albert Memmi, *The Colonizer and the Colonized* (Boston: Beacon Press, 1965), 71–75. Memmi constructed this same definition or model in other essays, books, or compilations, such as *Racism* (University of Minnesota Press, 2000), 95–100. I am indebted to Robert A. Williams, Jr., at the University of Arizona College of Law, for demonstrating Memmi's applicability to critical legal theory and American Indian policy.

[104] Van Kirk, *Many Tender Ties*, 171, 201, 236. Van Kirk analyzed how growing racial prejudice threatened family unity in the Red River community within the context of a member of Alexander Ross's family asking, "What if Mama is an Indian?"

[105] William Temple Hornaday, *The Extermination of the American Bison* (Washington, D.C.: Smithsonian Institution Press, 2002, reprinted and edited from the original, *The Extermination of the American Bison* in the *Annual Report of the Board of Regents of the Smithsonian Institution*, 1889), 441–51. Hornaday noted that the utilization of buffalo products included robes, hides, bones, pemmican, dried or jerked meat, fresh meat, hair, and buffalo "chips" for fuel.

[106] Letter from Henry M. Rice to Indian agent J. E. Fletcher, November 30, 1848, in *Report of Major Woods*, House Ex. Doc. 51, 8.

[107] Letter from Father G. A. Belcourt to General R. Jones, Adjutant General, U.S. Army, August 20, 1849, in *Report of Major Woods*, House Ex. Doc. 51, 41.

[108] Ibid., 44, 40. The Catholic French-Canadian priest George Antoine Belcourt (Bellecourt, Bellecours) and the Presbyterian Scot settler Alexander Ross described the returns of Red River and Pembina buffalo hunts in 1841 and 1845—twenty years after Long. Yet the plentitude of buffalo would only have been greater twenty years earlier, as Long noted, and the value of the pound sterling about the same.

[109] Alexander Ross, *Red River Settlement: Its Rise, Progress, and Present State; with Some Account of the Native Races and Its General History to the Present Day* (London: Smith, Elder and Co., 1856), 273, 256. He calculated a 1,200-pound sterling profit from an 1841 buffalo hunt.

[110] Prucha, *Documents*, 32. War Secretary Calhoun on Indian Trade, December 5, 1818: *American State Papers: Indian Affairs*, 2, 183; A. Irving Hallowell, "Northern Ojibwa Ecological Adaptation and Social Organization," in *Contributions to Anthropology: Selected Papers of A. Irving Hallowell*, ed., Raymond D. Fogelson (Chicago: University of Chicago Press, 1976), 335–36.


## CHAPTER 2 ENDNOTES

[1] Alexander Ramsey, *Journal of the United States Commission to Treat with the Chippewa Indians of the Pembina and Red Lake*, Minnesota Territory, August 18, 1851, concluded 20 September 1851, 8. Hereafter *1851 Treaty Journal*. ICC, Docket 18-A/Exhibit 2.

[2] *ARCIA* 1848.

[3] Warren, *Ojibway History*, 135.

[4] Keating, *Long Expedition Narrative*, 13.

[5] Treaty of Prairie du Chien (7 Stat., 272), August 19, 1825; Charles J. Kappler, *Affairs: Laws and Treaties*, Vol. 2: 250–55 (Washington, D.C.: Government Printing Office, 1904). The treaty line ran from what would become Chippewa Falls, Wisconsin, to Moorhead, Minnesota.

[6] Ibid.

[7] Dakota "winter counts" (i.e., elaborate pictographs on buffalo hides that served as tribal calendars of events) provided the source for Howard's dating and account of these events. ICC, Docket 113, Transcript, September 18, 1962, 81. Howard, along with Turtle Mountain Chippewa informant Charles Cree, Jr., located the site of the former village.

[8] Treaty of Prairie du Chien.

[9] Daniel K. Richter, "War and Culture: The Iroquois Experience," *William and Mary Quarterly* 40 (1983): 528–29. Richter asserted that Native American "non-state" armed conflict was as "rational" as European-derived nation-state or imperial warfare. Howard, *Plains-Ojibwa*, 19.

[10] *ARCIA* 1849, 94; Senate Doc. 444, No. XIII.

[11] Image 2, Indian Tribes before 1850 map, *State Maps on File* (North Dakota), New York: Facts on File, 1984, Figure 5.14 in the original. West of the Red River, the Ojibwe/Dakota "line" ran from the Turtle River, south and west to Devils Lake, and then farther west and slightly south to the junction of the Little Knife and Missouri Rivers.

[12] Warren, *Ojibway History*, 364.

[13] Ibid., 358–64, describes the exploits of Shappa, Wa-nah-ta, Flat Mouth, and Black Duck.

[14] Martha C. Bray, ed., *The Journals of Joseph N. Nicollet: A Scientist on the Mississippi Headwaters With Notes on Indian Life, 1836–37* (St. Paul: Minnesota Historical Society Press, 1970), 19; Kent McNeil, "Sovereignty on the Northern Plains: Indian, European, American and Canadian Claims," *Journal of the West* 39, no. 3 (Summer 2000): 16.

[15] Robert A. Williams, Jr., "Linking Arms Together: Multicultural Constitutionalism in a North American Indigenous Vision of Law and Peace," *California Law Review* 82 (July 1994): 987; Francis Jennings, *The Invasion of America: Indians, Colonialism, and the Cant of Conquest* (New York: W.W. Norton & Company, 1976), 123.

[16] ICC, Docket 113/Exhibit 9a, *Journal of the Treaty of August 19, 1825, at Prairie du Chien.*

[17] James D. Richardson, *Messages and Papers of the Presidents*, Vol. 2: 280–83.

[18] John Mack Faragher, "'More Motley than Mackinaw': From Ethnic Mixing to Ethnic Cleansing on the Frontier of the Lower Missouri, 1783–1833," in *Contact Points: American Frontiers from the Mohawk Valley to the Mississippi, 1750–1830*, eds., Andrew R. L. Clayton and Fredricka J. Teute (Williamsburg, VA: Omohundro Institute of Early American History and Culture, 1998), 304–26. I concur with Faragher's characterization that the use of the term Indian "removal" was nothing more than an "antiseptic" label for what could be more accurately described as "ethnic cleansing."

[19] In 1834, H. S. Tanner prepared the first official U.S. government map indicating a specific Pembina Chippewa area. In 1882, Commissioner Hiram Price referred to this map marking Chippewa territory from the Red River to the western extent of Devils Lake. See U.S. Congress, House, Report No. 1144 to accompany H.R. 1885, 1882; ICC, Docket 113/Exhibit 12.

[20] Treaty of Fond du Lac (7 Stat., 290), August 5, 1826, Kappler, *Treaties*, Vol. 2, 268–73.

[21] Ibid., 269.

[22] Warren, *Ojibway History*, 393. The fact that Cass and McKenney relied on the recommendations of selfish European American traders should come as no surprise. In 1817, Cass received payments totaling $35,000 from fur trade tycoon John Jacob Astor for undisclosed services. Such substantial remuneration would only be rendered to those influential public officials who furthered Astor's enterprises in the Northwest. Astor was the richest man in America, and a financial benefactor to Presidents Jefferson, Madison, and Monroe in support of their westward expansion policies. See Gustavus Meyers, *The History of the Great American Fortunes* (New York: Modern Library, 1936), 103.

[23] *ARCIA* 1850, Alexander Ramsey to Luke Lea, 60; Warren, *Ojibway History*, 393–94, 319, 135. Warren had intimate family knowledge of the local Lake Superior fur trade since his father (Lyman M. Warren) and uncle (Truman A. Warren) both married into, and took over, the fur trade concern of Michel Cadotte.

[24] Treaty of Fond du Lac, Kappler, *Treaties*, 270.

[25] Ibid., 269.

[26] Mary Jane Schneider, "An Adaptive Strategy and Ethnic Persistence of the Méchif of North Dakota," unpublished Ph.D. dissertation, University of Missouri, 1974, 85, 116.

[27] Warren, *Ojibway History*, 393.

[28] Treaty of Fond du Lac, Kappler, *Treaties*, 269. The allotments remained "under the direction of the President." The special provisions in treaties for "half-breed" relatives took varying forms: 1) money to traders' families; 2) land scrip certificates; 3) allotments on ceded lands; 4) allotments on public domain lands elsewhere. Federal policy wanted the mixed-bloods to sever their tribal affiliations, leaving the Native Americans in a weaker bargaining position.

[29] Ibid.

[30] Ibid.; William Cronon, *Changes in the Land: Indians, Colonists, and the Ecology of New England* (New York: Hill and Wang, 1983), 245.

[31] Treaty of Fond du Lac, Kappler, *Treaties*, 273.

[32] Erdrich, *Tracks*. The Turtle Mountain Chippewa writer Louise Erdrich begins her novel *Tracks* by linking the "spotted sickness of 1837" with a tuberculosis outbreak in 1912, and their horrific consequences for the Turtle Mountain people. Clyde D. Dollar, "The High Plains Smallpox Epidemic of 1837–38," *Western Historical Quarterly* 8, no. 1 (January 1977): 24. The 1837–1840 northern plains smallpox epidemic killed over 90 percent of the Mandan, 50 percent of the Assiniboine and the Arikara, 66 percent of the Blackfeet, 33 percent of the Crows, and 25 percent of the Pawnee, according to Dollar. His article refuted the long-held belief that the epidemic was spread deliberately through an infected blanket by the American Fur Company. Dollar's evidence suggested that three Arikara women passengers on the steamboat unknowingly spread the disease up the Missouri River and to the regional tribes.

[33] *Report of Major Woods, Relative to His Expedition to Pembina Settlement*, 31st Congress, 1st Session, 1850, House Executive Document 51, Serial set 577, Letter from G. A. Belcourt to Major Woods, August 20, 1849, 37.

[34] Ibid. While the lack of biological immunity to European diseases among Indigenous peoples is known widely as the natural cause for the waves of post-contact demographic disasters they suffered, in the case of the 1837 outbreak there was also an insidious and little known federal policy dimension to the affliction. See J. Diane Pearson, "Lewis Cass and the Politics of Disease: The Indian Vaccination Act of 1832," *Wicazo Sa Review* 18, no. 2 (Fall 2003): 9–6.

[35] *ARCIA* 1851, 324, referring to Sioux bands along the Missouri, Arkansas, and Platte Rivers.

[36] Ibid., 25. Alexander Ramsey to Secretary of the Interior A. H. H. Stuart, November 7, 1851. The Turtle Mountain Chippewa never entered into nor agreed to be included in the 1851 Fort Laramie Treaty.

[37] Edmund C. Bray and Martha C. Bray, eds., *Joseph N. Nicollet on the Plains and Prairies: The Expedition of 1838–39 with Journals, Letters, and Notes on the Dakota Indians* (St. Paul: Minnesota Historical Society Press, 1976), 198.

[38] *Report of Major Woods*, 14–15; Ibid., 128.

[39] *Report of Major Woods*, Letter from G. A. Belcourt to Major Woods, August 20, 1849, 36, 42.

[40] Livia Appel and Theodore C. Blegen, "Encouragement of Immigration," *Minnesota History Bulletin*, Vol. V (August 1923): 171. The 1849 Minnesota Territorial census indicated a non-Native population of 4,535.

[41] *General Land Office Commission Report of 1851*, 32nd Congress, 1st Session, 1851, Senate Document 1, Serial set 613.

[42] *ARCIA* 1849, p. 10.

[43] Alvin C. Gluek, *Minnesota and the Manifest Destiny of the Canadian Northwest: A Study in Canadian-American Relations* (Toronto: University of Toronto Press, 1975), 115.

[44] *ARCIA* 1850, Alexander Ramsey to Luke Lea, October 21, 1850, p. 57.

[45] *Report of Major Woods*, Letter from Captain John Pope, October 3, 1849, 54.

[46] Annie Heloise Abel, "Proposal for an Indian State, 1778–1878," in *Annual Report of the American Historical Association for the Year 1907*, Vol. 1: 103.

[47] Secretary of War William H. Crawford, "On Trade and Intercourse," March 13, 1816, *American State Papers: Indian Affairs*, 2:27.

[48] *Report of Major Woods*, Letter from Captain John Pope, October 3, 1849, 54.

[49] *ARCIA* 1854, 190–91. A written copy of a speech Green Setting Feather gave at St Joseph, September 14, 1852, as recounted by Isaac Stevens in a report to Commissioner George W. Manypenny, dated September 16, 1854, emphasis added. Father Belcourt tallied the number of Métis in Pembina County at "over two thousand" in his address to Commissioner Manypenny in Washington, D.C., November 20, 1854. See *Collections of the State Historical Society of North Dakota*, Volume I (1906): 214.

[50] *ARCIA* 1854, 190–91.

[51] Copway, *Life, History and Travels*.

[52] Wilcomb E. Washburn, *Red Man's Land, White Man's Law* (Norman: University of Oklahoma Press, 1971), 168.

[53] *Report of Major Woods*, Letter from Father G. A. Belcourt, November 20, 1845, 44. The map "Upland areas used by the *hivernant* Métis for wintering village sites," found in "Vernacular Houses and Farmsteads of the Canadian Métis," *Journal of Cultural Geography* 10, no. 1 (Fall/ Winter 1989): 21,

indicates that the Métis sited their wintering villages "in sheltered prairie uplands" like Pembina Mountain and Turtle Mountain, and other similar spots across North Dakota, Manitoba, and Saskatchewan.

[54] *ARCIA* 1854, 190–91. Steven's report labeled the Turtle Mountain Indians as "Prairie Chippewas," who "range[d] the country from east of the Red River to the Mouse [Souris] River valley,"189.

[55] The rest of Stevens's report described the expeditions of the "Red River hunters" in detail. Stevens, like Ramsey and Rice, but unlike Long, acquired a very positive impression of the Red River Métis. Stevens also put an end to the myth of the "Great American Desert" as asserted by Major Stephen Long. See Ramsey's letter in *ARCIA* 1849, 97. In contrast, Alexander Ross, *Red River Settlement*, disparaged the economic potential of the Métis inhabitants for any endeavor beyond buffalo hunting, along with many of the U.S. reports on the region. He characterized Pope's report as "totally at variance with facts, and calculated to mislead" (406). In general, he stated that "it is only the Americans who are gifted with the double sight [i.e., exaggerated estimates] that will have them a commercial and agricultural people" where none existed (407).

[56] *Report of Major Woods*, Captain John Pope's observations about Indians in the Red River Valley of the North, Pembina, and the Turtle Mountains, Father G. A. Belcourt's letters, and Henry M. Rice's report to the CIA on the Red River of the North inhabitants, ICC Docket 246/ Exhibit 211, 102, 106–107.

[57] Act of Congress (9 Stat. 544), September 30, 1850, 556.

[58] *1851 Treaty Journal*, 1.

[59] *ARCIA* 1849, 99. Ramsey referred particularly to the HBC's liquor trade with Native Americans and the global pretenses of the British Empire.

[60] *Treaty with the Pembina and Red Lake Chippewa*, 32nd Congress, 1st Session, September 20, 1851; Senate Confidential Executive Document 10, Serial 613, 1–3.

[61] *1851 Treaty Journal*, 5. It should be reiterated that Cherokee removal was an enormous financial windfall for the U.S. government, while the Cherokees had to pay for their own removal. ICC, Docket 191, Exhibits/ Plaintiff Exhibits 256 and 257, Map F.

[62] *ARCIA* 1851, 24. While never using the word annexation, Ramsey referred to it euphemistically as a "certain exigency" that might occur. *ARCIA* 1851, 27.

[63] *1851 Treaty Journal*, 8.

[64] *ARCIA* 1850, 63. Ramsey estimated 1,100 Métis in Minnesota Territory. Alexander Ross, *Red River Settlement*, 270, estimated 4,000 Métis in the Red River settlements of the British Possessions.

[65] *ARCIA* 1850, 63–64. Ramsey considered the Métis to be "considerably advanced in civilization," yet "practically without law." Like most European Americans, he did not comprehend their penchant for individual and collective autonomy, a political organization modeled on the Chippewa band structure, nor the strict laws governing their twice annual buffalo hunts. Jean Baptiste Wilkie was identified correctly by Ramsey but misspelled in the signatory section of the treaty as Battiste. Ross identified Wilkie as "an English half-breed brought up among the French" in Red River. His "good sound sense and long experience" gave him a prominence that can also be gleaned from the more significant fact that he had served as the "governor" or "chief" of the highly organized large-scale Red River Métis buffalo hunts. See *Red River Settlement*, 248, 271. Pierre Bottineau, son of a French-Canadian voyageur and an Ojibwe mother, was born in the Red River settlement. See Martha C. Bray, "Pierre Bottineau: Professional Guide," *North Dakota Quarterly* 32 (1964): 29–37.

[66] *Report of Major Woods*, Pope's report, 30–33, 1849. Indian agent J. E. Fletcher's reports in *ARCIA*, 1848–1849. Stevens' report, *ARCIA* 1849, 193. Ramsey came to the same conclusion during his trip to Pembina. See his letter in *ARCIA* 1851, 27.

[67] Warren, *Ojibway History*, 133; *1851 Treaty Journal*, 16; J. Wesley Bond, *Sketches by a Camp Fire: or Notes of a trip from St. Paul to Pembina and Selkirk Settlement on the Red River of the North* (New York: J. S. Redfield, 1854), 323.

[68] Prucha, *Documents*, 22.

[69] Joseph A. Wheelock, *Journal of the Proceedings Connected with the Negotiation of a Treaty with the Red Lake and Pembina Bands of Chippewas— Concluded at the Old Crossing of Red Lake River on the Second of October, 1863*, Treaty File, Records of the Bureau of Indian Affairs, National

Archives, Washington, D.C., 1863, 53, emphasis added. Hereafter referred to as *1863 Treaty Journal.*

[70] *ARCIA* 1850, 93. Ramsey spelled it as "Ojibewas." In his post–Pembina treaty letter to the CIA in 1851, the governor referred to "not more than three hundred Chippewas roam[ing] beyond the western boundary of the present purchase." See *ARCIA* 1851, 26. This population estimate excluded the more sizeable number of Métis at Turtle Mountain. The Turtle Mountain Band of Chippewa Indians of North Dakota are one of four federally recognized tribes descended from the Pembina Band of Chippewa Indians. The others include the White Earth Band of Minnesota Chippewa Indians, the Chippewa Cree Indians of the Rocky Boy's Reservation, Montana, and the Little Shell Tribe of Chippewa Indians of Montana. See https://www.pembinasettlement.com/ pembina/ and https://www.narf.org/ nill/documents/nlr/nlr31-1.pdf p. 1.

"The Turtle Mountain band was a constituent part of the Pembina band" at the 1851 treaty council at Pembina. ICC Docket 113, Briefs, "Petitioner's Proposed Findings of Fact," Finding No. 6, 19–20. This finding was affirmed in the decision of *Red Lake and Pembina Bands v. United States,* 6 Ind. Cl. Com. 247, 249 (Ind Cl. Comm. 1958).

[71] Ross, *Red River Settlement,* 412; Warren, *Ojibway History,* 47–48. In 1858, "Chief" Wilkie renewed the Sweet Corn treaty on behalf of the Turtle Mountain Métis and Little Shell II's band of Chippewa Indians, with the Dakota Indians. Details from ICC Docket 191/Exhibit 256, 4 fn 2: Report dated October 21, 1869, to General O. D. Greene. In regard to its relevance in the Sisseton-Wahpeton treaty of February 19, 1867, see ICC Docket 191/Exhibit 257, BIA Report to the Secretary of the Interior dated October 3, 1872. There are also the two (but since they are duplicates, I considered them one) May 4, 1892, affidavits allegedly "deposing" two Turtle Mountain Chippewa witnesses in Exhibit 31 (Michael Gladue, p. 151) and Exhibit 32 (Louis LaFromboise, p. 152) of Senate Doc. 444, compiled by Turtle Mountain attorney J. B. Bottineau. They recounted that a "grand council" was held in July 1858 somewhere north of the Sheyenne River, and west of Devils Lake, between the Turtle Mountain Band, the Yankton and Sisseton bands (and the French names of their chiefs), and the Metchifs represented by "Old Chief Wilkie." Although they inferred that Little Shell was present, they implied that Wilkie was "so respected" by Little Shell that he also represented the interests of the Turtle Mountain Band

of Chippewa at the meeting. The contending parties supposedly decided that the Sheyenne River was the "dividing or boundary line" between the Chippewa and the Dakota bands. The fact that each affidavit is identical indicates that they were not individual eyewitness accounts. Each witness made his mark, and therefore could not write. So, who wrote this account? I suspect it was J. B. Bottineau. I believe his purpose was to bolster the Turtle Mountain band's claim that the more southerly Sheyenne River, rather than the more northerly Goose River, was the southern extent of their land claim in North Dakota. However, the Davis-Nolin family history (in *St. Ann's Centennial*) stated that the Goose River marked the dividing line. Although Red Lake orator Little Rock referred to the Sheyenne River as being littered with the bodies of their Chippewa ancestors at the Old Crossing Treaty council in 1863, and reiterated "that is the reason we consider it belongs to us" (see *1863 Treaty Journal*, 60), such carnage indicated that the more northerly Goose River was most likely the safest southern landmark of the Turtle Mountain band's territory. The area between the Goose and Sheyenne Rivers was designated finally as Dakota land by the 1867 Sisseton-Wahpeton treaty with the United States.

72 *1851 Treaty Journal*: 22–25.

73 Prucha, *Documents*, 22. Quotation from President Thomas Jefferson in 1803.

74 Henry Knox, *American State Papers: Indian Affairs*, 1:14, 1789; ICC Docket 18-A: 7; These legal "standards," adopted since 1789 and supposedly governing U.S. relations with Native tribes, are referred to as the "canons of construction" by U.S. courts. Treaty language (e.g., "usual and accustomed places") should be interpreted by the courts as understood by the Native Americans, and ambiguities are to be resolved in favor of the Natives.

75 Letter from Flatmouth and Wawinchigun to President Millard Fillmore, October 6, 1851, Enclosed in Lea to Ramsey letter, November 14, 1851, Minnesota Field Office, BIA, Record Group 75, National Archives, Washington, D.C.

76 *ARCIA* 1851, Ramsey to CIA Luke Lea, 26–27.

77 *Report of Major Woods*, 20. The matted roots of prairie grasslands required a certain kind of plow. Up at the Red River settlements (i.e., Winnipeg), Woods noted bountiful crops of wheat, barley, oats, and potatoes.

[78] Kappler, *Treaties*, 2: 588–90, Treaty with the Sisseton and Wahpeton Bands, July 23, 1851 (10 Stat., 949); Kappler, *Treaties*, 2: 591–93, Treaty with the Mdewakanton and Wahpakoota Bands, August 5, 1851 (10 Stat., 954).

[79] The total cession approximated twenty-four million acres, the remainders located in Iowa and South Dakota. Since the inception of Minnesota Territory in 1849, lumbering and the Native trade comprised the two major lines of business. Lumbering alone accounted for $200,000 annually. The non-Native territorial population in 1849 was 4,535. "Impressions of Minnesota in 1849," *Minnesota History Bulletin* V (August 1923): 171.

[80] Letter from Henry H. Sibley to Ramsey, June 26, 1852, *Alexander Ramsey Papers*, Microfilm Roll 6. A major scandal ensued over these treaties, even though an 1853 Senate investigation cleared Ramsey of any wrongdoing. Nonetheless, as noted by Ramsey's successor as governor and superintendent of Indian Affairs in Minnesota, W. A. Gorman, the question of fact concerning the circumstances of the fraud was not disproved. The treaty monies promised to the Dakota bands were not paid to them. Most of it went to various self-dealing traders claiming debts owed. Gorman noted the "deep and bitter murmuring by [the Dakota] against the treatment they think they have received." *ARCIA* 1853, 298. Chapter three will note how Dakota resentment over the fraudulent circumstances of this treaty, plus subsequent broken promises and harsh treatment from their traders and agents, led directly to the murderous 1862 "Sioux uprising" in Minnesota.

[81] ICC, Docket 246/Exhibit 66. This petition was witnessed, and may have been written by, Father Belcourt and Norman Kittson. The priest wanted the mixed-bloods to become "civilized" farmers, while the trader did not want his Pembina Chippewa and Méti suppliers pushed out of their hunting grounds. The inability of the Métis to secure legal land title from the HBC represented one of their major long-standing grievances against the conglomerate.

[82] Linda W. Slaughter, "Leaves from Northwestern History," Introduction to Chapter II, and Belcourt's November 25, 1854, letter, 213–14, *Collection of the State Historical Society of North Dakota* Vol. I (1906). From the context of the entire letter, the reference to "Pembina" indicated the large extent of Pembina County extending as far west as the Missouri River, rather than the small village of Pembina on the Red River. Father Belcourt cited conflicting Indigenous population figures for the region. While estimating the "half-

breed" population to be "over 2,000," he also warned that "about" 5,000 "half-breeds" and Pembina Indian men threatened to sweep up the Missouri River from Fort Mandan and kill any other Natives or Métis whom they considered to be intruders, 214–15.

[83] Ibid., 214.

[84] W. L. Morton, "The Battle at the Grand Coteau, July 13 and 14, 1851," in *Historical Essays on the Prairie Provinces*, ed., Donald Swainson (Toronto: McClleland and Stewart Ltd., 1970), 58–59.

[85] See endnote 71 above. Also, *Sisseton and Wahpeton Indians v. United States*, 58 C. Cls. 302, 332–33. While Dakota informants referred to this agreement as the Sweet Corn treaty, some Turtle Mountain Chippewa informants also called it the Wilkie treaty. ICC, Docket 113/ Exhibit 200b, 34–37, 46.

[86] *ARCIA* 1851, 24–25.

[87] The Pembina Treaty of 1851 was one of 430 unratified Indian treaties. See the section, "Treaties and Agreements Rejected by Congress" in Vine Deloria, Jr., & Raymond J. DeMallie, *Documents of American Indian Diplomacy: Treaties, Agreements, and Conventions, 1775–1979* (Norman: University of Oklahoma Press, 2000), 798–801.

[88] Letter from Thomas Jefferson to Colonel Benjamin Hawkins, February 18, 1803; Reginald Horsman, *Expansion and American Indian Policy, 1783–1812* (Norman: University of Oklahoma Press, 1967), 104–14.

[89] Jeremy Adelman and Stephen Aron, "From Borderlands to Borders: Empires, Nation-States, and the Peoples in Between North American History," *American Historical Review* 104, no. 3 (June 1999): 814–15. Adelman and Aron defined a "borderland" as a "zone of intercultural penetration" where "geographic and cultural borders were not clearly defined."

[90] Kerwin Lee Klein, "Reclaiming the 'F' Word, Or Being and Becoming Postwestern," *Pacific Historical Review* 65, no. 2 (May 1996): 196, citing Forbes.

[91] Sheldon Hackney, "Borderland vs. Frontier: Redefining the West: A Conversation with Patricia Nelson Limerick," *Humanities* 17, no. 4 (September/October 1996): 4–14; Adelman and Aron, "From Borderlands to Borders," 817.

[92] Richard White, *The Middle Ground: Indians, Empires, and Republics in the Great Lakes Region, 1650–1815* (Cambridge University Press, 1991), ix–x. Also see Gary B. Nash, "The Hidden History of Mestizo America," *The American Journal of History*, 1995.

[93] *St. Ann's Centennial*, recollections of Emerise LaVallie, 300.

[94] White-Weasel, *History*, 300.

[95] Ibid. The Turtle Mountain reservation's central agency town of Belcourt was later named in his honor.

[96] The empire quote is Ramsey's. It and the *Minnesota Pioneer* reference are cited by Theodore C. Blegen in *Minnesota: A History of the State* (St. Paul: University of Minnesota Press), 19nn, 173. For the wider significance of the Fraser River boom, see Robert E. Fricken, "The Fraser River Humbug: Americans and Gold in the British Pacific Northwest," *Western Historical Quarterly* 33 (Autumn 2002): 297–313.

[97] The tonnage estimate is from the *ARCIA* 1859, 71. The fur sales dollar value is from the *St. Paul Press* of August 29, 1863, cited by Gluek, *Minnesota and the Manifest Destiny of the Canadian Northwest*, 152.

[98] The European American population estimates for Minnesota Territory from 1849 to 1860 were as follows: 1849—4,500; 1855—40,000; 1857—150,000; 1860—172,000; Appel and Blegen, "Encouragement of Immigration," *Minnesota History Bulletin* V (1923–1924): 171.

[99] See map from Nicholas C.P. Vrooman, "The Métis Red River Cart," *Journal of the West* 42, no. 2 (Spring 2003), 9; Nancy L. Woolworth, "Gingras, St. Joseph and the Métis in the Northern Red River Valley, 1843–1873," *North Dakota History* 42, no. 4 (1975): 18.

[100] Bertha R. Palmer, *Beauty Spots in North Dakota* (Boston: Gorham Press, 1928), 66; *Dunseith Herald* 45, no. 2 (May 21, 1886), 4.

[101] This characterization of North Dakota's overall historical development comes from Elwyn B. Robinson, *History of North Dakota* (Lincoln: University of Nebraska Press, 1966), xi.

[102] Theodore C. Blegen and Philip D. Jordan, eds., *With Various Voices: Recordings of North Star Life* (Saint Paul: Itasca Press, 1949), xi. For an excellent series of maps depicting the ever-shifting external and internal boundaries of North Dakota throughout the nineteenth century, see Luella

J. Hall, "History of the Formation of Counties in North Dakota," *Collections of the North Dakota State Historical Society* Vol. V (1923).

[103] *ARCIA* 1859, 71.

[104] Nancy O. Lurie, ICC, Docket 113, Transcript, September 19, 1962, 183. The Turtle Mountain Chippewa would protest on the exact same grounds from 1882–1905.

[105] *ARCIA* 1856 in Prucha, *Documents*, 92. It should be noted that each of these railroads went bankrupt as a result of the Panic of 1857. St. Paul had to wait until after the Civil War in 1867 to get linked up with Chicago by rail. Also, the eastern rail terminus ended up at Duluth, Minnesota, rather than Pembina, North Dakota.

[106] Nancy O. Lurie, ICC, Docket 113, Transcript, September 19, 1962, 183.

[107] *ARCIA* 1859, 56–57.

[108] Ibid., 71.

[109] *ARCIA* 1851, 27.

[110] *Journal of Proceedings in 1860*, ICC, Docket 18-A/Plaintiff Exhibit 255: 16, 18, 27, 29–30. *ARCIA*, 1860, 24.

[111] *ARCIA* 1860, 24–25.

[112] *ARCIA* 1859, 71.

[113] Robinson, *North Dakota History*, 216, 221.

[114] Howard R. Lamar, *Dakota Territory, 1861–1889* (Fargo: Institute for Regional Studies, North Dakota State University, 1997), 177.

[115] Securing citizen loyalty via land reform was an international phenomenon (also occurring in Mexico, Russia, Prussia, France, and Great Britain) during the mid- to late-nineteenth century that has eluded significant scholarly investigation. I am indebted to Tom Holm for making me aware of the global nature of this circumstance. In 1875, Congress passed the Indian Homestead Act of March 3, 1875 (18 Stat. 420), as an attempt to extend the provisions of the 1862 legislation to any U.S.-born adult male head of a Native American family "*who has abandoned, or may hereafter abandon, his tribal relations.*" See Section 15: 23 (emphasis added). Only a few Native Americans (e.g., the Winnebagos in 1881) accepted such terms out of a desperate need to survive. Most probably remained unaware

of the Act, did not want to sever their tribal relations, felt quite justified in assuming that they still possessed their land, or could not even meet the minimum requirements due to their poverty.

[116] *ARCIA* 1859, 71.

[117] March 2, 1861 (12 Stat. 239), Section 1.

[118] Ibid. David E. Wilkins and K. Tsianina Lomawaima, *Uneven Ground: American Indian Sovereignty and Federal Law* (Norman: University of Oklahoma Press, 2001): 181–83, 193.

[119] Bishop Henry B. Whipple, "The Indian System: Report of Commissioner of Indian Affairs, 1863; History of the Sioux War by I.V.D. Heard, 1863," *North American Review* 99 (1864): 449–50.

[120] Howard, ICC, Docket 113, Transcript, September 18, 1962, 144; ICC, Docket 113/ Plaintiff Exhibit 29, Letter from Agent W. W. Titson, to Clark W. Thompson, Superintendent of Indian Affairs, at St. Paul, November 21, 1862. Titson also identified two warriors of the Turtle Mountain band, Crane and Wolverine, as "soldiers of Little Shell." Among Copway's observations on Ojibwe governance, he noted that "a chief always had two braves at his side," *Life, History, and Travels*, 141. They served as bodyguards, messengers, or any other task assigned them by the chief. Summer Wolverine accompanied Little Shell to the Old Crossing council in 1863 and signed that treaty.

## CHAPTER 3 ENDNOTES

[1] Joseph A. Wheelock, *Journal of the Proceedings Connected with the Negotiation of a Treaty with the Red Lake and Pembina Bands of Chippewas– Concluded at the Old Crossing of Red Lake River on the Second of October, 1863.* Alexander Ramsey and Ashley C. Morrill were the official treaty commissioners, while Wheelock was the secretary. ICC, Docket 18-A/ Defendant's Exhibit 12. Hereafter *1863 Treaty Journal.*

[2] Russel L. Barsch and James Y. Henderson, *The Road: Indian Tribes and Political Liberty* (Berkeley: University of California Press, 1980), 270; Vine Deloria, Jr., "The Place of Indians in Contemporary Education," *American Indian Journal* 2, no. 21 (February 1976): 2.

[3] Native American tribes negotiated over 800 treaties with the United States, although the Senate ratified only 371 of them. See Charles Kappler,

*Indian Affairs, Laws and Treaties* (1904), for the most official, if incomplete, collection of the ratified treaties. Also see Vine Deloria, Jr., and Raymond J. DeMallie's *Documents of American Indian Diplomacy: Treaties, Agreements, and Conventions, 1775–1979* (1999). This collection supplements and expands Kappler's volumes by reprinting copies of hundreds of other treaties and agreements not published previously.

[4] *Barron's Dictionary of Legal Terms*, 35. "Bad faith" is the same as a "breach of faith," and connotes "dishonesty in fact in the conduct or transaction concerned."

[5] *ARCIA* 1863, 410.

[6] Vine Deloria, Jr., "The Subject Nobody Knows," *American Indian Quarterly* 19, no. 1 (Winter 1995): 143.

[7] Peter Nabokov, *A Forest of Time: American Indian Ways of History* (Cambridge, UK: Cambridge University Press, 2002), 25.

[8] Secretary of the Interior Caleb B. Smith to Commissioner of Indian Affairs William P. Dole, July 19, 1862, Commissioner Dole to treaty Commissioner Ramsey, July 24, 1863. Also see Melissa L. Meyer, *The White Earth Tragedy: Ethnicity and Dispossession at a Minnesota Anishinaabe Reservation, 1889–1920* (Lincoln: University of Nebraska Press, 1994), 40–49.

[9] ICC, Docket 18-A, Briefs, Plaintiff's Finding 32, 32.

[10] *ARCIA* 1863, 410.

[11] Gary Clayton Anderson, *Little Crow: Spokesman for the Sioux* (St. Paul, MN: Minnesota Historical Society Press, 1986), 172–74. Some Mdewakanton from Devils Lake "courted" the Turtle Mountain Chippewa and Métis at St. Joseph (e.g., Gingras and Bottineau). They traded food items in exchange for a large quantity of plundered goods from Little Crow's people when they sought refuge at Devils Lake and Pembina. Although the Ojibwe and Métis "seemed friendly," Pembina chief Red Bear expressed his disdain for Little Crow and wanted him and his followers to vacate the region.

[12] Martha C. Bray, "Pierre Bottineau: Professional Guide," *North Dakota Quarterly* 32 (1964): 29–37. Also see "Historical Accounts of Pierre, Charles, and Severe Bottineau," *Collections of the Minnesota Historical Society*. Pierre Bottineau was the father of Turtle Mountain Chippewa tribal Métis

member and lawyer, John Baptiste Bottineau, who represented the legal interests of Chief Little Shell III and the tribal council from 1878 until 1911. It should be noted that the final treaty documents of 1863 and 1864 did not identify Bottineau as an interpreter. They denoted Paul H. Beaulieu as "special interpreter" and T. A. Warren as "United States interpreter." Each of these men may have been suspect by the Native Americans because of their affiliation with the American Fur Company and the White Earth reservation. Pierre's brother, Charles Bottineau, participated in the "supplementary" negotiations for the amended 1864 treaty in Washington, D.C. The participation of both brothers indicated the importance placed by the Pembina and Turtle Mountain Chippewa on the value of their skills as trusted interpreters and advisors.

[13] *1863 Treaty Journal*, 2.

[14] The Old Crossing Treaty Historical Park is located on the Red Lake River near Huot, Minnesota.

[15] The following "enumeration" was made at the 1863 Old Crossing Treaty Council, *1863 Treaty Journal*, 38; Senate Doc. 444, 136. Enumeration of the band members in attendance (i.e., not the bands in their entirety) as "assembled by their chiefs":

| Chief | Indians | Half-Breeds | Total | Band |
|-------|---------|-------------|-------|------|
| Little Shell | 27 | 442 | 469 | Turtle Mtn |
| Red Bear | 325 | 221 | 546 | Pembina |
| TOTALS | 352 | 663 | 1,015 | |

David P. Delorme, "History of the Turtle Mountain Band of Chippewa Indians," *North Dakota History* 22 (1955): 127–28. The combined population of these bands equaled approximately 3,000 members.

[16] *1863 Treaty Journal*, 31. The term "half-breed" was used widely during this era, both by mixed-blood Natives to identify themselves and by European Canadians and Americans to distinguish them from Native Americans. Although sometimes used as such, the expression was not inherently pejorative. It became a negative label later in the 1880s and beyond. The word Métis is a modern appellation. See Appendix for an overview of the terminology used in this study.

[17] It should be noted that the direct ancestors and descendants of Summer Wolverine, Joseph Gourneau (spelled Gornon, or Little Thunder, the

adopted son of Old Wild Rice), and Joseph Montreuil, along with Pierre Bottineau, provide a straight-line link between the Pembina and Turtle Mountain bands of Chippewa Indians and their mixed-blood relations.

[18] *1863 Treaty Journal*, 4.

[19] Ibid., 5. Act of Congress, February 16, 1863 (12 Stat. 819). Ramsey did not mention the post facto treaty changes by the federal government without Native consent, the greed of the local traders, and delayed or stolen annuities and rations. Overlooking the reality of near starvation for many Dakota in the late summer of 1862, Ramsey concluded that "the conduct of the Sioux was without any excuse or apology." Their treachery resulted in being "stripped of everything." They were now without homes, land, food, or clothing of their own. Congress wielded its preemption power and revoked the treaties, abrogated the reservations, canceled their annuities, and "ethnically cleansed" the Dakota from Minnesota. See Gary Clayton Anderson, *Massacre in Minnesota: The Dakota War of 1862, the Most Violent Ethnic Conflict in American History* (Norman: University of Oklahoma Press, 2019).

[20] *ARCIA* 1859, 57: W. J. Cullen, Superintendent of Indian Affairs to CIA A. B. Greenwood.

[21] Ibid., 57–58.

[22] *1863 Treaty Journal*, 6–7; The *St. Paul Press* of 29 August 1863, cited by Gluek, *Minnesota and Manifest Destiny*, 152.

[23] Letters Received by the Office of Indian Affairs, Michigan Superintendency, 1863; Letter from Norman W. Kittson to Superintendent of Indian Affairs, Clark W. Thompson, November 2, 1862; ICC, Docket 18-A/Petitioner's Exhibit 259.

[24] Ibid. Kittson's letter is the earliest known document identifying specifically the Turtle Mountain Band of Chippewa Indians, with Little Shell (II) as principal chief. See ICC, Docket 113, Briefs, Petitioner's Proposed Findings of Fact, 88.

[25] Ibid. Episcopal Bishop Henry Benjamin Whipple had personal knowledge of various Chippewa and Dakota treaties in Minnesota during the 1860s. He concluded that they had been "usually conceived and executed in fraud," because while "the ostensible parties to the treaty are the government of the United States and the Indians; the *real* parties are

the Indian agents, traders [e.g., Kittson], and politicians." Whipple, "The Indian System," 450. As noted by Ojibwe scholar David Truer, "'the Indian problem' was and had always been a 'federal government problem.'" See *The Heartbeat of Wounded Knee: Native America from 1890 to the Present*, 255.

[26] Whipple, "The Indian System," 449; Gary Anderson and Alan R. Woolworth, eds., *Through Dakota Eyes: Narrative Accounts of the Minnesota Indian War of 1862* (St. Paul: Minnesota Historical Society Press, 1988), 1.

[27] Kittson letter, November 2, 1862.

[28] *1863 Treaty Journal*, 7.

[29] Harry Kelsey, "William P. Dole, 1861–65," in Robert M. Kvasnicka and Herman J. Viola, eds., *The Commissioners of Indian Affairs, 1824–1977* (Lincoln: University of Nebraska Press, 1979), 91.

[30] *1863 Treaty Journal*, 8.

[31] *Barron's Dictionary of Legal Terms*, 120. "Fraud differs from negligence in that it is an intentional wrong."

[32] Each of these individuals acted as incorporators and/or directors of various railroads and used their political influence to secure federal land grants for them.

[33] *1863 Treaty Journal*, 11.

[34] Ibid., emphasis added.

[35] Kent McNeil, "Aboriginal Rights in Canada: From Title to Land to Territorial Sovereignty," *Tulsa Journal of Comparative & International Law* 5 (Spring 1998): 271.

[36] *1863 Treaty Journal*, 12.

[37] Ibid.

[38] Ibid., 12–13.

[39] Ibid., 14.

[40] Ibid., 14–15.

[41] Ibid., 15.

[42] *ARCIA* 1859, 58.

[43] *1863 Treaty Journal*, 15.

[44] Ibid., 16.

[45] Ibid.

[46] Ibid., 17.

[47] Ibid.

[48] Ibid.

[49] Ibid.

[50] Ibid., 18.

[51] Ibid.

[52] Ibid.

[53] Ibid., 19.

[54] Reginald Horsman, "Science, Racism and the American Indian in the Mid-Nineteenth Century," *American Quarterly* 27, no. 2 (May 1975): 152–68; Robert E. Bieder, "Scientific Attitudes Toward Indian Mixed-Bloods in Early Nineteenth Century America," *Journal of Ethnic Studies* 8 (1980): 17–30.

[55] *1863 Treaty Journal*, 21.

[56] Robert A. Williams, Jr., *Linking Arms Together: American Indian Treaty Visions of Law and Peace, 1600–1800* (New York: Routledge, 1997), 54–56.

[57] *1863 Treaty Journal*, 21.

[58] Ibid., 23.

[59] Tom Holm et. al., "Peoplehood," *Wicazo Sa Review* 18, no. 1 (Spring 2003): 14. There are five major factors of Native American cultural identity that "overlap, entwine, interpenetrate and interact:" 1) sacred land (sense of place, environment); 2) knowledge of a sacred history (oral tradition); 3) family relations (kinship/clans) 4) ceremonial life, rituals (religion/spirituality); and 5) language. Together these attributes connote a worldview and sense of "peoplehood," or inherent sovereignty that differs from European-derived notions of statehood or nationhood: 11–15.

[60] *1863 Treaty Journal*, 23.

[61] Said, *Culture and Imperialism*, xii.

[62] *1863 Treaty Journal*, 23.

[63] Kittson letter, November 2, 1862.

[64] *1863 Treaty Journal*, 24.

[65] Ibid., 25.

[66] Ibid. Quote is from Tom Holm et. al., "Peoplehood," *Wicazo Sa Review* 18, no. 1 (Spring 2003): 14.

[67] Ibid., 26.

[68] Ibid., 27, emphasis added.

[69] Ibid.

[70] Ibid., 28, 55.

[71] Ibid., 56.

[72] Ibid., 28, emphasis original.

[73] Ibid., 27.

[74] Ibid., 28, emphasis added.

[75] Ibid., 33–34.

[76] Ibid., 29.

[77] Ibid., 36, emphasis original.

[78] Ibid., 37.

[79] Ibid., 37–38.

[80] Ibid., 40.

[81] *Report of Major Woods*, 22. Also, Father Belcourt's letter in same, 37.

[82] Kappler, *Treaties*, Treaty with the Sisseton and Wahpeton Bands, February 19, 1867 (15 Stat., 505), Article 2, 2: 956–59.

[83] *1863 Treaty Journal*, 40–41.

[84] Ibid., 41–42, 44.

[85] Ibid., 44–45.

[86] *Collection of the State Historical Society of North Dakota* Vol. 1 (1906): 220–21. Alexandre-Antonin Tache, *Sketch of the North-West of America.* Montreal: John Lovell, 1870. Approximately three hundred "Chippewa half-breeds" accompanied Father Andre from the St. Joseph and Pembina

missions. They provided information to General Henry H. Sibley, a prominent Minnesota politician and crony of Ramsey, on the movements of various fleeing Dakotas seeking allies, supplies, or refuge in the region. Bishop Tache confirmed this episode in his history of the region's Catholic missions. As a result of this initial contact, General Sibley hired Father Andre as a U.S. emissary in an attempt to pacify the "hostile" Dakota. Such acknowledged and helpful actions repudiated the treaty commissioner's misrepresentation of the facts.

[87] *1863 Treaty Journal*, 42.

[88] Anderson, *Through Dakota Eyes*, 1.

[89] *1863 Treaty Journal*, 42.

[90] Ibid., 44–45.

[91] Ibid., 43.

[92] Ibid. These assertions about the unique language of the Plains-Ojibwe bands were confirmed by informants of anthropologist James Howard. The southern boundary was confirmed by his archaeological investigations in the 1950s, as presented in his ICC, Docket 113, Transcript, September 18, 1962. Also see Howard, ICC, Docket 113, Map.

[93] *1863 Treaty Journal*, 44.

[94] Ibid., 46.

[95] Ibid.

[96] Ibid.

[97] Ibid.

[98] Ibid., 48, emphasis added.

[99] Confirmed by Bishop Whipple's critique that the entire "Indian system" was "carried out by fraud." Whipple, "The Indian System," 449. The requirement for establishing fraud is summarized as follows. "It is a well-established principle of the law of fraud, applied particularly by courts of equitable jurisdiction, that it is the duty of a person in whom confidence is reposed by virtue of the situation of trust arising out of a confidential or fiduciary relationship to make a full disclosure of any and all material facts within his knowledge relating to a contemplated transaction with the other party to such a relationship, and any concealment or failure to disclose such

facts is a fraud." ICC, Docket 18-A/Petitioner's Briefs: 61, citing *American Jurisprudence*: 858.

[100] *1863 Treaty Journal*, 48.

[101] Ibid., 49.

[102] Ibid., 51.

[103] *Cherokee Nation v. Georgia* 30 U.S. (5 Pet.) 1 (1831).

[104] *1863 Treaty Journal*, 52.

[105] Ibid., 53.

[106] Ibid., emphasis added. As the second most prominent signatory chief to the Pembina and Red Lake Chippewa Treaty of 1851, Little Shell II was identified as "Little Chief of Pembina."

[107] Ibid., 54, emphasis added. The Pillager Chippewa offer consisted of $150 per year per chief, a $500 first payment for each chief's house, $10,000 per year in goods for the band, and $20,000 to indemnify any alleged depredations. Ibid., 57.

[108] ICC, Docket 18-A, Briefs: 65.

[109] *1863 Treaty Journal*, 57, 59.

[110] Ibid., 58.

[111] Ibid.

[112] Ibid., 59.

[113] Ibid.

[114] Ibid., 60.

[115] Ibid., 64.

[116] Ibid., 68, 70.

[117] Ibid., 70.

[118] Ibid., 73.

[119] Treaty with the Chippewa—Red Lake and Pembina Bands, 1863, October 2, 1863, 13 Stat., 667. Ratified March 1, 1864.

[120] Treaty with the Chippewa—Red Lake and Pembina Bands, 1864, April 12, 1864, 13 Stat., 689. Ratified April 21, 1864.

[121] *1863 Treaty Journal*, 10. The ceded area ran close to 170 miles long, north and south, and around 120 miles wide, east and west, at the greatest extent of length and width. It contained approximately 9,000,000 acres according to Ramsey's estimate and report. Under the 1863 treaty, the United States paid $510,000 (which was reduced slightly by the 1864 treaty), or $.056 per acre, for the Red Lake and Pembina land cession. This pittance made the later "ten cent treaty" (i.e. the "purported" McCumber Agreement in 1892) seem beneficent. In 1958 the Indian Claims Commission ruled that the consideration paid to the Chippewa bands for the Old Crossing cession was "unconscionable." See *Red Lake, Pembina, & White Earth Bands v. United States, 6 Ind. Cl. Comm. 247.*

[122] Ella Hawkinson, "The Old Crossing Chippewa Treaty and Its Sequel," *Minnesota History* 25 (1934): 296.

[123] Treaty with the Chippewa—Red Lake and Pembina Bands, 1864, Articles Three and Five.

[124] This is not to say that other treaties distributed monies or lands to mixed-blood interpreters, witnesses, and traders, or white traders with Native wives and or children. Recall that Jean Baptiste Wilkie, as president, and a "council of the Half Breeds" signed the 1851 Pembina treaty. It made no land provisions for them, and any money for "mixed bloods" had to go through the Native chiefs. See Rhoda R. Gilman, "A Northwestern Indian Territory—the Last Indian Voice," *Journal of the West* 39, no. 1 (January 2000): 16–22, on the failed 1841 effort to create a "half-breed" homeland. Also, Article Nine of the 1830 Prairie du Chien treaty gave eastern Dakota mixed-bloods some land in Minnesota on which they never settled. The treaty of September 30, 1854, between the United States and the Chippewa of Lake Superior and the Mississippi, provided for the issue of land patents for certain mixed-blood members of those bands.

[125] *Use and Distribution of Pembina Chippewa Indians Judgement Funds*, 97th Congress, 2nd Session, June 17, 1982; Senate Select Committee on Indian Affairs Hearing, Microform Edition (Washington, D.C.: U.S. Government Printing Office, 1982): 138.

[126] Ibid. Scrip was issued to 464 Red Lake and Pembina half-breed Chippewa for 160 acres each, totaling 74, 240 acres. A Board of Visitors report in 1871 noted the failure of the allotment scheme and the often unlawful scramble for annuities.

[127] CIA Dole to treaty Commissioner Ramsey instructions issued on July 24, 1863.

[128] *St. Ann's Centennial*, 314–15.

[129] J. B. Bottineau, Chippewa Indians of Northern Dakota Territory: Will the Government Recognize Their Claim and Provide for Them? (Washington, D.C.: United States Department of the Interior, Thos. J. Brashears, 1878), 5, Hereafter Recognize Their Claim; ICC, Docket 113/ Petitioner's Exhibits 3, 58, 112, 166, p. 104, "Collection of Interpretive Maps . . . Prepared by Nancy O. Lurie."

## CHAPTER 4 ENDNOTES

[1] *ARCIA* 1871, 687.

[2] *Santa Clara County v. Southern Pacific Railroad* (1886).

[3] Cornell, Return of the Native, 225, fn 7. For the "disparagement of Indigenous cultures" as one of the "defining characteristics of imperial expansion," see Michael Hechter, *Internal Colonialism: The Celtic Fringe in British National Development, 1536–1996* (Berkeley, CA: University of California Press, 1975), 64.

[4] *ARCIA* 1864, 547–48.

[5] J. B. Bottineau, *Brief*, 2.

[6] Samuel P. Hays, *The Response of Industrialism, 1885–1914* (University of Chicago Press, 1995, 2nd ed.). Much of Hays's "pattern of colonialism" is in accord with the core-periphery thesis of Hechter's "internal colonialism" model in *Internal Colonialism: The Celtic Fringe in British National Development* (University of California Press, 1975). Another valuable source on the unequal nature of economic development in the American West and its impact on Native communities is Richard White's use of "dependency theory" in *The Roots of Dependency: Subsistence, Environment, and Social Change among the Choctaws, Pawnees, and Navajos* (University of Nebraska Press, 1983).

[7] The "democratizing" consequences of the Homestead Act, and its subsequent variations and emendations in the American West has been demythologized by many historians. Most notably, Paul W. Gates "challenged the conventional wisdom that the famous statute had

democratized the American land system." See the introduction, anthology and bibliography edited by Allan G. Bogue and Margaret Beattie Bogue, *The Jeffersonian Dream: Studies in the History of American Land Policy and Development* (Albuquerque: University of New Mexico Press,1996), x. Also, see Everett Dick, *The Lure of the Land: A Social History of the Public Lands from the Articles of Confederation to the New Deal* (Lincoln: University of Nebraska Press, 1970), 153–59.

[8] Report of Commissioner of General Land Office, November 5, 1868: 35–36.

[9] Robert P. Wilkins and Wynona H. Wilkins, *North Dakota: A Bicentennial History* (New York: W.W. Norton, 1977), 307. Commutation was a provision in the Homestead Act much abused by speculators. See Clement Lounsberry, *Early History of North Dakota* (Washington, D.C.: Liberty Press, 1919), 229.

[10] Gates, *Jeffersonian Dream*, xiv.

[11] Gerhard J. Ens, *Homeland to Hinterland: The Changing Worlds of the Red River Métis in the Nineteenth Century* (Toronto: University of Toronto Press, 1996), 173; Nicolas C. P. Vrooman, "The Metis Red River Cart," *Journal of the West* 42, no. 2 (Spring 2003): 16–17.

[12] Robinson, *History of North Dakota*, x–xi.

[13] U.S. Census 1870; Robinson, *History of North Dakota*, 122. For more data on homesteading in the Red River Valley from 1879 to 1895, see Stanley N. Murray, *The Valley Comes of Age: A History of Agriculture in the Valley of the Red River of the North, 1812–1920* (Fargo: North Dakota Institute for Regional Studies, 1967).

[14] Francis Paul Prucha, *Atlas of American Indian Affairs* (Lincoln: University of Nebraska Press, 1990), 88.

[15] White-Weasel, *History*, 9. Fort Abercrombie (1858–1877) had existed since 1858 to secure the Red River for steamboat traffic north of Wahpeton. The Sioux uprising of 1862 provided the impetus for more forts in the region. In western Dakota, the Missouri River represented the major strategic waterway. In 1864, Fort Berthold (1864–1867; replaced by Fort Stevenson [1867–1883]) was situated at the Southwest corner of the Turtle Mountain buffalo grounds on the Missouri River. By becoming the site of a reservation for the Three Affiliated tribes of the Arikara, Hidatsa,

and Mandan, it represented an illegal "taking" of 64,000 acres of Turtle Mountain territory. Fort Union (1864–1865; replaced by Fort Buford, 1866–1985) came into existence a bit farther up the Missouri on the western edge of North Dakota near the juncture of the Yellowstone River. Fort Totten (1867–1890) anchored the Southeast corner of the Pembina and Turtle Mountain domain at Devils Lake.

[16] Bottineau, *Recognize Their Claim*, 12; Kappler, *Treaties*, Treaty with the Sisseton and Wahpeton Bands, February 19, 1867 (15 Stat., 505).

[17] Report dated October 21, 1869, to General O. D. Greene. In regard to its relevance in the Sisseton-Wahpeton treaty of February 19, 1867, see BIA Report to the Secretary of the Interior dated October 3, 1872; ICC, Docket 191, Exhibits/Plaintiff Exhibits 256 and 257. On ICC Map F note overlap with the Pembina Chippewa land cession from the Old Crossing treaty. This section had long been fought over by the Plains-Ojibwe and Dakota bands.

[18] Nancy L. Woolworth, "Gingras, St. Joseph and the Métis in the Northern Red River Valley, 1843–1873," *North Dakota History* 42, no. 4 (1975): 26.

[19] Alvin J. Gluek, Jr., *Minnesota and the Manifest Destiny of the Canadian Northwest*, 262.

[20] Report of Major General Hancock, Department of Dakota, in *Annual Report of the Secretary of War*, 41st Congress, 3rd Session, 1870–1871; House Executive Document 1, 27–28.

[21] Mary Wilma M. Hargreaves, *Dry Farming in the Northern Great Plains, 1900–1925* (Cambridge: Harvard University Press, 1957), 33.

[22] Richard Franklin Bensel, *The Political Economy of American Industrialization, 1877–1900* (New York: Cambridge University Press, 2000); *Report of the Public Lands Commission, 1905*, 134. To get a complete sense of the mesh of railroads that eventually crisscrossed North Dakota, see map, Railroads on the Prairie—1915 in Wilkins and Wilkins, *North Dakota: A Bicentennial History*.

[23] *The* [Fargo] *Record*, December 1898, Northern Pacific Railroad Land Office advertisement.

[24] Prucha, *Documents*, 159, citing "General Sherman on the End of the Indian Problem," October 27, 1883.

[25] Prucha, *Documents*, 140–41, citing *ARCIA* 1872.

[26] Letter from Ka-kan-ne-wash to Assistant Commissioner of Indian Affairs, E. B. Meritt, March 10, 1917. Letters Received by the Office of Indian Affairs, Turtle Mountain Agency, RG 75. Federal Records Center, Kansas City, Missouri.

[27] I am indebted to Robert (Rob) A. Williams, Jr., for the "mopping up" insight. As a metaphor it aligns appropriately with the grab-bag analogy and model of federal policy options used in this study.

[28] On Hill's burgeoning railroad network see Albro Martin, *James J. Hill and the Opening of the Northwest* (New York: Oxford University Press, 1976), Part One, chapters 3–7; Robinson, *History of North Dakota*, xi.

[29] Robinson, *History of North Dakota*, xi. See map, "Great Northern RY. Lines in North Dakota," December 31, 1914, from *Early History of North Dakota*; Martin, *Hill*, 77, 202–203, 279, 338–39, 368–69; William C. Robbins, *Colony and Empire: The Capitalist Transformation of the American West* (Lawrence: University of Kansas Press, 1994), 72–73; Hays, *Industrialism*, 149–73.

[30] Margaret Susan Thompson, *The "Spider Web": Congress and Lobbying in the Age of Grant* (Ithaca: Cornell University Press, 1985), 35.

[31] *Bismarck Tribune*, June 17, 1874.

[32] There had been severe economic "panics" in 1837 and 1857 following the "industrial revolution," but before the advent of a national market dominated by major industrial corporations like the railroads.

[33] See Gerhard J. Ens, "Métis Agriculture in Red River During the Transition from Peasant Society to Industrial Capitalism: The Example of St. Francois Xavier, 1835 to 1870," in *Swords and Ploughshares: War and Agriculture in Western Canada*, ed., R. C. Macleod, 239–62 (Edmonton: University of Alberta Press, 1993).

[34] James W. Cheseboro, "Charles Joseph Bottineau, Sr., Techomehgood and Their Descendants." September 1, 1990, http://users.ap.net/~chenae/bottineau12.html

[35] Stanley N. Murray, *The Valley Comes of Age: A History of Agriculture in the Valley of the Red River of the North, 1812-1920*. Fargo: North Dakota Institute for Regional Studies, 1967, 98–99.

[36] Wilkins and Wilkins, *North Dakota*, 78–81; Murray, *The Valley Comes of Age*, 104–105; Robinson, *History of North Dakota*, 137. For example, a major bonanza farm area became Cass County, ND, named after NPRR President George W. Cass.

[37] Gates, *Jeffersonian Dream*, xiv.

[38] Robinson, *History of North Dakota*, xi; Wilkins and Wilkins, *North Dakota*, 79–81.

[39] Wilkins and Wilkins, *North Dakota*, 77.

[40] Murray, "The Turtle Mountain Chippewa," 22. The designation of Buffalo County occurred before being renamed Rolette County, where the Turtle Mountain reservation was located finally in 1882.

[41] Bottineau, *Brief*, 2.

[42] *Dunseith Herald*, March 6, 1890. Robinson, *History of North Dakota*, concluded that North Dakota development suffered from a "too-much mistake" pattern whereby more people than opportunities existed, 135, 155.

[43] Bensel, *The Political Economy of American Industrialization*, 293.

[44] Historian W. L. Morton coined the more fitting term of "resistance," rather than "revolt' or "rebellion" to the events at Red River in 1869–1870.

[45] Brown, *Strangers in Blood*, 210–20.

[46] In response to the Hudson's Bay Company's and the Dominion of Canada's initial disregard of their political right of representative government, and cultural rights protecting their language, schools, and religion, the Red River Métis created a Provisional Government under the leadership of Louis Riel in 1869–1870. This led to the passage of the Manitoba Act and creation of the Province Manitoba and its subsequent entry into the federation. Section 31 of the Manitoba Act reserved 1.4 million acres in the new province "toward the extinguishment" of "Aboriginal title" for people of part-Native ancestry. Unfortunately, these significant achievements failed ultimately to secure Métis land rights in Manitoba or the rest of Canada. See D. N. Sprague, *Canada and the Métis, 1869–1885* (Waterloo, ON: Wilfrid Laurier University Press, 1988).

[47] See Appendix for usage and meaning of the term Métchif.

[48] See D. N. Sprague and R. P. Frye, *The Genealogy of the First Métis Nation: The Development and Dispersal of the Red River Settlement, 1820–1900*

(Winnipeg: University of Manitoba Press, 1983). Then examine various Turtle Mountain Chippewa census rolls for place of birth data, and J. B. Bottineau's genealogical references.

[49] For the best source documenting how and why most Métis failed to secure land tenure within Manitoba, see D. N. Sprague, *Canada and the Métis, 1869–1885.*

[50] See Frederick E. Hoxie, *A Final Promise: The Campaign to Assimilate the Indians, 1880–1920* (Cambridge: Cambridge University Press, 1984).

[51] ICC, Docket 18-A, Briefs, Plaintiff's Finding 32, 32.

[52] *ARCIA* 1863, 410.

[53] Ibid.

[54] Wilcomb E. Washburn, *The Assault of Tribalism: The General Allotment Law (Dawes Act) of 1887* (Philadelphia: J. B. Lippincott Co, 1975), 24.

[55] Ibid., 24–25. The Indian Appropriations Act containing the treaty termination language is at 16 Stat. 566, March 3, 1871.

[56] In 1876 Dawes voted for the repeal of the 1866 Southern Homestead Act, thwarting the legislative intent to help freed African Americans acquire land legally. The repeal helped foster the sharecropping system of tenancy and debt peonage that left most southern African Americans landless and marginalized economically. It also kept down the cost of cotton production, which benefited the Massachusetts textile industry Dawes championed politically. The legislation's goals for granting property title to African Americans were about as effective as the similar provisions of the Indian Homestead Act of 1875. In terms of acquiring fee simple title to land, neither group benefited. The legislative intent of the 1887 Dawes General Allotment Act can be better understood within the context of these legislative precedents.

[57] *ARCIA* 1872, 9.

[58] Secretary of the Interior, *Annual Report for the Year 1872* (Washington: Government Printing Office, 1873), 235.

[59] ARCIA 1872, 9, 75–76. U.S. Congress, House, *General Sherman on the End of the Indian Problem*, 48th Congress, 1st Session, Oct. 27, 1883, House Executive Document 1, Serial set 2182, 45–46.

[60] "Minutes of General Council Meeting," February 15, 1905, 7; February 17, 1905, 1; Records of the Turtle Mountain Agency, ND, RG 75.19.121, NARA-Central Region (KC). It should be noted that Kah-ishpa Gourneau is also referred to in various documentary sources as Kaish-pah (in the October 1, 1892, census), Kaishpa, Kaishpar and Kaish-paw. They all refer to the same chief or sub-chief of the Turtle Mountain band who lived from 1817 until 1917. Since Charles J. Gourneau is a direct descendant, I adopted his spelling of the chief's name. After Little Shell III died in 1900, Kakenowash succeeded him as principal chief.

[61] Clement Lounsberry, *Early History of North Dakota*, 303, 307. Elwyn B. Robinson estimated that from 1878 to 1890 the population of North Dakota increased from 16,000 to 191,000, or more than 1,000 percent. Robinson, *History of North Dakota*, 134.

[62] Alexandre-Antonin Tache, *Sketch of the North-West of America*, ed., John Lovell (Montreal, 1870), 110. Father Belcourt came to a similar conclusion back in 1849. This testimony confirms modern anthropologist A. Irving Hallowell's thesis in *Culture and Experience* proposing a correlation between Ojibwe identity and cultural persistence.

[63] ICC, Docket 18-A/Plaintiff Exhibit 256,1864 Annuity Roll for Pembina Band of Chippewa Indians. The "chiefs share" of $500 had been stipulated under Article Five of the treaty.

[64] *ARCIA* 1873, 12.

[65] *ARCIA* 1871, 1008.

[66] U.S. Congress, House, *Report of Major General Hancock*, Department of Dakota, in *Annual Report of the Secretary of War*, 41st Congress, 3rd Session, 1870–1871, House Executive Document 1, Serial set 1503, 29.

[67] John E. Parsons, *West on the 49th Parallel: Red River to the Rockies, 1872–1876* (New York: William Morrow and Company, 1963); See "Northern Boundary Survey 1872–1876" map. Note how the Boundary Commission Trail skirted around the northern extent of Turtle Mountain. To catch a glimpse of its heavily wooded terrain, see the sketch entitled, "Turtle Mountain Cutting."

[68] *ARCIA* 1873, 179.

[69] Lounsberry, *Early History of North Dakota*, 303. They were "anticipating" the ratification of the February 19, 1867, Sisseton-Wahpeton land cession treaty.

[70] *ARCIA* 1873, 44, 12.

[71] Ibid., 11–12; Francis A. Walker, *The Indian Question* (Boston, J. R. Osgood, 1874), 101.

[72] Ibid., 9, 12.

[73] Letter from R. B. Marcy, Inspector General of Dakota Territory, August 5, 1868, Fort Pembina Papers, 1868–1895, State Historical Society of North Dakota, Bismarck, ND.

[74] *Memorial of the Legislative Assembly of Dakota Territory*, 42nd Congress, 3rd Session, 1873, House Miscellaneous Document 63, 1.

[75] Act of March 3, 1873 (17 Stat., 539); *ARCIA* 1873, 179, 12. The report cited 396 Pembina Chippewa, misidentified as a "band of Mississippi Indians."[76] Little Shell's letter from Pembina to the CIA, August 15, 1877; ICC, Docket 113/Petitioner's Exhibit 63.

[77] *ARCIA* 1873, 179, Agent E. Douglass's report; J. B. Bottineau, *Chippewa Indians of Northern Dakota Territory*, 1878, 10.

[78] *ARCIA* 1874, 30.

[79] *ARCIA* 1873, 12, 592, 182.

[80] Ibid., 592.

[81] Board of Visitors report in ARCIA 1871, 687. Further confirmation of this desire came from four elderly surviving witnesses who testified before the ICC in 1952 about the migration of many Pembina Chippewa to join their relations at Turtle Mountain: Mathias LaFromboise, Philip Allery, Louis Marion, and Isidore Peltier. They still resided there in 1952. ICC, Docket 113/ Petitioner's Exhibit 200a: 25–26, 53–54, 60; Exhibit 200b: 12–13.

[82] The 1871 BOV report on conditions at Turtle Mountain can also be found in ICC, Docket 13/ Petitioner's Exhibit 45: 3.

[83] *ARCIA* 1871, 7.

[84] Francis A. Walker, "The Indian Question," *North American Review* (April 1873): 385.

[85] Jack D. Forbes, "The Manipulation of Race, Caste and Identity: Classifying Afroamericans, Native Americans and Red-Black People," *Journal of Ethnic Studies* 17 (Winter 1990): 3, 4, 26.

[86] Walker, *North American Review*, 385.

[87] *ARCIA* 1873, 179, 592.

[88] Ibid., 594.

[89] *Chippewa Half-Breeds of Lake Superior*, 42nd Congress, 2nd Session, March 15, 1872, House Executive Document 193, Serial set 1513: CIA Walker to Department of the Interior, March 8, 1872, 3.

[90] *Chippewa Half-Breeds of Lake Superior*. 42nd Congress, 2nd Session, March 15, 1872, House Executive Document 193, Serial set 1513, 12.

[91] *ARCIA* 1873, 592.

[92] *Chippewa Half-Breeds of Lake Superior*. 42nd Congress, 2nd Session, March 15, 1872, House Executive Document 193, Serial set 1513, 12.

[93] Ibid., 13.

[94] Ibid.

[95] Ibid., 14.

[96] For an analysis of an even larger scale and parallel system of Métis scrip fraud in Manitoba, Canada, see Steve de Grosbois, *The Alienation of Métis Lands Through Federal Policy and Speculation: A Report to the Native Council of Canada* (Ottawa: National Library of Canada, 1979): 2–36.

[97] *ARCIA* 1873, 592.

[98] The July 15, 1830, Prairie du Chien treaty set aside a Sioux "half-breed" tract in Minnesota Territory.

[99] *Sioux Lands or Reservation in Minnesota Territory*. 33rd Congress, 2nd Session, April 28, 1854, House Report 138, 2.

[100] Murray, "The Turtle Mountain Chippewa," 19; Delorme, "History of the Turtle Mountain Band of Chippewa Indians," 128.

[101] *ARCIA* 1873, 592.

[102] Nancy L. Woolworth, "Gingras, St. Joseph and the Métis in the Northern Red River Valley, 1843–1873," *North Dakota History* 42, no. 4 (1975): 16–27.

[103] *New York Times*, November 21, 1874: 6.

[104] Senate Doc. 444, 155.

[105] White-Weasel, *History*, 136. Image 10 is a picture of the delegation.

[106] *Chippewa Indians of Turtle Mountain, Dakota Territory, Praying for Segregation and Confirmation of Tract of their Land to them, and that Certain Provisions be made for their Protection*, 44th Congress, 1st Session, February 23, 1875, Senate Miscellaneous Document 63, Serial set 1665, 1.

[107] *1863 Treaty Journal*, 53.

[108] *Chippewa Indians of Turtle Mountain*, Senate Miscellaneous Document 63, 1.

[109] Ibid. The memorial's claim of 35,000 square miles was overstated.

[110] Ibid., 2.

[111] Ibid.

[112] Ibid.

[113] Ibid.

[114] (19 Stat., 212)

[115] See *Montoya v. United States,* 180 U.S. 261 (1901), for the origins of what became known in federal law as the *Montoya* test for federal recognition of a tribe.

[116] *Report Authorizing Secretary of Interior to set aside reservation for Turtle Mountain band of Chippewa Indians*, 44th Congress, 1st Session, April 18, 1876, Senate Report 275, Serial set 1667, 1. Senator Lewis V. Bogy's report supported Senate Bill 669. Bogy had been the unconfirmed Commissioner of Indian Affairs in 1866–1867. He then became a Senator from Missouri and chairman of the Senate Select Committee on Indian Affairs.

[117] Angie Debo, *A History of the Indians of the United States* (Norman: University of Oklahoma Press, 1970), 305; ICC, Docket No. 113/ Petitioner's Exhibit, Proposed Findings of Fact and Brief: 8–9.

## CHAPTER 5 ENDNOTES

[1] Letters from CIA Hiram Price to the Secretary of the Interior, February 14, 1882, in Senate Doc. 444, Section XXI, 104.

[2] Prucha, *Documents*, 331, emphasis added.

[3] Ibid., 150. Citing *ARCIA* 1876.

[4] Ibid., 151.

[5] Ibid., 150–51.

[6] Nancy L. Woolworth, "Gingras, St. Joseph and the Métis in the Northern Red River Valley, 1843–1873," *North Dakota History* 42, no. 4 (1975): 16–18, 25–27; Thomas Flanagan, "Louis Riel and the Dispersion of the American Métis," *Minnesota History* 49, no. 5 (Spring 1985): 182. Turtle Mountain, North Dakota, to Milk River, Montana, is approximately 450 miles.

[7] Flanagan, "Louis Riel and the Dispersion of the American Métis," 181.

[8] Tanis C. Thorne, "'Breeds are Not a Tribe': Mixed-Bloods and Métissage on the Lower Missouri," in Lawrence J. Barkwell, Leah Dorion, and Darren R. Préfontaine, eds., *Métis Legacy: A Métis Historiography and Annotated Bibliography* (Winnipeg: Pemmican Publications Inc., 2001), 97; Roger L. Nichols, *Indians in the United States and Canada: A Comparative History* (Lincoln: University of Nebraska Press, 1998), 122.

[9] Flanagan, "Louis Riel and the Dispersion of the American Metis," 181.

[10] Ibid., 185.

[11] Prucha, *Documents*, 331 citing ARCIA 1879.

[12] Flanagan, "Louis Riel and the Dispersion of the American Metis," 185.

[13] Ibid.

[14] Records of the Turtle Mountain Agency, ND, Letter from J. B. Bottineau to Chief Kanick, September 15, 1910.

[15] ICC, Docket 113/Exhibit 162, J.B. Bottineau letter to the Secretary of the Interior, April 11, 1899.

[16] Bottineau and his family appeared on the Turtle Mountain Chippewa annuity rolls for 1869, 1870, and 1871. Also see ICC Docket 191 and 221/Exhibit 27, letter September 4, 1871, and "Excerpts from Report of the Special Commission in the Matters of Chippewa Scrip" in *ARCIA* 1871: 240, 256. Alexander Henry the Younger documented his grandfather Charles's work at the Pembina village trading post in 1802.

[17] Flanagan, "Louis Riel and the Dispersion of the American Metis," 185.

[18] Ibid., 187.

[19] Ibid., 189.

[20] Martha C. Bray, "Pierre Bottineau: Professional Guide," *North Dakota Quarterly* 32 (1964): 29–37. *Red Lake Falls Gazette*, August 3, 1895, obituary. In an 1896 legal brief on behalf of the Turtle Mountain Band of the Pembina Chippewa Indians, J. B. Bottineau even referred to himself as "an Indian." *Brief*, 7.

[21] J. B. Bottineau, *Chippewa Indians of Northern Dakota Territory: Will the Government Recognize Their Claim and Provide for Them?* (Washington, D.C.: United States Dept. of the Interior, Thos. J. Brashears, 1878), 3.

[22] Preamble of Board of Visitors report in *ARCIA* 1871, 687; Bottineau, *Chippewa Indians of Northern Dakota Territory*, 6.

[23] Treaty with the Chippewa—Red Lake and Pembina Bands, 1863, October 2, 1863, 13 Stat., 667, Ratified March 1, 1864, Article Five.

[24] Bottineau, *Chippewa Indians of Northern Dakota Territory*, 13–15. Bottineau included a detailed list of desired agricultural-related materials totaling $5,000.

[25] Ibid., 6.

[26] Ibid.

[27] Ibid., 6–7. Bottineau's presentation of Turtle Mountain Chippewa case to Secretary of the Interior Carl Schurz, February 1878, on file with the CIA, in Senate Doc 444, Item #33, where CIA Hayt's May 23 report to Schurz refers to Bottineau's letter of March 3.

[28] Bottineau, *Chippewa Indians of Northern Dakota Territory*, 12. In a deposition given for an ICC hearing at Belcourt, ND, on May 19, 1952, the Turtle Mountain member John Summer, aged nine in 1892, recounted testimony based on an eyewitness account given to him by Standing Chief. Summer stated that "Red Bear was not a chief of the Turtle Mountain Indians." ICC, Docket 113/Petitioner's Exhibit 200a.

[29] Bottineau, *Chippewa Indians of Northern Dakota Territory*, 12.

[30] Ibid., 13. Bottineau compiled a band census roll totaling 557 at the annual *le Pay* and council meeting with the Board of Visitors in 1871. He gave this roll to agent E.P. Smith, who then began making deletions of "half-breeds" to facilitate attempts to relocate the band in 1872.

31 *ARCIA* 1871, 592, 687.

32 Bottineau, *Chippewa Indians of Northern Dakota Territory*, 3, 12.

33 Senate Doc No. 444, Accompanying Papers No. XXXIII.

34 Records of the Turtle Mountain Agency, ND. Letter from J. B. Bottineau to Chief Kanick, October 14, 1910.

35 As noted tersely in *Shoshone Tribe v. United States*, 299 U.S. 476, 497–98 (1937), "spoliation is not management."

36 Dennis J. Palumbo, *Public Policy in America: Government Action* (New York: Harcourt Brace Jovanovich, Publishers, 1988), 87.

37 Robert A. Williams, Jr., "Jefferson, the Norman Yoke, and American Indian Land," *Arizona Law Review* 29, no. 2 (1987): 166; September 15, 1910, letter from J. B. Bottineau to Chief Kanick.

38 ICC, Docket 113/Petitioner's Exhibit 65, McLaughlin's Dec. 22, 1879, letter to General Charles Ewing, Catholic Commissioner of Indian Missions in Washington, D.C.

39 Robinson, *History of North Dakota*, 153; Laura T. Law, *History of Rolette County, North Dakota and Yarns of the Pioneers* (Minneapolis: Lund Press, Inc, 1953), 19.

40 *ARCIA* 1881, iv.

41 *New York Times*, February 13, 1882:5.

42 Robinson, *History of North Dakota*, 153; Bertha R. Palmer, *Beauty Spots in North Dakota* (Boston: Gorham Press, 1928), 160.

43 ICC, Docket 113/Exhibit 66, Letter from H. R. Vaughan to CIA, August 20, 1880; ICC, Docket 113/Exhibit 70, Letter from Agent at White Earth to CIA, September 25, 1880.

44 ICC, Docket 113/Exhibit 67, Letter from CIA to H.R. Vaughan, September 4, 1880.

45 ICC, Docket 113/Exhibit 73, Petition from the People of Pembina, October 12, 1880.

46 ICC, Docket 113/Exhibit 74, Letter from the Delegates of the Turtle Mountain Band to Agent James McLaughlin, October, 20 1880. A Chippewa lodge or family usually had five to seven members. Either these

self-reported figures do not reflect the usual demographic dominance of the mixed-bloods, or perhaps the Chippewa and the Métis each referred to the same number and location of peoples in slightly different ways.

[47] The northern boundary ran between the United States and the "British Possessions. The southern border headed westward up the middle fork of the Goose River, to Beaver Lodge, and to the headwaters of the Sheyenne River. It extended northwest to the Little Knife River, and then ran northwest along the western loop of the Souris River to the international border. At this meeting with McLaughlin, the delegation did not acknowledge the Old Crossing treaty cession, thus leaving the eastern border of their tract undefined. See ICC, Docket 113/Petitioner's Exhibit 3, "Turtle Mountain Chippewa Area as described in Little Shell Memorial of 1876" map prepared by Nancy O. Lurie (see Image 2).

[48] ICC, Docket 113/Exhibit 74, Letter from the Delegates of the Turtle Mountain Band to Agent James McLaughlin, October, 20 1880.

[49] Ibid.

[50] Ibid.

[51] ICC, Docket 113/Petitioner's Exhibit 79, Letter from Representatives of the Turtle Mountain Band (Little Bull, Red Thunder) to Agent James McLaughlin, July 28, 1881.

[52] Michael D. Cohen, James G. March and Johan P. Olsen, "A Garbage Can Model of Organizational Choice," *Administrative Science Quarterly* 17, no. 1 (March 1972):1–17. The authors refer to the jumble of problems, choices, solutions, and participants resulting in the lack of a clean decision-making process, as the "witches brew" of garbage can theory.

[53] Bruce E. Seely, "Pettigrew, Richard Franklin"; http://www.anb.org/ articles/05/05-00607.html; American National Biography Online (Oxford University Press, 2000). Pettigrew became one of South Dakota's first U.S. Senators in 1889.

[54] ICC, Docket 113/Petitioner's Exhibit 84, Letter from R.F. Pettigrew to C.I.A., May 2, 1881.

[55] Ibid.

[56] Ibid.

[57] By adapting the "policy process" model created by Randall B. Ripley and Grace A. Franklin, *Congress, the Bureaucracy, and Public Policy* (Homewood IL: Dorsey Press, 1980), this chapter outlines some of the most significant specific processes of federal policy formulation encountered by the Turtle Mountain Band of Pembina Chippewa during the 1880s.

[58] ICC, Docket 113/Petitioner's Exhibit 85, Letter from Acting GLO Commissioner E. J. Brooks to CIA, August 18, 1881.

[59] Ibid.

[60] ICC, Docket 113/Petitioner's Exhibit 87, Letter from R. F. Pettigrew, "Rights of Chippewa Lands in Dakota," to the Secretary of the Interior, 1882 [month and day obliterated]. It should be noted that since at least 1850, the federal policy in the Great Lakes region endeavored to centralize all the Chippewa tribes from Sault Ste. Marie to Red River on one or two reservations. See Ramsey's report in *ARCIA* 1863, 335.

[61] Ibid.

[62] ICC, Docket 113/Petitioner's Exhibit 84, Letter from R. F. Pettigrew to CIA, May 2, 1881.

[63] Ibid.

[64] *Brief*, 39.

[65] ICC, Docket 113/Petitioner's Exhibit 84, Letter from R. F. Pettigrew to CIA, May 2, 1881, emphasis added.

[66] Note that Graham's Island is not really an island. Recall that Graham's Island had been a Plains-Ojibwe site identified by James Howard as site # 5. Points of interest on Creel's map include the Turtle Mountain-Mouse River trail heading northwest to connect the agency at Ft. Totten with the Turtle Mountain reservation. Lt. Creel's trail of 1880 is indicated in two places. Also note the existence of Creel City in the upper left-hand corner. This site was located outside of either the Red Lake-Pembina Chippewa cession of 1863–1864, or the Sisseton-Wahpeton cession of 1867. Therefore, it remained in unceded Turtle Mountain Chippewa territory. *Collection of the State Historical Society of North Dakota* Volume III (1910): 209.

[67] *Collection of the State Historical Society of North Dakota* Volume III (1910): 195.

[68] Records of the Turtle Mountain Agency, ND, Lt. H. M. Creel's Report cited in a Letter to CIA Price, December 29, 1881. Hereafter *Creel's Report*.

[69] *Report of Major Woods*, Letter from Father G. A. Belcourt, November 20, 1845, to G. W. Manypenny, November 20, 1854. The White Earth River in western North Dakota should not be confused with the White Earth Reservation in western Minnesota.

[70] Ibid.

[71] ICC, Docket 18-A/Plaintiff's Finding 26: 28.

[72] *Creel's Report.*

[73] Ibid., emphasis added.

[74] Ibid.

[75] Ibid.

[76] Ibid. ICC, Docket 113/Petitioner's Exhibit 77, Letter from H. M. Creel to General F. M. Cockrall, forwarded to Secretary of Interior Samuel J. Kirkwood on March 25, 1881.

[77] ICC, Docket 113/Petitioner's Exhibit 82, Letter from H. M. Creel to R. F. Pettigrew inquiring into "the nature of the unceded Chippewa lands," April 17, 1881.

[78] ICC, Docket 113/Petitioner's Exhibit 76, Settlers Petition to Congress to Open the Turtle Mountain Tract for Settlement, March 28, 1881.

[79] White-Weasel, *History*, 140–42, citing Letter of April 19, 1881, from Archives of Assumption Abbey, Richardton, North Dakota.

[80] ICC, Docket 113/Petitioner's Exhibit 88, Letter from Major J. S. Conrad, February 9, 1882.

[81] ICC, Docket 113/Petitioner's Exhibit 83, Letter from Agent James McLaughlin to CIA, April 18, 1881, referring to ICC, Docket 113/ Petitioner's Exhibit 82, Letter from H. M. Creel to Agent McLaughlin, April 17, 1881.

[82] Records of the Turtle Mountain Agency, North Dakota, Letter from J. B. Bottineau to Chief Kanick, October 14, 1910.

[83] Teller was appointed by President Chester A. Arthur and took office as Secretary of the Interior on April 17, 1882.

[84] Letters from CIA Hiram Price to the Secretary of the Interior, February 14, 1882, in Senate Doc. 444, Section XXI, and March 11, 1882, in Senate Doc. 444, Section XXII.

[85] Senate Doc. 444, Section XXI.

[86] *ARCIA* 1881, 50; Senate Doc. 444, Section XXI: 104.

[87] *ARCIA* 1881, 50.

[88] Senate Doc. 444, Section XXI.

[89] Ibid. See ARCIA 1881 map noting that the land of the Turtle Mountain Indians "has not been extinguished."

[90] ICC, Docket 113/Petitioner's Exhibit 97, Telegram from Governor Ordway of Dakota Territory to Secretary of the Interior Teller, June 26, 1882.

[91] ICC, Docket 113/Petitioner's Exhibit 98, Letter from Agent John W. Cramsie to CIA Hiram Price, June 30, 1882, 8–9.

[92] E. E. Schattschneider, *The Semi-Sovereign People: A Realist's View of Democracy in America* (New York: Holt, Rinehart and Winston, 1960), vii.

[93] ICC, Docket 113/Petitioner's Exhibit 92, Letter from R. F. Pettigrew to Secretary of the Interior Henry M. Teller, May 2, 1882.

[94] ICC, Docket 113/Petitioner's Exhibit 99, July 3, 1882; "Dakota Lands for Settlers," *New York Times*, September 28, 1882, 2.

[95] Letter from CIA Hiram Price to the Secretary of the Interior, February 14, 1882, in Senate Doc. 444, Section XXI, 2.

[96] Ibid., 3, emphasis added.

[97] Ibid., 4.

[98] Ibid., 3.

[99] These prices did not reflect the real market value of good wheat lands. Everett Dick recounted that in 1885, land near Great Northern rail lines, many of which crossed Turtle Mountain territory, "was offered at $6.00 to $8.00 an acre." Everett Dick, *The Lure of the Land: A Social History of the Public Lands from the Articles of Confederation to the New Deal* (Lincoln: University of Nebraska Press, 1970), 177. In 1886, the *Dunseith Herald* reported the sale of lands in Dakota to a syndicate for $2.00 an acre. *Dunseith*

*Herald*: August 5, 1886, vol. 3, no. 4: 1. The "syndicate" was probably the Northern and Dakota Trust Company.

[100] Letter from CIA Hiram Price to the Secretary of the Interior, February 14, 1882, in Senate Doc. 444, Section XXI, 4.

[101] Ibid.

[102] This figure turned out to be only $125,000 less than the October 19, 1891, Turtle Mountain Chippewa Grand Council proposal. Such a comparison shows that the lack of a final mutual settlement did not derive from significant disagreement over the amount of compensation the U.S. was willing to consider, or the band was willing to accept.

[103] Cohen, March, and Olsen, "A Garbage Can Model of Organizational Choice," 16.

[104] Act of March 3, 1873 (17 Stat., 539).

[105] Letter from CIA Hiram Price to the Secretary of the Interior, February 14, 1882, in Senate Doc. 444, Section XXI, 5.

[106] Ibid.

[107] Ibid.

[108] Ibid.

[109] Ibid.

[110] William Temple Hornaday, *The Extermination of the American Bison* (Washington, D.C.: Smithsonian Institution Press, 2002; Reprinted and edited from the original, *The Extermination of the American Bison* in the *Annual Report of the Board of Regents of the Smithsonian Institution*, 1889), 511. Hornaday's 1889 report called the "systematic slaughter" of the bison "a disgrace to the American people in general, and the Territorial, State, and General Government in particular" (486).

[111] LeRoy Barnett, "The Buffalo Bone Commerce On the Northern Plains," *North Dakota History* 39, no. 1 (Winter 1972): 23. This fine article includes many excellent photographs.

[112] Ibid., 23–24. Barnett figured 5,000 boxcars of buffalo bones shipped annually grossing about $500,000. In total, he estimated that the collection and shipment of 2,000,000 million tons of buffalo bones produced $40,000,000 in revenue.

[113] Ibid., "The Minot Bone Trade."

[114] Price, March 11, 1882, letter and report in Senate Doc. 444, Section XXII; *Brief*, 13.

[115] *Mitchel v. United States*, 9 Pet. (34 U.S.) 711, 746 (1835).

[116] Letter from CIA Hiram Price to the Secretary of the Interior, February 14, 1882, in Senate Doc. 444, Section XXI, 5–6.

[117] Ibid.

[118] Ibid., 5.

[119] Ibid., 6.

[120] Ibid.

[121] *Brief*, 3.


## CHAPTER 6 ENDNOTES

[1] *Brief*, 8.

[2] ICC, Docket 113, Petitioner's Proposed Findings of Fact and Brief, Finding 7, 34; *Brief*, 13.

[3] *ARCIA* 1881, 50.

[4] Letter from CIA Hiram Price to the Secretary of the Interior, February 14, 1882, in Senate Doc. 444, 6. "It seems to me that these Indians are justly entitled to the recognition of their claim on the part of the Government to the lands in question, and the files and records abound in evidence showing that this office bas long recognized such claim." Senate Doc. 444, 160.

[5] U.S. Congress. House. *Turtle Mountain Band of Chippewa Indians*, 47th Congress, 1st Session, 1882. House Report 1144, Nathaniel C. Deering, Committee of Indian Affairs, to Accompany Bill H.R. 1885, April 28, 1882, emphasis added.

[6] Ibid.

[7] *ARCIA* 1881, 110.

[8] Deering Report, *Turtle Mountain Band of Chippewa Indians*.

[9] Records of the Turtle Mountain Agency, ND, Lt. H. M. Creel's report cited in a letter from CIA Price, December 29, 1881.

[10] Ibid.

[11] *ARCIA* 1881: 50. Letter from CIA Hiram Price to the Secretary of the Interior, February 14, 1882, in Senate Doc. 444, Section XXI; Deering Report, *Turtle Mountain Band of Chippewa Indians*, April 28, 1882.

[12] Deering Report, *Turtle Mountain Band of Chippewa Indians*. The original quote mistakenly used the word "recognized" instead of extinguished. The disavowal of the Turtle Mountain claim by some local agents (e.g., Agent Stowe's repudiation at White Earth in 1874 that they did not "own one inch of land") was contradicted immediately by a Nov. 2 letter from Ennegahbowh to Bishop Whipple, when a Turtle Mountain delegation stopped off on their way to Washington, D.C. The preponderance of official government testimony acknowledged their rightful ownership. Implicit legal recognition of the Turtle Mountain Chippewa land claim derived from the Prairie du Chien and Sweet Corn treaties of 1825 and 1858, the Old Crossing treaties of 1863–1864, the Sisseton-Wahpeton treaty of 1867, and the rediscovery of the Sweet Corn treaty in 1869. Explicit acknowledgement came from various reports by federal agents and treaty commissioners. Most notable was Alexander Ramsey's reports on the unratified 1851 Pembina treaty and the Old Crossing treaty. Concerning the latter, he stated that "the Pembina bands . . . retain for themselves a tract of country claimed by them . . . north and northwest of Devils Lake." Commissioner of Indian Affairs Hayt cited this extract in his Report to the Secretary of the Interior, May 23, 1878. Hayt's report became Exhibit No. XXXIII in J. B. Bottineau's Senate Document No. 444, June 6, 1900. Thus, the United States and its federal level representatives (e.g., a treaty commissioner in 1851 and 1863, the Commissioners of Indian Affairs in 1871, 1872, 1874, and 1878, and the Board of Visitors in 1871), not just the Interior Department, "recognized" the "Indian title" of the Pembina and Turtle Mountain bands and the "justice of their request." Board of Visitors 1871 Report: 3. The confusion over the question of Congress's "recognition," or lack thereof, further complicated the issue.

[13] *Prayer*, 8–9.

[14] *Brief*, 10, 14.

[15] Palumbo, *Public Policy in America*, 87.

[16] Hesketh, "History of the Turtle Mountain Chippewa," 119–20. This happened on June 25, 1882.

[17] *Dunseith Herald* 2, no. 45 (May 21, 1886), 4, Microfilm, North Dakota Historical Society, Bismarck, North Dakota. Hereafter *DH*.

[18] *Brief*, 12 citing Price, March 11, 1882, *DH* 7, no. 12 (September 25, 1890), 4.

[19] *Brief*, 39.

[20] These events took place from July 11 to July 15, 1882. Charles Montgomery, Charles Gladeau, and Kah-ishpa affixed their names to the sign. *Winnipeg Daily Sun*, July 29, 1882, 7; Laura T. Law, *History of Rolette County, North Dakota and Yarns of the Pioneers* (Minneapolis: Lund Press, Inc, 1953), 22.

[21] Hesketh, "History of the Turtle Mountain Chippewa," 119–20; "The Turtle Mountain Indians," *NYT* July 27, 1882, 2.

[22] "The Turtle Mountain Indians," *NYT* July 27, 1882, 2.

[23] *Brief*, 21.

[24] Bureau of Indian Affairs, Report of the Secretary of War I, August 30, 1882, 91. The squatters returned on September 3, 1882.

[25] Ibid., 90–91.

[26] Howard R. Lamar, *Dakota Territory, 1861–1889* (Fargo: Institute for Regional Studies, North Dakota State University, 1997), 52.

[27] Ibid., 238.

[28] ICC, Docket 113, Petitioner's Proposed Findings of Fact and Brief: 50, note 154.

[29] ICC, Docket 113/Petitioner's Exhibit 92, Letter from R. F. Pettigrew to Secretary of the Interior Henry M. Teller, May 1, 1882.

[30] *ARCIA* 1883, 38–39, emphasis added.

[31] "Dakota Land for Settlers," *NYT* September 28, 1882, 2; "Notes from Washington," *NYT* October 7, 1882, 5, emphasis added.

[32] *Prayer*, 7, emphasis added.

[33] *Brief*, 38.

[34] Letter from CIA Hiram Price to the Secretary of the Interior, March 11, 1882, in Senate Doc. 444, Section XXII; *Brief*, 12.

[35] Act to Provide for Temporary Government for Territory of Dakota, Section 1: 27, emphasis added. Also see Hesketh, "History of the Turtle Mountain Chippewa," 110–11.

[36] Ibid.

[37] David E. Wilkins and K. Tsianina Lomawaima, *Uneven Ground: American Indian Sovereignty and Federal Law* (Norman: University of Oklahoma Press, 2001), 212.

[38] ICC, Docket 113/Petitioner's Exhibit 103, Meeting of Secretary Teller with Chief Little Shell and the Turtle Mountain delegation, December 19, 1882.

[39] Ibid. The italicized emphasis in original comes from *Brief*, 19.

[40] Palumbo, *Public Policy in America*, 87.

[41] Executive Order. President Chester A. Arthur, December 21, 1882; *Prayer*, 6 citing CIA and Teller report to Congress. This reservation, referred to subsequently as the "original" or "large" reservation, entailed all of present-day Rolette County, North Dakota, except the easternmost range of townships. ICC, Docket 113/Petitioner's Exhibit 166, 101. See map on back cover, section labeled Turtle Mountain Reservation, 1882.

[42] Murray, "The Turtle Mountain Chippewa, 1882–1905," 23.

[43] *Brief*, 12.

[44] *Prayer*, 6.

[45] Tanis C. Thorne, *The Many Hands of My Relations: French and Indians on the Lower Missouri* (Columbia: University of Missouri Press, 1996), 136.

[46] *Brief*, 8

[47] Ibid.

[48] Ibid., 13.

[49] *Brief*, 13; *Prayer*, 5.

[50] *Brief*, 12; U.S. Congress, House, *Turtle Mountain Band of Chippewa Indians*, 47th Congress, 1st Session, 1882, House Report 1144, Nathaniel C. Deering, Committee of Indian Affairs, to Accompany Bill H.R. 1885 and S. 925, April 28, 1882.

[51] Elmer Ellis, *Henry Moore Teller: Defender of the West* (Caldwell ID: Caxton Printers, 1941), 134.

[52] ICC, Docket 113/Petitioner's Exhibit 103, Meeting of Secretary Teller with Chief Little Shell and the Turtle Mountain delegation, December 19, 1882.

[53] Executive Order, President Chester A. Arthur, March 29, 1884; *Brief*, 27; Debo, *A History of the Indians of the United States*, 354; Murray, "The Turtle Mountain Chippewa, 1882–1905," 23; Delorme, "History of the Turtle Mountain Band of Chippewa Indians," 133; *Prayer*, 6. A subsequent Executive Order of June 3, 1884, exchanged one adjacent township for another with slightly better prospects for farming. Yet only one-third of the diminished reservation had farming potential, with equal amounts of grazing and timber lands. *Prayer*, 3. The two townships, named Couture and Ingebretson, existed within Rolette County of Dakota Territory.

[54] *ARCIA* 1885, 310.

[55] Washburn, *Assault on Tribalism*, 19.

[56] *Prayer*, 15; U.S. Congress, House, *Estimate to purchase seeds for Turtle Mountain band of Chippewa Indians*, 50th Congress, 2nd Session, 1889, House Executive Document 63, Serial set 2651.

[57] Leonard A. Carlson, *Indians, Bureaucrats, and Land: The Dawes Act and the Decline of Indian Farming* (Westport, Connecticut: Greenwood Press, 1981), 136. Carlson concluded that "allotment policy as a means of promoting self-sufficient farming among Indians was a failure." E. A. Schwarz's online article, "What Were the Results of Allotment?" concluded similarly that the Dawes (General Allotment) Act never intended to transform Indians into farmers" (5).

[58] *Prayer*, 15.

[59] Ibid., 15–16.

[60] ICC, Docket 113/Petitioner's Exhibit 105, Report from Special Agent Cyrus Beede to Secretary of the Interior Henry M. Teller, July 19, 1883; *Prayer*, 4; *Brief*, 28.

[61] Brian W. Dippie, *The Vanishing American: White Attitudes and U.S. Indian Policy* (Lawrence: University of Kansas Press, 1982), 41. Some reformers associated with federal policy did want to save Native Americans from

extinction, but by draconian modes of assimilation. Richard Henry Pratt advocated "killing the Indian but saving the man" or woman by cajoling or compelling Native children to attend boarding schools.

[62] Francis Walker, "Indian Question," *North American Review* (April 1873): 7.

[63] *Prayer*, 10.

[64] Louis Riel, "The Métis: Louis Riel's Last Memoire" in A. H. de Tremaudan, ed., *Hold High Your Heads* (History of the Métis Nation in Western Canada), (Winnipeg: Pemmican Publications, 1982), 205. The detailed developments between the Métis aspirations for self-governance, cultural preservation, and secure land tenure (river lots) at the Red River communities in 1870 and the South Saskatchewan settlements in 1885 remain beyond the scope of this study. The best sources on these events are the works cited by Morton, Peterson, and Brown, and Ens, Sprague, and Flanagan.

[65] Sprague, *Canada and the Métis, 1869–1885*, 169.

[66] Wallace Stegner distilled the "local attitude" towards the landless Chippewa-Cree and the Métis around the time of World War I. In his autobiographical novel *Wolf Willow*, he noted that European American and European Canadian settlers in Saskatchewan, North Dakota, and Montana "brought fully developed prejudices with them which we inherited without question or thought." They believed that "an Indian was a thieving, treacherous, lousy, unreliable, gut-eating vagabond, and . . . a halfbreed was worse" (50). Stegner also noted that "we never so much heard the word *métis*" (57). Father Genin called the international boundary "the magical cage line" in his May 11, 1888, letter to the *Duluth Journal*; also see Slaughter, *Leaves*, 289.

[67] Métis scholar Gail Morin's study of the 1885 half-breed North West Territory scrip applications explains the major regional Métis habitations, ranging from Turtle Mountain; Cypress Hills; Wood Mountain; Milk River; Glasgow, MT; St. Boniface, Manitoba; St. Laurent and Duck Lake, Northwest Territories. Also see Lawrence Barkwell (Coordinator of Metis Heritage and History Research Louis Riel Institute), *North Dakota Métis of the Cypress Hills Hunting Band*, December 2018.

[68] *DH*, May 21, 1886, 4. See map from *Out of Many*, 529.

[69] Dusenberry, "Waiting for a Day That Never Comes," 119.

[70] *ARCIA* 1884, 34–35.

[71] Gerhard J. Ens, "After the Buffalo: The Reformation of the Turtle Mountain Métis Community, 1879–1904," in *New Faces of the Fur Trade: Selected Papers of the Seventh North American Fur Trade Conference, Halifax, Nova Scotia, 1995* (East Lansing: Michigan State University Press, 1997), 147. Ens gained his insights on this point from WPA oral histories collected from Turtle Mountain members in the 1930s, preserved on microfilm in the State Historical Society of North Dakota Archives.

[72] *Prayer*, 10; Senate Doc 444, Section XX.

[73] *Brief*, 34, citing testimony of Bishop Walker; *DH* vol. 6, no. 37 (March 20, 1890), 4, citing Bishop Stanley and Father Stephen.

[74] *Collection of the State Historical Society of North Dakota*, Vol. III: 207; *DH* vol. 6 no. 37 (March 20, 1890), 4.

[75] Hesketh, "History of the Turtle Mountain Chippewa," 119–24; E. W. Brenner's August 11, 1888, letter in *ARCIA* 1888, 41. Brenner was the government agent or farmer-in-charge for the Turtle Mountain reservation from 1887–1904.

[76] *Prayer*, 11.

[77] Ibid.

[78] See report from R. V. Belt, Senate Doc. 444, 117, for breakdowns of annual gratuitous and destitution appropriations by Congress from 1884 to 1892.

[79] Bureau of Indian Affairs, Letter from Agent John Waugh to the Office of Indian Affairs, December 20, 1886, and Agent John Cramsie's letter to the CIA of January 17, 1887. Fortuitous circumstances rather than negligence seemed to be at the heart of this untimely occurrence.

[80] *DH* (May 21, 1886), 4. These realities of life on the northern plains contrasted radically with the euphemistic boosterism featured prominently in such local newspapers.

[81] *ARCIA* 1886, Cramsie to CIA, 60.

[82] *ARCIA* 1887, 35. The agent provided a detailed itemized list of expenditures.

[83] Ibid.

[84] *ARCIA* 1886, Cramsie to CIA, 61.

[85] *Prayer*, 9; *DH* vol. 2, no. 47 (June 4, 1886), 4; *DH* vol. 3, no. 10 (September 16, 1886), 1.

[86] *Brief*, 25. This became the exact finding of the Indian Claims Commission (ICC) in 1974. See *Turtle Mountain Band of Chippewa Indians, et al. v. United States*, Appeal No. 6-72 Court of Claims 203 Ct. Cl. 426; 490 F.2d 935, 1974 U.S. Ct. Cl. January 23, 1974, Prior History: Section II (c) (1) "since the power of Congress to eliminate aboriginal title is exclusive, the creation of the Turtle Mountain reservation in Rolette County, North Dakota, by Executive Orders of December 21, 1882, and March 29, 1884, did not extinguish Indian title prior to the 1905 McCumber Agreement since there is no adequate showing that Congress authorized the extinguishment of the aboriginal title via an Executive Order reservation or that the Indians accepted such reservation as quid pro quo for giving up their claims."

[87] *Prayer*, 9.

[88] *DH* vol. 3, no. 5 (August 12, 1886), 4. At this date L. Q. C. Lamar was Secretary of the Interior. President Grover Cleveland vetoed the railroad bill. Senator Henry Dawes, known as a "friend of the Indian," sought to override the veto.

[89] ICC, Docket 113/Petitioner's Exhibit 118, Report from CIA Atkins to Secretary of the Interior, "The Title and Matter of the Claim of the Turtle Mountain band of Chippewa Indians to certain land in Dakota Territory," February 17, 1887, 2.

[90] Teller fulfilled Secretary of War John C. Calhoun's insistence in 1818 that Native communities "must be overwhelmed by the might torrent of our population." *American State Papers*, Indian Affairs, 2: 182–84.

[91] *ARCIA* 1886, 61.

[92] ICC, Docket 113/Petitioner's Exhibit 118, Report from CIA Atkins to Secretary of the Interior, "The Title and Matter of the Claim of the Turtle Mountain band of Chippewa Indians to certain land in Dakota Territory," February 17, 1887, 2.

[93] The BIA's stakeholders were not their "Indian wards." Federal policy formulations moved from solutions to problems, rather than the reverse.

The Department of the Interior and the BIA initiated actions before analysis, and then sought the best rationale for the action taken. This observation accords with the grab-bag or garbage-can model of decision making. See Palumbo, *Public Policy in America*, 87, 151.

[94] ICC, Docket 113/Petitioner's Exhibit 119, Letter from Assistant Attorney General to Acting Secretary of the Interior, March 29, 1887, 2.

[95] Ibid.

[96] Ibid., 3.

[97] *Prayer*, 15.

[98] Bureau of Indian Affairs, Letter from Farmer-in-Charge E. W. Brenner to Major John Cramsie, August 10, 1887.

[99] Howard, *The Plains-Ojibwa*, 23–24. Howard did not provide a source for this statement.

[100] *Duluth Journal*, May 11, 1888, cited by Slaughter, *Leaves*, 289. For the full text see "Starvation in the Turtle Mountains," posted on 3/2/2012 by Kade M. Ferris at http://www.chippewaheritage.com/heritage-blog; Murray, "The Turtle Mountain Chippewa," misdated this tragedy as occurring in the "winter of 1886–1887," 24. Yet Hornaday, *The Extermination of the American Bison*, conveyed the deadly nature of this preceding winter. He stated that "during the winter of 1886–87, destitution and actual starvation prevailed to an alarming extent among certain tribes of Indians in the Northwest territory who once lived bountifully on the buffalo," 526.

[101] "Indians Preparing for War," *NYT*, June 1, 1884, 2.

[102] *Brief*, 25.

[103] Bureau of Indian Affairs, Letter from Major John Cramsie to CIA John H. Oberly, November 27, 1888.

[104] "Indians Preparing for War," *NYT*, June 1, 1884, 2.

[105] Frank Alonzo Wilder, "The Lignite Coals of North Dakota," *Economic Geologist* 1, no. 7 (1906): 674–81. Wilder reported that "one important outlier of the Laramie [lignite area] is found in the Turtle Mountains," specifically in "northeastern Bottineau and north Rolette counties" (674). Also see *Prairie Past and Mountain Memories: A History of Dunseith, North Dakota, 1882–1892* (Dunseith, ND: Dunseith Centennial Committee, 1982), 190–91, and Wilder, 680–81.

[106] *DH* vol. 8, no. 31 (February 4, 1892), 2. Bottineau had a law office at various Washington, D.C., addresses.

[107] Bureau of Indian Affairs, Letter from Joseph Rolette, on behalf of Little Shell and tribal council, to the CIA, March 14, 1892.

[108] Neither Hesketh's, Delorme's, Howard's, Murray's, nor Camp's published articles acknowledged this significant causal factor for the radical reduction of the Turtle Mountain Chippewa reservation on March 29 and June 3, 1884.

[109] *Brief*, 30.

[110] Senate Doc. 444, Section XXXIV, 157.

[111] Bureau of Indian Affairs, Letter from Major John Cramsie to CIA John D. C. Atkins, March 12, 1887; Letter from Chief Little Shell to Secretary of the Interior L. Q. C. Lamar, April 22, 1887.

[112] Hesketh, "History of the Turtle Mountain Chippewa," 122.

[113] *Prayer*, 15.

[114] *DH* vol. 6, no. 37 (March 20, 1890), 4, citing report of Bishop Stanley of Jamestown, ND, and Father Stephen from the Catholic Indian Bureau of Washington, D.C., after an investigative tour of the Turtle Mountain Chippewa reservation.

[115] Bureau of Indian Affairs, Letters Received, Letter from Chief Little Shell to Secretary of the Interior L. Q. C. Lamar, April 22, 1887; *Brief*, 28. St. Mary's school, Bishop Walker's school, and three government schools had a combined enrollment of 372 children, although far fewer attended. Little Shell sent his children to the Episcopal school. See *ARCIA* 1897, 213.

[116] Bureau of Indian Affairs, Letters Received, Letter from Chief Little Shell to Secretary of the Interior L. Q. C. Lamar, April 22, 1887.

[117] Ibid.

[118] *DH* vol. 5, no. 37 (March 21, 1889), 4. Such occurrences contrasted pointedly with newspaper boosterism touting "free homes" and "the ease with which a good farm can be secured" by European Americans or Canadians. See *DH* vol. 6, no. 32 (February 12, 1890), 1. The article's subtitle was "How to Get a Start in North Dakota and Become an Independent Property Owner."

[119] Letter from Little Shell, Red Thunder, and Henri Poitras ("the half-breed chief") to Father Genin, April 29, 1888, cited by Slaughter, *Leaves*, 288.

[120] Hesketh, "History of the Turtle Mountain Chippewa," 121–22.

[121] *Brief*, 39–40. Also see Orlan J. Svingen, "Jim Crow, Indian Style," *American Indian Quarterly* 11 (Fall 1987): 275–86; Jeremy Mumford, "Métis and the Vote in 19th-Century America," *Journal of the West* 39, no. 3 (Summer 2000): 38–45, and Verne Dusenberry, "Waiting for a Day That Never Comes."

[122] Hesketh, "History of the Turtle Mountain Chippewa," 125.

[123] *Duluth Journal*, May, 14, cited by Slaughter, *Leaves*, 288.

[124] *Brief*, 12.

[125] Ibid., 16.

[126] Ibid., 30.

[127] Ibid.

[128] *Prayer*, 11.

[129] Cohen, March, and Olsen, "A Garbage Can Model of Organizational Choice," 16.

[130] Bureau of Indian Affairs, Letter from Farmer-in-Charge E. W. Brenner at Turtle Mountain to Major John Cramsie at Fort Totten, July 22, 1888.

[131] *Turtle Mountain Band of Chippewa Indians v. United States* 490 F.2d 935 (Ct. Cl. 1974): 945-946. For more details on this decision, see Conclusion.

[132] *Brief*, 7. *Prayer*, 8.

[133] *Prayer*, 9.

[134] *Turtle Mountain Band of Chippewa Indians v. United States* 490 F.2d 935 (Ct. Cl. 1974): 947.

[135] *Brief*, 8.

[136] Bureau of Indian Affairs, Agent John Cramsie to CIA John H. Oberly, November 27, 1888.

# CHAPTER 7 ENDNOTES

[1] Senate Doc. 444, 5.

[2] Robinson, *History of North Dakota*, 153, xi. The Turtle Mountain population estimates come from *ARCIA* 1886 and Bureau of Indian Affairs, Letters received, Report of William F. Canfield, Superintendent of Indian School, Agent-in-Charge at Fort Totten.

[3] *Prayer*, 2.

[4] ICC, Docket 113/Petitioner's Exhibit 125, "Talk with the Turtle Mountain Chippewas," February 15, 1889. This Joseph Rolette was "Jolly Joe's" son. Joseph "Jolly Joe" Rolette, Jr., died in 1871. See Bruce M. White, "The Power of Whiteness, or the Life and Times of Joseph Rolette, Jr.," *Minnesota History* 56, no. 4 (Winter 1998–99): 178–97. From the documentary evidence surveyed, I could not discern how Joseph Rolette, Jr., became a member of the Turtle Mountain Chippewa. The Pembina fur trade connection provides the most plausible explanation. White did not mention that he appeared on the 1868 and 1869 tribal annuity rolls. Some scholars object to the "jolly" characterization as a stereotype that disparages Métis people. Contrary to many older accounts, White cites other scholars who claim that the Rolettes were French Canadians with perhaps a very distant Ottawa grandmother. While some claim that Joseph Rolette, Jr., was one-eighth Native, others claim the Rolettes were not "half-breeds," mixed bloods, or Métis. Joseph Rolette III appeared on the 1888 (at age 42), 1889, 1890, and 1892 Turtle Mountain Agency census rolls. Only on the infamous 1892 McCumber roll is Rolette, his wife (his wife's mother was a Poitras, a mixed-blood family long associated with the band and its leadership), and six children identified as "mixed bloods on the reservation." This may have been a convenient mischaracterization engineered by Agent Waugh. See below for the controversies surrounding the McCumber roll. Rolette's role as an interpreter indicates that he probably spoke English, French, Ojibwe, and Michif. He also knew how to write in English, e.g., his March 14, 1892, letter to the CIA on behalf of Little Shell's council.

[5] ICC, Docket 113/Petitioner's Exhibit 125, "Talk with the Turtle Mountain Chippewas," February 15, 1889.

[6] Ibid.

[7] *DH* 7, no. 12 (September 25, 1890), 4.

8 ICC, Docket 113/Petitioner's Exhibit 125, "Talk with the Turtle Mountain Chippewas," February 15, 1889.

9 Ibid.

10 Ibid.

11 Bureau of Indian Affairs, Letters Received, Letter from Agent John Cramsie to CIA T. J. Morgan, March 29, 1890.

12 Brief, 23.

13 Murray, "The Turtle Mountain Chippewa, 1882–1905," 25.

14 Ibid.

15 Commissioner of Indian Affairs R. V. Belt, Report to Secretary of the Interior, in Senate Doc. 444: 116, September 21, 1890.

16 Bureau of Indian Affairs, Letters Received, Letter from Agent John Waugh to CIA T. J. Morgan, August 7, 1890, enclosing E. W. Brenner's letter of August 4, 1890, requesting military assistance to restore order. Sometime between April and August 1890, John H. Waugh replaced J. W. Cramsie as the federal agent in charge at Devils Lake. This agency had administrative responsibility for the Turtle Mountain reservation.

17 Ibid.

18 Congress appointed the commission under the Act of August 19, 1889 (26 Stat., 354), ICC, Docket 113/Petitioner's Exhibit 139. Acting CIA R. V. Belt instructed the Mahone Commission on October 4, 1890, ICC, Docket 113/Petitioner's Exhibit 128.

19 NYT, "The Indians Dangerous," November 21, 1890, 5; NYT, January 11, 1891, 1.

20 DH 6, no. 37 (March 20, 1890), 4.

21 ICC, Docket 113/Petitioner's Exhibit 132, February 9, 1891; ICC, Docket 113/Petitioner's Exhibit 139, May 25, 1891.

22 NYT, "The Turtle Mountain Band," January 6, 1891, 5.

23 ICC, Docket 113/Petitioner's Exhibit 135, Letter from Acting Secretary of the Interior to Agent John H. Waugh at Fort Totten, May 25, 1891.

24 ICC, Docket 113/Petitioner's Exhibit 130, Resolutions of January 7, 1891; Senate Doc. 444, Section XXIII: 110.

[25] ICC, Docket 113/Petitioner's Exhibit 130, Preamble and Resolution of the Turtle Mountain Chippewa Indians, letter from J. B. Bottineau to the Secretary of the Interior, January 24, 1891 (corrected preamble date August 22, 1891); *Turtle Mountain band of Chippewa Indians v. United States and the Mahone Commission*, suit brought by J. B. Bottineau as "attorney for claimants."

[26] ICC, Docket 113/Petitioner's Exhibit 136, Letter from Little Shell, Chief of the Turtle Mountain Band of Chippewas, to CIA, August 28, 1891.

[27] CIA letter to Secretary of the Interior, Sept. 21, 1891, in Senate Doc 444, 115. The CIA claimed that the reservation requested at Turtle Mountain encompassed nineteen townships, or 446,670 acres. Other sources mention "approximately" twenty townships at both locations. J. B. Bottineau estimated that the December 21, 1882, Turtle Mountain reservation encompassed 491,520 acres, or just over twenty-one townships. *Brief*, 23.

[28] ICC, Docket 113/Petitioner's Exhibit 136, Letter from Little Shell, Chief of the Turtle Mountain Band of Chippewas, to CIA, August 28, 1891.

[29] Bureau of Indian Affairs, Letter from CIA T. J. Morgan to agents Brenner and Waugh, May 29, 1891.

[30] *Brief*, 41. ICC, Docket 113/Petitioner's Exhibit 135, Letter from Acting Secretary of the Interior to Agent John H. Waugh at Fort Totten, May 25, 1891; ICC, Docket 113/Petitioner's Exhibit 138, July 28, 1891.

[31] *ARCIA* 1892, 353, emphasis added.

[32] Revision of Letter of Oct. 14, 1910, p. 11, dated Nov. 4/10, 1900, from John B. Bottineau; Hallowell, Berens River, p. 68.

[33] Erdrich, *Tracks*, 109.

[34] *ARCIA* 1892, 78.

[35] ICC, Docket 113/Petitioner's Exhibit 137, Proposition of the Turtle Mountain Chippewa, September 1, 1891.

[36] This conclusion was reached by tracing the first five signatories of the proposition, and discerning their age, status and affiliation via tribal annuity and census records: 1) Joseph Bruce (two of them—one 28, the other 38, "mixed bloods on reservation"); 2) Daniel Turcotte (20, Family 229; #1009–1011, "mixed bloods on reservation); 3) Vital Turcotte (33, Family 74; #355– 362) "mixed bloods in vicinity of reservation"; 4) Martin Jerome

(34, since 1868 TM annuity roll; Family 128; #550–556, "mixed bloods on reservation"; and 5) Louis Jerome (since 1868 TM annuity roll, not on 1892 McCumber roll).

[37] ICC, Docket 113/Petitioner's Exhibit 137, Proposition of the Turtle Mountain Chippewa, September 1, 1891.

[38] Ibid., see Image 7.

[39] *DH*, May 21, 1886, vol. 5, no. 2, p. 4.

[40] In *Elk v. Wilkins*, 112 U.S. 94, 102 (1884), a divided ruling by the U.S. Supreme Court stated that: "Indians born within the territorial limits of the United States, members of, and owing immediate allegiance to, one of the Indian tribes (an alien, though dependent, power), although in a geographical sense born in the United States, are no more born in the United States and subject to jurisdiction thereof, within the meaning of the first section of the Fourteenth Amendment, than the children of subjects of any foreign government born within the domain of that government, or the children born within the United States, of ambassadors or other public ministers of foreign nations." Therefore, federal bureaucratic classification of "American" versus "Canadian" Natives constituted a false representation of fact. As attorney Bottineau noted, "there is a great prejudice existing in the Indian office against the half-breed and other Indians of mixed blood, charging that they are British or Canadian subjects, and not entitled to a like consideration with the full-bloods; this question should not have any weight in deciding this case, because the Pembina band of Chippewa Indians are well aware of who are and who are not descendants of the Chippewa tribe belonging to their band." *Protest*, 48. "To our great misfortune the more white blood predominates in the mixture with the Indian the worse we fare." The "half or mixed blood Indian . . . would seem as if he had no rights to be respected." *Brief*, 38–39.

[41] ICC, Docket 113/Petitioner's Exhibit 137, Proposition of the Turtle Mountain Chippewa, September 1, 1891, 2–3. While the proposal stated specific numbers of years pertaining to certain items, it did not mention a term for the $30,000 annual payment. Based on a subsequent proposal to the McCumber Commission the following year, one can infer that they foresaw a one-hundred-year annuity accruing to $3,000,000. The itemized list of the articles, stock, and implements included oxen, mares, stallions, wagons, cows, bulls, sheep, harnesses, plows, binders, rakes, mowers,

threshers, seeders, and a grist mill. A detailed list of annual provisions needed for the next twenty-five years stipulated quantities of beef, pork, flour, rice, beans, sugar, salt, tea, soap, oatmeal, cattle feed, and seed for two years or after in case of drought. They also requested clothing and bedding, their own Indian agency, blacksmith, carpenter, and farmer, plus an additional two schools.

[42] ICC, Docket 113/Petitioner's Exhibit 139, Letter from CIA Morgan to the Secretary of the Interior, October 19, 1891. The commissioner estimated the total cost of the Turtle Mountain Chippewa proposal to be $2,043,500. This figure did not include school maintenance, the cost of the seven additional townships, or buying out 256 European American properties and improvements. He estimated the buyout cost by calculating a price of $3.75 per acre or $600 for 160 acres. The purchase price of 256 quarter sections equaled $153,600. This made the grand total equivalent to $2,250,000.

[43] Ibid., 5.

[44] See chapter five for Price's calculations in Letter from CIA Hiram Price to the Secretary of the Interior, February 14, 1882, in Senate Doc. 444, Section XXI, 4. See chapter six for Cramsie's compensation cost estimates in *ARCIA* 1887, 35.

[45] *Handbook of American Indians North of Mexico*, "Government Policy" (Bureau of American Ethnology: Washington, D.C.), 1905.

[46] Richardson, *Messages and Papers of the Presidents*, Vol. 8, 355–58.

[47] *Brief*, 32. The federal government had also granted near-border reserves to Blackfeet bands in Montana and the Lake Superior Chippewa in Minnesota.

[48] They also support Robinson's "colonial hinterland" thesis. The 1890 census of wealth explained this apparent anomaly by stating that the "valuation per capita of some counties situated in sections recently settled is relatively very high, owing it is thought, to a large portion of the property being held by non-residents." See U.S. 1890 *Census of Wealth*, 9. Imported capital drove up the per capita value of real estate. As noted by Robinson, places like Rolette County and most of North Dakota became dependent on "outside finance, trade, and manufacturing." The specialized wheat farming economy remained dependent on access to markets controlled by "the

owners and managers of the railroads, the flour mills, the grain elevators and exchanges, and the banks which furnished the credit for the whole complex operation." Robinson, *North Dakota History*, xi.

[49] For greater insight into Sioux land rights during this period, see Jo Lea Wetherilt Behrens, "In Defense of 'Poor Lo': National Indian Defense Association and *Council Fire's* Advocacy for Sioux Land Rights," *South Dakota History* 24, no. 4 (Winter 1994): 170.

[50] Richardson, *Messages and Papers of the Presidents*, Vol. 8, 307.

[51] Ibid., 355–58. The decisive difference that led to the Sioux land restoration derived from their treaty with the United States. The Turtle Mountain Chippewa had sought a treaty since 1871, but had been unable to secure one during the intervening twenty years.

[52] July 13, 1892 (27 Stats. 139).

[53] Only McCumber, an outsider with no first-hand knowledge of tribal politics, and in pursuit of a foregone federal political agenda, used the term "factions" to describe the Turtle Mountain band's political in-fighting. ICC, Docket 113/Petitioner's Exhibit 144, Letter from McCumber to CIA from Belcourt, ND, September 29, 1892. In terms of "misrepresentation and concealment," the commission never revealed the federal government's goal of removal (to either the White Earth, Red Lake or Fort Berthold reservations), as stated in the Indian Appropriation Act of August 19, 1890, and July 13, 1892. *Brief*, 23.

[54] Howard, *Plains-Ojibwa*, 74–75.

[55] Gregory S. Camp, "Working Out Their Own Salvation: The Allotment of Land in Severalty and the Turtle Mountain Chippewa Band, 1870–1920." *American Indian Culture and Research Journal* 14 (1990): 19–38; Stanley N. Murray, "The Turtle Mountain Chippewa, 1882–1905," *North Dakota History* 51, no. 1 (1984): 14–37.

[56] ICC, Docket 113/Petitioner's Exhibit 144, Letter from McCumber to CIA from Belcourt, ND, September 29, 1892; *Brief*, 41; *Protest*, 3.

[57] Sources vary on the exact figure. Bottineau's *Brief*, 42, cited a letter from sub-agent Brenner claiming that the committee "expelled" 512 individuals.

[58] Father Genin, Letter from Church of St. Anthony at Bathgate, ND, to *Duluth Journal*, May 6, 1897, *Collections of the State Historical Society of North Dakota*, Vol. I, 1906: 297.

[59] Senate Doc. 444, 33–34, "Minutes of the Grand Council Proceedings of January 29, 1892," Section No. XXIV of Senate Doc. 444, 119.

[60] Senate Doc. 444, 34.

[61] Bureau of Indian Affairs, Letter from Agent J. W. Cramsie to CIA T. J. Morgan, March 29, 1890.

[62] Senate Doc. 444, Documents D, G and I, 40–43. ICC, Docket 113/Petitioner's Exhibit 114, Letter from Robert S. Gardner, Indian Inspector, to the Secretary of the Interior, August 26, 1885; ICC, Docket 113/Petitioner's Exhibit 113, Letter from Robert S. Gardner, Indian Inspector, to the Secretary of the Interior, August 28, 1885.

[63] ICC, Docket 113/Petitioner's Exhibit 144, Letter from McCumber to CIA from Belcourt, ND, September 29, 1892; *Brief*, 42.

[64] ICC, Docket 113/Petitioner's Exhibit 188, Tribal Council Minutes on Enrollment Decisions, June 26–29, 1906.

[65] In a letter dated November 25, 1910, Bottineau outlined the genealogy of his family and 123 other families in five generations of descent across "consanguinity and affinity" relations. Apparently, this invaluable documentation was stolen after his death in 1911. The 1910 Turtle Mountain Census Roll tallied 2,684 total members, including 2,009 (or 75 percent) mixed-bloods. Bureau of Indian Affairs, Record Group 75, Records of the Turtle Mountain Agency, ND, National Archives, Central Plains Region, Kansas City, Missouri. Also see chapter one, fn 12 and Appendix.

[66] *Brief*, 42.

[67] Ibid., 43.

[68] Turtle Mountain Agency, Ward Shepard, "Land and Self-Government for Indians," May 24, 1934, 1; *Prayer*, 7.

[69] *ARCIA*, 1906, 154–55.

[70] Senate Doc. 444, Letter from agents Waugh and Brenner to J. B. Bottineau, October 15, 1892, 41.

[71] ICC, Docket 113/Petitioner's Exhibit 144, Letter from McCumber to CIA from Belcourt, ND, September 29, 1892. The source used the word "advise" incorrectly, instead of advice.

[72] *Brief*, 17, 41.

[73] ICC, Docket 113/Petitioner's Exhibit 200a, 27, Testimony at Belcourt, ND on May 19, 1952. Mathias LaFramboise's testimony, at age eighty-eight. He lived on the reservation for sixty-four years. Belcourt Creek is known locally as Ox Creek, but also as Sibising—The Little Creek That Sings.

[74] Ibid.

[75] *Brief*, 17. As noted in a 2007 Turtle Mountain Community College publication on the North Dakota State University website, "The McCumber Agreement is what we commonly refer to today as . . . 'The Ten-Cent Treaty'; however, the U.S. Congress stopped making treaties with Indian tribes after 1871, but continued to make agreements with tribes that are similar to treaties through Acts of Congress or Executive Orders. The McCumber Agreement is one of these, but it is not formally a treaty." Les LaFountain, Orie Richard, and Scott Belgarde, *Who I Am: A Guide to Your Turtle Mountain Home*, Project Peacemaker, Turtle Mountain Community College, August 20, 2007, p. 8. https://www.ndsu.edu/fileadmin/centers/americanindianhealth/files/Who_I_Am_20Aug07.pdf

[76] Ibid., 17.

[77] McCumber Agreement, as Amended and Ratified by Congress, April 21, 1904 (33 Stat. 194). See back cover, section labeled Turtle Mountain Reservation, 1884.

[78] *Prayer*, 1; ICC, Docket 113/Petitioner's Exhibit 200a, May 19, 1952. A deponent named John Summer, aged nine in 1892, recounted these events based on an eyewitness account given to him by Standing Chief.

[79] Senate Doc. 444, No. II and D, 31–39, *Protest* Document No. 1, 1–12. In making their legal case to various Indian Affairs committees, commissions, or officials, Turtle Mountain Métis Attorney John B. Bottineau compiled a 178-page history of their tribal growth and change throughout the nineteenth century, entitled *Papers Relative to an Agreement with the Turtle Mountain Band of Chippewa Indians in North Dakota*. "A protest was submitted by the Turtle Mountain Indians, in the State of North Dakota, against the ratification" of the McCumber Agreement. The grievances compiled by Bottineau derived from "the proceedings of Chief Little Shell and the council of the tribe, held October 24, 1892." This Native testimony, although derived almost exclusively from European American sources, and primarily from government documents, recounted their terms of membership, leadership, and territorial claims, along with the development

of their economic and political relationships with European Americans and the U.S. government. The narrative also revealed the cultural beliefs and behaviors supporting their legal claim. Although not derived from the band's oral tradition, such a chronicle still embodied fundamental elements of Native "peoplehood": a kinship-related community's shared sense of a common history and homeland. Their legal claims rested solidly upon this sense of "peoplehood." See chapter one, fn 66, for sources pertaining to this insightful concept from Tom Holm.

[80] *Prayer*, 2; Senate Doc. 444, 33. The McCumber Census was finalized on October 1, 1892. It tallied 1,759 members for the Turtle Mountain band of Chippewa Indians, with 1,114 mixed- bloods on the reservation, 283 full bloods, and 362 mixed-bloods outside of the reservation.

[81] Senate Doc. 444, 35.

[82] Ibid., 20, 37. The specific neighboring tribes consisted of the Arikara, Mandan, Gros Ventre, and Sisseton Sioux.

[83] Ibid., 33.

[84] Ibid., 37–38.

[85] Ibid., 37.

[86] Ibid., 38.

[87] Ibid., 37.

[88] Senate Report 693, 7.

[89] ICC, Docket 113/ Petitioner's Brief, Finding No. 1, October 14, 1964, 4.

[90] *Brief*, 18.

[91] Senate Doc. 444, 37; *Brief*, 17, 20.

[92] Senate Report 693, 3.

[93] *Brief*, 18

[94] Prayer, 2.

[95] ICC, Docket 191–221/Petitioner's Exhibit 87, Letter from CIA Browning, July 6, 1893, 94.

[96] "Memorial of Turtle Mountain Band of Chippewa Indians on Treaty on Devils Lake, North Dakota," Senate Document 239, 54th Congress, 1st session, May 2, 1896, Serial set 3354. Agent Ralph Hall certified that the memorial and its 216 signatures represented "the wishes of the majority of

male adults of the Turtle Mountain Band of Chippewa Indians in North Dakota." Joseph Rolette acted as their interpreter.

[97] Tribal Chairman Richard LaFromboise, Select Committee on Indian Affairs hearing, U.S. Senate, 97th Congress, 2nd Session, June 17, 1982, on S. 1735, 81.

[98] *NYT*, March 28, 1900, 1.

[99] *DH*, vol. 6, no. 44, May 8, 1890, 4.

[100] *NYT*, August 15, 1900, 7, cited "twenty-four hospital cases," with others "quarantined at home." Similar outbreaks occurred among the Dakota Natives, the Flathead in Montana, and some Cree in Canada. Kappler, 1900 Census—full-bloods = 277, mixed-bloods on the reservation = 1, 484, mixed-bloods off the reservation = 421, mixed-bloods on the reservation but unrecognized = 421, total = 3, 410, plus 325 Pembina Chippewa at White Earth reservation in Minnesota.

[101] ICC, Docket 113/Petitioner's Exhibit 164, Letter from Bottineau to Secretary of the Interior, C. K. Davis, January 4, 1900, protest of the McCumber Agreement and request for a hearing before the Interior Secretary.

[102] H.R. 3541, 54th Congress, 1st Session, January 9, 1896; *Brief*, 3. The acting CIA was Frank C. Armstrong.

[103] Senate Doc. 444, 162, letter from the Chief and all the Councilmen to J. B. Bottineau, January 26, 1898; Hearing before the Select Committee on Indian Affairs, U.S. Senate, 97th Congress, 2nd Session, June 17, 1982, on S. 1735, Statement of Little Shell Band of Chippewa Indians of Montana on S. 1735, 143–44. James Howard noted that Little Shell III had a son named Thomas. Howard described him as a "good and upright citizen," but he "showed little inclination or ability for the office" of principal chief. Still, "no tribal ceremony was considered quite complete unless he was present." *Plains-Ojibwa*, 75; James M. Reardon, *George Anthony Belcourt: Pioneer Catholic Missionary of the Northwest, 1803–1874* (St. Paul: North Central Publishing Company, 1955), 22.

[104] *Turtle Mountain Band of Chippewa Indians*, 56th Congress, 1st Session, March 22, 1890, Senate Report 693, Serial set 3889, 7.

[105] Ibid., 3.

[106] *ARCIA* 1901, 295—report from agent W. O. Getchell.

[107] Ward Shepard, "Land and Self-Government for Indians," May 24, 1934, 4.

[108] *DH*, March 6, 1890, 1, and September 25, 1890, 4.

[109] Ward Shepard, "Land and Self-Government for Indians," May 24, 1934, 1.

[110] ICC, Rule 7C, Petitioner's Brief, December 3, 1962, 8.

[111] *Report Amending Senate Bill 196 to Ratify Agreement with Turtle Mountain Indians of North Dakota,* January 25, 1904, Senate Report 471, 58th Congress, 2nd Session, Serial 4571.

[112] *Congressional Record*, Senate, March 21, 1904, 3458–459.

[113] Ibid.

[114] Ibid. McCumber's valuation has been confirmed by subsequent scholarship. "Between 1900 and 1910 the acre value of farm real estate in northwestern and central North Dakota quadrupled." See Hargreaves, *Dry Farming*, 428–29. Emphasis added.

[115] *Brief*, 31–32.

[116] *Congressional Record*, Senate, March 21, 1904, 3458–459.

[117] Ibid.

[118] *Brief*, 32.

[119] Turtle Mountain Agency Superintendent letter, July 8, 1932. Record Group 75, Records of the Turtle Mountain Agency, ND, National Archives, Central Plains Region, Kansas City, Missouri.

[120] ICC, Docket 191–221, September 1962: 304–16. Dussome became recognized as the leader or president of the Little Shell Band of Montana during the 1920s. He gave this account, at the age of 83, during his testimony before the Indian Claims Commission.

[121] Ibid.

[122] Ibid. The Little Shell Tribe of Chippewa Indians of Montana finally received official federal recognition on December 20, 2019, 127 years after the 1892 McCumber "agreement." As noted by Chickasaw Native legal scholar Kevin Washburn, "The best evidence that the Little Shell Band is legitimate and deserving of federal recognition is the sheer persistence of its leadership. Persistence is the single most important trait of any tribal

nation in the United States." He continued, "I have always told my law students that persistence is the most important trait of American Indians . . . If our ancestors had lacked that, we would have been wiped from the earth long ago." https://www.washingtonpost.com/national/a-big-moment-finally-comes-for-the-little-shell-federal-recognition-of-their-tribe/2019/12/20/72f5ee86-204d-11ea-bed5-880264cc91a9_story. Html.

[123] Ibid.

[124] Land allotted to band members ranged from Graham's Island near Devils Lake, to the Trenton Service Area in western North Dakota, and farther west in Montana near Great Falls and Lewiston. *ARCIA* 1906, 293; *ARCIA* 1907, 59–60.

[125] *Congressional Record*, Senate, March 21, 1904, 3458–459.

[126] Articles IV, V, VIII, and XI were amended. See Senate Doc. 471, 1904, 2–6, Turtle Mountain Band of Chippewa Indians: *Release and Satisfaction to Accept and Ratify the Amended Agreement as Ratified by Congress on April 21, 1904*, February 17, 1905.

[127] ICC, Docket 113/Petitioner's Exhibit 200a; Minutes of Meeting of General Council of the Turtle Mountain Band of Chippewa Indians Called by Chas. L. Davis, Acting Indian Agent, February 15–17, 1905. Record Group 75, Records of the Turtle Mountain Agency, ND, National Archives, Central Plains Region, Kansas City, MO.

[128] Ibid.

[129] White-Weasel, *Pembina and Turtle Mountain Ojibway History*, 322.

[130] ICC, Docket 113/Petitioner's Exhibit 181.

[131] ICC, Docket 113/Petitioner's Exhibit 178, Letter from agent Davis to CIA, February 19, 1905 (mislabeled as January 19), with an attached letter of protest by J. B. Bottineau forwarded to agent Davis at Fort Totten by Farmer-in-Charge E. W. Brenner at Turtle Mountain. No public notice of this important proceeding was published in either of the nearby Rolla or Dunseith newspapers. It should be noted that Bottineau's daughter, Marie Louise Bottineau, also signed the protest letter. She had been the "first woman of color" to receive a law degree from the Washington College of Law at American University in Washington, D.C.; Lawrence J. Barkwell, "Bottineau-Baldwin, Marie Louise," Virtual Museum of Metis History and

Culture, January 13, 2014. In 1905, she assisted her nearly seventy-year-old father with his still active law practice.

[132] *Brief*, 7. Bottineau stated that he quoted from a "special Committee of the American Bar Association on Indian Legislation" report.

[133] ICC, Docket 113/Petitioner's Exhibit 200a, 16.

[134] Ibid., 49.

[135] Ibid., 41.

[136] *Brief*, 20–21.

[137] Letter from Kakenowash to CIA, February 10, 1917; Statements of Louis Marion, Gregoire Brien, Louis Gourneau, William Davis, et. al., Turtle Mountain School, Belcourt, ND, August 16, 1921, Record Group 75, Records of the Turtle Mountain Agency, ND, National Archives, Central Plains Region, Kansas City, MO.

[138] Letter from Acting CIA Meritt to Kakenowash, March 10, 1917, Record Group 75, Records of the Turtle Mountain Agency, ND, National Archives, Central Plains Region, Kansas City, MO.

[139] Letter from Bottineau to Chief Kanick and the members of the Standing Committee of the Turtle Mountain Indians, September 15, 1910, Record Group 75, Records of the Turtle Mountain Agency, ND, National Archives, Central Plains Region, Kansas City, MO.

[140] Letter from Bottineau to Chief Kanick and the members of the Standing Committee of the Turtle Mountain Indians, October 14, 1910, Record Group 75, Records of the Turtle Mountain Agency, ND, National Archives, Central Plains Region, Kansas City, MO.

[141] *Prayer*, 23; Statements of Louis Marion, Gregoire Brien, Louis Gourneau, William Davis, et. al., Turtle Mountain School, Belcourt, ND, August 16, 1921.

[142] Letter from Bottineau to Chief Kanick and the members of the Standing Committee of the Turtle Mountain Indians, January 1, 1911, Record Group 75, Records of the Turtle Mountain Agency, ND, National Archives, Central Plains Region, Kansas City, MO. Bottineau died eleven months later on December 1, 1911, in Washington, D.C., https://archive.org/details/ inmemoriamjeanba00jnbh.

## CONCLUSION ENDNOTES

[1] John W. Cramsie, Indian Agent for the Turtle Mountain Indians, 1886, in "Statement of Little Shell Tribe on Chippewa Indians of Montana on S. 1735," June 17, 1982, before the Senate Select Committee on Indian Affairs, "Use and Distribution of Pembina Chippewa Indian Judgment Funds," 143.

[2] Delorme, Dissertation, Appendix X, 256.

[3] ICC Docket No. 113/Exhibit 161, March 5, 1898, letter from J. B. Bottineau to Willis Van Devanter, Assistant Attorney General of the United States.

[4] *Brief*, 24.

[5] *Prayer*, 7–8; *Brief*: 7–8, 12; CIA Price March 11, 1882, letter.

[6] *Miami Herald*, February 24, 1985, "Indians in Fact, Indians in Fiction: A Conversation with Louise Erdrich," William Robertson, Herald Book Editor, 7E.

[7] *Brief*, 40.

[8] Delorme, Dissertation, Appendix X, 256. "Because our claim has not been settled," the Turtle Mountain Chippewa rejected the federal policy reforms of the Indian Reorganization Act in 1934 and the reactionary termination policy impositions of House Concurrent Resolution 108 in 1954. In both eras, they wanted their long-standing legal claims settled prior to *any* change in the treaty-derived trust relationship with the federal government.

[9] *Brief*, 31–32.

[10] Frank Pommersheim, *Braid of Feathers: American Indian Law and Contemporary Tribal Life* (Berkeley: University of California Press, 1995), 34.

[11] The U.S. Congress created the Indian Claims Commission by an act of August 13, 1946 (60 Stat. 1049). It "heard and determined claims against the United States on behalf of any tribe, band, or other identifiable group of American Indians residing within the United States." An Act of Congress on October 8, 1976 (90 Stat. 1990) abolished the commission effective September 30, 1978. The original $52,527,337.97 award was offset by $250,000 in non-treaty-related gratuities allocated by the U.S. government in support of the Turtle Mountain band from July 1, 1882, to June 30, 1951. The final award amounted to $52, 277,337.97. *Turtle Mountain Band of Chippewa Indians v. United States*, 43 Ind. Cl. Comm. 251 (1978).

Affirmed by *United States v. Turtle Mountain Band of Chippewa Indians*, 222 Ct. Cl. 1, 612 F.2d 517 (1979). In his June 17, 1982, testimony before the Senate Select Committee on Indian Affairs, tribal chairman Richard J. LaFramboise accepted the award, but still protested the less than "fair market value" of $6.50 per acre recompense considering the good farmland and numerous subsurface oil and gas deposits within the band's original unceded territory, 80–81. See David Wishart, "Belated Justice? The Indian Claims Commission and the Waitangi Tribunal." See *American Indian Culture and Research Journal* 25, no. 1 (2001): 99, for map labeled "Fair Market Value Established by the Indian Claims Commission," showing the [Turtle Mountain] Chippewa cession in northern North Dakota. But, forty-two years after the 1980 award, a class-action lawsuit, filed originally by the Turtle Mountain Band of Chippewa Indians (*Peltier v. Haaland*) and litigated by the Native American Rights Fund, finally resulted in a $59 million settlement in 2021. See https://www.indiangaming. com/interior-department-statement-on-pembina-judgment-fund-settlement/.

[12] The Turtle Mountain Band of Chippewa Indians acted as the plaintiff in Indian Claims Commission (ICC) Docket No. 113 from May 23, 1951, until September 29, 1978, when the case was transferred to the Court of Claims. The nexus of their claim sought fair compensation for the 9,000,000 to 10,000,000 acre area relinquished in the McCumber Agreement. The ICC determined that the band held "Indian title" to most of the area given up under the McCumber Agreement, which the United States acquired formally in February 1905 when a non-authorized and non-majority group of band members confirmed the cession legally. The Turtle Mountain Band brought suit on this claim, asserting a cause of action under Clauses 3 and 4 of Section 2 of the Indian Claims Commission Act, 25 USC § 70a (1946). Section 2 Clause 3 dealt with "claims which would result if the treaties, contracts, and agreements between the claimant and the United States were revised on the ground of fraud, duress, unconscionable consideration, mutual or unilateral mistake, whether of law or fact, or any other ground cognizable by a court of equity." Section 2 Clause 4 considered "claims arising from the taking by the United States, whether as the result of a treaty of cession or otherwise, of lands owned or occupied by the claimant without the payment for such lands of compensation agreed to by the claimant." 23 Ind. Cl. Comm. 315 (1970). The ICC found the consideration of the "ten-cent treaty" to be "unconscionable." It should also be noted that in ICC Docket No. 18-A, the Red Lake and Pembina Chippewa sued the

United States for the "unconscionable" recompense they received from the 1863 Old Crossing Treaty cession. The ICC verified the "Aboriginal title" of both bands and deemed "unconscionable" the $510,000 consideration proffered by Alexander Ramsey on behalf of the United States for the 11,000,000-acre land cession. *Red Lake and Pembina Chippewa et. al. v. United States*, 6 Ind. Cl. Comm. 247 (1958).

[13] Chairman LaFromboise used the phrase "object of hope" in praise of the persistence of his people "for 80-odd years," 81, 83; *Brief*, 25. The ICC ruled that "since the power of Congress to eliminate aboriginal title is exclusive, the creation of the Turtle Mountain reservation in Rolette County, North Dakota, by Executive Orders of December 21, 1882, and March 29, 1884, did not extinguish Indian title prior to the 1905 McCumber Agreement since there is no adequate showing that Congress authorized the extinguishment of the aboriginal title via an Executive Order reservation or that the Indians accepted such reservation as quid pro quo for giving up their claims, (2) that since the Executive Order reservation was ineffective, under the circumstances, to extinguish Indian title, it follows that the acts of private white citizens were also insufficient, (3) that the findings of the Commission based on apparently reliable evidence that the Chippewa did not give up their ties or claims to the land have substantial support." *Turtle Mountain Band of Chippewa Indians, et al. v. The United States* Appeal No. 6-72 United States Court of Claims 203 Ct. Cl. 426; 490 F.2d 935; 1974 U.S. Ct. Cl. January 23, 1974, Decided.

[14] Sidney L. Harring, *Crow Dog's Case: American Indian Sovereignty, Tribal Law, and United States Law in the Nineteenth Century* (Cambridge: University of Cambridge Press, 1994), 12–13.

[15] Senate Doc. 444, 5.

[16] *Barron's Law Dictionary*, 81, defines "color of law" as "the semblance of legal right" that has the "apparent authority of law but is actually contrary to law."

[17] "Minutes of a General Council Meeting of the Turtle Mountain Band of Chippewa Indians Called by Chas. L. Davis, Acting Indian Agent, February 15–17, 1905." Bureau of Indian Affairs, Record Group 75.19.121, Records of the Turtle Mountain Agency, ND, National Archives, Central Plains Region, Kansas City, MO. The Turtle Mountain spokespersons still declared that "they want to have justice," February 16, 1905, 3.

[18] Ignatia Broker and Steven Premo, *Night Flying Woman: An Ojibway Narrative* (St. Paul: Minnesota Historical Society Press, 1983), 8.
[19] *Brief*, 2; ICC Docket No. 113/Exhibit 161, March 5, 1898, letter from J. B. Bottineau to Willis Van Devanter, Assistant Attorney General of the United States.

## ABBREVIATIONS

| | |
|---|---|
| AAG | Assistant Attorney General |
| AFC | American Fur Company |
| ARCIA | Annual Report Commissioner of Indian Affairs |
| BIA | Bureau of Indian Affairs |
| BIC | Board of Indian Commissioners |
| BOV | Board of Visitors |
| CIA | Commissioner of Indian Affairs |
| *DH* | *Dunseith Herald* |
| EO | Executive Order |
| GLO | General Land Office |
| HBC | Hudson's Bay Company |
| ICC | Indian Claims Commission (New York: Clearwater Publishing Co.) microfiche |
| |  ICC, Docket No., Decisions |
| |  ICC, Docket No., Transcript |
| |  ICC, Docket No., Briefs |
| |  ICC, Docket No., Exhibits |
| |  ICC, Docket No., Journal |
| NWC | North West Company |
| *NYT* | *New York Times* |
| RG | Record Group |

## PRIMARY SOURCES

GOVERNMENT DOCUMENTS

American State Papers

U.S. Board of Indian Commissioners

U.S. Census Bureau

U.S. Commissioner of Indian Affairs

U.S. Congress, *Congressional Record*

U.S. Congress. House

U.S. Congress. Senate

U.S. *Statutes at Large*

1887 *U.S. Statutes at Large*, 24 St. 388 Vol. 27.

## STATE OF MINNESOTA DOCUMENTS

Minnesota Historical Society, St. Paul, MN.

> The Alexander Ramsey Papers and Records. Microfilm Roll 6.

## STATE OF NORTH DAKOTA DOCUMENTS

State Historical Society of North Dakota, Bismarck, ND.

> *Dunseith Herald*, Newspaper Microfilm
>
> Fort Pembina Papers, 1868–1895

## UNITED STATES DOCUMENTS

National Archives and Records Administration—Central Region, Kansas City, MO. National Archives Building, Washington, D.C.

Government Printing Office, 1946.

Department of the Interior, Office of Indian Affairs, Letter to A. H. Mahone, William Hoyne, and Isaac Fennimore, Commissioners to Negotiate with the Turtle Mountain Band of Chippewa Indians. Washington, D.C., October 4, 1890.

Exhibit I, *Printed Protest of Turtle Mountain Indians*. Committee on Indian Affairs, 53d Cong., 2d sess., *Turtle Mountain Indians*, Documents of Record in the Interior Department, Indian Office, Documents 1–16, pp. 1–153.

*Joint Resolution of Congress.* April 6, 1876 (19 Stat., 212).

*Report of the Secretary of War*, 1882, 1885, 1889.

United States Indian Claims Commission, *Final Report*, 1978.

*U.S. Congress House Documents.*

*Report of Major General Hancock*, Department of Dakota, in *Annual Report of the Secretary of War*. 41st Congress, 3rd Session, 1870–1871. House Executive Document 1, Serial set 1503.

*Estimate to purchase seeds for Turtle Mountain band of Chippewa Indians.* 50th Congress, 2nd Session, 1889. House Executive Document 63, Serial set 2651.

Stevens, Isaac. "Reports of Explorations and Surveys, to Ascertain the Most Practicable and Economical Route for a Railroad from the Mississippi River to the Pacific Ocean." 33rd Congress, 2nd Session, 1855. House Executive Document 91, Serial 791.

_____. "Narrative and Final Report of Explorations for a Route for a Pacific Railroad," 36th Congress, 1st Session, 1857. House Executive Document 56.

*Chippewa Half-Breeds of Lake Superior.* 42nd Congress, 2nd Session, March 15, 1872. House Executive Document 193, Serial set 1513.

*Commercial Relations with British America.* 39th Congress, 1st Session, June 12, 1866. House Executive Document 128, Serial set 1263.

*Report of the Turtle Mountain Commission.* Turtle Mountain Indians: Message from the President of the United States, "Communication from the Secretary of the Interior accompanied by an agreement between the Turtle Mountain Indians and the McCumber Commission, appointed July 13, 1892." 52nd Congress, 2nd Session, December 3, 1892. House Executive Document 229, Serial set 3105.

*Report of Major Woods, Relative to His Expedition to Pembina Settlement.* 31st Congress, 1st Session, 1850. House Executive Document 51, Serial set 577. Letter from G.A. Belcourt (November 25, 1845): 44–52; translated into English in *North Dakota History* 38, no. 3 (Summer 1971): 335–48. Letter from G. A. Belcourt to U.S. Congress, 31st Congress, 1st Session, August 20, 1849, 36-43.

*General Sherman on the End of the Indian Problem.* 48th Congress, 1st Session, October 27, 1883. House Executive Document 1, Serial set 2182.

*Memorial of the Legislative Assembly of Dakota Territory.* 42nd Congress, 3rd Session, 1873. House Miscellaneous Document 63.

*Turtle Mountain Band of Chippewa Indians.* 47th Congress, 1st Session, 1882. House Report 1144, Nathaniel C. Deering, Committee of Indian Affairs, to Accompany Bill H.R. 1885, April 28, 1882.

*Turtle Mountain Band of Chippewa Indians.* H.R. Rep. No. 820, 55th Cong., 2nd Sess. March 24, 1898.

Committee on Indian Affairs, *Reservation of Sioux Indians in Dakota,* House Report 3645, 50th Congress, 2nd Session, Serial set 2673.

Gifford, Oscar S. *Report on bill authorizing negotiations for surrender of reservation in in North Dakota and consolidation with Minnesota Chippewas.* United States Congress, 51st Congress, 1st Session, March 4, 1890. House Report 632, Serial set 2808.

*To Refer Turtle Mountain Band of Chippewa Indians to Court of Claims.* House Report 820, 55th Congress, 2nd Session, March 24, 1898, Serial set 3719. Contains the *Sweet Corn Treaty* of 1858.

*Turtle Mountain Chippewa Indians of North Dakota.* United States Congress, 75th Congress, 3rd Session, February 8, 1938. House Report 1770.

U.S. Congress Senate Documents.

"Letter from the Secretary of the Interior relative to Agreement between the Turtle Mountain Indians in North Dakota and the Commission Appointed under the Act of July 13, 1892." 54th Congress, 1st Session, Senate Document 23, Serial set 3347.

"Memorial of Turtle Mountain Band of Chippewa Indians on Treaty on Devils Lake, North Dakota." Senate Document 239, 54th Congress, 1st session, May 2, 1896, Serial set 3354.

Kyle, James H. and John B. Bottineau. *Turtle Mountain Band of Pembina Chippewa Indians*: Mr. Kyle presented the January 26, 1898 petition and memorial of Turtle Mountain Band of Chippewa Indians, in the state of North Dakota, praying for the reference of their claim to the Court of Claims under the Bowman Act, March 3, 1883 (22 Stat., 485), for advice to the committee on the disputed questions of law and fact in the case, for the segregation of their unceded lands and for their relinquishment, under the provision of H.R. 2279, 55th Congress, 1st Session, February 23. 1898, Senate Document 154, Serial set 3600.

*Chippewa Indians of Turtle Mountain, Dakota Territory, Praying for Segregation and Confirmation of Tract of their Land to them, and that Certain Provisions be made for their Protection.* 44th Congress, 1st Session, February 23, 1876. Senate Miscellaneous Document 63, Serial set 1665.

*Turtle Mountain Band of Chippewa Indians.* 56th Congress, 1st Session, March 22, 1890. Senate Report 693. Serial set 3889.

*Turtle Mountain Band of Chippewa Indians.* 56th Congress, 1st Session, June 6, 1900. Senate Document 444. Serial set 3878.

"Use and Distribution of Pembina Chippewa Indian Judgement Funds." *Hearing before the Select Committee on Indian Affairs, United States Senate*, 87th Congress, 2nd Session, on S. 1735, "To Provide for the Use and Distribution of Funds Awarded the Pembina Chippewa Indians in Dockets Numbered 113, 191, 221, and 246 of the Court of Claims." June 17, 1982.

"Turtle Mountain Band of Chippewa Indians." 55th Congress, 2nd Session, Serial 3600, February 23, 1898.

"To Ratify Agreement with Turtle Mountain Band of Chippewa Indians in North Dakota *Senate Report 393*, 56th Congress, 1st session, Serial 3889, 1900.

*Report of the Public Lands Commission, 1905.* Senate Document 189, 58ᵗʰ Congress, 3ʳᵈ Session.

*Treaty with the Pembina and Red Lake Chippewa.* 32ⁿᵈ Congress, 1ˢᵗ Session, September 20, 1851. Senate Confidential Executive Document 10. Serial set 613.

Senate Executive Document No. 61, 33ʳᵈ Congress, 1ˢᵗ Session, Serial set 699.

Ramsey, Alexander. *Senate Miscellaneous Documents No. 4 and 22,* 40ᵗʰ Congress, 2ⁿᵈ Session, Serial 1319.

"Report Authorizing Secretary of Interior to set aside reservation for Turtle Mountain band of Chippewa Indians." 44ᵗʰ Congress, 1ˢᵗ Session, April 18, 1876. Senate Report 275, Serial set 1667.

"Use and Distribution of Pembina Chippewa Indians Judgment Funds." 97ᵗʰ Congress, 2ⁿᵈ Session, June 17, 1982. Senate Select Committee on Indian Affairs Hearing. Microform Edition, Washington, D.C.: U.S. Government Printing Office, 1982.

Bottineau, John B. "Turtle Mountain Band of Chippewa Indians," Senate Document 444, 56ᵗʰ Congress, 1ˢᵗ Session, June 6, 1900: 1–178.

"Report Amending Senate Bill 196 to Ratify Agreement with Turtle Mountain Indians of North Dakota," January 25, 1904, from Senate Report 471, 58ᵗʰ Congress, 2ⁿᵈ Session, Serial set 4571.

*Report Amending Senate Bill 196 to Ratify Agreement with Turtle Mountain Indians of North Dakota.* 58ᵗʰ Congress, 2ⁿᵈ Session, January 25, 1904. Senate Report 471, Serial set 4571.

Pope, Captain John. "The Report of an Exploration of the Territory of Minnesota," 31ˢᵗ Congress, 1ˢᵗ Session 1850. Senate Executive Document 42, Serial set 558.

_____. "Report to the Secretary of War," 31ˢᵗ Congress, 1ˢᵗ Session, 1850. Executive Document 10, Serial set 577. "Report of the Public Lands Commission," 58ᵗʰ Congress, 3rd Session, 1905. Senate Document 187, Serial set 4766.

## CENSUS REPORTS

Census of Half Breed Chippewas of Turtle Mountain, Dakota Territory, 1884, 1885, 1886, 1888, 1889, 1890.

Dakota Territorial Census, 1860.

McCumber Census of the Turtle Mountain band of Chippewa Indians, Belcourt, North Dakota, October 1, 1892.

Turtle Mountain Allotment and Census Records. Record Group 75, National Archives RG 75, Kansas City, MO; Microfilm copy.

Turtle Mountain Chippewa, Pembina Band. Annuity Payments: 1865, 1868, 1869, 1870, 1871, 1872, 1873, 1874.

*Turtle Mountain Census*: 1884, 1885, 1886, 1887, 1888, 1889, 1890, 1892, 1900. Gail Morin (ed.). Pawtucket, RI: Quintin Publishing, 2000.

U.S. Bureau of the Census, *1850 Minnesota Territorial Census*, Pembina District.

St. Paul, Minnesota: Minnesota Historical Society, 1972.

U.S. Census Office, 11th Census, 1890. "Report on Wealth, Debt, and Taxation." "Report on Farms and Homes: Proprietorship and Indebtedness."

## MISCELLANEOUS

*Chippewa Indians VII: Indian Claims Commission Findings*. New York, Garland Publishing Inc., 1974.

*Deposition of Louis Marion, Gregoire Brien, Louis Gourneau, et. al.* Turtle Mountain School, Belcourt, North Dakota. August 16, 1921.

*Guide to the Lands of the Northern Pacific Railroad.* New York: Northern Pacific Land Department, 1872.

*Minutes of Meeting of General Council of the Turtle Mountain Band of Chippewa Indians,* Called by Chas. L. Davis, Acting Indian Agent, February 15, 1905.

*North Dakota: A Guide to the Northern Prairie State.* Fargo: Federal Writers Project of the Works Progress Administration, 1938.

*Ojibwe Peoples Dictionary.* https://ojibwe.lib.umn.edu/

*St. Ann's Centennial: 100 Years of Faith, 1885-1985; Turtle Mountain Indian Reservation, Belcourt, North Dakota.* Rolla, ND: Star Printing, 1985.

Baraga, Bishop Frederic. *A Dictionary of the Otchipwe Language.* Minneapolis: Ross and Haines, 1965.

Belcourt, G. A. "Letter of Father Belcourt Describing a Buffalo Hunt (Nov. 25, 1845)." *Collection of the State Historical Society of North Dakota* 5 (1923): 134–54.

_____. "Letter of Father Belcourt to the Commissioner of Indian Affairs, G. W. Manypenny, (Nov. 29, 1854)." *Collection of the State Historical Society of North Dakota* 1 (1906): 213–16.

Bond, J. Wesley. *Sketches by a Camp Fire: or Notes of a trip from St. Paul to Pembina and Selkirk Settlement on the Red River of the North.* New York: J. S. Redfield, 1854.

Bottineau, J. B. *Chippewa Indians of Northern Dakota Territory: Will the Government Recognize Their Claim and Provide for Them?* Washington, D.C.: United States Dept. of the Interior, Thos. J. Brashears, 1878: 1–15.

_____. Prayer and Address of the Turtle Mountain Band of the Pembina Chippewa Indians Historical Society of Wisconsin, Microfilm 621 I 1000, February 14, 1895: 1-24.

_____. *The Turtle Mountain Band of the Pembina Chippewa Indians: Brief and Points in Support of H.R. Bill No. 3541 Now Pending.* Historical Society of Wisconsin, Microfilm 621 I 1002, May 29, 1896: 1-44.

_____. *Letter to My Dear Chief and Kinsmen*, September 15, 1910.

_____. *Letter to My Dear Chief and Kinsmen*, October 14, 1910.

_____. *Letter to My Dear Chief and Kinsmen*, Revision of October 14, 1910 Letter. November 4/10, 1910.

Bray, Edmund C. and Martha C. Bray, eds. *Joseph N. Nicollet on the Plains and Prairies: The Expedition of 1838-39 with Journals, Letters, and Notes on the Dakota Indians.* St. Paul: Minnesota Historical Society Press, 1976.

Copway, George. *Life, History, and Travels.* Philadelphia: J. Harmstead, 2d ed., 1846.

Harrer, C.M. *Mineral Resources and Their Potential on Indian Lands: Turtle Mountain Reservation, Rolette County, North Dakota, Preliminary Report 140.* Denver, CO: Bureau of Mines, August 1961.

Harrison, Jonathan Baxter. "A Typical Indian Removal: An Account of the Condition and Treatment of the Chippewa Indians on the Turtle Mountain Reservation," from the Boston evening transcript of the Indian Rights Association, December 17, 1887. Philadelphia: Indian Rights Association, 1887.

Harvard, V. *The French Half-breeds of the North West*, Smithsonian Institution, Annual Report for 1879. Washington, D.C.: 309–27.

Henry, Alexander (the elder). *Travels and Adventures in Canada and the Indian Territories.* Toronto: Vermont Tuttle Co. Inc., 1809, 1969.

Henry, Alexander and David Thompson, Elliot Coues, ed. *New Light on the Early History of the Greater Northwest: The Manuscript Journals of Alexander Henry and David Thompson, 1799–1814*, New York: F. P. Harper, 1897.

Holst, John B. *Report of Progress in the Preparation of a Turtle Mountain Chippewa Roll*, January 10, 1941. Indian census rolls, 1910–1912. Turtle Mountain (Chippewa Indians) National Archives Microfilm Publications, Microcopy Roll 595, 1910–12.

Jefferson, Thomas. *Papers of Thomas Jefferson*, Vol. IV, ed. Julian P. Boyd. Princeton: Princeton University Press, 1950.

Jones, Peter. *History of the Ojebway Indians*. Freeport, NY: Books for Libraries Press, 1970. First published in 1861.

Kappler, Charles J. *Indian Affairs: Laws and Treaties.* Washington: Government Printing Office, 1904. http://digital.library.okstate.edu/kappler/

Kittson, Norman. "Letter from Red River, Nov. 2, 1862, to Clark W. Thompson, Superintendent of Indian Affairs, St. Paul." Forwarded by W. T. Otto, Acting Secretary, Interior Department to William P. Dole, Commissioner of Indian Affairs, May 21, 1863.

Letter from Flatmouth and Wawinchigun to President Millard Fillmore, October 6, 1851. Enclosed in Lea to Ramsey letter, November 14, 1851. Minnesota Field Office, BIA, Record Group 75, National Archives, Washington, D.C.

Long, Stephen H., William H. Keating, ed., *Narrative of an Expedition to the Source of St. Peter's River.* London: Geo. B. Whittaker, 1825.

MacLeod, John. "Diary of Chief Trader John MacLeod, Senior of Hudson's Bay Company, Red River Settlement, 1811." *Collections of the State Historical Society of North Dakota*, II (1908): 115–34. Mayer, Frank B. *With Pen and Pencil on the Frontier in 1851.* St Paul: Minnesota Historical Society Press, 1932.

Ramsey, Alexander. *Journal of the United States Commission to Treat with the Chippewa Indians of the Pembina and Red Lake*, Minnesota Territory, August 18, 1851, concluded 20th September, 1851. Alexander Ramsey Papers and Records.

Records of the Adjutant General's Office. Petition from Louis Riel to Nelson A. Miles, August 20, 1880, Record Group 94, National Archives, Washington D.C.

Richardson, James D., ed. *A Compilation of the Messages and Papers of the Presidents, 1789–1897,* Volumes 1–10. Washington, D.C.: Government Printing Office, 1896.

Riel, Louis. *The Collected Writings of Louis Riel,* Vol. 2, ed. Gilles Martel. Edmonton: University of Alberta Press, 1985.

Royal Commission on Aboriginal Peoples. "Restructuring the Relationship," Vol. 2 Part 1, Ottawa: Canada Communication Group, 1996.

Ross, Alexander. *The Red River Settlement: Its Rise, Progress, and Present State.* Minneapolis: Ross and Haines, 1957 (published originally in 1856).

Schoolcraft, Henry R. "Travels Among the Aborigines: The Chippewa Indians." *North American Review* 27 (July 1828): 89-114.

Tache, Alexandre-Antonin. *Sketch of the North-West of America.* Montreal: John Lovell, 1870.

Tanner, John. *A Narrative of the Captivity and Adventures of John Tanner.* Introduction by Louise Erdrich. Reprint of the G. & C. & H. Carvill 1830 edition. New York: Penguin Books, 1994.

Teller, Henry M. *Report of the Secretary of the Interior 1882.* Washington: D.C.: Government Printing Office, 1883.

_____. *Report of the Secretary of the Interior 1883.* Washington: D.C.: Government Printing Office, 1884.

_____. Report of the Secretary of the Interior 1885. Washington: D.C.: Government Printing Office, 1886.

Turtle Mountain Band of Chippewa Indians: *Release and Satisfaction to Accept and Ratify the Amended Agreement as Ratified by Congress on April 21, 1904.* February 17, 1905.

Warren, William W. "Answers to Inquiries Regarding Chippewas." *Minnesota Pioneer,* December 5, 12, 19, 26, 1849. Reprinted in Minnesota Archaeologist 13 (January 1947): 5–21.

_____. "Sioux and Chippewa Wars." *Minnesota Chronicle & Register,* June 3 and 10, 1850. Reprinted in *Minnesota Archaeologist* 12 (October 1946): 95–107.

_____. "History of the Ojibways, Based Upon Traditions and Oral Statements." *Collections of the Minnesota Historical Society* 5 (1885): 21–394.

Wheelock, Joseph A. *Journal of the Proceedings Connected with the Negotiation of a Treaty with the Red Lake and Pembina Bands of Chippewas—Concluded at the Old Crossing of Red Lake River on the Second of October, 1863.* ICC, Docket 18-A/Defendant's Exhibit 12. National Archives, Washington, D.C.

Wilson, John W. and W. Woodville Fleming, Letter from Members of the McCumber Commission, to Commissioner of Indian Affairs, October 22, 1892.

## COURT CASES

*Cherokee Nation v. Georgia*, 30 U.S. (5 Pet.) 1 (1831)

*Chippewa Nation v. United States,* 301 U.S. 358 (1937)

*Elk v. Wilkins*, 112 U.S. 94 (1884)

*Johnson v. McIntosh*, 21 U.S. (8 Wheat.) 543 (1823)

*Lone Wolf v. Hitchcock*, 187 U.S. 553 (1903)

*Maddux v. Bottineau*, 34 App. D.C. 119 (1909)

*Mitchel v. United States*, 9 Pet. (34 U.S.) 711 (1835)

*Montoya v. United States*, 180 U.S. 261 (1901)

*Morgan v. Vandal, Grant et. al.*, (1910)

*Red Lake, Pembina, and White Earth Bands, and Minnesota Chippewa Tribe v. United States*, 1 Ind. Cl. Comm. 575, 588 (Ind. Cl. Comm. 1951)

*Red Lake, Pembina, & White Earth Bands v. United States*, 6 Ind. Cl. Comm., 247, 249 (Ind. Cl. Comm. 1958)

*Red Lake, Pembina, & White Earth Bands v. United States*, 9 Ind. Cl. Comm. 315 (Ind Cl. Comm. 1961)

*Red Lake, Pembina, & White Earth Bands v. United States*, 164 Ct. Cl. 389 (Ct. Cl. 1964)

*Red Lake & Pembina Bands v. Turtle Mountain Band of Chippewa Indians*, 355 F.2d 936 (Ct. Cl. 1965)

*Turtle Mountain Band of Chippewa Indians v. United States*, 490 F. 2d 935 (Ct. Cl. 1974)

*Turtle Mountain Band of Chippewa Indians, et al. v. United States*, Appeal No. 6–72 Court of Claims 203 Ct. Cl. 426; 490 F.2d 935; 1974 U.S. Ct. Cl. January 23, 1974, Decided.

*Turtle Mountain Band of Chippewa Indians, Red Lake Band, & Peter Graves v. United States*, 43 Ind. Cl. Comm. 251 (Ind. Cl. Comm. 1978)

*Turtle Mountain Band v. United States,* 23 Ind. Cl. Comm. 315 (Ind. Cl. Comm. 1970)

*United States v. Higgins,* 103 Fed. 348 D. Mont. (1900)

*United States v. Santa Fe Pacific Railroad Company,* 314 U.S. 339 (1941)

*United States v. Turtle Mountain Band of Chippewa Indians,* 612 F.2d 517 (Ct. Cl. 1979)

*Voight v. Bruce,* 44 L.D. 524 (1916)

*Worcester v. Georgia,* U.S. (6 Pet.) 515 (1832)


## NEWSPAPERS

*Bismarck Tribune*

*Dunseith Herald*

*Fargo Record*

*Grand Forks Plaindealer*

*Miami Herald*

*Minnesota Pioneer*

*Minnesota Chronicle & Register*

*New York Times*

*Turtle Mountain Star*

*Winnipeg Daily Sun*


## SECONDARY SOURCES

*Albert Gatschet Ojibwe Materials: 1878 Bottineau Vocabulary.* February 7, 2020 https://miidashgeget.wordpress.com/2020/02/07/gatschet-1878-bottineau/.

Abel, Annie Heloise. "Proposal for an Indian State, 1778–1878," in *Annual Report of the American Historical Association for the Year 1907,* Vol. 1.

Archambeault, William G.  Personal communication to the author. 10 Feb. 2000.

Adelman, Jeremy and Stephen Aron. "From Borderlands to Borders: Empires, Nation-States, and the Peoples in Between North American History," *American Historical Review* 104, no. 3 (June 1999): 814–44.

Anaya, S. James. *Indigenous Peoples in International Law.* New York: Oxford University Press, 1996.

Anderson, Gary Clayton. *Little Crow: Spokesman for the Sioux.* St. Paul, MN: Minnesota Historical Society Press, 1986.

_____. *Massacre in Minnesota: The Dakota War of 1862, the Most Violent Ethnic Conflict in American History.* Norman: University of Oklahoma Press, 2019.

Anderson, Gary and Alan R. Woolworth, eds. *Through Dakota Eyes: Narrative Accounts of the Minnesota Indian War of 1862.* St. Paul: Minnesota Historical Society Press, 1988.

Appel, Livia and Theodore C. Blegen. "Impressions of Minnesota in 1849." *Minnesota History Bulletin,* Vol. V (August 1923).

Axtell, James. "The White Indians of Colonial America." *William and Mary Quarterly,* 37 (January 1975): 55–88.

Babcock, Willoughby M. "With Ramsey to Pembina: A Treaty-Making Trip." *Minnesota History* 38, no. 1 (March 1962): 1–10.

Bakker, Peter. *A Language of Our Own: The Genesis of Michif, the Mixed Cree-French Language of the Canadian Metis.* New York: Oxford University Press, 1997.

Baraga, Reverend Frederick. *Chippewa Indians As Recorded by F. Baraga in 1847.* New York: Studia Slovenica, 1976.

Barkwell, Lawrence J., Leah Dorion, and Darren R. Préfontaine, eds. *Métis Legacy: A Métis Historiography and Annotated Bibliography.* Winnipeg: Pemmican Publications Inc., 2001.

Barnett, LeRoy. "The Buffalo Bone Commerce On the Northern Plains." *North Dakota History* 39, no. 1 (Winter 1972): 23–40.

Barsch, Russel L. and James Y. Henderson. *The Road: Indian Tribes and Political Liberty.* Berkeley: University of California Press, 1980.

Behrens, Jo Lea Wetherilt. "In Defense of 'Poor Lo': National Indian Defense Association and *Council Fire's* Advocacy for Sioux Land Rights." *South Dakota History* 24, no. 4 (Winter 1994):153–173.

Bell, Catherine. "*Metis* Constitutional Rights in Section 35(1)." *Alberta Law Review* 36 (December 1997): 180–217.

Bensel, Richard Franklin. *The Political Economy of American Industrialization, 1877–1900.* New York: Cambridge University Press, 2000.

Berkhofer, Robert F. "The Political Context of a New Indian History." *Pacific Historical Review* 40, no. 3 (August 1971): 357–82.

_____. *The White Man's Indian: Images of the American Indian from Columbus to the Present*. New York: Vintage Books, 1978.

Bieder, Robert E. "Scientific Attitudes Toward Indian Mixed-Bloods in Early Nineteenth Century America." *Journal of Ethnic Studies* 8 (1980): 17–30.

Binnema, Theodore, Gerhard J. Ens, and R. C. MacLeod, eds. *From Rupert's Land to Canada*. Edmonton: University of Alberta Press, 2001.

Blegen, Theodore C. *Minnesota: A History of the State*. Minneapolis: University of Minnesota Press, 1963.

Blegen, Theodore C. and Philip D. Jordan, eds. *With Various Voices: Recordings of North Star Life*. Saint Paul: Itasca Press, 1949.

Branch, E. Douglas. *The Hunting of the Buffalo*. Lincoln: University of Nebraska Press, 1997. New Bison Books Edition by Andrew C. Isenberg.

Bray, Martha C. "Pierre Bottineau: Professional Guide." *North Dakota Quarterly* Vol. 32 (1964): 29–37.

_____. ed. *The Journals of Joseph N. Nicollet: A Scientist on the Mississippi Headwaters With Notes on Indian Life, 1836–37*. St. Paul: Minnesota Historical Society Press, 1970.

Broker, Ignatia and Steven Premo. *Night Flying Woman: An Ojibway Narrative*. St. Paul: Minnesota Historical Society Press, 1983.

Brown, Jennifer S. H. *Strangers in Blood: Fur Trade Company Families in Indian Country*. Norman: University of Oklahoma Press, 1980.

Brown, Jennifer S. H. and Robert A. Brightman, eds. *The Orders of the Dreamed: George Nelson on Northern Ojibwa Religion and Myth, 1823*. St. Paul: Minnesota Historical Society Press, 1988.

Bumsted, J. M. "Crisis at Red River." *The Beaver* (June/July 1995): 23–34.

Calloway, Colin G. *Crown and Calumet: British-Indian Relations, 1783–1815*. Norman: University of Oklahoma Press, 1987.

Campbell, Marjorie Wilkins. *McGillivray, Lord of the Northwest*. Toronto: Clark, Irwin, 1962.

Camp, Gregory S. "The Chippewa Fur Trade in the Red River Valley of the North, 1790-1830." In *The Fur Trade in North Dakota*, ed. Virginia L. Heidenreich, 33–46. Bismarck: State Historical Society of North Dakota, 1990.

_____. "The Chippewa Transition from Woodland to Prairie, 1790–1820." *North Dakota History* 51, no. 3 (Summer 1984): 39–47.

_____. "The Turtle Mountain Plains-Chippewas and Métis, 1797–1935." unpublished Ph.D. dissertation, University of New Mexico, 1987.

_____. "Working Out Their Own Salvation: The Allotment of Land in Severalty and the Turtle Mountain Chippewa Band, 1870–1920." AmericanIndian Culture and Research Journal 14 (1990): 19–38.

_____. "Commerce and Conflict: A History of Pembina, 1797–1895." North Dakota History 60, no. 4 (1993): 22–33.

Carlson, Leonard A. Indians, Bureaucrats, and Land: The Dawes Act and the Decline of Indian Farming. Westport, CT: Greenwood Press, 1981.

Catlin, George. Letters and Notes on the North American Indians. New York: Penguin Paperback Edition, 1995; original edition 1832.

Champagne, Duane. "American Indian Studies Is for Everyone." American Indian Quarterly 20, no. 1 (Winter 1996): 77–82.

Chavkin, Allan and Nancy Feyl Chavkin, eds. Conversations with Louise Erdrich & Michael Dorris. Jackson: University Press of Mississippi, 1994.

Cheseboro, James W. "Charles Joseph Bottineau, Sr., Techomehgood and Their Descendants." September 1, 1990. http://users.ap.net/~chenae/bottineau12.html.

Chippewa Indians VII: Indian Claims Commission Findings. New York: Garland Publishing Inc., 1974.

Clark, W. Leland. "The Place of the Metis Within the Agricultural Economy of the Red River During the 1840s and 1850s." Canadian Journal of Native Studies 3, no. 1 (1983): 69–84.

Cohen, Felix S. "Original Indian Title." Minnesota Law Review 28 (1947): 32–35.

Cohen, Michael D., James G. March, and Johan P. Olsen. "A Garbage Can Model of Organizational Choice." Administrative Science Quarterly 17, no. 1 (March 1972): 1–17.

Colebatch, H. K. Policy. Buckingham, UK: Open University Press, 1998.

Cornell, Stephen. The Return of the Native: American Indian Political Resurgence. New York: Oxford University Press, 1988.

Coulter, John L. "Industrial History of the Valley of the Red River of the North," Collections of the State Historical Society of North Dakota Vol. III (1910): 529–671.

Cowger, Thomas W. "Dr. Thomas A. Bland, Critic of Forced Assimilation." *American Indian Culture and Research Journal* 16 (1992): 77–97.

Coyle, Michael. "Traditional Indian Justice in Ontario: A Role for the Present." *Osgoode Hall Law Journal* 24, no. 3 (1986): 605–33.

Crawford, John C. "Introduction." *The Michif Dictionary: Turtle Mountain Chippewa Cree*, ed. Patline Laverdure and Ida Rose Allard, vii–x. Winnipeg: Pemmican Publication, Inc., 1983.

_____. "Speaking Michif in Four Metis Communities." *Canadian Journal of Native Studies* 3 (1983): 47–55.

_____. "What Is Michif? Language in the Métis Tradition." *The New Peoples: Being and Becoming Metis in North America.* Eds., Jacqueline Peterson and Jennifer S. H. Brown. Minneapolis: Minnesota Historical Society Press, 1985.

Cronon, William. *Changes in the Land: Indians, Colonists, and the Ecology of New England.* New York: Hill and Wang, 1983.

Debo, Angie. *A History of the Indians of the United States.* Norman: University of Oklahoma Press, 1970.

Deloria, Philip J. "Historiography." Eds., Deloria and Neal Salisbury. *A Companion to American Indian History.* Malden, MA: Blackwell Publishers, 2002.

_____. "From Nation to Neighborhood: Land, Policy, Culture, Colonialism, and Empire in U.S.- Indian Relations." *The Cultural Turn in U.S. History: Past, Present, and Future.* Eds. James W. Cook, Lawrence B. Glickman, and Michael O'Malley. Chicago: 2008.

Deloria, Jr., Vine. "The Place of Indians in Contemporary Education." *American Indian Journal* 2, no. 21 (February 1976).

_____. "Laws Founded in Justice and Humanity: Reflections on the Content and Character of Federal Indian Law." *Arizona Law Review* 31, no. 2 (1989): 203–23.

_____. "The Subject Nobody Knows." *American Indian Quarterly* 19, no. 1 (Winter 1995):143–47.

Deloria, Jr., Vine and Raymond J. DeMallie. *Documents of American Indian Diplomacy: Treaties, Agreements, and Conventions, 1775–1979.* Norman: University of Oklahoma Press, 2000.

Deloria, Jr., Vine and Clifford M. Lytle. *American Indians, American Justice.* Austin: University of Texas Press, 1983.

Deloria, Jr., Vine and David E. Wilkins. *Tribes, Treaties, and Constitutional Tribulations*. Austin: University of Texas Press, 1999.

Delorme, David P. "Emancipation and the Turtle Mountain Chippewas." *American Indian* 7, no. 1 (1954): 11–20.

_____. "A Socio-Economic Study of the Turtle Mountain Band of Chippewa Indians and a Critical Evaluation of Proposals Designed to Terminate Their Federal Wardship Status." Unpublished Ph.D. dissertation. University of Texas, 1955.

_____. "History of the Turtle Mountain Band of Chippewa Indians." *North Dakota History* 22 (1955): 121–34.

DeMallie, Raymond J. "Kinship: The Foundation for Native American Society." *Studying Native America: Problems and Prospects*. Ed., Russell Thornton. Madison: University of Wisconsin Press, 1998.

DeMers, Anne, et. al. *St John: City at the End of the Rainbow*. Grafton, ND: Printers, 1982.

Densmore, Frances. "Chippewa Customs." *Bureau of American Ethnology*. Bulletin 45. Washington, D.C., 1929.

de Grosbois, Steve. *The Alienation of Métis Lands Through Federal Policy and Speculation: A Report to the Native Council of Canada*. Ottawa: National Library of Canada, 1979.

Dick, Everett. *The Lure of the Land: A Social History of the Public Lands from the Articles of Confederation to the New Deal*. Lincoln: University of Nebraska Press, 1970.

Dickason, Olive P. *Canada's First Nations: A History of Founding Peoples from Earliest Times*. New York: Oxford University Press, 2001, 3rd edition.

Dippie, Brian W. *The Vanishing American: White Attitudes and U.S. Indian Policy*. Lawrence: University of Kansas Press, 1982.

Doenecke, Justus D. *The Presidencies of James A. Garfield and Chester A. Arthur*. Lawrence: The Regents Press of Kansas, 1981.

Dollar, Clyde D. "The High Plains Smallpox Epidemic of 1837–38." *Western Historical Quarterly* 8 no. 1 (January 1977): 15–38.

Dorris, Michael. "Indians on the Shelf." *The American Indian and the Problem of History*. Ed., Calvin Martin. New York: Oxford University Press, 1987.

Dusenberry, Verne. "Waiting for a Day That Never Comes: The Dispossessed *Métis* of Montana." *The New Peoples: Being and Becoming*

*Métis in North America.* Eds., Jacqueline Peterson and Jennifer H. Brown. Minneapolis: Minnesota Historical Society Press, 1985.

Drache, Hiram M. *The Day of the Bonanza: A History of Bonanza Farming in the Red River Valley of the North.* Fargo: North Dakota Institute for Regional Studies, 1964.

_____. *The Challenge of the Prairie: Life and Times of Red River Pioneers.* Fargo: North Dakota Institute for Regional Studies, 1970.

Ellis, Elmer. *Henry Moore Teller: Defender of the West.* Caldwell ID: Caxton Printers, 1941.

Ens, Gerhard J. "Métis Agriculture in Red River During the Transition from Peasant Society to Industrial Capitalism: The Example of St. Francois Xavier, 1835 to 1870." *Swords and Ploughshares: War and Agriculture in Western Canada.* Ed., R. C. Macleod. Edmonton: University of Alberta Press, 1993.

_____. *Homeland to Hinterland: The Changing Worlds of the Red River Métis in the Nineteenth Century.* Toronto: University of Toronto Press, 1996.

_____. "After the Buffalo: The Reformation of the Turtle Mountain Métis Community, 1879–1904." *New Faces of the Fur Trade: Selected Papers of the Seventh North American Fur Trade Conference, Halifax, Nova Scotia, 1995.* East Lansing: Michigan State University Press, 1997, 139-151.

Epstein, Richard A. "Property and Necessity." *Harvard Journal of Law & Public Policy* 13, no. 1 (Winter 1990): 2–9.

Erdrich, Louise. "Where I Ought to Be: A Writer's Sense of Place." *New York Times Book Review,* July 28, 1985.

_____. *Tracks.* New York: Harper & Row, 1988.

Ewers, John C. "Ethnological Report on the Chippewa Cree Tribe of the Rocky Boy Reservation and the Little Shell Band of Indians." *Chippewa Indians VI.* New York: Garland Publishing Inc., 1974: 9–182.

Faragher, John Mack. "'More Motley than Mackinaw': From Ethnic Mixing to Ethnic Cleansing on the Frontier of the Lower Missouri, 1783–1833." *Contact Points: American Frontiers from the Mohawk Valley to the Mississippi, 1750–1830.* Eds., Andrew R. L. Clayton and Fredricka J. Teute. Williamsburg, VA: Omohundro Institute of Early American History and Culture, 1998.

Farrell, Alfred C. "A Calendar of Principal Events of the French and Indians of Early Dakota." *Collections of the State Historical Society of North Dakota* Vol. 1 (1906).

Ficken, Robert E. "The Fraser River Humbug: Americans and Gold in the British Pacific Northwest." *Western Historical Quarterly* 33 (Autumn 2002): 297–313.

Fixico, Donald L. "Ethics and Responsibilities in Writing American Indian History," *American Indian Quarterly* 20 (1996): 29–39.

_____. "Methodologies in Reconstructing Native American History." *Rethinking American Indian History*. Ed. Donald L. Fixico. Albuquerque: University of New Mexico Press: 1997.

Flanagan, Thomas. "Louis Riel and Aboriginal Rights." *As Long As the Sun Shines and Water Flows*. Eds., Ian A. L. Getty and Antoine S. Lussier. Vancouver: University of British Columbia Press: 247–62, 1983.

_____. "Louis Riel and the Dispersion of the American Metis." *Minnesota History* 49, no. 5 (Spring 1985): 179–90.

Folwell, William Watts. *Minnesota*. Boston: Houghton Mifflin Company, 1908.

Forbes, Jack D. "The Manipulation of Race, Caste and Identity: Classifying Afroamericans, Native Americans and Red-Black People." *Journal of Ethnic Studies* 17, no. 4 (Winter 1990): 1–51.

Francis, R. Douglas and Howard Palmer. *The Prairie West: Historical Readings*, 2nd Edition. Edmonton: University of Alberta Press, 1992.

Friesen, Gerald. *The Canadian Prairies: A History*. Toronto: University of Toronto Press, 1984.

_____. *River Road: Essays on Manitoba and Prairie History*. Winnipeg: University of Manitoba Press, 1996.

Fritz, Henry Eugene. *The Movement for Indian Assimilation, 1860–1890*. Philadelphia: University of Pennsylvania Press, 1963.

Gates, Paul W. *Fifty Million Acres: Conflicts Over Kansas Land Policy, 1854–1890*. Ithaca: Cornell University Press, 1954.

_____. "Indian Allotments Preceding the Dawes Act." *The Frontier Challenge: Responses to the Trans-Mississippi West*. Ed., John G. Clark. Lawrence: University of Kansas Press, 1971.

_____. *Landlords and Tenants on the Prairie Frontier*. Ithaca: Cornell University Press, 1973.

_____. *The Rape of Indian Lands*. New York: Arno Press, 1979.

_____. *The Jeffersonian Dream: Studies in the History of American Land Policy and Development*. Eds., Allen G. Bogue and Margaret Beattie Bogue. Albuquerque: University of New Mexico Press, 1996.

Gaustad, Edwin S. *Liberty of Conscience: Roger Williams in America*. Grand Rapids, MI: William B. Eerdsmans Publishing Company, 1991.

Geertz, Clifford. *The Interpretation of Cultures*. New York: Basic Books, 1973.

Gifis, Steven H. *Barron's Dictionary of Legal Terms*. Hauppauge, NY: Barron's Educational Series, Inc., 1993.

Gilman, Rhoda R., Carolyn Gilman, and Deborah M. Stultz. *The Red River Trails: Oxcart Routes between St. Paul and the Selkirk Settlement, 1820–1870*. St. Paul: Minnesota Historical Society, 1979.

Gilman, Rhoda R. "A Northwestern Indian Territory—The Last Indian Voice." *Journal of the West* 39, no. 1 (January 2000): 16–22.

Gillette, J. M. "Advent of the American Indian Into North Dakota." *North Dakota History Quarterly* 6, no. 3 (April 1932): 210–20.

Gluek, Alvin C. "The Riel Rebellion and Canadian-American Relations." *Canadian Historical Review* 36, no. 3 (September 1955): 199–221.

_____. *Minnesota and the Manifest Destiny of the Canadian Northwest: A Study in Canadian-American Relations*. Toronto: University of Toronto Press, 1975.

Gourneau, Patrick. *History of the Turtle Mountain Band of Chippewa Indians*, 7th Ed. Belcourt, ND: Self-published, 1980.

Gourneau, Charles J. *Old Wild Rice: "The Great Chief."* Belcourt, ND: Self-published, 1988.

Goyette, Linda. "The X Files: *Metis* Scrip." *Canadian Geographic* 123, no. 2 (March/April 2003): 70–80.

Grace, Thomas L. "Journal of Trip to Red River August and September 1861." *Acta et Dicta* 1 (1908): 176–79.

Hackney, Sheldon. "Borderland vs. Frontier: Redefining the West. A Conversation with Patricia Nelson Limerick." *Humanities* 17, no. 4 (September/October 1996): 4–14.

Hagen, Dalia. "Nations, Migration, and Metis Subsistence, 1860–1940." *Race and Displacement: Nation, Migration, and Identity in the Twenty-First Century*. Ed., Maha Marouan and Merinda Simmons. Tuscaloosa: University of Alabama Press, 2013.

Hall, Luella J. "History of the Formation of Counties in North Dakota." *Collections of the State Historical Society*, 5 (1923): 167–250.

Hallowell, A. Irving. *Culture and Experience*. Philadelphia: University of Pennsylvania Press, 1955.

_____. "Ojibway Ontology, Behavior and World View." *Culture in History*. Ed., Stanley Diamond. New York: Columbia University Press, 1960.

_____. "Northern Ojibwa Ecological Adaptation and Social Organization." *Contributions to Anthropology: Selected Papers of A. Irving Hallowell*. Ed., Raymond D. Fogelson. Chicago: University of Chicago Press, 1976.

_____. *The Ojibwa of Berens River, Manitoba*. Ed., Jennifer S. H. Brown. Fort Worth: Harcourt Brace Jovanovich, 1992.

Hamilton, A. C. and C. M. Sinclair. "'Justice Systems' and Manitoba's Aboriginal People: An Historical Survey." *The Canadian Prairies: A History*. Ed., Gerald Friesen. Toronto: University of Toronto Press, 1984.

Hargrave, Joseph James. *Red River*. Montreal: Lovell, 1871.

Hargreaves, Mary Wilma M. *Dry Farming in the Northern Great Plains, 1900–1925*. Cambridge: Harvard University Press, 1957.

Harmon, Alexandra. "When Is an Indian Not an Indian? The 'Friends of the Indian' and the Problems of Indian Identity." *Journal of Ethnic Studies* 18 (1990): 95–123.

Harring, Sidney L. *Crow Dog's Case: American Indian Sovereignty, Tribal Law, and United States Law in the Nineteenth Century*. Cambridge: University of Cambridge Press, 1994.

Hawkinson, Ella. "The Old Crossing Chippewa Treaty and Its Sequel." *Minnesota History* 25 (1934): 282–300.

Hayes, Derek. *First Crossing: Alexander Mackenzie, His Expedition Across North America, and the Opening of the Continent*. Seattle: Sasquatch Books, 2001.

Hays, Samuel P. *The Response to Industrialism, 1885–1914*, 2nd Edition. Chicago: University of Chicago Press, 1995.

Heard, Issac V. *History of the Sioux War and Massacres of 1862 and 1863*. New York: Harpers, 1863.

Hechter, Michael. *Internal Colonialism: The Celtic Fringe in British National Development, 1536–1996*. Berkeley, CA: University of California Press, 1975.

_____. "Group Formation of the Cultural Division of Labour."
*American Journal of Sociology* 84 (1978): 283–318.

Hesketh, John. "History of the Turtle Mountain Chippewa." *Collections of the State Historical Society of North Dakota* 5 (1923): 85–124.

Hickerson, Harold. "The Genesis of a Trading Post Band: The Pembina Chippewa." *Ethnohistory* 3 (1956): 289–345.

_____. "Journal of Charles Jean-Baptist Chaboillez, 1797–1798." *Ethnohistory* 6, no. 3 (Summer 1959): 265–316.

_____. "The Southwestern Chippewa: An Ethnohistorical Study." *American Anthropologist* 64 (1962): Part 2, 1–110.

Hilger, Sister M. Inez. "Some Customs of the Chippewa." *North Dakota History*. 26, no. 3 (Summer 1959): 123–25.

Hinderaker, Eric. *Elusive Empires: Constructing Colonialism in the Ohio Valley, 1673–1800*. Cambridge: Cambridge University Press, 1997.

Hobsbawm, Ian and Terence Ranger. *The Inventing of Tradition*. Cambridge: Cambridge University Press, 1983.

Hockett, Charles. "The Proto Central Algonquian Kinship System." *Explorations in Cultural Anthropology: Essays in Honor of George Peter Murdock*. Ed., Ward H. Goodenough. New York: McGraw-Hill Book Company, 1964: 239–57.

Holm, Tom. "Indian Concepts of Authority and the Crisis in Tribal Governments." *The Social Science Journal* 19, no. 3 (July 1982): 59–71.

_____. "Politics Came First: A Reflection on Robert K. Thomas and Cherokee History." *A Good Cherokee, A Good Anthropologist: Papers in Honor of Robert K. Thomas*. Ed., Steve Pavlik. Los Angeles: University of California American Indian Studies Center, 1998: 41–55.

Holm, Tom, J. Diane Pearson, and Ben Chavis. "Peoplehood: A Model for the Extension of Sovereignty in American Indian Studies." *Wicazo Sa Review* 18, no. 1 (Spring 2003):7–24.

Hornaday, William Temple. *The Extermination of the American Bison*. Washington, D.C.: Smithsonian Institution Press, 2002. Reprinted and edited from the original, *The Extermination of the American Bison* in the *Annual Report of the Board of Regents of the Smithsonian Institution*, 1889.

Horsman, Reginald. *Expansion and American Indian Policy, 1783–1812*. Norman: University of Oklahoma Press, 1967.

_____. "Science, Racism and the American Indian in the Mid-Nineteenth Century." *American Quarterly* 27, no. 2 (May 1975): 152–68.

_____. *Race and Manifest Destiny: The Origins of American Racial Anglo-Saxonism.* Cambridge: University of Harvard Press, 1981.

Howard, James H. "The Sun Dance of the Turtle Mountain Ojibwa." *North Dakota History* 19, no. 4 (1952): 249–64.

_____. "The Turtle Mountain 'Chippewa.'" *North Dakota Quarterly* 26, no. 2 (1958): 37–46.

_____. *The Plains-Ojibwa or Bungi: Hunters and Warriors of the Northern Prairies with special reference to the Turtle Mountain Band.* University of South Dakota, Reprints in Anthropology 7. Lincoln, NE: J. & L. Reprint Company, 1977.

Hoxie, Frederick E. *A Final Promise: The Campaign to Assimilate the Indians, 1880–1920.* Cambridge: Cambridge University Press, 1984.

Jackson, John C. "Brandon House and the Manitoba Connection." *North Dakota History* 49, no. 1 (Winter 1982): 11–19.

Jaenen, Cornelius. "French Sovereignty and Native Nationhood during the French Regime." *Sweet Promises: A Reader On Indian-White Relations in Canada.* Ed., J. R. Miller. 1991.

Jennings, Francis. *The Invasion of America: Indians, Colonialism, and the Cant of Conquest.* New York: W.W. Norton & Company, 1976.

Johnston, Basil. *Ojibway Heritage.* Toronto: McClelland & Stewart, 1976.

Kane, Lucille M. "The Sioux Treaties and the Traders." *Minnesota History* 32, no. 2 (June 1951): 65–80.

Kelsey, Vera. *Red River Runs North!* New York: Harper & Brothers Publishers, 1951.

Klein, Kerwin Lee. "Reclaiming the 'F' Word, Or Being and Becoming Postwestern." *Pacific Historical Review* 65, no. 2 (May 1996): 179–215.

Kvasnicka, Robert M. and Herman J. Viola, Eds. *The Commissioners of Indian Affairs, 1824–1977.* Lincoln: University of Nebraska Press, 1979.

LaBlanc, Rosella. "The Development of Turtle Mountain Indian Reservation." *The American Benedictine Review,* 407–20.

Lamar, Howard R. *Dakota Territory, 1861–1889.* Fargo: North Dakota Institute for Regional Studies, 1997.

Landes, Ruth. *The Ojibwa Woman.* New York: W.W. Norton, 1938.

_____. *Ojibwa Religion and the Midewiwin*. Madison: University of Wisconsin Press, 1968.

Lass, William E. *Minnesota: A History*. New York: W.W. Norton & Company, 1998.

Lasswell, Harold. *Politics: Who Gets What, When, How*. Cleveland: Meridian Books, 1958.

LaViolette, Gontran. *The Sioux Indians in Canada*. Regina, SK: Marian Press, 1944.

Law, Laura T. *History of Rolette County, North Dakota and Yarns of the Pioneers*. Minneapolis: Lund Press, Inc, 1953.

Leonard, Arthur Gray. "The Lignite Deposits of North Dakota." *North Dakota Quarterly* 6, no. 3 (April 1916): 234–40.

Limerick, Patricia Nelson. *The Legacy of Conquest: The Unbroken Past of the American West*. New York: W.W. Norton & Company, 1987.

Loew, Patty. "Hidden Transcripts in the Chippewa Treaty Rights Struggle: A Twice Told Story, Race, Resistance, and the Politics of Power." *American Indian Quarterly* 21 (1997): 713–28.

Lounsberry, Clement. *Early History of North Dakota*. Washington, D.C.: Liberty Press, 1919.

Martin, Albro. *James J. Hill and the Opening of the Northwest*. New York: Oxford University Press, 1976.

McCloud, Lise. "Heart of the Turtle." *North Dakota Quarterly* 59, no. 4 (Fall 1991): 89–97.

McKenzie, James. "'Sharing What I Know': An Interview with Francis Cree." *North Dakota Quarterly*, 59, no. 4 (Fall 1991): 98–112.

McLean, Don. *Home from the Hill: A History of the Métis in Western Canada*. Regina, SK: Gabriel Dumont Institute of Native Studies and Applied Research, 2nd printing, 1988.

McNeil, Kent. *Common Law Aboriginal Title*. Oxford: Clarendon Press, 1989.

_____. "Aboriginal Rights in Canada: From Title to Land to Territorial Sovereignty." *Tulsa Journal of Comparative & International Law* 5 (Spring 1998): 253–98.

_____. "Sovereignty on the Northern Plains: Indian, European, American and Canadian Claims." *Journal of the West* 39, no. 3 (Summer 2000): 10–18.

McNickle, D'Arcy. "The Federal-Indian Relationship." *Indian Health Care*. U.S. Congress. Office of Technology Assessment. Washington, D.C.: Government Printing Office, 1986.

Memmi, Albert. *The Colonizer and the Colonized*. Boston: Beacon Press, 1965.

Menig, D. W. *The Shaping of America: A Geographical Perspective on 500 Years of History*. Volume 2, *Continental America 1800–1867*. New Haven: Yale University Press, 1993.

Meyer, Melissa L. *The White Earth Tragedy: Ethnicity and Dispossession at a Minnesota Anishinaabe Reservation, 1889–1920*. Lincoln: University of Nebraska Press, 1994.

Meyers, Gustavus. *The History of the Great American Fortunes*. New York: Modern Library, 1936.

Milloy, John S. *The Plains Cree: Trade, Diplomacy and War, 1790 to 1870*. Winnipeg: University of Manitoba Press, 1988.

Miner, H. Craig. *The Corporation and the Indian: Tribal Sovereignty and Industrial Civilization in Indian Territory, 1865–1907*. Columbia: University of Missouri Press, 1976.

Momaday, N. Scott. "The Man Made of Words." *Nothing But the Truth: An Anthology of Native American Literature*. Eds., John L. Purdy and James Rupert. Upper Saddle River, NJ: Prentice Hall, 2001.

Monette, Gerald. E-mail to author, 25 June 2001.

Monette, Richard A. "A New Federalism for Indian Tribes: The Relationship Between the United States and Tribes in Light of Our Federalism, and Republican Democracy." *University of Toledo Law Review* 25: 617–72.

Morin, Gail, Ed. *Manitoba Scrip*. Pawtucket, Rhode Island: Quinton Publications, 1996.

_____. 1885 *Half-Breed North West Territory scrip applications*. Copyright Gail Morin, 1998.

Morton, W. L. *Manitoba: The Birth of a Province*. Altona, MB: D.W. Friesen & Sons Ltd., 1965.

_____. "The Battle at the Grand Coteau, July 13 and 14, 1851." *Historical Essays on the Prairie Provinces*. Ed., Donald Swainson. Toronto: McClleland and Stewart Ltd., 1970.

Mumford, Jeremy. "Métis and the Vote in 19th-Century America." *Journal of the West* 39, no. 3 (Summer 2000): 38–45.

Murphy, Lucy Eldersveld. "Public Mothers: Native American and *Metis* women as Creole Mediators in the Nineteenth-Century Midwest." *Journal of Women's History* 14, no. 4 (Winter 2003): 142–67.

Murray, Stanley N. "Railroads and the Agricultural Development of the Red River Valley of the North, 18701890." *Agricultural History*. XXVI (October 1957): 57–66.

_____. *The Valley Comes of Age: A History of Agriculture in the Valley of the Red River of the North, 1812-1920.* Fargo: North Dakota Institute for Regional Studies, 1967.

_____. "The Turtle Mountain Chippewa, 1882–1905." *North Dakota History* 51, no. 1 (1984): 14–37.

Nabokov, Peter. *A Forest of Time: American Indian Ways of History.* Cambridge, UK: Cambridge University Press, 2002.

Nash, Gary B. "The Hidden History of Mestizo America." *The American Journal of History* (1995): 941–62.

Nichols, Roger L. *Indians in the United States and Canada: A Comparative History.* Lincoln: University of Nebraska Press, 1998.

Norgren, Jill. *The Cherokee Cases: The Confrontation Between Law and Politics.* New York: McGraw Hill, 1996.

*North Dakota: A Guide to the Northern Prairie State.* Fargo: Federal Writers Project of the Works Progress Administration, 1938.

Newton, Nell Jessup. "Introduction." *Arizona Law Review* 31, no. 2 (1989).

O'Brien, Sharon. *American Indian Tribal Governments.* Norman: University of Oklahoma Press, 1989.

Owens, Louis. *Other Destinies: Understanding the American Indian Novel.* Norman: University of Oklahoma Press, 1992.

Otis, D. S., F. P. Prucha, Eds. *The Dawes Act and the Allotment of Indian Lands.* Norman: University of Oklahoma Press, 1973.

Palumbo, Dennis J. *Public Policy in America: Government Action.* New York: Harcourt Brace Jovanovich, Publishers, 1988.

Palmer, Bertha R. *Beauty Spots in North Dakota.* Boston: Gorham Press, 1928.

Pannekoek, Frits. *A Snug Little Flock: The Social Origins of the Riel Resistance of 1869–70.* Winnipeg, MB: Watson & Dwyer Publishing, 1991.

Paredes, J. Anthony, Ed. *Anishinabe: 6 Studies of Modern Chippewa.* Tallahassee: University Press of Florida, 1996.

Parsons, John E. *West on the 49th Parallel: Red River to the Rockies, 1872–1876.* New York: William Morrow and Company, 1963.

Pascoe, Peggy. "Miscegenation Law, Court Cases, and Ideologies of 'Race' in Twentieth-Century America." *Journal of American History* 83, no. 1 (June 1996).

Pearson, J. Diane. "Lewis Cass and the Politics of Disease: The Indian Vaccination Act Of 1832." *Wicazo Sa Review* 18, no. 2 (Fall 2003): 9–35.

Peterson, Jacqueline. "Gathering at the River: The Métis Peopling of the Northern Plains." *The Fur Trade in North Dakota.* Ed., Virginia L. Heidenreich. Bismarck: State Historical Society of North Dakota, 1990.

Peterson, Jacqueline and Jennifer S. H. Brown, Eds. *The New Peoples: Being and Becoming Métis in North America.* Winnipeg: University of Manitoba Press, 1985.

Pettipas, Leo. *Aboriginal Migrations: A History of Movements in Southern Manitoba.* Winnipeg: Manitoba Museum of Man and Nature, 1996.

Pike, Zebulon M., Elliot Coues, Eds. *The Expeditions of Zebulon Montgomery Pike,* in Two Volumes. New York: Dover Publications, Inc., 1987.

Poitra, Patricia F. & Karen L. *The History and Culture of the Turtle Mountain Band of Chippewa.* Bismarck: Office of Indian Education, North Dakota Department of Public Instruction. (online version)

Polyani, Karl. *The Great Transformation.* Boston: Beacon Hill Press, 1944.

Pommersheim, Frank. *Braid of Feathers: American Indian Law and Contemporary Tribal Life.* Berkeley: University of California Press, 1995.

*Prairie Past and Mountain Memories: A History of Dunseith, North Dakota, 1882–1892.* Dunseith, ND: Dunseith Centennial Committee, 1982.

Pritchett, John Perry. *The Red River Valley, 1811–1849: A Regional Study.* New Haven: Yale University Press, 1942.

Priest, Loring Benson. *Uncle Sam's Stepchildren: The Reformation of United States Indian Policy, 1865–1887.* Lincoln: University of Nebraska Press, 1975.

Prucha, Francis P., Ed. *Documents of United States Indian Policy.* Lincoln: University of Nebraska Press, 1990.

_____. *The Great Father: The United States Government and the American Indian.* Lincoln: University of Nebraska Press, 1984.

_____. *Atlas of American Indian Affairs.* Lincoln: University of Nebraska Press, 1990.

_____. "The Challenge of Indian History." *Journal of the West* 34, no. 1 (January 1995): 3–4.

Reardon, James M. *George Anthony Belcourt: Pioneer Catholic Missionary of the Northwest, 1803–1874.* St. Paul: North Central Publishing Company, 1955.

Richter, Daniel K. "War and Culture: The Iroquois Experience." *William and Mary Quarterly* 40, no. 4 (October 1983): 528–59.

_____. *Facing East from Indian Country: A Native History of Early America.* Cambridge, MA: Harvard University Press, 2001.

Rife, Clarence W. "Norman W. Kittson, A Fur Trader at Pembina." *Minnesota History* 3 (September 1925): 225–52.

Ripley, Randall B. and Grace A. Franklin, *Congress, the Bureaucracy, and Public Policy.* Homewood, IL: Dorsey Press, 1980.

Ritterbush, Lauren W. "Fur Trade Posts at Pembina: An Archeological Perspective of North Dakota's Earliest Fur Trade Center." *North Dakota History* 59, no. 1 (Winter 1992): 16–29.

Robbins, William G. *Colony and Empire: The Capitalist Transformation of the American West.* Lawrence: University of Kansas Press, 1994.

Robinson, Elwyn B. *History of North Dakota.* Lincoln: University of Nebraska Press, 1966.

Ronda, James P. *Lewis and Clark among the Indians.* Lincoln: University of Nebraska Press, 1984.

Ross, Alexander. *Red River Settlement: Its Rise, Progress, and Present State; with Some Account of the Native Races and Its General History to the Present Day.* London: Smith, Elder and Co., 1856.

St. Ann's Centennial Committee. *St. Ann's Centennial: 100 Years of Faith, 1885–1985; Turtle Mountain Indian Reservation. Belcourt, North Dakota.* Rolla, ND: Star Printing, 1985.

St. Germain, Jill. *Indian Treaty-Making Policy in the United States and Canada, 1867–1877.* Lincoln: University of Nebraska Press, 2001.

St-Ong, Nicole. "Uncertain Margins: Métis and Saulteaux Identities in St-Paul des Saulteaux, Red River 1821–1870." *Manitoba History* 53 (Oct 2006): 1–15.

Said, Edward W. *Culture and Imperialism.* New York: Vintage Books/ Random House, 1993.

Satz, Ronald N. *Chippewa Treaty Rights: The Reserved Rights of Wisconsin's Chippewa Indians in Historical Perspective.* Madison: Wisconsin Academy of Sciences, Arts and Letters, 1991.

Schattschneider, E. E. *The Semi-Sovereign People: A Realist's View of Democracy in America.* New York: Holt, Rinehart and Winston, 1960.

Schenck, Theresa. *"The Voice of the Crane Echoes Afar": The Sociopolitical Organization of the Lake Superior Ojibwa, 1640–1855.* New York: Garland Publishing Inc., 1997.

Schneider, Mary Jane. "An Adaptive Strategy and Ethnic Persistence of the Méchif of North Dakota." Unpublished Ph.D. dissertation, University of Missouri, 1974.

Schwarz, E. A. "What Were the Results of Allotment?" In "Allotment Data" available from Native American Documents Project, https:// public.csusm.edu/nadp/asubject.htm.

Scott, James C. *Domination and the Arts of Resistance: Hidden Transcripts.* New Haven: Yale University Press, 1990.

Scott, L. Lee. *Turtle Mountain Michif: A People and Their Language.* July 2, 2007.  https://web.archive.org/web/20140729004358/http:// voices.yahoo.com/the-turtle-mountain-michif-people- their-language-418374.html.

Seely, Bruce E. "Pettigrew, Richard Franklin"; American National Biography Online. Oxford University Press, 2000. http://www.anb. org/articles/05/05- 00607.html

Shannon, Fred A. *The Farmer's Last Frontier: Agriculture, 1860–1897,* Vol. V. The Economic History of the United States. New York: Holt, Rinehart and Winston, 1963.

_____. "The Homestead Act and the Labor Surplus." *The Public Lands: Studies in the History of the Public Domain.* Ed., Vernon Carstensen. Madison: University of Wisconsin Press, 1968.

Shattuck, Petra T. and Jill Norgren. *Partial Justice.* Providence: Berg Publishers, 1993.

Sheehan, Bernard. "Indian-White Relations in Early America." *William and Mary Quarterly* 3, no. 26 (1969): 267–86.

Skinner, Alanson. "Political Organization, Cults and Ceremonies of the Plains-Ojibway." *Anthropological Papers of the American Museum of Natural History* 11 (1914): 475–511.

_____. "The Cultural Position of the Plains-Ojibway." *Anthropological Papers of the American Museum of Natural History* 16 (1914): 314–18.

Slaughter, Linda W. "Leaves from Northwestern History." *Collection of the State Historical Society of North Dakota,* Vol. I (1906): 200–92.

Slotkin, Richard. *The Fatal Environment: The Myth of the Frontier in the Age of Industrialization, 1800–1890.* New York: Harper Perennial, 1985.

Smandych, Russell and Rick Linden. "Co-existing forms of Aboriginal and Private Justice: An Historical Study of the Canadian West." *Legal Pluralism and the Colonial Legacy: Indigenous Experiences of Justice in Canada, Australia, and New Zealand.* Ed., Kayleen M. Hazlehurst. Brookfield, VT: Ashgate Publishing Company, 1995.

Smith, James G. E. *Leadership among the Southwestern Ojibwa.* Ottawa: National Museum of Canada, 1973.

Smith, Maurice G. *Political Organization of the Plains Indians, with Special Reference to the Council.* Lincoln: University of Nebraska, 1924.

Sprague, D. N. *Canada and the Metis, 1869–1885.* Waterloo, ON: Wilfrid Laurier University Press, 1988.

Sprague, D. N. and R. P. Frye. *The Genealogy of the First Métis Nation: The Development and Dispersal of the Red River Settlement, 1820–1900.* Winnipeg: University of Manitoba Press, 1983.

*State Maps on File* (North Dakota). New York: Facts on File, 1984

Stegner, Wallace. *Wolf Willow: A History, a Story, and a Memory of the Last Plains Frontier.* Lincoln: University of Nebraska Press, 1980, reprint. (Printed originally in 1955).

Stevens, O. A. "Turtle Mountains of North Dakota." *The American Botanist* 28, no. 1 (February 1922): 9–14.

Strickland, Rennard. *Fire and the Spirits.* Norman: University of Oklahoma Press, 1982.

Stuart, Paul. *The Indian Office: Growth and Development of an American Institution, 1865–1900.* UMI Research Press, 1979.

Sturtevant, William. "Anthropology, History and Ethnohistory." *Ethnohistory* 13, nos. 1, 2 (Winter/Spring 1966): 1–52.

Sutton, Imre. *Indian Land Tenure.* New York: Clearwater Publishing Co., 1975.

_____. Ed. *Irredeemable America: The Indians' Estate and Land Claims.* Albuquerque: University of New Mexico Press, 1985.

Svingen, Orlan J. "Jim Crow, Indian Style." *American Indian Quarterly* 11 (Fall 1987): 275–86.

Swan, Ruth and Edward A. Jerome. "The History of the Pembina Métis Cemetery: Inter-Ethnic Perspectives on a Sacred Site." *Plains Anthropologist* 44, no. 170 (1999): 81–94.

Swierunga, Robert P. "Land Speculation and Its Impact on American Economic Growth and Welfare: A Historiographical Review." *Western Historical Quarterly* 8, no. 3: 283–301.

Tanner, Helen Horbeck. *The Ojibwas: A Critical Bibliography.* Bloomington: Indiana University Press, 1976.

Tanner, John. *A Narrative of the Captivity and Adventures of John Tanner.* Introduction by Louise Erdrich. Reprint of the G. & C. & H. Carvill 1830 edition. New York: Penguin Books, 1994.

Teillet, Jean. *The Northwest Is Our Mother: The Story of Louis Riel's People: The Métis Nation.* Toronto: HarperCollins, 2019.

Terrell, John Upton. *Zebulon Pike: the Life and Times of an Adventurer.* New York: Weybright and Talley, 1968.

Thompson, Margaret Susan. *The "Spider Web": Congress and Lobbying in the Age of Grant.* Ithaca: Cornell University Press, 1985.

Thorne, Tanis C. *The Many Hands of My Relations: French and Indians on the Lower Missouri.* Columbia: University of Missouri Press, 1996.

Tinker, George E. *Missionary Conquest: The Gospel and Native American Cultural Genocide.* Minneapolis: Fortress Press, 1993.

Treuer, Anton, Ed. *Living Our Language: Ojibwe Tales & Oral Histories.* St. Paul: Minnesota Historical Society Press, 2001.

_____. *Warrior Nation: A History of the Red Lake Ojibwe.* St. Paul: Minnesota Historical Society Press, 2015.

Treuer, David. *The Heartbeat of Wounded Knee: Native America from 1890 to the Present.* New York: Riverhead Books, 2019.

Turner, Frederick Jackson. *Frontier and Section: Selected Essays of Frederick Jackson Turner.* Englewood Cliffs, NJ: Prentice Hall, 1961.

Turtle Mountain Community College and North Dakota State Department of Public Instruction. *The History and Culture of the Turtle Mountain Band of Chippewa.* Bismarck, North Dakota: North Dakota State Department of Public Instruction, 1997.

Tweton, D. Jerome. "North Dakota in the 1890s: Its People, Politics and Press." *North Dakota History* 24, no. 2 (1957): 113–18.

Tyrell, J. B., Ed. *David Thompson's Narrative of His Explorations in Western America, 1784–1812.* Toronto: The Champlain Society, 1916.

Van Kirk, Sylvia. *Many Tender Ties: Women in Fur Trade Society, 1670–1870.* Norman: University of Oklahoma Press, 1983.

Verbicky-Todd, Eleanor. *Communal Buffalo Hunting Among the Plains Indians: An Ethnographic and Historic Review.* Alberta Culture Historical Resources Division, 1984.

Vizenor, Gerald. "Three Anishinaabeg Writers." *The People Called Chippewa: Narrative Histories.* Minneapolis: University of Minnesota Press, 1984.

Vrooman, Nicholas C. P. "Buffalo Voices." *North Dakota Quarterly* 59, no. 4 (Fall 1991): 113–21.

_____. "The Metis Red River Cart." *Journal of the West* 42, no. 2 (Spring 2003): 8–20.

_____. *The Whole Country was . . . One Robe: The Little Shell Tribe's America.* Drumlummon Institute and Little Shell Tribe of Chippewa Indians of Montana, 2013.

Walker, Francis A. "The Indian Question." *North American Review* (April 1873).

_____. *The Indian Question.* Boston, J. R. Osgood, 1874.

Washburn, Wilcomb E., Ed. *The American Indian and the United States: A Documentary History.* New York: Random House, 1973.

_____. *The Assault of Tribalism: The General Allotment Law (Dawes Act) of 1887.* Philadelphia: J. B. Lippincott Co, 1975.

_____. *Red Man's Land, White Man's Law.* Norman: University of Oklahoma Press, 1971.

Wexler, Alex and Molly Braun. (Carl Waldman, editorial consultant). *The Atlas of Westward Expansion.* New York: Facts on File, Inc, 1995.

Wheeler-Voegelin, Erminie and Harold Hickerson. *Chippewa Indians I: The Red Lake and Pembina Chippewa.* New York: Garland Publishing, 1974.

Whipple, Bishop Henry B. "The Indian System: Report of Commissioner of Indian Affairs, 1863." *North American Review* 99 (October 1864): 449–64.

_____. *Lights and Shadows of a Long Episcopate*. Minneapolis, 1900.

White, Bruce M. "'Give Us a Little Milk': The Social and Cultural Significance of Gift Giving in the Lake Superior Fur Trade." *Minnesota History* 48, no. 2 (Summer 1982): 60–71.

_____. "The Power of Whiteness, or the Life and Times of Joseph Rolette Jr." *Minnesota History* 56, no. 4 (Winter 1998–99): 178–97.

White, Leonard D. *The Republican Era: 1869–1901, A Study in Administrative History*. New York: The MacMillan Company, 1958.

White, Richard. *The Middle Ground: Indians, Empires, and Republics in the Great Lakes Region, 1650–1815*. Cambridge University Press, 1991.

_____. *The Roots of Dependency: Subsistence, Environment, and Social Change among the Choctaws, Pawnees, and Navajos*. Lincoln: University of Nebraska Press, 1983.

White-Weasel, Charlie. *Pembina and Turtle Mountain Ojibway (Chippewa) History*. Belcourt, North Dakota, 1995.

Widder, Keith R. *Battle for the Soul: Metis Children Encounter Evangelical Protestants at Mackinaw Mission, 1823–1837*. East Lansing: Michigan State University Press, 1999.

Wilder, Frank Alonzo. "The Lignite Coals of North Dakota." *Economic Geologist* 1, no. 7 (1906): 674–81.

Wilkins, David E. "Modernization, Colonialism, Dependency: How Appropriate Are These Models for Providing an Explanation of North American Indian 'Underdevelopment'?" *Ethnic and Racial Studies* 16, no. 3 (July 1993): 390–419.

Wilkins, David E. and K. Tsianina Lomawaima. *Uneven Ground: American Indian Sovereignty and Federal Law*. Norman: University of Oklahoma Press, 2001.

Wilkins, Robert P. and Wynona H. Wilkins. *North Dakota: A Bicentennial History*. New York: W.W. Norton, 1977.

Williams, Jr., Robert A. *The American Indian in Western Legal Thought: The Discourses of Conquest*. Oxford University Press, 1990.

_____. "Jefferson, the Norman Yoke, and American Indian Lands." *Arizona Law Review* 29, no. 2 (1987): 165–94.

_____. *Linking Arms Together: American Indian Treaty Visions of Law and Peace, 1600–1800*. New York: Routledge, 1997.

_____. "Linking Arms Together: Multicultural Constitutionalism in a North American Indigenous Vision of Law and Peace." *California Law Review* 82 (July 1994): 981–1049.

_____. "'The People of the States Where They Are Found Are Often Their Deadliest Enemies': The Indian Side of the Story of Indian Rights and Federalism." *Arizona Law Review* 38, no. 3 (Fall 1996): 981–97.

Williams, Walter L. "From Independence to Wardship: The Legal Process of Erosion of American Indian Sovereignty, 1810–1903." *American Indian Culture and Research Journal* 7 (1984): 5–32.

Wishart, David. "Belated Justice? The Indian Claims Commission and the Waitangi Tribunal." *American Indian Culture and Research Journal* 25, no. 1 (2001): 81–111.

Woolworth, Nancy L. "Gingras, St. Joseph and the Métis in the Northern Red River Valley, 1843–1873." *North Dakota History* 42, no. 4 (1975): 16–27.

Wub-e-ke-niew. *We Have a Right to Exist.* New York: Black Thistle Press, 1995.

# INDEX

Page numbers in **bold** type indicate photographs or illustrations.

John M. Shaw grew up where George Washington led the Continental Army across the Delaware River and surprised the Hessian garrison at Trenton, New Jersey, on Christmas day, 1776. One of John's earliest childhood memories recalls his parents bundling him up on Christmas mornings to watch the annual reenactment. This tradition sparked his lifelong interest and passion for history, culminating in an M.A. in American Indian Studies and a Ph.D. in History, both from The University of Arizona.

In graduate school, a colleague informed John about a compelling microfilm of an eloquent prayer, address, and legal brief on behalf of the Turtle Mountain Band of the Pembina Chippewa. Compiled by Métis tribal citizen and attorney John B. Bottineau, these inspiring documents provided a unique Indigenous perspective on the injustices of federal Indian policy. The tribe's legal struggle for land, sovereignty, and justice derived from the power to narrate their own side of the story through articulate chiefs and delegations, confirming that North Dakota's most populace Indigenous community remain a powerful people with a compelling history.

John contributed multiple entries to *Making it in America: A Sourcebook on Eminent Ethnic Americans* (2000) and *The Encyclopedia of United States-American Indian Policy, Relations, and Law* (2008), as well as several book reviews for UCLA's *American Indian Culture and Research Journal* and the *New Mexico Historical Review*. He has taught Native American and U.S. History courses for the departments of American Indian Studies, American Multicultural Studies, and History at The University of Arizona (1996–2003), Minnesota State University Moorhead (2004–2005), and Portland (Oregon) Community College (2005–present).

# ABOUT THE PRESS

North Dakota State University Press (NDSU Press) exists to stimulate and coordinate interdisciplinary regional scholarship. These regions include the Red River Valley, the state of North Dakota, the plains of North America (comprising both the Great Plains of the United States and the prairies of Canada), and comparable regions of other continents. We publish peer reviewed regional scholarship shaped by national and international events and comparative studies.

Neither topic nor discipline limits the scope of NDSU Press publications. We consider manuscripts in any field of learning. We define our scope, however, by a regional focus in accord with the press's mission. Generally, works published by NDSU Press address regional life directly, as the subject of study. Such works contribute to scholarly knowledge of region (that is, discovery of new knowledge) or to public consciousness of region (that is, dissemination of information or interpretation of regional experience). Where regions abroad are treated, either for comparison or because of ties to those North American regions of primary concern to the press, the linkages are made plain. For nearly three-quarters of a century, NDSU Press has published substantial trade books, but the line of publications is not limited to that genre. We also publish textbooks (at any level), reference books, anthologies, reprints, papers, proceedings, and monographs. The press also considers works of poetry or fiction, provided they are established regional classics or they promise to assume landmark or reference status for the region. We select biographical or autobiographical works carefully for their prospective contribution to regional knowledge and culture. All publications, in whatever genre, are of such quality and substance as to embellish the imprint of NDSU Press.

Our name changed to North Dakota State University Press in January 2016. Prior to that, and since 1950, we published as the North Dakota Institute for Regional Studies Press. We continue to operate under the umbrella of the North Dakota Institute for Regional Studies, located at North Dakota State University.